Media Scholarship in a Transitional Age

Research in Honor of Pamela J. Shoemaker

Carol M. Liebler and Tim P. Vos, Editors

PETER LANG
New York • Bern • Berlin
Brussels • Vienna • Oxford • Warsaw

Library of Congress Cataloging-in-Publication Data

Names: Liebler, Carol M. editor. | Vos, Tim P. editor. | Shoemaker, Pamela J. honoree.
Title: Media scholarship in a transitional age: research in honor of
Pamela J. Shoemaker / Carol M. Liebler and Tim P. Vos, editors.
Description: New York: Peter Lang, 2018.
Series: Mass communication and journalism; vol. 25 | ISSN 2153-2761
Includes bibliographical references and index.
Identifiers: LCCN 2017057042 | ISBN 978-1-4331-4772-2 (hardback: alk. paper)
ISBN 978-1-4331-4777-7 (paperback: alk. paper) | ISBN 978-1-4331-4778-4 (ebook pdf)
ISBN 978-1-4331-4779-1 (epub) | ISBN 978-1-4331-4780-7 (mobi)
Subjects: LCSH: Communication. | Digital media—Social aspects.
Online journalism—Social aspects.
Classification: LCC P87.3.S48 M33 2017 | DDC 302.2—dc23
LC record available at https://lccn.loc.gov/2017057042
DOI 10.3726/b11654

Bibliographic information published by **Die Deutsche Nationalbibliothek.**
Die Deutsche Nationalbibliothek lists this publication in the "Deutsche
Nationalbibliografie"; detailed bibliographic data are available
on the Internet at http://dnb.d-nb.de/.

The paper in this book meets the guidelines for permanence and durability
of the Committee on Production Guidelines for Book Longevity
of the Council of Library Resources.

29 Broadway, 18th floor, New York, NY 10006
www.peterlang.com

Printed in the United States of America

We dedicate this book to Pamela J. Shoemaker,
our mentor, colleague and friend.

Table of Contents

The "Mediated" Method

Reflections on the Transitional Age

Figures

Tables

Acknowledgements

We are indebted to the S.I. Newhouse School of Public Communications at Syracuse University for financial support and to our Editorial Assistant Ji Won Kim. We also thank Tatsiana Karaliova for her assistance.

Foreword

MICHAEL ROLOFF*

At the end of 2015, Pam Shoemaker retired from her position as Professor in the S. I. Newhouse School of Public Communications at Syracuse University. To say that she was an accomplished scholar is an understatement. Pam completed her doctorate in 1982 and during the next 33 years amassed an impressive publication record. She wrote or edited ten books/monographs, twenty-three book chapters, twenty-four refereed journal articles, fifteen invited articles, and sixty conference papers. Since the beginning of her career, Pam has had a strong interest in news. Early on she studied how the media covered deviant political groups and later became renowned for her research on media gatekeeping.

Pam is not only a prolific researcher, but her work is well-regarded and influential. In 2015, she received the Paul J. Deutschmann Award for Excellence in Research from the Association for Education in Journalism and Mass Communication, and in 2014, she received the Guido H. Stempel III Award for Research in Journalism and Mass Communication from the E.W. Scripps School of Journalism at Ohio University.

Based on citation activity, Pam's accolades are well deserved. Using Google Scholar as the database, I examined the frequency with which her scholarship is referenced. Forty-four of her publications have been referenced and have a total of 5,072 citations. She has an H-index of 30, which is impressive. Her books are among her most referenced publications, including *Gatekeeping Theory* coauthored

* Michael Roloff is Professor in the Department of Communication Studies at Northwestern University. Email: m-roloff@northwestern.edu

with Tim Vos (2009; 606 citations), *Gatekeeping* (1991, 496 citations), *News Around the World* coedited with Akiba Cohen (2006; 240 citations), *How to Build Social Science Theories* coauthored with James Tankard and Dominic Lasorsa (2002, 217 citations) and *Mediating the Message in the 21st Century* coauthored with Stephen Reese (2013; 171 citations). The range of dates of the aforementioned works shows that her published research from various points in her career has been influential. Indeed, some her most referenced journal articles were published in 2001, 1996, 1987 and 1984.

Pam's impressive record of scholarship reflects all but one of her major contributions. She is an excellent educator. Over her career, she directed forty-six master's theses and thirty-three doctoral dissertations. In 2007, she received the Distinguished Educator Award from the Mass Media and Society Division of the Association for Education in Journalism and Mass Communication.

Pam also has been strongly committed to the field. Her service included serving on editorial boards and journal editing. From 1997 through 2016, Pam and I coedited *Communication Research*. Prior to taking on that role, Pam and I met to make sure that we were compatible. We were. We shared a strong commitment to publishing research that was theory driven and that used rigorous quantitative methods. We wanted to make sure that the review process was efficient and constructive. Pam noted that the field was broadening both with respect to the topics that were being investigated and the nationality of the researchers. She argued that CR should maintain its established focus on political communication while encouraging submissions on all communication topics and from international researchers. Finally, she argued that CR should serve a mentoring function for young scholars. The reviews should be constructive in tone and suggestive of ways to improve research.

Looking back at our editorship, Pam played a key role in fulfilling our vision for the journal. Pam handled the logistics of journal submissions and issue content, and based on metrics such as time in review, CR was among the top journals published by SAGE. Furthermore, from 1999 through 2015, only once did the three-year impact factors for CR fall below those of the top ten of communication journals, and for seven years the impact factors were in the top five. When we began editing, all submissions were paper, which slowed the review process. Pam oversaw the complicated and difficult conversion to electronic submissions. The topics of the articles became increasingly diverse, as did the nationality of the authors. And we often published articles that were a gateway for the research programs for new scholars. Pam was the driving force behind all of this.

Much of what I have written is about Pam's past accomplishments. This in no way implies that retirement has ended her contributions. She has indicated that she will continue to write. Moreover, the chapters in this volume clearly indicate that her scholarship continues to influence her students and collaborators. I have no doubt but that she will remain a highly influential scholar.

CHAPTER ONE

Introduction

Examining Media in a Transitional Age

TIM P. VOS* AND CAROL M. LIEBLER†

It has certainly become a truism to say that media are being transformed in the digital age (Peters & Broersma, 2016). It is perhaps less of a truism, but a truth nonetheless, to say that media scholarship is also being transformed. However, in noting these transformations we are not holding out digital technologies as the sole driver of change. Human beings are cultural creatures whose values, attitudes, and ideas reflect, refract, and deflect the inclusion and intrusion of digital technologies. One can argue that digitalization—the ubiquity and integration of all things digital in the cultural, institutional, and material world—has precipitated much of the change we see today (Castells, 2010). That is why it's called a digital age, after all. But, we can also add some important caveats to that claim. In fact, it is the caveats that drive this book.

The first caveat is that digital dominance is indeed real, but it is not complete. We have not completely left behind the analogue world, the world of mass media, or the media theories rooted in the twentieth century world (or before). True; the analogue world no longer captures our research imaginations as it once did, mass media are more limited than in the past, and we seek out new ways of conceptualizing the new media landscape (O'Sullivan & Carr, 2017). But, the transition to a

* Tim P. Vos is Chair and Associate Professor of Journalism Studies in the School of Journalism at the University of Missouri. Email: vost@missouri.edu.

† Carol M. Liebler is Professor at the S.I. Newhouse School of Public Communications at Syracuse University. Email: cmlieble@syr.edu.

digital age is not complete. We are still—for better or worse—in a transitional age. While the digital world offers new research opportunities, we should not neglect our scholarly obligation to account for the world as it is (Shoemaker, Tankard, & Lasorsa, 2004)—and that is a world in transition.

The second caveat is that while digitalization is almost certainly a real phenomenon, our scholarly obligation is to embrace this claim in all its nuance. Thus, while we point to the insertion and intrusion of the digital into our world, we must closely account for the cascade of conceptually distinct transformations implicit in the notion of digitalization. Globalization, for example, comes about—at least in part—because of the digital means of communication, but is nevertheless its own kind of transformation (Castells, 2010). And globalization not only shapes the new mediated world that is the subject of our enquiries, it shapes our ability to collaborate across borders, adding comparative perspectives and opening up new insights (Waisbord & Mellado, 2014). Likewise, the introduction of digital technologies has involved economic and institutional adjustments in news media and other media that are worthwhile objects of study in their own right. Networks are not just digital phenomena, they are social and cultural phenomena as well, and must be examined as such.

The final caveat that drives this book is that not everything has changed. Although media scholarship has been invigorated, some methods and concepts have been validated or substantiated during this time of transition. It is worth taking stock of these anchors in our scholarly work, lest theory building become chaotic or unfocused. Transition refers to an easing from one state to another. This describes the world as we see it, but it also offers our normative assessment—our scholarship should ease forward. Claims of revolution can be self-fulfilling: We are convinced that all is changed, so we proceed to try to change everything. We think, however, there is much in our media scholarship that is worth preserving and that doing so serves the purpose of orderly theory building.

Out of these caveats comes this volume—a book that examines the media's digital *transformation*, the cultural and institutional *refraction* of digital pressures on media, and the *validation* of certain scholarly concepts and methods in a transitional age. We do this, inspired by scholars who have long been attentive to media transitions and who have carefully eased the scholarly way forward. One of those scholars is Pamela J. Shoemaker. She represents but one degree of separation from each of the authors represented in the volume. But, it is also her research approach and program that informs the scope of the transitions we explore here. Hence, the volume engages in the work of (re)theorizing key media-related processes; offers a set of original empirical studies, each of which thinks about the media against a backdrop of digitalization, globalization, and (re)institutionalization; considers validated methods of media research; and eases the way forward by reflecting about the past and the future.

THEORIZING THE TRANSITIONAL AGE

Digitalization has left a distinct mark on how social movements operate. In Chapter 2, Hyunjin Seo puts forward a theoretical framework that identifies how collaborative digital networks instigate social movements to address an array of issues, from the local to the global. These networks are both digital and social; that is, they have both structural and behavioral dimensions. In fact, Seo argues that the dynamic nature of these social movements can best be understood by accounting for the interactions between digital infrastructure and behavioral factors. The chapter underscores the ways in which political communication can be explored in fresh ways, raising policy issues and sensitizing scholars to the global dimensions of mediated communication moving forward.

In Chapter 3, Gina Masullo Chen offers a theoretical framework for understanding the place of online commenting in public deliberation. Digitalization brings with it some largely unwelcome social side effects, namely incivility. These nasty verbal attacks raise important policy and normative issues and call into question the efficacy of public deliberation. Chen concludes that democratic deliberation naturally involves some incivility but that the "cure is more speech, not less". The chapter highlights the ways in which democratic traditions refract and deflect the digitalization of society. Online comments present an array of challenges, but Chen argues that deliberative speech is nevertheless possible.

Chapters 4–6 address the selection and construction of news. In Chapter 4, Kevin Han and Josh Shear offer a new theoretical framework for understanding the place of audience feedback in the production of news in both analogue and digital media. The authors put forward several hypotheses about the effect of audience feedback on news media content. The analysis points to the ways digitalization, in the form of digital audience feedback, has transformed some aspects of news production, has refracted some forms of feedback making them function differently in a digital, as opposed to an analogue environment, and has validated some of what we have long understood about audience feedback. In Chapter 5, Marcos Paulo da Silva posits a pendulum metaphor as the basis for a theoretical model for the "news selection process and cultural construction of everyday regularity". The chapter validates traditional considerations of news selection—availability and suitability—but also offers an original conceptualization of how regularity and irregularity drive considerations of newsworthiness. In Chapter 6, Suman Lee also looks at newsworthiness, exploring its theoretical importance for public relations scholarship. Lee contends that the public relations field largely overlooks the newsworthiness of events, foregrounding instead the intentions of public relations practitioners. Drawing on Shoemaker and Cohen's (2006) work, he examines the concepts of deviance and social significance and their impact on news content. Lee concludes that scholars must expand their understanding of newsworthiness, particularly in identifying factors that influence national image in news, a key concern in the subfield of public diplomacy. Newsworthiness remains a valid concept and an important anchor for work in the sociology of news.

In Chapter 7, Dominic Lasorsa explores how digitalization—in the form of Internet use—shapes civic engagement. The chapter contextualizes it arguments by exploring the many ways communication concepts have been central to concerns of the social sciences. Lasorsa theorizes how different forms of communication ties contribute to social capital and in turn to civic engagement. The chapter concludes that Internet use has had a transformative effect on civic engagement—both suppressing engagement in some contexts and promoting engagement in other contexts. The chapter demonstrates the complicated course that digitalization brings to traditional communication worlds.

As noted at the outset, media scholars have begun to revisit classic communication theories in the light of digitalization and accompanying transitions. In Chapter 8, Elena Vartanova considers the state of agenda setting theory in a Russian-digital context. The rise of social media and mobile devices has changed the information ecosystem in Russia, leading to a change in the equilibrium of media to audience agenda setting. Vartanova proposes that "social media create personal news agendas based on individual preferences and news demand" and that this "changes not only the production and distribution of news by professional news rooms, but also the traditional theoretic understanding of the agenda-setting process, its players, filters and barriers". Vartanova ultimately finds value in traditional communication concept, but also demonstrates how real world digitalization significantly transforms the meaning of the concept.

THE EMPIRICAL LANDSCAPE IN A TRANSITIONAL AGE

This section of the book picks up where the previous section left off, looking to explore transitions in real world media behavior. The section offers a variety of empirical studies—studies that explore not only digitalization, but the accompanying transformations in a global mediated environment.

In Chapter 9, Maxwell McCombs, Pei Zheng, and Paro Pain do a sophisticated network analysis to examine and compare the agenda setting function of a top US and a top Chinese newspaper. The idea is to establish which countries appear in the psychological space that news media create. The picture that emerges is one of a truly globalized representational world, where "the psychological geography agendas" of the two countries newspapers strongly correlate. A slightly different picture emerges in the next two chapters. In Chapter 10, Di Zhang, Pan Shuya, and Xiuli Wang examine news media influence on political communication in China. Here, globalization seems to have less to contribute than in the previous chapter. The results show the local information structure and local culture play important roles in accounting for media influence on civic engagement. Meanwhile, in Chapter 11, Akiba A. Cohen examines whether Israelis' interest in foreign news has grown in the last 25 years, during a time in which citizens have been more thoroughly exposed to the world-wide reach of the Internet. The study shows that digitalization has its limits—his study found a declining interest in foreign news, although it also found an interest in a hybrid form of news, particularly news about Jews and Israeli interests abroad. The studies underscore the place of media in transitional age, where there is indeed change, but not revolutionary change.

Chapter 12 returns to the matter of newsworthiness, this time in an empirical study that again validates the usefulness of the concept. Jong Hyuk Lee and Yun Jung Choi ultimately call for expanding Shoemaker's (1996) perspective by exploring evolutionary psychology, cultural evolution, and gene culture co-evolution to better understand how deviance and social significance predict attention to news. The chapter demonstrates that considerations of newsworthiness can be driven both by local, global, and biological forces. Chapter 13 focuses on another key theoretical contribution of Shoemaker (1991)—the concept of gatekeeping. Nick Michael and Tim P. Vos examine gatekeeping in an online, networked environment, particularly in the emerging field of micro-documentaries. The online publication of these documentaries exposes filmmakers to similar gatekeeping forces seen in other, legacy news organizations. However, the chapter also demonstrates how digitalization is refracted in the networked setting, opening up a new bridge-keeping role in addition to the more traditional gatekeeping role. This section of empirical studies concludes with a look at news coverage of political candidates. Elizabeth A. Skewes shows how news media play an important political role, especially early in the election, in assigning some candidates to a second-tier status. News media then reinforce that status in the kind and amount of coverage given to second tier candidates. Skewes' study validates long established theoretical constructs in the field, namely agenda setting and framing.

Finally, in Chapter 15, John Wolf explores the impact on mobile communication devices, empirically investigating the cultural phenomenon of sexting—the sending and receiving of sexually explicit text and visual messages. At a basic level, the chapter explores the digitalization of sexual communication. But like all forms of digitalization, digital technology is but one part of the transition underway. Wolf explores the complicated motivations that drive sexting, and points to psychosocial context for understanding mediated sexual communication. Thus, the chapter demonstrates the ways sexual communication is refracted in the new digital environment.

While scholars have eagerly explored new phenomena in the digital world, sometimes those new phenomena are usefully understood through the lenses of venerable communication concepts and theories. But, as the chapters in this section demonstrate, careful attention to new communication settings also demonstrate how even these traditional concepts can take on new meaning or can provide leverage to identify new processes in a new media world. So, for example, studying gatekeeping in the networked, online environment opens up awareness of a heretofore neglected function, bridge building. Thus, in a time of transition in media scholarship the old and the new can happily and helpfully coexist.

THE "MEDIATED" METHOD IN THE TRANSITIONAL AGE

Digitalization has also affected how media scholars do their work, not only opening up new topics to explore but providing new means for doing research. Through digital scraping technologies, huge social media datasets, machine learning and coding, and other means, media researchers are able to address new questions and arrive at new conclusions. The era of "big data" has clearly arrived. Nevertheless, here too talk of a transformation can be over done. Our research tools are becoming more sophisticated and our data sets are becoming much bigger, but our research logic is unaltered and the fundamentals of our methodologies have changed little (Webster, 2016).

In this section of the book, three chapters outline the "art and science" of content analysis research, touching on a variety of methodological issues and other methods in the process. The picture is one of transition—moving the field forward but reinforcing the fundamentals of research design. In Chapter 16 Erica Scharrer outlines the principles of sound and effective content analysis. In doing so, she points to the new digital tools available to the content analyst and outlines the research challenges and opportunities that come with computer algorithms, computational techniques, not to mention the content of interactive media. Scharrer underscores that the new digital, scientific techniques do not negate the "art" of content analysis.

In Chapter 17, Michael J. Breen poses a tension between news coverage of sexual crimes and official statistics about those crimes. He points to the Sexual Abuse and Violence in Ireland (SAVI) report as a backdrop for interpreting content in mainstream news coverage. He argues that "sexual crime in Ireland is not well represented in the mainstream media, that some types of sex crimes are prioritized in reporting above others, and that the representation of sex crime perpetrators is deeply unrepresentative of the reality". Finally, in Chapter 18, Carol M. Liebler performs a content analysis of news coverage of missing children. By using a database of posters of missing children, Liebler documents how age, race, attractiveness and the circumstances of the children's disappearance all play a role in the visibility of those children in news coverage. Liebler sees in content analysis—turned both on media content and on posters of missing children—the tools to identify evidence of mediated erasure, that is, the absence of news coverage based on a child's age, race, or other characteristics. Thus, both Breen and Liebler point to the importance of extra-media content in analyses of news content. It is often what is not depicted that is the most telling.

REFLECTIONS ON THE TRANSITIONAL AGE

In the book's final section the individual authors reflect on the challenges that bridge eras and traditions of media scholarship. In Chapter 19, in a poignant contribution, the late Guido Stempel traced his 60-year long career as a mass communication researcher, as he challenged the "dubious conclusions" with which he was confronted. Stempel's experiences provide insight for how today's researchers can approach their scholarship, particularly in terms of relationships with the journalism profession. In Chapter 20, Brenda Wrigley confronts the structures and assumptions about gender and diversity that shape hiring and promotion practices in corporate and agency communication roles. By building on the levels of influence developed in Shoemaker's work (1991; Shoemaker & Reese, 2013; Shoemaker & Vos, 2009), Wrigley poses that media scholars document the range of ways in which women and members of marginalized groups continue to face discrimination in salary and promotion in public relations and corporate communication management.

In Chapter 21, Stephen Reese revisits the pointed musings of C. Wright Mills to craft fresh guidance "on life-structuring as young scholars contend with the pressing demands of career expectations and the digital firehose of information". Reese confronts the relentless intrusion of digitalization into the academic life—replete with algorithmic citation counts—and points to methods of refraction; that is, to ways of making the academic life a balanced and sustainable undertaking. Standards of productivity have certainly changed, but Reese offers the means for easing scholars into a productive and healthy workflow.

The research world is filled with revolutionary tools—useful tools that can lead to better and more insightful research—but scholars who are intellectual craftsmen must be mindful of the validated concepts, theories, and methods of the past if they are to help media scholarship transition into the future. This book is inspired by a role model who made this all look easy: Pamela J. Shoemaker. Thus, it is her outlook, her research program, and her exacting standards that shape the commitments of this volume.

REFERENCES

Castells, M. (2010). *The rise of the network society* (2nd ed.). Chichester; Malden, MA: Wiley-Blackwell.

O'Sullivan, P. B., & Carr, C. T. (2017). Masspersonal communication: A model bridging the mass-interpersonal divide. *New Media & Society*, 1–17. doi:10.1177/1461444816686104

Peters, C., & Broersma, M. J. (2016). *Rethinking journalism again: Societal role and public relevance in a digital age.* New York, NY; London: Routledge.

Shoemaker, P. J. (1991). *Gatekeeping.* Newbury Park, CA: Sage Publications.

Shoemaker, P. J. (1996). Hardwired for news: Using biological and cultural evolution to explain the surveillance function. *Journal of Communication, 46*(3), 32–47.

Shoemaker, P. J., & Cohen, A. A. (2006). *News around the world: Practitioners, content and the public.* New York, NY: Routledge.

Shoemaker, P. J., & Reese, S. D. (2013). *Mediating the message in the 21st century: A media sociology perspective* (3rd ed.). New York, NY: Routledge.

Shoemaker, P. J., Tankard, J. W., & Lasorsa, D. L. (2004). *How to build social science theories.* Thousand Oaks, CA: Sage.

Shoemaker, P. J., & Vos, T. P. (2009). *Gatekeeping theory.* New York, NY: Routledge.

Waisbord, S., & Mellado, C. (2014). De-westernizing Communication Studies: A reassessment. *Communication Theory, 24*(4), 361–372. doi:10.1111/comt.12044

Webster, J. G. (2016). Why study measures of exposure? From exposure to attention. *Communication Methods and Measures, 10*(2–3), 179–180. doi:10.1080/19312458.2016.1150974

Theorizing the Transitional Age

CHAPTER TWO

Social Change IN THE Networked Information Age

HYUNJIN SEO*

INTRODUCTION

How does social change take place? What are social movements, and why do some succeed while others fizzle? These questions have piqued scholars in many disciplines to explore various aspects of interactions among actors in society (Bastos, Mercea, & Charpentier, 2015; Benkler, 2006; Bennett & Segerberg, 2013; Bimber, Flanagin, & Stohl, 2012; Dutta, 2015). In fact, social change and social influence were the topics that Kurt Lewin, widely considered father of gatekeeping perspectives, focused on in his group dynamics research (Lewin, 1947a, 1947b). Lewin contended that social change could be measured by focusing on actors in key positions of influence who served as gatekeepers to the flow of ideas and information. Shoemaker and Vos (2009) noted that "scholars studying 21st century mass media must return to Lewin's original application of the theory—studying social change" (p. 132).

Analyzing social change dynamics has arguably become more complex as digital communication technologies have enabled actors other than traditional intermediaries such as government and mainstream media outlets to occupy positions of influence. Consider as examples the Occupy Wall Street movement and popular uprisings in the Middle East and North Africa in recent years (Bastos et al., 2015;

* Hyunjin Seo is Associate Professor and Docking Faculty Scholar in the William Allen White School of Journalism and Mass Communications at the University of Kansas. Email: hseo@ku.edu.

Gleason, 2013; Howard & Hussain, 2011; Seo & Thorson, 2012). Not only movement organizers but also informally associated citizens used social media to share information and mobilize people for social change. In addition, traditional mass media such as *The New York Times* makes use of Twitter streams and YouTube videos to gather information about those movements and report on them.

The development of the global Internet has had important consequences for human collaborations within and across borders and news flows and consumption (Benkler, 2006; Castells, 2011; Shoemaker, Cohen, Seo, & Johnson, 2011). Moreover, the emergence of digital-facilitated social collaborative networks has brought a shift from "the mass-mediated social spaces to a networked public space" (Benkler, 2006). Information is generated, filtered, and exchanged without necessarily going through traditional intermediaries. The result is the rapid emergence and extinction of networked spaces as well as gatekeepers within and between those spaces. These spaces are dynamic and can quickly adapt to changes in infrastructure and the requirements of particular social or political movements. Somewhat paradoxically, as the distribution of information becomes more decentralized, there is increased dependence upon underlying and enabling communication protocols. These protocols remain largely under the centralized control of governments and large-scale service providers.

In this chapter, I propose a theoretical framework for identifying conditions under which digital media-facilitated social collaborative networks catalyze social movements for social change while taking into account both structural (the architecture of connectedness) and behavioral (social manifestations) aspects of those movements. The proposed framework is derived from my conceptual and empirical research (Seo, 2013, 2014; Seo & Ebrahim, 2015; Seo, Houston, Knight, Kennedy, & Inglish, 2014; Seo & Kinsey, 2013; Seo & Thorson, 2012) and informed by Shoemaker's scholarship in gatekeeping and international communication (e.g., Shoemaker & Cohen, 2006; Shoemaker et al., 2011; Shoemaker & Vos, 2009). I conclude with a discussion of scholarly and policy implications of this research with special focus on the areas of digital and international communication.

NETWORKED INFORMATION SOCIETY AS A CONTEXT

The increased use of Internet-based communication tools has changed the ways people and organizations connect with one another. Increasingly available and affordable network-based communication tools influence how people and organizations connect with one another and have helped both with extending existing social relationships and forging new ones (Ahn, 2012; Duggan, Ellison, Lampe, Lenhart, & Madden, 2014; Seo et al., 2014). Digital communication technologies have also had a significant influence on public arenas, as demonstrated during political campaigns for the 2016 U.S. presidential election (McCabe, 2015; Sanders, 2015) and popular uprisings in the Middle East and Asia in recent years (BBC, 2014; Howard & Hussain, 2011; Parker, 2014; Seo & Thorson, 2012). Political candidates and activists have mobilized publics via wide-scale and low-cost digital communication tools, and these new communication channels have enabled citizens to participate in activities traditionally reserved for government representatives (Benkler, 2006, 2011; Chadwick, 2006; Hindman, 2009; Howard & Hussain, 2011). As Benkler (2006) puts it, the Internet has changed "the cultural practice of public communication" (p. 180).

These changes in the nature of interactions between actors in society, facilitated by increasingly available information communication technologies (ICTs), are described in many different terms such as *information society* (Webster, 2006), *network society* (Castells, 2000, 2004, 2011), and *networked information economy* (Benkler, 2006). Castells (2000, 2004, 2011) used the term network society to describe the impact of ICTs on different levels of interactions in society. According to Castells (2004), a network society is "a society whose social structure is made of networks powered by microelectronics-based information and communication technologies" (p. 3).

Benkler (2006) argues that ICTs have brought about a networked information economy characterized by information decentralization, nonproprietary strategies, nonmarket mechanisms, and more effective large-scale non-hierarchical cooperation. Examples of the networked information economy include wikis, blogs, and open-source software through which an unlimited number of individuals can collaborate to produce and share information and ideas. According to Benkler, the networked information economy is replacing the industrial information economy that relied on capital-intensive and professional production. Traditionally published and distributed newspapers and broadcast networks belong to the industrial information economy. The networked information economy has created a new environment for public discourse where the influence of traditional mass media, which used to maintain an almost exclusive control over gatekeeping, is reduced (Benkler, 2006, p. 12). Internet-based information and communication technologies have brought about important changes in our society, particularly with regard to producing and sharing information and knowledge (Benkler, 2006, 2011). Some (e.g., Hindman, 2009) argue these changes do not eliminate the exclusivity of traditional gatekeepers but only shift "the bar of exclusivity from the production to the filtering of political information" (p. 13). Recent examples indicate that the increasing decentralization in information production and sharing has reduced the relative influence of some traditional gatekeepers (Benkler, 2006) while perhaps increasing the influence of others. These underlying changes have significant implications for movements for social change. I argue that both digital communication infrastructure and behaviors in networked spaces enabled by the infrastructure should be taken into account to have a more complete understanding of social change dynamics in the networked information age.

NETWORK INFRASTRUCTURE-BEHAVIOR INTERACTIONS AND SOCIAL CHANGE

Communication networks provide affordances for the flow of messages among communicators (Monge & Contractor, 2003). As such, the structure of those networks is not neutral to the forms and content of information that traverses them. Behaviors of individuals and organizations are patterned and often enabled by structural aspects of systems within which they operate (Benkler, 2011; Seo & Thorson, 2012). Changes in the communication system influence types of communication tools used, how groups interact, and modes of shared content. Thus, it is important to understand both communication systems and behavioral aspects and interactions between the two in analyzing social movements in the networked information age.

Communication networks or systems are key factors for mobilization, organization, and diffusion of social and political movements, influencing the sharing of news and information among actors. By empowering ordinary citizens to create and share information and content rather than simply acting as passive consumers of information, the Internet plays a significant role in contemporary political and social movements (Benkler, 2006, 2011; Howard & Hussain, 2011; Seo & Thorson, 2012). In addition, the emergence of digital media-facilitated social collaborative networks has brought a shift from "the mass-mediated social spaces to a networked public sphere" (Benkler, 2011; Seo & Thorson, 2012). These networked public spaces facilitate dynamic creation, sharing, and deletion of various modes of communication content—text, still image, video, and audio—in one-to-one or one-to-many communication conditions. And, as discussed below, these have produced new dynamics for political and social movements for social change.

Information communication technologies (ICTs) were significant in facilitating the so-called Arab Spring—popular political movements in some Middle Eastern and North African countries such as Tunisia, Egypt and Syria since 2010—though debates still continue as to specific contributions of ICTs in motivating and spreading those movements in the region (Halverson, Ruston, & Trethewey, 2013; Howard & Hussain, 2011; Seo & Thorson, 2012). In addition, protesters in Hong Kong in 2014 utilized social media services for organizing and sustaining their movements calling for election reform (Parker, 2014). Social media have been an important part of political movements in South Korea—one of the world's most wired countries where the Internet plays a large role in social relations (Seo, 2013; Seo & Kinsey, 2013). In the wake of the South Korean Sewol ferry disaster, South Koreans used social media channels such as Kakao Talk to mobilize protests against the South Korean government for its perceived "mishandling of the situation" (BBC, 2014). While these protests may have taken place even without these digital networks, information infrastructure certainly influenced their immediacy and scope (Seo & Thorson, 2012) by providing channels for both activists and citizens to express dissatisfaction and to create a collective identity (Halverson et al., 2013).

Not surprisingly, digital communication networks and infrastructure have become a target of governments attempting to control citizens' protests. In response to popular uprisings in Libya, the Muammar Gaddafi regime severed Internet access and international phone calls in eastern Libya (Hill, 2011). The Bashar al-Assad government used the Syrian Electronic Army, dubbed as "Assad's cyber warriors", to closely monitor and track down dissenters and shut down websites critical of the Assad regime (Harding & Arthur, 2013). Similarly, the Chinese government intensified its crackdown on Internet users who were involved in or demonstrated sympathy for the Hong Kong protests (Parker, 2014). In South Korea, it has been reported that the Park Geun-hye government monitored messages on Kakao Talk, a mobile messaging app used by 70 percent of South Korea's population, in an attempt to identify people thought to be spreading "insults and rumors" related to the ferry incident (BBC, 2014).

These attempts by the governments to disrupt communication forced activists to find ways of circumventing the government interruption (BBC, 2014; Hill, 2011; Parker, 2014). In Libya, when Gaddafi shut down mobile providers and ordered telecommunication companies to close Internet access, a relatively new mobile service provider in Libya, which was less centralized and less affected by the Gaddafi government, used home location register (HLR) and other means to help support a mobile phone system in some areas and provided free service throughout the uprising (Coker & Levinson, 2011; Hill, 2011). In addition, foreign companies arrived in Libya to open a new cellphone network in 2011. Limited Internet connections supported by these efforts enabled use of Skype calls and MSN chats in and from Libya, helping the uprising to keep its momentum (Hill, 2011).

During the pro-democracy protests in Hong Kong in 2014, protesters tried to get around automatic filters by the Chinese government by intentionally misspelling words or writing in code (Parker, 2014). Moreover, FireChat—an "off-the-grid" smartphone app developed by a Silicon Valley start-up—emerged as an important communication tool among protesters as the Internet connectivity significantly slowed down in the area (Cohen, 2014; Shadbolt, 2014). During the first two weeks of the protests, FireChat registered about 500,000 downloads in Hong Kong with 10.2 million chat sessions and 1.6 million chatrooms (Shadbolt, 2014). FireChat served as "a giant megaphone" during the Hong Kong protest, as the app is not limited to a user's circle but messages on FireChat available for everybody to see.

Amid the Park Geun-hye government's pledge to prosecute people spreading rumors about her dealing with the Seowol ferry incident in 2014, South Koreans migrated from the popular Kakao Talk chat app to an encrypted messaging service called Telegram Messenger to avoid government censorship (BBC, 2014). Telegram Messenger utilizes end-to-end encryption providing a "secret chat" option and reportedly gained 1.5 million new South Korean users within seven days (BBC, 2014).

As discussed above, digital communication infrastructure has provided affordances for creating networked spaces for interactions among active or loose participants in political and social movements. In the following section, I propose a preliminary theoretical framework for social change research that takes into account both structural (the architecture of connectedness) and behavioral (social manifestations) aspects of network-facilitated movements.

MULTILEVEL FRAMEWORK FOR SOCIAL CHANGE IN NETWORKED INFORMATION AGE

Social interactions in the networked information age can be understood and predicted by integrating information from several distinct levels—communication network infrastructure, networked space, and communication behavior. Communication network infrastructure provides opportunities to create networked spaces and consequently motivating particular communication behaviors in those networked spaces. Digital network infrastructure consists of multiple components including Internet Protocol (IP) connectivity and physical parts such as broadband, router, and fiber. Creation and mutation of these components will influence affordances for social movements provided at the network infrastructure level. That is why authoritarian governments or other forces, which attempt to suppress social or political movements for social change, often resort to network infrastructure disruptions (Fisher, 2013; Hill, 2011). In addition, changes in the communication infrastructure level (e.g., disruption of Internet connectivity) influence types of communication tools used and how groups interact. For example, to circumvent the Chinese government's censorship to quell democracy movements in Hong Kong, activists migrated from the global Internet to peer-to-peer wireless mesh networks and mobile ad-hoc networks (Parker, 2014).

Networked spaces are digital media-facilitated social communities such as Facebook groups or online chat rooms. This networked space level is dynamic and adaptable to changes in the infrastructure and needs of particular social or political movements. In the previous section, I discussed how participants in social or political movements moved from one system to another to maintain a space in the face of disruptions—such as South Koreans transferring from Kakao Talk to Telegram Messenger in 2014 (BBC, 2014; Parker, 2014). It is in these networked spaces where some citizens function as content producers and gatekeepers influencing behaviors of other citizens. I call these citizens *social influencers* to distinguish them from traditional influencers or intermediaries of information such as mainstream media outlets. While citizens are traditionally labeled as audience members or content consumers, these network spaces and technological affordances available in these spaces allow them to be effective content producers with influence on their peers (Li & Bernoff, 2011). That is, in these network spaces, information propagation and diffusion is less and less influenced by traditional intermediaries such as mass media with the gap filled by social influencers.

It should be noted that technological affordances available in a particular networked space influence types of communication behavior. That is, specific interactive or privacy features allowed in a particular infrastructure (Facebook group vs. Yik Yak group) affect interactions and connections among actors and types of content generated by actors.

The interactions between the three levels are non-linear and flow both ways. While digital network infrastructure influences creation and mutation of a networked space, activities in the networked space can influence the network infrastructure. For example, in the case of Libya, continued movements in networked spaces encouraged other Internet and mobile network providers to support necessary infrastructure when Gaddafi shut down mobile providers and ordered telecommunication companies to close Internet access to suppress social movements (Coker & Levinson, 2011; Hill, 2011).

Examining interactions between different levels enables a more robust picture of social interactions and supports high-level situational awareness in rapidly changing, often highly non-linear, operating environments. The effects of changes in each level on the other levels and how those changes combine to help us understand the role of each level should be examined. Multilevel theoretical frameworks—informed by longitudinal, interdisciplinary empirical research incorporating network analysis, content analysis, and field experiments—are crucial to developing predictive causal understandings of social interactions. In particular, there are multiple aspects of social interactions in networked spaces that should be analyzed and integrated in the multilevel and interdisciplinary model. Next, I illustrate the multilevel framework by considering the ongoing civil war in Syria.

CASE STUDY: SYRIA

Syria, officially Syrian Arab Republic, is a MENA (Middle East and North Africa) country that shares borders with Turkey, Lebanon, Iraq, Israel, and Jordan. Syrian President Bashar Hafez al-Assad assumed the presidency in 2000 when his father, Hafez al-Assad, died after ruling the country for 30 years (Erlich, 2014). The popular uprising in Syria began in March 2011, with pro-democracy demonstrators gathering in the southern city of Derra in protest against the government's arrest and torture of several teenagers who wrote anti-government graffiti on a school wall (BBC, 2015). Government forces responded by shooting at the demonstrators, which was followed by more citizens joining the pro-democracy protests. Demonstrations spread across Syria with hundreds of thousands taking to the streets by July 2011 (BBC, 2015). Protesters demanded an end to the authoritarian practices of the Assad regime and the resignation of President Bashar al-Assad. The Assad regime used deadly forces in his attempt to quell the opposition movement, and armed opposition groups fought against the government. Amid confrontations between the Assad regime and opposition forces, as of 2015 more than 6.5 million Syrians had been displaced in Syria and about 4.1 million Syrians had sought refugee in other countries (UNHCR, 2015). In particular, the Assad regime tried to further restrict and control information by attacking media organizations and journalists. For example, Syrian government forces raided the nonprofit Syrian Center for Media and Freedom of Expression and arrested its officials (Freedom House, 2015). The Committee to Protect Journalists (2015) reported that at least 81 journalists have been killed in Syria since the 2011 uprising, "making it the second deadliest conflict for journalists" since the committee began comprehensive records in 1992.

The Syrian case highlights the importance of examining the interplay of the communication infrastructure, networked spaces, and behavioral aspects to develop a more robust understanding of political/social movements in the context of networked digital information. Pro-democracy movements on the streets of Syria in 2011 quickly garnered support on popular social media sites such as Facebook and Twitter, generating social interactions within Syria and with supporters outside Syria at the networked spaces afforded by digital communication technologies (Sadiki, 2012; Seo & Ebrahim, 2015; Shehabat, 2012). Activists in Syria used social media to expose actions of the Assad regime to the international community, to exchange information and tactics with other revolutionaries both within and outside of Syria, and to spread their messages related to resistance activities (Seo & Ebrahim, 2015). Their social media use also helped them to develop and spread a revolutionary narrative of support for democratic change and opposition to the Assad regime. For example, rebels used YouTube to show brutalities of the Assad regime and tell their stories. As of 2015, there were a dozen active Facebook accounts that claimed to be accounts of the official Syrian opposition. These sites include Facebook pages named "National Coalition of Syrian Revolution and Opposition Forces", "Syrian National Council", and "Local Coordination Committees of Syria" (Seo & Ebrahim, 2015). As of November 2015, about 6.4 million people in Syria used the Internet with the penetration rate of 28.1 percent (Internet World Stats, 2015). This is a significant increase from 30,000 in 2000, and is in line with increased Internet connectivity in the MENA region in recent years (Internet World Stats, 2015; Seo & Thorson, 2012).

Recognizing the importance of information and communication technologies (ITCs) in controlling its citizens and its image outside the country, Syrian President

Bashar al-Assad's government has attempted to disrupt networked spaces of the opposition by influencing communication network infrastructure. For example, in November 2012 and May 2013 the Syrian government shut down the Internet across the country and cut cellphone services in certain areas where opposition forces were active (Fisher, 2013). While rebels in Syria were struggling to create alternative social collaborative spaces online, Syrian diaspora activists have supported the Syria-based opposition's efforts by telling stories of civilian sufferings in Syria via social media (Andén-Papadopoulos & Pantti, 2013). In both 2012 and 2013, the Internet connectivity was restored within days.

In addition to the disruption at the network infrastructure level, the Syrian government directly attacked the opposition's social collaborative networks created in the networked spaces. The Syrian government shut down websites critical of the regime and trolled Twitter accounts and Facebook pages. In addition, it monitored and tracked down dissenters, and on occasion subjected them to torture for more information. The Syrian government has accomplished these largely through the Syrian Electronic Army, dubbed as "Assad's cyber warriors" and considered an extension of the regime itself (Harding & Arthur, 2013). The activities of the Syrian Electronic Army have extended to other countries. For example, it hacked the Twitter account of the Associated Press and proclaimed that U.S. President Barack Obama had been injured in an attack on the White House, causing the U.S. stock market to dive within minutes (Thompson, 2013). In 2015, the Syrian Electronic Army claimed credit for taking down the U.S. Army's public website (Vinton, 2015). Syrian President Bashar al-Assad's government has also capitalized on social media to promote its political agenda (Harding & Arthur, 2013; Seo & Ebrahim, 2015; Shehabat, 2012).

As illustrated in this example, examining the three different levels help us better understand how movements for social change are facilitated or disrupted at multiple levels. In the following section, I discuss policy and scholarly implications of this study and agenda for future research.

CONCLUSION

In this chapter, I have proposed a preliminary theoretical framework for analyzing social change in the networked information age. I argue mechanisms and outcomes of interactions of the three levels presented in the framework—communication network infrastructure, networked space, and communication behavior—should be considered to understand social change dynamics in the digital media age. The framework should be refined based on additional empirical research studies in the area. For example, one could analyze political movements in countries that offer varying degrees in terms of country network infrastructure, social media use, and

Internet policy. Examining communication phenomena in different countries or cultures is essential to develop a more comprehensive understanding of communication dynamics in the digital media age (Shoemaker & Cohen, 2006; Shoemaker et al., 2011). Empirical data for this could include domestic and international Internet connectivity, levels and characteristics of activities in networked spaces, patterns of connections among actors, and visual and textual messages generated in the networked spaces. Identifying social influencers and understanding their roles in the process of information propagation is also essential. In addition, social media platforms have become important channels for spreading images with both manifest and latent meanings in conflict situations, as demonstrated by Twitter images during recent Israeli-Hamas conflicts and graphic Internet videos by the self-proclaimed Islamic State (Seo, 2014). Visuals will continue to rise in popularity in this digital media age, as people opt for content that is attention-grabbing and easy to understand. Consequently, it is important to understand both textual and visual content. Additionally, cultural variability needs to be considered. As widely documented, culture shapes both verbal and nonverbal communication behaviors (Gudykunst, 2003) and cultural variability should be considered at the three levels to more accurately capture the role of culture in formation and dissemination of communication cues in social interactions. Culture provides an important context for understanding social change initiatives in a particular society (Dutta, 2015).

In empirically testing the multilevel framework, it will prove useful to adopt an interdisciplinary research approach incorporating concepts and methods from disciplines including sociology, political science, economics, and computer science. Theory-driven empirical studies will help illuminate the evolution of communication structures as well as the affordances that evolution provides for social change. Moreover, speedy disintermediation in networked spaces and interactions between the three levels in this process provides an opportunity for better understanding gatekeeping in this rapidly changing media environment.

REFERENCES

Ahn, J. (2012). Teenagers' experiences with social network sites: Relationships to bridging and bonding social capital. *The Information Society, 28*(2), 99–109. http://doi.org/10.1080/01972243.2011.649394

Andén-Papadopoulos, K., & Pantti, M. (2013). The media work of Syrian diaspora activists: Brokering between the protest and mainstream media. *International Journal of Communication, 7*, 2185–2206.

Bastos, M. T., Mercea, D., & Charpentier, A. (2015). Tents, tweets, and events: The interplay between ongoing protests and social media. *Journal of Communication, 65*(2), 320–350. http://doi.org/10.1111/jcom.12145

BBC. (2014). *#BBCtrending: Why South Koreans are fleeing the country's biggest social network.* Retrieved from http://www.bbc.com/news/blogs-trending-29555331

BBC. (2015). *Syria: The story of the conflict*. Retrieved from http://www.bbc.com/news/world-middle-east-26116868

Benkler, Y. (2006). *The wealth of networks: How social production transforms markets and freedom contract*. New Haven, CT: Yale University Press. Retrieved from http://site.ebrary.com/lib/alltitles/docDetail.action?docID=10170022

Benkler, Y. (2011). Network theory | Networks of power, degrees of freedom. *International Journal of Communication, 5*, 721–755.

Bennett, W. L., & Segerberg, A. (2013). *The logic of connective action: Digital media and the personalization of contentious politics*. Cambridge: Cambridge University Press.

Bimber, B., Flanagin, A., & Stohl, C. (2012). *Collective action in organizations: Interaction and engagement in an era of technological change*. Cambridge: Cambridge University Press.

Castells, M. (2000). Materials for an exploratory theory of the network society. *The British Journal of Sociology, 51*(1), 5–24. http://doi.org/10.1111/j.1468-4446.2000.00005.x

Castells, M. (Ed.). (2004). *The network society: A cross-cultural perspective* (illustrated edition). Cheltenham; Northampton, MA: Edward Elgar Pub.

Castells, M. (2011). *The rise of the network society: The information age: Economy, Society, and Culture*. New York, NY: John Wiley & Sons.

Chadwick, A. (2006). *Internet Politics: States, Citizens, and New Communication Technologies* (1st ed.). New York, NY: Oxford University Press.

Cohen, N. (2014, October 5). Hong Kong protests propel FireChat phone-to-phone app. *The New York Times*. Retrieved from http://www.nytimes.com/2014/10/06/technology/hong-kong-protests-propel-a-phone-to-phone-app-.html

Coker, M., & Levinson, C. (2011, April 13). Rebels hijack Gadhafi's phone network. *Wall Street Journal*. Retrieved from http://www.wsj.com/articles/SB10001424052748703841904576256512991215284

Committee to Protect Journalists. (2015). *How many more? CPJ remembers journalists killed*. Retrieved December 29, 2015 from http://committeetoprotectjournalists.tumblr.com/post/113800746974/how-many-more-cpj-remembers-journalists-killed

Duggan, M., Ellison, N. B., Lampe, C., Lenhart, A., & Madden, M. (2014). *Social Media Update 2014*. Retrieved from http://www.pewinternet.org/2015/01/09/social-media-update-2014/

Dutta, M. J. (2015). Decolonizing communication for social change: A culture-centered approach. *Communication Theory, 25*(2), 123–143. http://doi.org/10.1111/comt.12067

Erlich, R. (2014). *Inside Syria: The backstory of their civil war and what the world can expect*. Amherst, NY: Prometheus Books.

Fisher, M. (2013, May 8). How did Syria cut off the entire country from the Internet? *The Washington Post*. Retrieved from https://www.washingtonpost.com/news/worldviews/wp/2013/05/08/how-did-syria-cut-off-the-entire-country-from-the-internet/

Freedom House. (2015). *Syria | Country report | Freedom of the Press | 2015*. Retrieved from https://freedomhouse.org/report/freedom-press/2015/syria

Gleason, B. (2013). #Occupy Wall Street: Exploring informal learning about a social movement on Twitter. *American Behavioral Scientist, 57*(7), 966–982. http://doi.org/10.1177/0002764213479372

Gudykunst, W. B. (2003). *Cross-cultural and intercultural communication*. Thousand Oaks, CA: SAGE.

Halverson, J. R., Ruston, S. W., & Trethewey, A. (2013). Mediated martyrs of the Arab Spring: New media, civil religion, and narrative in Tunisia and Egypt. *Journal of Communication, 63*(2), 312–332. http://doi.org/10.1111/jcom.12017

Harding, L., & Arthur, C. (2013, April 30). Syrian electronic army: Assad's cyber warriors. *The Guardian*. Retrieved from http://www.theguardian.com/technology/2013/apr/29/hacking-guardian-syria-background

Hill, E. (2011). How "rebel" phone network evaded shutdown – Al Jazeera English. *Al Jazeera*. Retrieved from http://www.aljazeera.com/indepth/features/2011/04/20114233530919767.html

Hindman, M. (2009). *The myth of digital democracy*. Princeton, NJ: Princeton University Press.

Howard, P. N., & Hussain, M. M. (2011). The role of digital media. *Journal of Democracy, 22*(3), 35–48. http://doi.org/10.1353/jod.2011.0041

Internet World Stats. (2015). *Middle East Internet Statistics, Population, Facebook and Telecommunications Reports*. Retrieved from http://www.internetworldstats.com/stats5.htm#me

Lewin, K. (1947a). Frontiers in group dynamics: Concepts, method and reality in science; social equilibria and social change. *Human Relations, 1*, 5–40.

Lewin, K. (1947b). Frontiers in group dynamics II. Channels of group life: Social planning and action research. *Human Relations, 1*, 143–153.

Li, C., & Bernoff, J. (2011). *Groundswell: Winning in a world transformed by social technologies*. Boston, MA: Harvard Business Press.

McCabe, D. (2015). Welcome to the social media election. *The Hill*. Retrieved from http://thehill.com/policy/technology/251185-welcome-to-the-social-media-election

Monge, P. R., & Contractor, N. S. (2003). *Theories of communication networks*. Oxford: Oxford University Press.

Parker, E. (2014, October 1). Social media and the Hong Kong protests. *The New Yorker*. Retrieved from http://www.newyorker.com/tech/elements/social-media-hong-kong-protests

Sadiki, L. (2012). The professionalisation of revolution in Syria – Al Jazeera English. *Al Jazeera*. Retrieved from http://www.aljazeera.com/indepth/opinion/2012/01/201211313229137341.html

Sanders, S. (2015). Instagram: The new political war Room? *NPR.org*. Retrieved from http://www.npr.org/sections/itsallpolitics/2015/09/03/436923997/instagram-the-new-political-war-room

Seo, H. (2013). Online social relations and country reputation. *International Journal of Communication, 7*, 1–20.

Seo, H. (2014). Visual propaganda in the age of social media: An empirical analysis of Twitter images during the 2012 Israeli–Hamas conflict. *Visual Communication Quarterly, 21*(3), 150–161. http://doi.org/10.1080/15551393.2014.955501

Seo, H., & Ebrahim, H. (2015, May). *Social media and visual propaganda: A comparative analysis of Facebook images during Syrian conflicts*. Paper presented at the International Communication Association, Puerto Rico.

Seo, H., Houston, J. B., Knight, L. A. T., Kennedy, E. J., & Inglish, A. B. (2014). Teens' social media use and collective action. *New Media & Society, 16*(6), 883–902. http://doi.org/10.1177/1461444813495162

Seo, H., & Kinsey, D. F. (2013). Three Korean perspectives on U.S. internet public diplomacy. *Public Relations Review, 39*(5), 594–596. http://doi.org/10.1016/j.pubrev.2013.06.006

Seo, H., & Thorson, S. (2012). Networks of networks: Changing patterns in country bandwidth and centrality in global information infrastructure, 2002–2010. *Journal of Communication, 62*(2), 345–358. http://doi.org/10.1111/j.1460-2466.2012.01631.x

Shadbolt, P. (2014). FireChat, the app behind Hong Kong's protests. *CNN*. Retrieved from http://www.cnn.com/2014/10/16/tech/mobile/tomorrow-transformed-firechat/index.html

Shehabat, A. (2012). The social media cyber-war: The unfolding events in the Syrian revolution 2011. *Global Media Journal, 6*(2), 1–9.

Shoemaker, P. J., & Cohen, A. A. (2006). *News around the world: Content, practitioners, and the public.* New York, NY: Routledge.

Shoemaker, P. J., Cohen, A. A., Seo, H., & Johnson, P. (2011). Comparing news on foreign and international affairs. In *The Handbook of Comparative Communication Research.* Routledge. Retrieved from http://www.routledgehandbooks.com/doi/10.4324/9780203149102.ch21

Shoemaker, P. J., & Vos, T. P. (2009). *Gatekeeping theory.* New York, NY: Routledge.

Thompson, N. (2013, May 8). Why did Syria shut down the internet? *The New Yorker.* Retrieved from http://www.newyorker.com/news/daily-comment/why-did-syria-shut-down-the-internet

UNHCR. (2015). *Total number of Syrian refugees exceeds four million for first time.* Retrieved from http://www.unhcr.org/559d67d46.html

Vinton, K. (2015, June 8). Syrian electronic army claims responsibility for hacking U.S. army website. *Forbes.* Retrieved from http://www.forbes.com/sites/katevinton/2015/06/08/syrian-electronic-army-claims-responsibility-for-hacking-army-website/

Webster, F. (2006). *Theories of the information society* (3rd ed.). New York, NY: Routledge.

CHAPTER THREE

Online Incivility and Public Deliberation

GINA MASULLO CHEN*

When terrorists attacked Paris on November 13, 2015, resulting eventually in the death of 130 people (Rubin, 2015), the response online was swift. In the first 24 hours after the attack, 430 million online interactions—including likes, comments, posts, and tweets—took place to show support for the French (Laurent, 2015). The #PrayforParis hashtag and other hashtags surfaced almost immediately on Twitter. An image that combines a peace sign and an Eiffel Tower began to show up as profile pictures on Facebook or be shared fervently on Instagram. Almost as quickly, the online conversation shifted from outpourings of support and grief to fear. A tide of anti-refugee, anti-Muslim sentiment swelled in the days after the Paris attacks (Bosman, 2015), leading governors from 31 U.S. states to oppose letting Syrian refugees into their states for fear terrorists might be among their numbers after reports that a suspect in the Paris attack had entered Europe as a Syrian refugee. The governors' outcry was symbolic, as refugee resettlement is a federal issue, not a state one. The online response was brutal. Pictorial memes depicting refugees as terrorists filled Facebook feeds. People debated the issue in online comments and through tweets and Facebook posts, with vitriol marking the discourse on all sides of the issue. Republican presidential candidates fueled the fire, with Ben Carson comparing refugees to rabid dogs (Frumin, 2015) and Donald Trump urging that all Muslims be banned from travel to the United States (Diamond, 2015). As Charles M. Blow (2015), a columnist for *The New York*

* Gina Masullo Chen is Assistant Professor in the School of Journalism at The University of Texas at Austin. Email: gina.chen@austin.utexas.edu.

Times, asserted: "The tone of anti-Muslim musings post-Paris attack has become so poisonous that it cannot portend anything positive".

This chapter will examine the issue of incivility in user-generated comments by reviewing the literature on commenting in general and how these comments relate to public debate. My aim is to pull together strands of divergent research to put forth a more consistent theoretical understanding of the role of online commenting on public deliberation by addressing one over-arching questions: Can uncivil discourse allow for deliberation? This chapter relies on the idea of democratic deliberation, a belief that the public use of arguments and reasoning among free and equal individuals (Landemore, 2012) is important to our society. In this chapter, I define incivility as nasty, attacking remarks mired with profanity; name-calling; words in all capital letters to signify yelling in computer-mediated speech; or racist, sexist, or stereotypical undertones (Berry & Sobieraj, 2014; Chen & Lu, 2017; Papacharissi, 2004; Sobieraj & Berry, 2011; Stroud, Scacco, Muddiman, & Curry, 2015). I will begin by explaining the relevance and importance of this topic. Then I explore the key concepts under discussion in this chapter before reviewing the germane literature. Finally, I will sum up the major assertions of this chapter.

Some foundational beliefs underlie this essay. First, I believe that online discourse—even disagreement—is vital to an open society. Without discussion or debate, without disagreement, we cease to be a truly free society. Moral disagreement, defined as "conflicts about fundamental values" (Gutmann & Thompson, 1996, p. 1), is an essential component of a political structure, such as ours, that encourages discussion before decision. Free citizens must be able to criticize their government, their politicians, even each other, and, hopefully, truth and justice emerge from these open discussions. Any harm that comes from this disagreement, while troubling, is a necessary evil. A free society is better than a constrained society, even if that freedom offers people the means to hurt each other's feelings. Second, incivility is a natural part of the human condition, though it may make us cringe. An understanding of empathy explains why. From an evolutionary perspective, empathy has confounded researchers for decades because it seems to operate in contrast to one's self interest. It is intrinsically unselfish (De Waal, 2008) yet evolution suggests that people behave in a manner that helps them survive and pass on their genes. So why would people be empathetic? The way psychologists explain this phenomenon is through the inherent human need for social connection, or belongingness (Baumeister & Leary, 1995). This line of research argues that people are not really being selfless when they are empathetic, although it appears so. They are fulfilling their own need for human connection through empathetic acts, which cement their relationships with others (De Waal, 2008). Using this reasoning, incivility becomes logical. It allows people to exert control over others, assert their own position, and jockey for power. It also can be used to hurt others and decrease their value as a means to restore one's own value (Brett et al., 2007). In an evolutionary world where we all are competing against each other to survive and pass on our genes, incivility is a natural expression of the need to elevate oneself compared with others. What restrains our natural urge to be uncivil is our need to belong (Baumeister & Leary, 1995), to get along with others, and to form human connections that help us survive. In other words, incivility is a natural outgrowth of the tension between asserting oneself to gain control without damaging one's connection with the group.

INCREASING ONLINE INTERACTIVITY

The backdrop for the topic is that online interactivity—user-generated comments on news stories, social media posts, blogs, and chat services like Snapchat—is one of the most significant shifts regarding computer-mediated news that has taken place in decades. The public's ability to discuss and debate topics in the news went from static signed letters to the editor that may or may not be published to today's always-on, instant environment that makes it possible for people to say almost anything they want at any time. News organizations increasingly encourage readers to comment on stories, share items through social media, and engage with news topics across a wider audience (Brost, 2013) in a search for clicks and page views. News sites added interactive features in a quest to drive up readership and, ultimately, advertising revenue (Chock, Wolf, Chen, Schweisberger, & Wang, 2013; Huang, 2007; Tremayne, Schmitz, & Alves, 2007). News consumers flocked to these features, but some distinct patterns emerged. For example, news audience members are more likely to comment on stories about politics or public affairs, compared with general news (Boczkowski & Mitchelstein, 2012; Tenenboim & Cohen, 2015), and this effect is heightened during key political moments, such as Election Day (Boczkowski & Mitchelstein, 2012). News that is controversial, negative, has high social impact, or is focused on one's own nation are more likely to elicit comments, confirming that values traditionally associated with newsworthiness also influence commenting (Weber, 2014). People are also more likely to comment when they perceive a story as biased (Chung, Munno & Moritz, 2015), perhaps as a means of setting the record straight. Commenters tend to be more deliberative, expressing more balanced views and offering a higher-quality conversation, when discussing political news content on websites, rather than on Facebook (Rowe, 2015). This suggests that commenting offers great potential—perhaps untapped—for public deliberation on important topics, such as politics or public affairs.

However, these virtual free-for-alls of online discourse leave the commenter, rather than the journalist, in charge of what is said (Stroud et al., 2015). In a sense, online interaction obliterates part of journalists' traditional gatekeeping role. Instead of journalists deciding which letters to the editor to publish, the public gets a chance to say whatever it wants through online conversation. Media scholars Pamela J. Shoemaker and Tim P. Vos call this a "secondary gatekeeping process" (2009, p. 7) where the active audience plays a pivotal role in controlling the traditional gates that open or close to allow news and information to flow. All too often in this untethered environment these discussions turn acrimonious (Anderson, Brossard, Scheufele, Xenos, & Ladwig, 2014; Brooks & Geer, 2007; Coe, Kenski & Rains, 2014; Santana, 2014). In fact, one study of 6,444 comments posted on 310 news stories over 21 days found that one in five comments contained some marker of incivility, such as name-calling, profanity, or pejorative speech (Coe et al., 2014). Yet, other research suggests that the majority of online conversations are civil and polite, supporting the "Internet's potential to revive the public sphere, provided the greater diversity and volume of discussion is present" (Papacharissi, 2004, p. 259). Allowing people to comment anonymously, in particular, has been linked to greater incivility (Santana, 2014). Researchers also have found that the way people comment conforms to norms of the website they are using. When thoughtful and civil comments dominate a site, other commenters were likely to follow suit (Ruiz et al., 2011; Sukumaran, Vezich, McHugh, & Nass, 2011), but uncivil comments tended to beget uncivil replies (Chen & Lu, 2017). In fact, even one person can influence the deliberative norms in online conversation. One study found that if a recognizable reporter engaged in a comment stream, commenters were more civil and more likely to use evidence in their comments (Stroud et al., 2015), rather than merely spout off. This suggests that reporters engaging with commenters can influence and increase deliberation. Serious topics with clear sides, such as guns, abortion, the economy, politics, law and order, taxes, and foreign affairs tend to elicit uncivil comments, while posts about education, health, lifestyle, journalism, and technology do not (Stroud et al., 2015). Research also has found that news organizations can control the incivility on their sites by requiring people to register and use real names to comment and rigorously moderating comments can help discourage incivility (Ksiazek, 2015). Yet, even with these efforts, online incivility persists. The topic of incivility is important because it has been found to lead to distrust in government (Mutz & Reeves, 2005), more polarized viewpoints (Anderson et al., 2014), and negative perceptions of those engaging in debate (Ng & Detenber, 2005). Overall, incivility online may discourage people to comment or create a negative experience for those who do choose to join the conversation. In this context, much of the deliberative potential of online commenting may be lost. In addition, clearly incivility causes emotional pain (Chen, 2015; Chen & Lu, 2017; Sobieraj & Berry, 2011), so it is intrinsically negative to the human experience.

INCIVILITY DEFINED

Before moving forward with my argument about how incivility fits into democratic deliberation, it makes sense to explicate what is meant by incivility. In many ways, the concept can be a slippery notion. One person's sense of incivility may be another's definition of impassioned speech. Scholars have defined civility in a variety of ways, with many equating it with politeness or good manners. Communications scholar Zizi A. Papacharissi argues persuasively that this is a mistake: "Civility is misunderstood when reduced to interpersonal politeness because this definition ignores the democratic merit of robust and heated discussion. ... It is adherence to etiquette that frequently restricts conversation by making it reserved, less tepid, less spontaneous" (2004, p. 260). In that sense, it is impossible to separate incivility from the larger concept of disagreement, an exchange of views different from one's own beliefs (Klofstad, Sokhey, & McClurg, 2013). When people speak in a deliberative fashion, intrinsic to that discussion is the idea of "moral disagreement" (Gutmann & Thompson, 1996, p. 1). There is little point to a discussion on important issues of the day, such as politics or crime, if people are considered uncivil by merely expressing a counter view. Therefore, equating incivility with impoliteness leaves little room for the healthy debate of a free society (Landemore, 2012; Santana, 2014). One might find any challenge to one's view as impolite, but that negates the belief that it is valuable to express divergent views. In fact, some research has found that any type of disagreement—either civil or uncivil—may lead to negative emotions or even aggressive intentions (Chen & Lu, 2017). This suggests that incivility must be worse than mere impoliteness to differentiate it from civil disagreement.

Therefore, I propose that incivility includes impolite speech but goes well beyond impoliteness. It is best understood if one imagines a continuum ranging from impoliteness to virulent hate speech. Incivility operates at the midpoint between these concepts and encompasses all the speech from that point on up to and including hate speech. As a result, expressing a counter view online may be impolite but not uncivil, yet racist epithets would constitute incivility, as well as fit into the more nefarious category of flaming, defined as insulting, swearing or using offensive language in online communication expressed with intent to violate norms (Moor, Heuvelman, Verleur, 2010; O'Sullivan & Flanagin, 2003). Based on this viewpoint, the definition of incivility becomes clearer. It is defined as mean-spirited or nasty remarks that attack a person or idea, express anger or frustration with a disrespectful tone, and is intended to spark a response (Borah, 2014; Coe et al., 2014). As such, this speech is marked by specific affordances, including profanity or other forms of abusive language; name-calling; use of capital letters to indicate a raised tone in computer-mediated speech; xenophobic or hateful expressions, epithets, or racial slurs; and racist or bigoted statements that disparage or assign stereotypes (Borah, 2014; Chen & Lu, 207; Coe et al.,

2014; Papacharissi, 2004; Sobieraj & Berry, 2011; Stroud et al., 2015). For online communication to be considered uncivil, it need not include each of these affordances of incivility. The presence of one is enough to mark it as uncivil (Stroud et al., 2015), although multiple markers of incivility would deem the speech more uncivil than communication with fewer attributes.

INCIVILITY AS DEVIANCE

As much as people bemoan the incivility on news sites and social media, they seem drawn to it. Part of the reason may be because incivility deviates from norms of polite speech. Grice's (1969) maxims on politeness propose that people expect conversations to be truthful, relevant, clear, and contribute only what is necessary (Chen & Ng, 2016; Papacharissi, 2004), even when communicating online (Reeves & Nass, 1996). When people violate these norms of politeness, their speech stands out because it differs from typical communication. Incivility, which I have already argued goes beyond mere politeness, does not merely violate these norms; it tramples them. This relies on a normative understanding of deviance; deviant speech is speech that violates social rules (Shoemaker, 1982, 1984). Shoemaker's (1996) work is helpful to understand why people might be drawn to speech that is so outside the norm. She argues that humans are biologically "hardwired to survey their environment and to prefer news about deviant and otherwise threatening events" (p. 44). She traces this to our primitive roots when early humans had to attend to what was threatening, or risk physical harm. As a result, attending to the deviant gave "early humans a reproductive advantage" (Shoemaker, 1996, p. 35), meaning those who paid attention to what was deviant were more likely to survive long enough to pass on their genes to a future generation. Shoemaker was writing about news, but her theorizing applies equally well to user-generated information, such as online comments. People pay attention and respond to uncivil comments because they stand out as deviant. This effect may be heightened in the computer-mediated space, which in many ways has blurred the lines between public and private (Chen & Mandell, 2016; Papacharissi, 2013), fostering an online environment where pretty much anything goes. In this context, incivility violates norms and also reifies the Internet as a place where the rules do not apply. For example, incivility is fairly common online, suggesting a virtual space where norms are less entrenched, yet incivility is driven most by infrequent commenters (Coe et al., 2014) who may be less attuned to norms. This suggests that people may feel freer to speak out uncivilly online but that normative forces still restrict them and influence how others perceive this incivility.

PUBLIC DELIBERATION

Given this definition of incivility, the question becomes: Can incivility ever be truly deliberative? First, we must consider what we mean by deliberation and why that may be a positive value for society. Political theorist Hannah Arendt (1958) argues that to be political means that decisions are made through discussion and persuasion, not battles. Implicit in this view is the idea that people will debate or disagree because as Arendt notes, "everybody sees and hears from a different position" (1958, p. 57). This give and take is the heart of deliberation. A deliberative disagreement is when people differ on basic moral views but seek to see the other side and resolve the difference (Gutmann & Thompson, 1996). In fact, this deliberation can generate communicative power (Habermas, 1994) to influence political elections and legislation. This discussion may take place in Congress, the courts, or the media. Political scientists Amy Gutmann and Dennis Thompson assert this debate also should occur in what they call the "land of middle democracy" (1996, p. 12), defined as any place where citizens come together. This deliberation is essential to the democratic process because it allows a wide range of voices to take part in the collective decision-making of a democracy, rather than limit that debate to a few. As political theorist Hélène Landemore explains: "In politics, the best knower is the group itself" (2012, p. 252). "Public talking" (Jacobs, Cook, & Delli Carpini, 2009, p. 4) is part of this vital deliberation because it identifies the issues that people see as important, thereby helping to inform the political process. Under this view, deliberation is not just a benefit of a free society but essential to maintaining freedom. We cannot be a nation of the people and for the people unless the people are part of the decision-making. Political scientist Harold D. Lasswell summed it up well years ago: "Democratic government acts upon public opinion and public opinion acts openly and continually upon government. This open interplay of opinion and policy is the distinguishing mark of popular rule" (1941, p. 15).

Scholars suggest deliberation must be universal, meaning it applies to everyone, not just elites; be inclusive, involve a diversity of voices; be rational, be rooted in reason; and also promote both agreement and political efficacy among the electorate (Jacobs et al., 2009). In other words, while deliberation undoubtedly includes disagreement, that disagreement should lead to consensus and improve the confidence of citizens in their own political knowledge. Gutmann and Thompson (1996) explain deliberation along similar lines. They argue that "moral disagreement" (p. 1)—conflict about fundamental issues—is at the root of deliberation. They submit that deliberation must be reciprocal, meaning it embraces different views; public, conducted in the view of others; and accountable, including justification for a particular viewpoint. In essence, deliberation does not mean that people do not argue or disagree even pointedly. It means they offer evidence of their viewpoints, they hear other sides, and they have open minds. It does not require politeness necessarily, just openness to ideas. When people disagree, "they should be deliberative with one another, seeking moral agreement when they can, and maintaining mutual respect when they cannot" (Gutmann & Thompson, 1996, p. 346).

DIGITAL DELIBERATION

Public deliberation can take place in many forms, including face-to-face and through collective group discussions, such as formal meetings (Jacobs et al., 2009). However, in this chapter, I am focused on deliberation only in the digital sphere, which has been touted as a more equalitarian space for debate but also criticized for reinforcing normative inequalities (Baek, Wojcieszak, & Delli Carpini, 2012; Dahlberg, 2011; Papacharissi, 2004). In the online space, deliberation tends to foment negative emotions and is less likely to lead to consensus and political action, but it also involves more diverse viewpoints, when compared with face-to-face deliberation (Baek et al., 2012). These diverse viewpoints are a key aspect of successful deliberation. It is important to note that people choose the media they pay attention to, and this selective exposure may increase the polarization of the electorate because people often select media messages that reinforce their own viewpoints (Stroud, 2011). Online this effect is most evident, as people easily can sort through information and choose what to read, share, or comment on. As they share and comment on what suits their interests, this can artificially inflate the importance of a particular viewpoint because it becomes popular online, even if it has little substantiation. Yet, deliberation has been found to take place in comments. One study found that discussions at *The New York Times* and *The Guardian* websites exhibited respect among commenters, diversity of ideas, and argumentation—hallmarks of sociologist Jürgen Habermas' principles of a democratic debate that are virtual re-enactments of eighteenth century cafés (Ruiz et al., 2011). However, the same study found a lack of these attributes in other newspapers, where comments expressed little diversity of opinion, derogatory messages were common, and commenters did not appear to be receptive to the views of other commenters. The commenters were sharing a view, but not deliberating in any real sense.

Deliberation, either online or off, is important because it is one of three key conditions for a democratic system to thrive. Communication and politics scholar James S. Fishkin (1991) suggests that democracy cannot occur without political equality, the absence of tyranny, and deliberation. As early as the days of James Madison, deliberation was seen as a means for the public to influence government, as part of the democratic process (Fishkin, 1991). Deliberation also can be seen as a method to identify issues that the public deems important, as a means to motivate government to address these topics (Jacobs et al., 2009). In the online environment deliberation also serves the role of communicating political information to other citizens, rather than influencing the government (Hoffman, Jones, & Young, 2013). People understand that some acts of political engagement, such as voting, influence government, but posting comments on news sites or liking or friending politicians online are about communicating information to other citizens, not to public officials (Hoffman et al., 2013). However, online deliberation has been found to influence people's knowledge of political issues, political efficacy, and willingness to participate in political activities (Min, 2007). Talking online, therefore, becomes a value in and of itself. The discussion of an issue with other interested citizens is part of ensuring an engaged electorate but also of spreading information among people, leading to a spiraling effect on the exchange of ideas. From this standpoint, it is important that topics are discussed, weighed, and even debated uncivilly. The benefit is that deliberation takes place, even if it becomes mired at times in harsh words, hurtful tones, or misinformation.

DELIBERATION AMID INCIVILITY

This brings us to the key question of this chapter: Can uncivil discourse allow for deliberation? My analysis of the literature suggests the answer is yes. Incivility suggests that people are likely facing an issue of moral disagreement (Gutmann & Thompson, 1996) when they speak out uncivilly online about the news of the day. Trivial matters, or those without clear sides (Stroud et al., 2014), are unlikely to generate enough emotional response to provoke incivility. When people feel strongly about an issue, and when an issue is important and offers clear sides, incivility is more likely (Stroud et al., 2015). In fact, incivility about an important issue may even spark people's intention to get politically engaged in that topic and fight for their viewpoint (Borah, 2014; Chen, 2016; Mutz & Reeves, 2005). One study found that incivility in online comments about abortion produced a negative emotional response, which in turn triggered women to feel greater intention to become politically involved in support of their view on abortion (Chen, 2016). Another study found that uncivil comments about same-sex marriage before the June 2015 U.S. Supreme Court decision that legalized gay marriage produced a similar effect. Dubbed the "defensive effect", this study showed that people confronted with uncivil comments experienced negative emotion that in turned prompted their intention to become involved politically in this issue (Chen & Zheng, 2016). These studies suggest that while incivility may harm by fostering negative emotions, it may also jumpstart political activity. An engaged electorate is the essence of what a democracy should be. Without an emotional response to news and information, people are bound to grow complacent and uninvolved. So there may be some limited merit when incivility stirs the pot so to speak and gets people engaged. The anecdote that started this chapter of virulent anti-refugee speech in the wake of the

Paris terrorist attack provides a compelling example. Much of the speech around that issue was abhorrent. However, it did raise the issue of how refugees should be handled and provoked refugee resettlement agencies and politicians to speak out in more measured ways. It fostered a dialogue. It encouraged the electorate to talk about the issue. It engaged politicians around the topic. Deliberation did occur despite the mire of harsh and hateful words.

However, caution should be taken. Other research has found that uncivil political talk induces feelings of anger and aversion, which increases anti-deliberative attitudes (Gervais, 2013). In addition, incivility has been found to make it more likely that people will respond back uncivilly (Chen & Lu, 2017), creating a dangerous cycle. Of course, I do not mean to suggest that incivility should be encouraged merely to foment political involvement. The best form of discourse is civil and deliberative, not uncivil. However, I do submit that seeing incivility as only a wide swath of speech with no value is shortsighted. Some incivility may encourage the political action and debate that is necessary in a democratic society. Tainted free speech is better than no speech. If online speech must be absent any shred of incivility to be tolerable, we may miss out on valuable viewpoints that should be heard. Indeed, one recent study suggests that incivility can interrupt the spiral of silence, which holds that people remain silent when they hold a minority viewpoint, by encouraging people to speak out, even when they see their view as unpopular (Chen, Fadnis, & Lu, 2016).

In addition, this analysis suggests that deliberation can take place through commenting, even when it is uncivil. The essence of deliberation is disagreement on a moral issue (Gutmann & Thompson, 1996). Disagreement can easily slip into incivility when emotions run hot. Even when this happens, however, it does not necessarily mean all deliberative qualities are absent. For example, uncivil comments certainly may offer alternative views, be conducted in public, and include a justification for the commenter's viewpoint, three essential tenets of public deliberation (Gutmann & Thompson, 1996). People can certainly swear and use harsh words but still make a case for their own point of view. Incivility fails to be deliberative when it lacks an open, rational mind that is inclusive to all and promotes agreement and political efficacy (Jacobs et al., 2009) or when it includes racist, sexist, xenophobic, or bigoted speech that obscures any deliberative qualities. It seems unlikely that incivility could foster agreement or make people feel open to join a conversation. This distinction is important because I argue our goal should not necessarily be to seek an end to all incivility, but rather to foster deliberation even in uncivil discourse. Research suggests we can do this by monitoring comments, requiring people to register before commenting and use real names (Santana, 2014), and by encouraging journalists to join the online conversations (Stroud et al., 2015) to foster a normative environment that is conducive to civility.

In summary, the research suggests that incivility is a more complicated concept than merely offensive or disrespectful speech. Solving the problem of incivility is not just about cleaning up speech. Incivility is both part of the human condition and normatively deviant. It creates speech that people shun but that also attracts them. It fosters emotions that may spark people to speak out, get politically involved, or to become less deliberative. In other words, incivility certainly offers harm, but is also can foster discussion. In a democratic society, even discourse that is not favored should be permitted. The chance that some deliberation may take place in online commenting, even if that chance is slight, makes this form of discourse important. This analysis suggests that the goal should be to foster deliberative speech through creating a normative atmosphere for this discourse, rather than focusing on prohibiting every hint of objectionable speech. The cure for uncivil online speech is more speech, not less. As Papacharissi (2004) explains: "One could argue that impoliteness is not so bad; it implies emotion, and emotion implies compassion, which in turn implies humanity. It is incivility without a trace of politeness, 'impeccable incivility,' that should frighten us" (p. 279).

REFERENCES

Anderson, A. A., Brossard, D., Scheufele, D. A., Xenos, M. A., & Ladwig, P. (2014). The "nasty effect": Online incivility and risk perceptions of online technologies. *Journal of Computer-Mediated Communication, 19*(3), 373–387.

Arendt, H. (1958). *The human condition*. Chicago, IL: University of Chicago Press.

Baek, Y. M., Wojcieszak, M., & Delli Carpini, M. X. (2012). Online versus face-to-face deliberation: Who? Why? What? With what effects? *New Media & Society, 14*(3), 363–383.

Baumeister, R. F., & Leary, M. R. (1995). The need to belong: Desire for interpersonal attachments as a fundamental human need. *Psychological Bulletin, 117*(3), 497–529.

Berry, J. M., & Sobieraj, S. (2014). *The outrage industry: Political opinion media and the new incivility*. New York, NY: Oxford University Press.

Blow, C. M. (2015, November 23). Anti-Muslim is anti-American. *The New York Times*. Retrieved from http://www.nytimes.com/2015/11/23/opinion/anti-muslim-is-anti-american.html

Boczkowski, P. J., & Mitchelstein, E. (2012). How users take advantage of different forms of interactivity on online news sites: Clicking, e-mailing, and commenting. *Human Communication Research, 38*(1), 1–22.

Borah, P. (2014). Does it matter where you read the news story? Interaction of incivility and news frames in the political blogosphere. *Communication Research, 41*(6). 809–827.

Bosman, J. (2015, November 23). A chill grips a Michigan haven for Syrian families. *The New York Times*. Retrieved from http://www.nytimes.com/2015/11/24/us/syrian-refugees-cling-to-a-longtime-haven-in-michigan.html

Brett, J. M., Olekalns, M., Friedman, R., Goates, N., Anderson, C., & Lisco, C. C. (2007). Sticks and stones: Language, face, and online dispute resolution. *Academy of Management Journal, 50*(1), 85–99.

Brooks, D. J., & Geer, J. G. (2007). Beyond negativity: The effect of incivility on the electorate. *American Journal of Political Science, 51*(1), 1–16.

Brost, L. F. (2013). Editors have mixed feelings on user-generated content. *Newspaper Research Journal, 34*(3), 101–115.

Chen, G. M. (2015). Losing *face* on social media: Threats to *positive face* lead to an indirect effect on retaliatory aggression through negative affect. *Communication Research, 42*(6), 819–838.

Chen, G. M. (2016, April). *News story comments indirectly increase intention to participate politically for women, mediated through negative affect.* Paper presented to the Mass Communication Division of the Southern States Communication Association at its annual meeting, Austin, Texas.

Chen, G. M., Fadnis, D., & Lu, S. (2016, June). *Unspiraling the silence: Online incivility and likelihood to speak out about safety of childhood vaccines.* Paper presented to the Health Communication Division of the International Communication Association at its annual conference, Fukuoka, Japan.

Chen, G. M., & Lu, S. (2017). Online political discourse: Exploring differences in effects of civil and uncivil disagreement in news website comments. *Journal of Broadcasting & Electronic Media, 61*(1): 108–125.

Chen, G. M., & Mandell, H. (2016). Conclusion: Predicting a new scandal environment in the 21st century. In H. Mandell & G.M. Chen (Eds.), *Scandal in a digital age.* New York, NY: Palgrave Macmillan.

Chen, G. M., & Ng, Y. M. M. (2016). Third-person perception of online comments: Civil ones persuade you more than me. *Computers in Human Behavior, 55,* 736–742.

Chen, G. M., & Zheng, P. (2016, August). *Online public discourse: Exploring differences in responses to civil and uncivil disagreement in news story comments.* Paper presented to the Mass Communication and Society Division of the Association for Education in Journalism and Mass Communication at its annual conference, Minneapolis, MN.

Chock, T. M., Wolf, J., Chen, G. M., Schweisberger, V. N., & Wang, Y. (2013). Social media features attract college students to news websites. *Newspaper Research Journal, 34*(4), 96–108.

Chung, M., Munno, G. J., & Moritz, B. (2015). Triggering participation: Exploring the effects of third-person and hostile media perceptions on online participation. *Computers in Human Behavior, 53,* 452–461.

Coe, K., Kenski, K., & Rains, S. A. (2014). Online and uncivil? Patterns and determinants of incivility in newspaper website comments. *Journal of Communication, 64*(4), 658–679.

Dahlberg, L. (2011). Re-constructing digital democracy: An outline of four positions. *New Media & Society, 13*(6), 855–872.

De Waal, F. B. M. (2008). Putting the altruism back into altruism: The evolution of empathy. *Annual Review of Psychology, 59,* 279–300.

Diamond, J. (2015, November 8). Donald Trump: Ban all Muslim travel to U.S. *CNN*.com. Retrieved from http://www.cnn.com/2015/12/07/politics/donald-trump-muslim-ban-immigration/

Fishkin, J. S. (1991). *Democracy and deliberation: New directions for democratic reform.* New Haven, CT: Yale University Press.

Frumin, A. (2015, November 19). 6 extreme responses to the Syrian refugee crisis. *MSNBC.com.* Retrieved from http://www.msnbc.com/msnbc/6-extreme-responses-the-syrian-refugee-crisis

Gervais, B. T. (2013, September). *Incivility in online political discourse and anti-deliberative attitudes: An experimental analysis.* Paper presented at the annual meeting of the American Political Science Association, Chicago, IL.

Grice, H. P. (1969). Utterer's meaning and intention. *The Philosophical Review, 78*(2), 147–177.

Gutmann, A., & Thompson, D. (1996). *Democracy and disagreement*. Cambridge, MA: Harvard University Press.

Habermas, J. (1994). Three normative models of democracy. *Constellations, 1*(1), 1–10.

Hoffman, L. H., Jones, P. E., & Young, D. G. (2013). Does my comment count? Perceptions of political participation in an online environment. *Computers in Human Behavior, 29*(6), 2248–2256.

Huang, E. (2007). Use of rich media differs at newspapers, TV web sites. *Newspaper Research Journal, 28*(3), 85–97.

Jacobs, L. R., Cook, F. L., & Delli Carpini, M. X. (2009). *Talking together: Public deliberation and political participation in America*. Chicago, IL: University of Chicago Press.

Klofstad, C. A., Sokhey, A. E., & McClurg, S. D. (2013). Disagreeing about disagreement: How conflict in social networks affects political behavior. *American Journal of Political Science, 57*(1), 120–134.

Ksiazek, T. B. (2015). Civil interactivity: How news organizations' commenting policies explain civility and hostility in user comments. *Journal of Broadcasting & Electronic Media, 59*(4), 556–573.

Landemore, H. (2012). Democratic reason: The mechanism of collective intelligence in politics. In H. Landemore & J. Elster (Eds.), *Collective wisdom: Principles and mechanisms* (pp. 251–289). New York, NY: Cambridge University Press.

Lasswell, H. D. (1941). *Democracy through public opinion*. Menasha, WI: George Banta Publishing.

Laurent, O. (2015, November 16). 70 million people shared their prays for Paris on Instagram this weekend. *Time*. Retrieved from http://time.com/4114288/paris-instagram/

Min, S. (2007). Online vs. face-to-face deliberation: Effects on civic engagement. *Journal of Computer-Mediated Communication, 12*(4), 1369–1387.

Moor, P. J., Heuvelman, A., & Verleur, R. (2010). Flaming on YouTube. *Computers in Human Behavior, 26*(6), 1536–1546.

Mutz, D. C., & Reeves, B. (2005). The new videomalaise: Effects of televised incivility on political trust. *American Political Science Review, 99*, 1196–1211.

Ng, E. W. J., & Detenber, B. H. (2005). The impact of synchronicity and civility in online political discussions on perceptions and intentions to participate. *Journal of Computer-Mediated Communication, 10*(3), n.p.

O'Sullivan, P. B., & Flanagin, A. J. (2003). Reconceptualizing 'flaming' and other problematic messages. *New Media & Society, 5*(1), 69–94.

Papacharissi, Z. (2004). Democracy online: Civility, politeness, and the democratic potential of online political discussion groups. *New Media & Society, 6*(2), 259–283.

Papacharissi, Z. (2013). *A private sphere: Democracy in a digital age*. Malden, MA: Polity Press.

Reeves, B., & Nass, C. (1996). *The media equation*. Cambridge, MA: Cambridge University Press.

Rowe, I. (2015). Deliberation 2.0: Comparing the deliberative quality of online news user comments across platforms. *Journal of Broadcasting & Electronic Media, 59*(4), 539–555.

Rubin, A. J. (2015, December 15). 3 held in connection with Paris attacks in January and November. *The New York Times*. Retrieved from http://www.nytimes.com/2015/12/16/world/europe/3-held-in-connection-with-paris-attacks-in-january-and-november.html

Ruiz, C., Domingo, D., Micó, J. L., Díaz-Noci, J., Meso, K., & Maship, P. (2011). Public sphere 2.0? The democratic qualities of citizen debates in online newspapers. *The International Journal of Press/Politics, 16*(4), 463–487.

Santana, A. D. (2014). Virtuous or vitriolic: The effect of anonymity on civility in online reader comment boards. *Journalism Practice, 8*(1), 18–33.

Shoemaker, P. J. (1982). The perceived legitimacy of deviant political groups: Two experiments on media effects. *Communication Research, 9*(2), 249–286.

Shoemaker, P. J. (1984). Media treatment of deviant groups. *Journalism Quarterly, 61*(1), 66–82.
Shoemaker, P. J. (1996). Hardwired for news: Using biological and cultural evolution to explain the surveillance function. *Journal of Communication, 46*(3), 32–47.
Shoemaker, P. J., & Vos, T. P. (2009). *Gatekeeping theory.* New York, NY: Routledge.
Sobieraj, S., & Berry, J. M. (2011). From incivility to outrage: Political discourse in blogs, talk radio, and cable news. *Political Communication, 28*(1), 19–41.
Stroud, N. J. (2011). *Niche news: The politics of news choice.* New York, NY: Oxford University Press.
Stroud, N. J., Scacco, J. M., Muddiman, A., & Curry, A. L. (2015). Changing deliberative norms on news organizations' Facebook sites. *Journal of Computer-Mediated Communication, 20*(2), 188–203.
Sukumaran, A., Vezich, S., McHugh, M., & Nass, C. (2011). *Normative influences on thoughtful online participation.* Proceedings of the CHI 2011 Session: Incentives & User Generated Content, Vancouver, British Columbia.
Tenenboim, O., & Cohen, A. A. (2015). What prompts users to click and comment: A longitudinal study of online news. *Journalism, 16*(2), 198–217.
Tremayne, M., Schmitz, A., & Alves, R. C. (2007). From product to service: The diffusion of dynamic content in online newspapers. *Journalism & Mass Communication Quarterly, 84*(4), 825–839.
Weber, P. (2014). Discussions in the comments section: Factors influence participation and interactivity in online newspapers' reader comments. *New Media & Society, 16*(6), 941–957.

CHAPTER FOUR

Influences of Audience Feedback on News Content in Traditional and New Media

A Theoretical Evaluation

GANG (KEVIN) HAN* AND JOSH SHEAR†

Web 2.0 has changed the field of mass communications from a broadcast model of one-way, one-to-many communications to an on-demand, interactive model where many-to-many communications predominate. We believe that Internet-based media increase the importance of understanding both sides of the media equation, namely content production and content reaction.

Little theoretical work has been done, however, regarding the influence of audience feedback on news content either for traditional media or for new media. Existing models of mass communication acknowledge the existence of audience feedback but research has primarily focused on the effects of media content on the audience, not vice-versa. The paradigms concerning media effects, which treat audience feedback as an important assumption, nevertheless, have been able to dominate the field of mass communication for decades. While the prior art of mass communication research provides an adequate basis for the study of some parts of

* Gang (Kevin) Han is Associate Professor in Greenlee School of Journalism and Communication at Iowa State University. Email: ghan@iastate.edu.

† Josh Shear is a senior producer for Advance Digital's National Desk, a co-creator of the Josh & Kelvin World Domination Podcast, and the creator of Josh: The Podcast. Email: jshear@advance.net.

feedback processes, no theoretical or operational definitions of feedback were found in the literature and so had to be constructed for the purposes of this discussion.

In this chapter, first, we try to explicate the concept of feedback from both outside and inside the mass communication field, followed by a discussion on audience's influences on media content. It paves the way to a better understanding of the concept from a broader interdisciplinary background. Second, we review the theoretical perspectives related to the role of Internet-based media in news production. After assessing the assumptions underlying our endeavor for theory building, we then propose a variety of attributes of audience feedback and evaluate several theoretical hypotheses that address the influence of feedback on both traditional and online media production. Finally, we provide a summary and further elaboration on our theoretical ideas regarding feedback, as well as suggest opportunities for future research.

FEEDBACK

Feedback: The Lexicographical Significance

Originally, feedback is a noun that refers to the return to the input of a part of output of machine, system or process as for producing changes in an electronic circuit that improve performance or in an automatic control device that provides self-corrective action (Merriam-Webster's, 1993, p. 427). Defined as the partial reversion of the effects of a process to its source or to a preceding stage, feedback also means the transmission of evaluative or corrective information to the original or controlling source about an action, event or process. It can thus be used to refer to the information so transmitted. Dividing feedback, the noun, into two words, then to feedback becomes a verbal phrase that describes the behavior or action from the information receiver to its sender as a kind of response. As Norbert Wiener, the father of cybernetics, writes, "in its simplest form the feedback principle means that a behavior is tested with reference to its result and success or failure of this result influences the future behavior" (Wiener, 1958, p. 55; see also Underwood, 2003).

Feedback: A Multi-Disciplinary Concept

Feedback has become a key concept in a number of disciplines. From the early days of electronics, feedback has been emphasized for studies in engineering and applied sciences. For example, one of the original uses of feedback was to improve the quality of early electronic amplifiers (Brignell, 2004).

Feedback is also used in biological systems to maintain stability. Brignell (2004) raises the example of homeostasis, and points out that this process keeps conditions in the healthy human body constant, regardless of a wide variation of magnitudes in external stimuli. Disrupting such processes can cause illness and death.

In computer models, feedback was once regarded as a powerful but dangerous concept (Brignell, 2004). Models with multiple feedback loops are likely to be chaotic (very small changes in coefficients produce very large changes of behavior). Feedback can exaggerate the effects of computational errors (noise) and systems can become capable of operating on the noise alone regardless of any inputs.

Golec (2004) provides a model (Figure 4.1) when he discusses feedback in economics. He emphasizes the importance of feedback mechanisms and their ubiquity in our life, and then introduces a simplifying division between the systemic view of feedback and the decision-making view of feedback. The former is understood as a regularly interacting or interdependent group of items forming a unified whole, in which there are two basic kinds of feedback, namely: positive and negative feedback. A feedback mechanism is positive if the resulting action goes in the same direction as the condition that triggers it and negative if the resulting action goes in the opposite direction to the condition that triggers it.

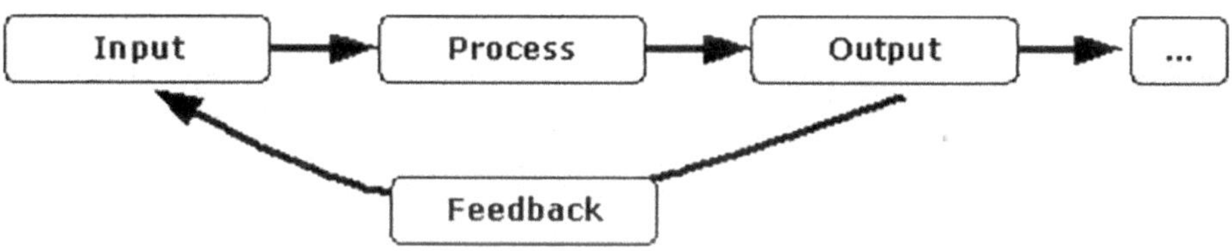

Figure 4.1: Feedback Mechanisms (source: www.economicswebinstitute.org/glossary/feedback.htm)

From the point of view of decision-making, attention is put on the processes controlled by humans, as opposed to the processes controlled by artificial intelligence. Golec points out that we have to notice the qualitative change in the weight of positive and negative feedback. A decision-maker receiving positive feedback tends to be motivated to continue with the previously chose course of action, with or without slight modifications of it. If provided with negative feedback, the decision-maker has a tendency to feel demotivated and search for other alternatives to solve the problem. In this sense, consumer behavior and brand loyalty can be viewed as "a trial-and-error" process in marketing.

Based on modern control theory, Lewis (1992) further explains a related concept, feedback control, as the use of difference signals, determined by comparing the actual values of system variables with their desired values, as a means of controlling a system. It is the basic mechanism by which systems, whether mechanical, electrical, or biological, maintain their equilibrium or homeostasis. Lewis argues that a primary contribution of Charles Darwin was the theory that feedback over long time periods is responsible for the evolution of species. In this sense, feedback controls not only people-made systems such as those used to control aircraft and industrial processes, but also natural systems such as those that occur in living organisms or in social systems. Lewis maintains that although feedback control is an engineering discipline, the development of mass communications at the beginning of the twentieth century indeed affected the progress of social feedback control.

Feedback: As a Component of Communication Models

Shannon and Weaver (1949), two forerunners of information theory, propose a general model of communication. Although primarily applied to telecommunication technology, their model has served as one of the important cornerstones upon which human communication study achieved further development. This model suggests that all communication must include six elements: source, encoder, message, channel, decoder and receiver. Emphasizing mainly the transmission and reception of information, communication here is viewed as a one-way process, although the modified model (see Figure 4.2) mentions feedback initiated from the receiver.

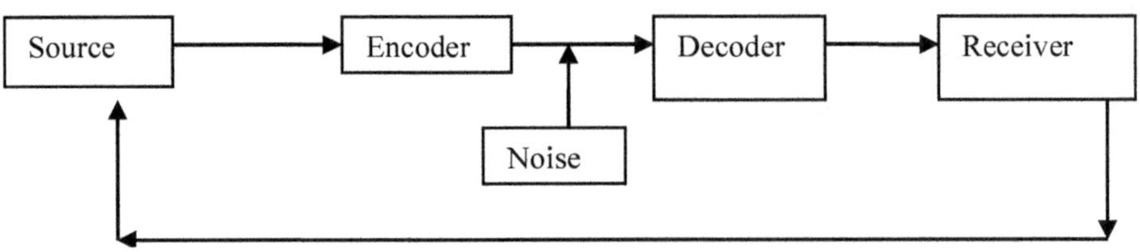

Figure 4.2: The Modified Shannon-Weaver Information Model of Communication

At the same time, Lasswell (1948) categorizes mass communication processes into his well-known 5-W's model that underlies many endeavors in mass communication theory construction in the U.S. Although including audience in the model, however, Lasswell does not explicitly mention feedback as a component of a communication process.

Viewing it as a vital part of communication, Underwood (2003) emphasizes the importance of feedback. For example, he suggests that the lack of feedback explains why people do not like getting voice mail when they make a phone call. Conveyed in the visual channel through body language, feedback also makes face-to-face interaction meaningful in interpersonal communication. Likewise, the public's feedback is crucial to advertisers, broadcasters, and politicians through mass communication, where marketing surveys, TV ratings and opinion polls have been employed as routine vehicles for either receiving or retrieving feedback. As

Underwood (2003) further points out, positive feedback, by showing interest, will encourage the communicator or information sender to continue in the same fashion. Negative feedback, by showing dullness, will conversely force the content to be changed or discontinued.

AUDIENCE'S INFLUENCES ON MEDIA CONTENT

It should be noted that "mass communication research has been dominated by an effects-orientation" (Lowery & DeFleur, 1995, p. viii; see also Bryant & Zillmann, 2002), as media effects have "traditionally fascinated communications researchers" (Shoemaker & Reese, 1996, p. 22) at least for several decades.

Throughout the evolution of paradigms from a powerful effects model (e.g., "magic bullet theory") in early days of communication research to a limited-or moderate-effects model then returning to a strong-effects model, the individual audience is always treated as one of the key variables. The audience serves as either the starting point (e.g., information seeking, see Sears & Freedman, 1971; uses and gratifications, see Katz, 1959), or the destination of effects (e.g., cultivation, see Gerbner, Gross, Jackson-Beeck, Jeffries-Fox, & Signorielli, 1978). Whether media have impact on audience members, to a certain extent, depends on how the audience respond in one way or another after using the media or getting exposed to media content. In this respect, the process, form and structure of feedback are usually implied as assumptions for effects studies. We could not measure the effect or impact of mass communication or media content on individuals, or vice-versa, without examining their feedback in some ways.

Furthermore, the feedback loop can serve as an indispensable component in the process of communication not only because it may carry out certain effects on the audience, on one hand, but also because it will bring back responses from the public to communicators, on the other hand.

Shoemaker and Reese's hierarchical model (1996) assesses the audience as a component of influences on content from outside of media organizations, where feedback is not explicitly examined. They point out that the assumption for those studies that focus on target audiences is that "media workers actually do know what the desired target audience wants" (p. 192). They also argue, "the problem is that even if they want to know what the audience wants, journalists may have little knowledge—or incorrect information—about the audience they communicate with" (p. 192). Moreover, they find that "for most commercial media, audiences are important only because their attention can be sold to advertisers" (p. 192). In this respect, it is the advertisers, not the audiences, who influence the relationship among audiences, the media and their content. The direct or pure influence of the audience feedback on content, therefore, needs to be further investigated. In this chapter, we argue that feedback has become a bonding point that sets up a linkage among media effects, audience analysis and the factors at individual levels that influence media content production.

"NEW" MEDIA

We explicated the interdisciplinary concept, feedback, in the previous section. We then linked it to news work that narrows our discussion to a more specific context related to journalism and mass communication, focusing on how audience feedback may affect media content in a mass communication process. In this section we clarify the characteristics of "new media", i.e., Internet-based mass media, that may have reshaped news production. This section serves as a reference point for our further discussion on a variety of attributes of audience feedback and the role audience feedback plays in news production involving both "traditional" and "new" media.

"New media", where the Internet serves as the primary infrastructure for information distribution, have drawn increasing scholarly attention since the late 1990s. The elements of new media both as a diffuse continuum and as discrete entities have distinguished them from their predecessors, which are conventionally termed as "traditional media": principally print, radio, television and film, and all other forms of media in existence at the inception of the Internet in 1969. On one hand, new media facilitate the online consumption of large amounts of content of a broad variety. On the other hand, in comparison with "traditional media", new media, including social networking sites, significantly differ in ways an audience can produce content and react to it. Computers and the Internet have removed or reduced financial, geographic, political, cultural and time constraints on producers and audiences and increase access to mass media. Rapid publication cycles and the labile nature of digital formats allow content to be ever more quickly updated, superseded, altered, and rescinded. New media provide venues where news organizations and audience interact with each other more frequently, in many cases, in real time. The public's feedback to news items thus can be readily heard by the journalists and the producers. Audience members can also more easily publish their reactions to content, and interact with each other and with the world at large to constitute a reaction stream, the flow of ideas and processes that forms in the wake of publication.

In recent years, scholars (e.g., Biven, 2014) have seen a shift of news production from a "vertical" mode of traditional media—few producers, many consumers and little interaction between the two (p. 8)—to a "horizontal" one, where the public has the ability to broadcast news through social networking platforms (p. 7). Public participation with increased use of new media thus blurs the border between news production and news consumption, as well as offers and expands the "opportunities for exploitation of feedback loops" (Biven, 2014, p. 124) in newsrooms. When production streams are more easily influenced through reaction streams than ever before, the ideas of the audience become part of a production stream that result in content.

Meanwhile, it should be noted that the production of new media content is dominated by not one but legions of nominal publishers—people whose daily activities generate content incidental to the primary purpose of their efforts. Nominal publishers take many forms in new media. In addition to online magazines and newspapers, there are personal websites and interactive sites that facilitate content creation by private individuals acting on their own. Wikis, weblogs, message boards, podcasts, and the likes of Facebook, Twitter and Instagram can drive content. Nominal publishers operate in an environment of instant communication where the mediation stream flows unimpeded and some content is produced directly by audiences. For this reason, content produced by these nominal publishers should be more dynamic and cover a greater diversity of subject matter than content produced by traditional media.

This is not to say that new media limit the social effects of content produced by nominal publishers, though specific forms of new media are likely to pick producers. For purposes of achieving a state of public awareness in the public sphere of new media, aggregation favors large numbers over loud voices so nominal publishers, who create the most content related to a specific subject, or, more likely, a specific cause, are at a vantage point.

Online communities, blogs, public listservs and similar forms of organized publication, along with social networking sites, are more likely to bring a subject to public awareness through the mechanism of realization confluence. Individuals intent on publishing news are more likely to form, or seek out and join, some organized online effort and in doing so exploit realization confluence than publishing information on their own.

Moreover, nominal producers of new media are often considered to be less bounded by barriers of institutional structure and entrenched media routines that act to filter the flow of feedback to producers of traditional media, although some online news producers have mimicked their traditional media counterparts in the use of journalistic routines (Boczkowski, 2005).

Today, new media producers of news are able to adopt more interactive practices to better incorporate audience feedback into news production. With regard to this study, we think the influence of direct feedback from individual audience members to individual news producers will become increasingly important and indirect feedback has greater influence on content production (see Figure 4.3).

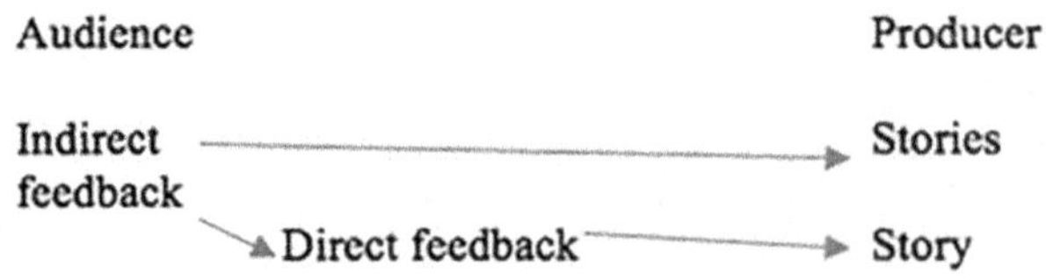

Figure 4.3: Direct Feedback and Indirect Feedback Affecting News Content

ASSUMPTIONS

Before proposing theoretical hypotheses on audience feedback and content production, we first discuss the underlying assumptions.

Assumption 1: Only two significant forms of mass communication exist: traditional analog media such as print, radio, television, and film; and new media in which information is created and transmitted in digital formats over the Internet, on computers, portable or mobile devices or through other digital formats.

The following is the context of this assumption. News organizations have experimented widely with different forms of digital news publication since the latter part of the last century. The Internet has caught on whereby many forms of digital publishing or digital media (such as videotext and facsimile transmission) have faded out or been abandoned. New forms of digital publication involving mobile phones and other wireless devices are becoming important media and they incorporate Internet protocols to function. It should be noted that this assumption does not mean the two forms of mass communication must exist separately. Rather, some forms of media may probably coexist in a symbiotic relationship with the Internet in a way that amplifies audience feedback because media outlets have been developing interactive applications that use emerging technologies.

Assumption 2: Mass communication is characterized by the presence of a mass audience.

Such an assumption about traditional media is automatic and hardly questionable, and in fact is the primary defining characteristic of mass communication. Conventional broadcast and cable media are inherently media of mass communication because they publish stories produced by few and consumed by many. Mass publication of newspapers, books and magazines is the same.

However, the existence of a mass audience apparently does not mean that the entire audience is consuming the same content. The current trend toward increasing customization of content and format has led to a situation in which the audience for a particular media outlet is consuming different content formatted in different ways for each member. In this case it seems clear that the definition of mass audience itself could be changing in a way that affects feedback.

Assumption 3: Some forms of computer-mediated communication are forms of mass communication, which we term computer-mediated mass communication (CMMC).

Following the previous assumptions, CMMC is any form of computer-mediated communication that is consumed by a mass audience. Included are not only online representations of traditional media but also newer forms such as list-servs, weblogs, Wikis, microblogging (e.g., Twitter), multi-user domains (MUDs), social networking media (e.g., Facebook), and online learning communities.

Assumption 4: Feedback from an audience to producers of online and traditional media takes the same or similar forms, including:

- Synchronous and direct such as personal contact, telephone calls, online comments, chat, and direct tweets.
- Asynchronous and direct such as e-mails and letters to the editor.
- Asynchronous and indirect such as survey results, weblogs, microblogging, message boards, posts on social media, reviews, and so forth.

The basis for this assumption is the observation that producers of all media have access to all existing forms of communication. Moreover, feedback in this article mainly refers to an active, meaningful way to respond to news content conventionally produced by mainstream media either in traditional ways or via social channels (e.g., comments posted on social networking sites), but not on a) mainstream media's active solicitation of news stories from the public, b) the more recent, social recommendation or distribution of news stories, such as "most emailed", "liking" or "sharing", which is viewed more often as news consumption rather than production, and c) user-generated content (UGC) that initiates a post or publication of a story through breaking news at social networking platforms by non-professional reporters or ordinary users, which is viewed more often from the perspective of citizen journalism. We still count in UGC that starts with a public contribution to professional news production by providing news organizations with such materials as texts, photos and videos that can be adopted or incorporated into professionally edited news items (Biven, 2014, p. 19). It is the news organization, producers and professional journalists who decide whether and how to include the public's feedback in their professionally edited or updated news items.

In addition, it should be noted that the forms of feedback keep updating or evolving as some "new" forms fade in while some "old" fade out, against the ever-changing media landscape. It is thus a plausible argument that this study does not aim to exhaust all potential or newly emerging feedback forms in discussion. Related to Assumption 4, there could be a possible fourth option of feedback form—synchronous and indirect, which was not examined in this study. For example, Web or digital analytics, a process of tracking user activity (e.g., traffic) or interaction on websites, social networking platforms and mobile applications, may fall into this category. The data and reports derived from web analytics are mainly used to evaluate the effectiveness of an organization's online presence, in order to attract more visitors, increase sales, or improve user engagement or retention (Thurstradius, 2017). Likewise, in journalism, editors employ web analytics in decision making mostly on selection and placement of news stories on webpage, as well as on distribution and promotion of stories through social networking. For an instance, news stories got good traffic would get more "updates and follow-ups", and popular topics would thus "get assigned more" (Tandoc, 2014, p. 567). Although journalists may also use web metrics to determine how to edit headlines for eye-catching or how to choose visual stuff to accompany a story, webpage traffic seems to be the primary concern of editors in adopting web analytics in newsroom. Audience feedback, in this sense, is "reduced to news page views and clicks" (p. 569). Therefore, this type of "feedback", collected often with audience measurement tool (ratings or circulation figures can be other examples) or algorithm-based metrics in an "unobtrusive" way, may be more closely related to online marketing or promotion (even for news websites or certain stories) than to the audience's substantive contribution specifically to news facts included in news content production per se, at least at this stage.

Assumption 5: Feedback refers to news stories published by the specific media outlet on which they are received and not to stories by a different media outlet that may belong to the same parent media organization. In such cases it is assumed that feedback will be distinguishable as to the particular story referenced.

For instance, it is conceivable that viewers of a television show could react to a story by posting a message on the website of the media organization that owns the television station and which may also have produced an online version of the same story. It is also possible that audiences may choose to respond to a story published by one media outlet on another, different media outlet. The occurrence of situations like these can only add to the difficulty of studying feedback.

Assumption 6: Increasing amounts of feedback in new media formats will facilitate the study of feedback at the same time that they increase the influence of feedback on the production of news content.

Feedback in new media formats tends to be persistent and publicly accessible and therefore should be more easily captured for study. Although it appears that the amounts of accessible (online, digital) feedback are growing, it could also be that the amounts of inaccessible (offline, analog) feedback are also growing and that the influences of these two forms of feedback are different.

HYPOTHESES

In this study, we propose three hypotheses that can be refined in future studies to test the influence of audience feedback on content production in both traditional and new media.

Hypothesis 1: Indirect feedback has more influence on content than direct feedback.

Here, feedback type is treated as the independent variable and refers to the extent to which messages from an audience to a news producer are either direct or indirect. Feedback can be direct, as in a message received from an audience member by a producer such as an email, letter, telephone call, or chat message; or indirect as in a message received from an audience member by a producer that is mediated through an agent such as a person or group of people, or a publication such as a newspaper, blog, message board, a poll, or a survey.

As a dependent variable, feedback influence assesses the extent to which a news producer creates or alters the content of news stories in response to messages received from audience members.

Theoretically, we may notice that feedback mediated through some agency is likely to be formalized, aggregated, and bear some degree of institutional authority. As a result, it may be delivered with an expectation of action by the producer and is less easily ignored than feedback from a single individual delivered directly.

This hypothesis describes a positive linear relationship between the type of feedback (direct and indirect) and the influence that feedback has on the content or publication of a news story. This hypothesized relationship is given in Figure 4.4.

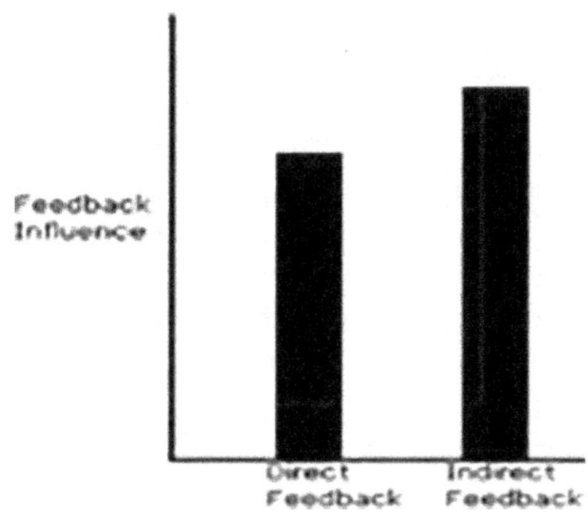

Figure 4.4: Hypothesized Relationship Between Feedback Type and Feedback Influence on News Stories

Boundary conditions for Hypothesis 1: a) This may be true only for media outlets located in countries which have little or no governmental regulation or influence in content production. b) This may be true only in countries where adequate infrastructure exists so that audiences can have easy access to communications technology that allows them to provide feedback.

Hypothesis 2: The more variety of feedback, the more likely the feedback is to be used as media content. Specifically, the more privileged forms of feedback are available, the more likely the feedback is to be used as media content; meanwhile, the more the categories of feedback received, the more likely the feedback is to be used as media content.

The independent variable, feedback variety, is defined as a) the number of privileged forms in which messages can be provided to a media outlet, and b) the number of feedback categories present in the content of a message.

Privileged forms can be a designated physical address, a designated email address, a dedicated feedback form, a dedicated telephone number, an online comment form, an online message board, a blog, a wiki, or a chat applet, to name a few.

Types of feedback content are opinion, comments, or supplemental information that are relevant to a news story.

The dependent variable, feedback content, mentions the extent to which content from feedback is included in a news story. For example, the number of times that content from a feedback message is quoted or paraphrased in the content of a news story; or the amount in words, inches or duration of content from a feedback message used as content in a news story.

Media outlets that provide many privileged forms for feedback are likely to receive more feedback and more valuable feedback than outlets that provide fewer privileged forms. The greater amount of feedback and the greater value assigned to it the greater the likelihood that excerpts from feedback will be included in news items.

This hypothesis predicts a positive relationship among the number of forms that feedback can take (or the number of categories of feedback given) and the amount of (or the frequency of) content from feedback that is used as content in news stories. Figures 4.5–4.8 illustrate the two linkages that show the combinations of the two independent variables (the form and kinds of feedback) and the two dependent variables (amount used and number of times used).

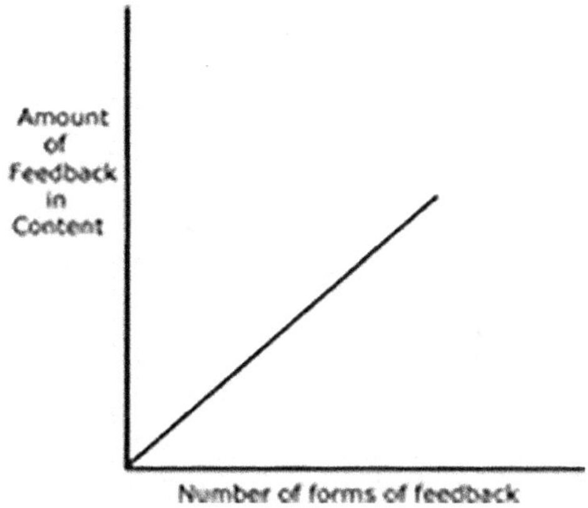

Figure 4.5: Hypothesized Relationship Between the Number of Privileged Forms of Feedback and the Amount of Content from Feedback that is Included in a News Story

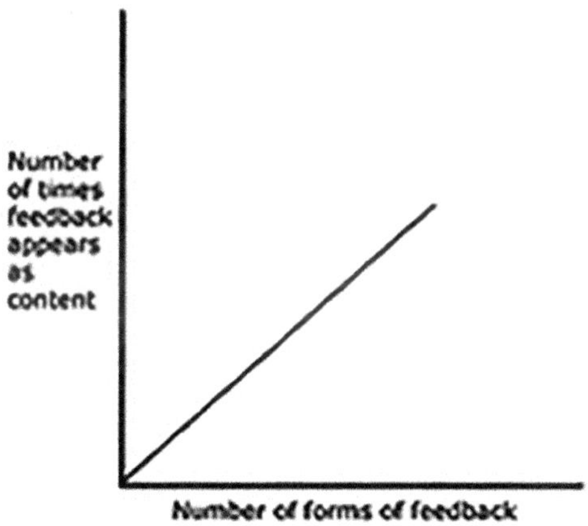

Figure 4.6: Hypothesized Relationship Between the Number of Privileged Forms of Feedback and the Number of Times Feedback Appears as Content in News Stories

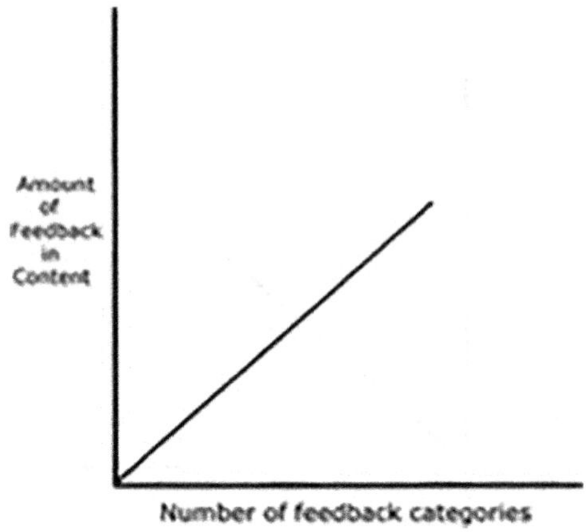

Figure 4.7: Hypothesized Relationship Between the Number of Feedback Categories and the Amount of Feedback Included as Content in News Stories

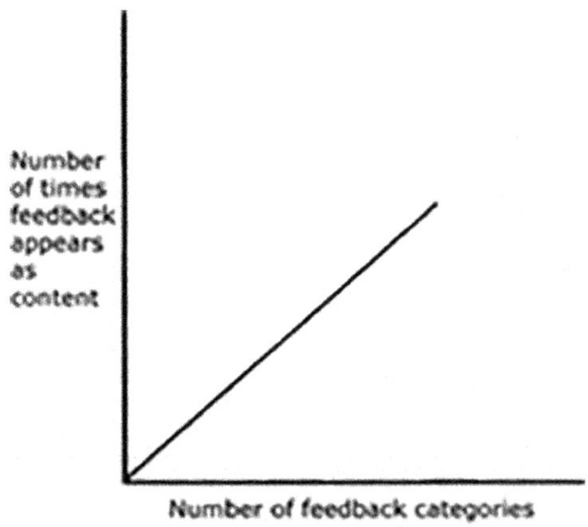

Figure 4.8: Hypothesized Relationship Between the Number of Feedback Categories and the Number of Times Feedback Appears as Content in News Stories

Boundary conditions for Hypothesis 2: This may be true only for media outlets that have a means to supply accessible forms of feedback such as a website, or a social media account. Indirect feedback may exist but may not be known or accessible to researchers, thus nullifying the hypothesis.

Hypothesis 3: The more newsworthy the feedback is, the more likely the feedback is to be used as news content.

Newsworthiness, as the independent variable, refers to the news determinants that are present in feedback content, including timeliness, proximity, relevance, novelty, deviance, significance, etc. (e.g., Shoemaker & Cohen, 2006; Shoemaker, Lee, Han, & Cohen, 2007).

Feedback content, as the dependent variable, is similar to that in Hypothesis 2 and suggests the extent to which content from feedback is included in a news story, in terms of the number of times that content from a feedback message is quoted or paraphrased in a news story, or the number of words, inches or duration of content from a feedback message that is used in a news story.

Studies on news making and gatekeeping have found that newsworthy information is more likely to be included as content in a news story than ordinary information. Feedback can be a convenient source of newsworthy information; therefore, it is likely to be included as content in a news story.

This hypothesis predicts a positive relationship between news value that feedback has and the amount of (or the frequency of) content from feedback that is used as content in news stories. Figures 4.9 and 4.10 demonstrate the two linkages that show the combinations of the independent (news values) and two dependent variables (amount used and number of times used).

Boundary conditions for Hypothesis 3: This may not be true for media outlets that lack audiences for which commonality of new values can be established. For instance, an online newspaper may have a global audience, in which case news values may not apply across all audience segments. Likewise, stories may be timely for one audience segment and lack timeliness for another audience segment. Therefore, news values may be interpreted ambiguously by such media outlets.

Figure 4.9: Hypothesized Relationship Between the Number of News Determinants and the Amount of Feedback Included as Content in News Stories

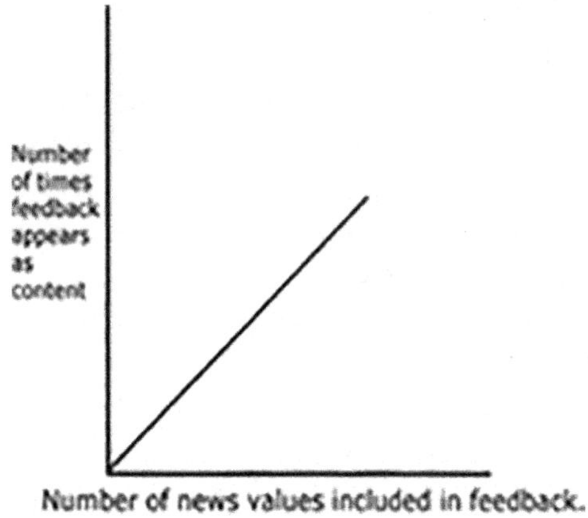

Figure 4.10: Hypothesized Relationship Between the Number of News Determinants and the Number of Times Feedback Appears as Content in News Stories

DISCUSSION

In this chapter, we explicate the concept of feedback and outline a theoretical framework examining the role the audience feedback plays in news production. This endeavor is expected to facilitate a better understanding of audience's influence on media content, accommodating today's trend toward a decentralized and interactive model of mass communication.

News production in traditional media is dominated by established routines of centralized newsgathering. These routines include provision of formal mechanisms for feedback that have taken the forms of letters (such as "letters to the editor"), telephone calls (as are sometimes solicited during radio and television shows), and audience surveys and focus groups.

With regard to the offline-online, hybrid production of news, earlier observation (Boczkowski, 2005) found that online versions of newspapers typically copied their traditional routines despite experimentation with what he terms distributed construction practices. Broadcast and cable outlets such as NBC, CNN and the BBC have likewise integrated their online news production into their established newsroom processes. To some extent, the early online operations of traditional media outlets persisted in limiting feedback mechanisms in order to retain their gatekeeping roles.

With the rapid growth of Internet-based or computer-mediated mass communication, however, traditional media have gradually but quickly picked up and adopted additional online feedback mechanisms in which the audience may have a stronger say that contributes to content. It should be noted (Boczkowski, 2005), meanwhile, when interacting with their fellow members online, audiences generally did not provide content related to news stories. Rather, they hosted the communities as integrated parts of the online presence or the websites of the media outlet. This phenomenon may raise questions about the definition of feedback, especially in new media.

In traditional media, privileged forms of contact mechanisms automatically define the audience's role in such communications as feedback. The online versions of traditional media replicate these privileged mechanisms, for instance through the provision of online feedback forms and email accounts designated for receiving feedback. However, as with newer modalities of online communication, not all messages received by a news producer from an audience can be strictly characterized as feedback. Depending on the format available to the audience, the content of their communication can range from commentary about a news story to the complete construction of a news story itself. It can also be completely unrelated to news (e.g., the data collected through web analytics tool as discussed above). While a particular format can allow and promote content of a particular type, it is the content itself that is the distinguishing feature.

In this chapter we considered feedback as the response from an audience in reaction to media content. Specifically, feedback is the effect of media content by which the audience makes comments and voices opinions to the producer in order to provide additional information, correction, or evaluation.

This definition distinguishes contact between producer and audience on the basis of initiation and intent rather than the form of communication. For instance, source content would be provided by a person contacted by a producer. The information this person provided would not be characterized as feedback. Likewise, a press release received by the producer could be considered source material or feedback depending on whether or not it mentioned a published news item.

The production of news does not occur in a vacuum, however. It is possible and likely that communications between audience members and producers may be indirect and may contain content that is in reaction to news items meeting our conditions of informing, correcting or evaluating only intangibly. It is even likely that the most important effects of feedback on the production of news content occur in reaction to indirect feedback, rather than to direct feedback. The methodology of the study of feedback is complicated by this situation. Direct feedback can be measured by observing flows of information through privileged channels such as counting letters and emails, and conducting content analyses, perhaps in conjunction with experiments that manipulate the news items. As for indirect feedback, it requires greater effort to identify as well as higher degrees of subjective interpretation to analyze. Surveys, focus groups, and ethnographic/participatory observation are possible methodological approaches.

With some forms of audience-to-producer communication, the boundary between feedback and communications other than feedback are not distinct, even with the application of a strict definition. For instance, certain websites provide a means by which the audience can construct a news story in its entirety. It is difficult to know in such cases whether the story itself was created spontaneously or was motivated by a desire to inform, correct or evaluate some prior story.

Likewise, the persistence of online news items combined with the practice of syndication (as through RSS) creates situations where feedback may be relevant to a story originated by a producer who is not a mediator of the outlet on which the story appeared and to which the feedback is directed, even if the feedback is received through privileged feedback channels. The disconnection between producer and outlet has, to a lesser degree, always existed in traditional media outlets but is common online. Should these communications be considered feedback? If a producer reacts to such communications in the creation of new stories then it would seem that they are, indeed, feedback. This raises the question of whether producer mediation should be considered in the definition of feedback in addition to the conditions of informing, correcting, and evaluating.

Mediation is itself changed in new media outlets. In traditional media it is necessary for a journalist of the subscribing media outlet to review syndicated news items and make decisions about the selection, editing, and formatting of the syndicated content. In new media, an algorithm often replaces this journalistic decision making process, to the point where syndicated content appears verbatim in an online outlet. The limits of machine automation are being expanded from the simple ability to clone news stories across many websites by news aggregators such as news.google.com to more advanced personalized selection of news feeds on social networking sites such as Facebook. No research has been done on the effects of such artificial intelligence systems on content production, yet they promise to bring about great changes in media routines. These systems certainly play a role in establishing the importance of a news story at both regional and global levels, but how do they receive, accept, process and respond to audience feedback? The newer mechanisms for feedback should be addressed in future research.

New mediation roles are emerging in new media as well. Wherever an online news outlet includes formats such as message boards, blogs, Wikis, social media sharing options, and the like, interactive mediation can become part of the media routines and may influence the creation of news items. There is significant potential for indirect feedback to influence content production because such formats favor the establishment of virtual social relationships. The influence of virtual relationships on content production is an area where future study is also needed.

Scholars (e.g., Boczkowski, 2004) argue that it is media routines rather than structural determinacy that govern the production of news content in new media, as a heritage from traditional news outlets. However, technology is becoming increasingly influential on media routines. With time, their influence could come to dominate news production. We usually consider technology to facilitate communication processes, but is there provision in these mechanisms for feedback? Is the influence of feedback limited by such technology?

Our theoretical evaluation on feedback only begins to explain the effect of feedback on the production of news content. It establishes limits on the scope of audience messages that should be considered as feedback, thus making the study of feedback manageable. These limits are susceptible to the changing landscape of media modalities or formats that are the result of technological advances. However, our theoretical perspective establishes the independence of feedback from media format, thus providing a predictive tool for the assessment of feedback effects on content production across time. Feedback, meanwhile, is an integral part of media effects. We feel that paying more attention to feedback would enrich the literature of media effects research as well.

Our theoretical deliberation is yet to be expanded in further studies. We have so far considered fairly general ideas with regard to the influence of feedback on news content production, and these mostly regard direct feedback in tangible forms. More work is needed to operationalize indirect feedback in intangible forms, as these forms are likely to be more influential on news content production than tangible forms.

In addition, the process of news production should be regarded as a system, not merely a mechanism. Besides discussing the effect of feedback, we also need to consider the interactive effect between feedback and the feedback control exercised by internal or external influencing agencies on media content production. Moreover, the valence of feedback content (i.e., positive vs. negative) should be involved in our thoughts, which is assumed to have independent influence on media content.

REFERENCES

Biven, R. (2014). *Digital currents: How technology and the public are shaping TV news.* Toronto, Canada: University of Toronto Press.

Boczkowski, P. J. (2004). The processes of adopting multimedia and interactivity in three online newsrooms. *Journal of communication, 54*(2), 197–213.

Boczkowski, P. J. (2005). *Digitizing the news: Innovation in online newspapers.* Cambridge, MA: The MIT Press.

Brignell, J. (2004). *Feedback.* Retrieved April 6, 2006 from http://www.numberwatch.co.uk/feedback.htm

Bryant, J., & Zillmann, D. (Eds.). (2002). *Media effects: Advances in theory and research.* Mahwah, NJ: LEA.

Gerbner, G., Gross, L., Jackson-Beeck, M., Jeffries-Fox, S., & Signorielli, N. (1978). Cultural indicators: Violence profile No.9. *Journal of Communication, 28*(3), 176–207.

Golec, P. (2004). *Feedback.* Retrieved April 6, 2006 from http://www.economicswebinstitute.org/glossary/feedback.htm

Katz, E. (1959). Mass communication research and the study of popular culture: An editorial note on a possible future for this journal. *Studies in Public Communication, 2*, 1–6.

Lasswell, H. D. (1948). The structure and function of communication in society. In L. Bryson (Ed.), *The communication of ideas.* New York, NY: Harper & Bros.

Lewis, F. L. (1992). *Applied optimal control and estimation.* Upper Saddle River, NJ: Prentice-Hall.
Lowery, S. A., & DeFleur, M. L. (1995). *Milestones in mass communication research* (3rd ed.). White Plains, NY: Longman.
Merriam-Webster's Collegiate Dictionary (10th ed.). (1993). Springfield, MA: Merriam-Webster, Inc.
Sears, D. O., & Freedman, J. L. (1971). Selective exposure to information: A critical review. In W. Schramm & D.F. Roberts (Eds.), *The process and effects of mass communication.* (rev. ed.). (pp. 209–234). Urbana, IL: University of Illinois Press.
Shannon, C., & Weaver, W. (1949). *The mathematical theory of communication.* Urbana, IL: University of Illinois Press.
Shoemaker, P. J., & Cohen, A. A. (2006). *News around the world: Content, practitioners, and the public.* New York, NY: Routledge.
Shoemaker, P. J., Lee, J. H., Han, G., & Cohen, A. A. (2007). Proximity and scope as news values. In E. Devereux (Ed.), *Media studies: Key issues and debates* (pp. 231–248). Los Angeles, CA: Sage.
Shoemaker, P. J., & Reese, S. D. (1996). *Mediating the message* (2nd ed.). White Plains, NY: Longman.
Tandoc, E. C. Jr. (2014). Journalism is twerking? How web analytics is changing the process of gate-keeping. *New Media & Society, 16*(4), 559–575.
Thurstradius. (2017). Web analytics tools. Retrieved January 25, 2017 from https://www.trustradius.com/web-analytics.
Underwood, M. (2003). *Communication studies, cultural studies, media studies infobase.* Retrieved April 6, 2006 from http://www.cultsock.ndirect.co.uk/MUHome/cshtml/introductory/
Wiener, N. (1958). *Nonlinear problems in random theory.* Cambridge, MA: MIT Press & Wiley.

CHAPTER FIVE

Journalism, Rationality and Common Sense

A Theoretical Model for Relations Between News Selection and Cultural Construction of Everyday Regularity*

MARCOS PAULO DA SILVA†

There is a Brazilian traditional song by Vinicius de Moraes and Toquinho, *Cotidiano número dois* (in English, *Everyday number two*), that says within the poetry of its stanzas that "the day always tells the same stories".[1] The verse, evidently, does not refer properly to the "uniqueness"[2] of everyday facts—or of the news—narrated day after day by journalism (Genro Filho, 2012). The relevance of the poetic meaning, however, may reside in a wider and more complex relationship that is present in the journalistic way of narrating reality: the "back-and-forth" between everyday life and its narration modes.

* This chapter systematizes some of main reflections built on the PhD dissertation "A construção cultural da narrativa noticiosa: noticiabilidade, representação simbólica e regularidade cotidiana" (*Cultural construction of news narrative: newsworthiness, symbolic representation and everyday regularity*), concluded in January 2013, at Methodist University of São Paulo (UMESP), São Paulo, Brazil. The development of an internship as visiting scholar at the *John Ben Snow Research Team* of the Newhouse School of Public Communication at Syracuse University, under supervision of Pamela Shoemaker, during the Fall 2011, was essential for the improvement of the theoretical model proposed in the dissertation. Special thanks to David Victor-Emmanuel Tauro and Tim P. Vos for reading and reviewing this English version.

† Marcos Paulo da Silva is Professor of Journalism Studies at Federal University of Mato Grosso do Sul (UFMS), Campo Grande, Brazil. E-mail: marcos.paulo@ufms.br.

Accordingly, in the same way as Herbert Gans (2004) suggests the involvement of two basic steps—*availability* and *suitability*—in the process of news selection, the construction of the journalistic narrative can also be interpreted by the scope of two complementary processes rooted in the symbolic level: the characterization of everyday paradoxes by the newsworthiness criteria (from an understanding of the word "paradox" based on its Greek etymology as something beyond—prefix "*para*"—the *doxa*[3]) and the comprehension of a modality of narrative that can "dissolve" (at the symbolic level) their most dissonant aspects beyond the immediacy of the facts. So it is, once the dissemination of the news narrative is "supported" by a cultural pattern of regularity and "instrumental rationality" that "endorses" the everyday experience in modernity.

In terms of social and critical theory, Brendan Earley (2009, p. 1) says, "instrumental rationality is often seen as a specific form of rationality focusing on the most efficient or cost-effective means to achieve a specific end, but not in itself reflecting on the value of that end". The construction of the journalistic narrative consists, in this context, in a circular process of mutual influences (moved by transcoding and dissemination steps) involving both the journalistic way of narrating the reality and the parameters of rationality that guide the modern way of life—as it is shown in Figure 5.1:

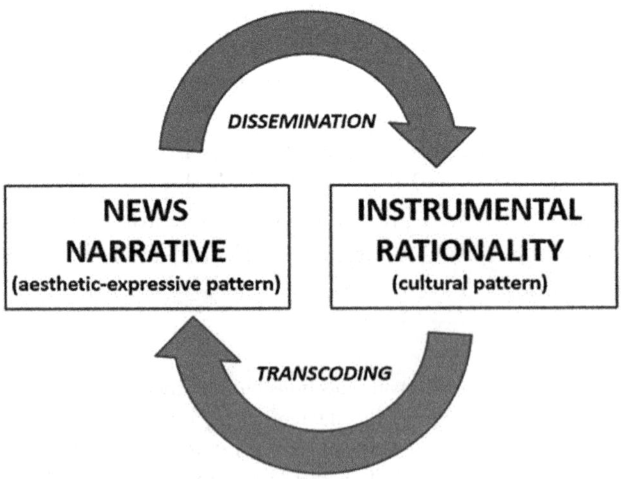

Figure 5.1: Representation of Transcoding and Dissemination Relations of Instrumental Rationality Pattern by the News Narrative

Source : Author.

Ordinary meaning in modern life finds its resonance exactly in the ordinary sense of everyday life—"the day always tells the same stories", that Vinícius de Moraes e Toquinho sings about. The news narrative is, in this horizon, established as a typical narrative of the everyday mode of life in modernity—regular, rational and instrumental (Adorno & Horkheimer, 1985)—contributing to the spread of a cultural trace of ordering of the most *paradoxical* meanings contained in the experience of the day-to-day. In other words, it represents a way of narrating the world that gets purpose through the breakup of the ordinary expectations of *doxa*, or of the common sense.

In what mode, however, do relations between the journalistic practice and the cultural construction of everyday regularity manifest themselves in the narrative level? That is no a simple answer. It involves a group of symbolic components and narrative resources that go beyond the level of content, reaching a news narrative aesthetic. In sum, the events provided with newsworthiness are understood as elements rupturing an established symbolic order that is instituted relative to common sense. At the same step, the news narrative, with its transcoded cultural patterns of rationality and regularity, is characterized as an instance that may attenuate those "bifurcations"[4] of everyday life.

In this context, in order to lend structure to the debate, a rhythmic nature metaphor takes shape and finds legitimacy in the creation of an interpretive model for the triad between *journalism*, *rationality* and *common sense*. That is, once considered the theoretical premise that both the selection of news events and the spread of journalistic narrative are intrinsically related processes to a cultural pattern of regularity, few metaphors are more suitable than an instrument historically used to mark the pace of the capitalist mode of production: the pendulum, a mechanism that introduces the idea of regularity—coming from the circular conception of time—inside the linearity provided by the productive routines of the capitalist mode of production. The theoretical and conceptual model that follows is based on this rhythmic analogy.

JOURNALISM, DOXA AND *EVERYDAY PARADOXES*: A PENDULUM METAPHOR

Historically, different analogies and explanatory models have been used in journalism studies to illustrate the news selection process and the news narrative construction process. The most classic of these models are the "inverted pyramid" metaphor and the famous analogy of gatekeeping (White, 1950), direct derivations of the paradigms of impartiality and objectivity that became relevant in Western journalism in the twentieth century (Schudson, 1978).

With the inevitable historical progress of theoretical and conceptual discussions, however, new and more complex metaphors have been established. For example, the French theorist Patrick Charaudeau (2003) uses the metaphor of a "machine" to elucidate the various stages of construction and feasibility of "communicative contracts" between enunciators and the enunciated. In the specific case of Brazilian studies about journalism, one of the most emblematic metaphoric models is that suggested by Adelmo Genro Filho (2012) to deconstruct the classic analogy of the "inverted pyramid" and to reveal the "secret" beyond the "pyramid" based on the relationship between the Hegelian concepts of "uniqueness" and "universality" applied to news.

Nevertheless, despite the relevance of these metaphorical models, it is suggested in this chapter that the relationship between journalism and the conceptions of common sense and *everyday paradoxes* can be inserted into another peculiar interpretive framework. That framework is based on the analogy proposed by Muniz Sodré between journalistic practice and the rhythm of a musical composition. Or, in the Brazilian thinker's own words: "the micro aspects of the facts, as the notes, flow rhythmically in a 'metric', which is the temporality marked as 'everyday'" (Sodré, 2009, p. 92).[5] In turn, this rhythm has a differentiated cyclic time, which brings the news to have "a cycle whose duration varies, in practice, according to the value journalistically attributed to the fact" (Sodré, 2009, p. 94).[6]

Such a metaphorical relation proposed by Sodré (2009) enables the development of a new metaphor, from a kinetics analogy, based on a pendulum: in other words, while journalistic activity depends of *everyday paradoxes* (translated as events endowed with "news values") to build its narrative structure, it also establishes itself as an essential cultural practice for constitution—and dissemination—of a daily pattern. That is, transcoding and, at the same time, disseminating cultural patterns of rationality (fruits of the everyday experience in modernity), the journalistic practice—as a social activity inscribed into the *doxa* (Barthes, 1988), into *common sense*—contributes to a process of attenuating to the *paradoxical senses* of everyday life, rationalizing them (the *everyday paradoxes*) and returning them to a consensual symbolic order. This is illustrated in Figure 5.2:

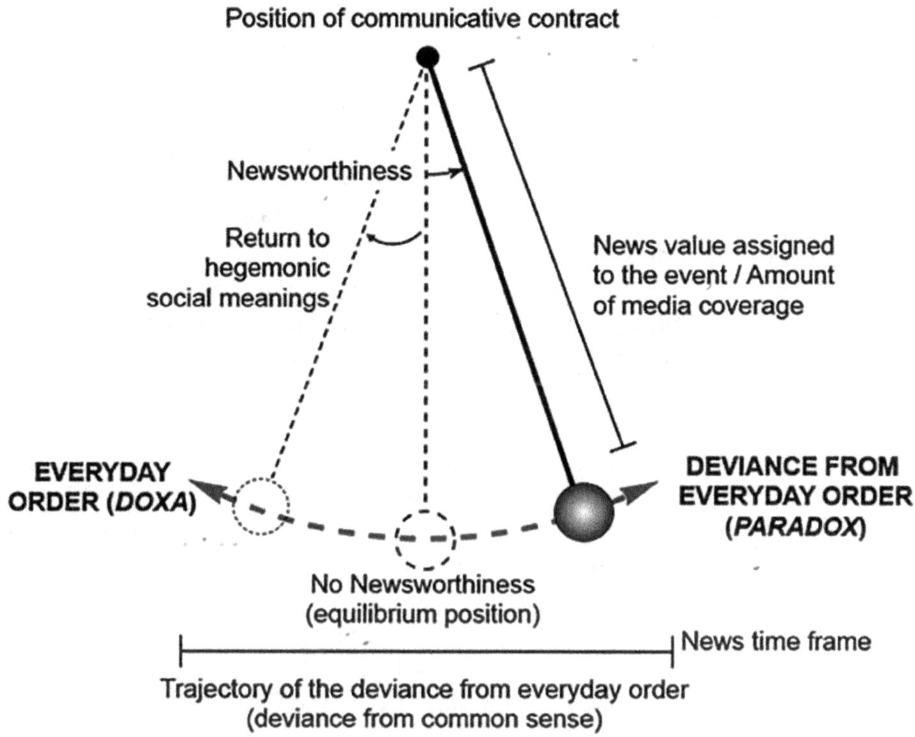

Figure 5.2: Graph Model for the Relation Between Journalism, *Doxa* and *Paradoxes*
Note: This metaphorical model was substantially improved during the author's internship as visiting scholar at the Newhouse School of Public Communication of Syracuse University. It is important, therefore, to thank the opinions and comments about the model made by Professor Pamela Shoemaker and by other members of the *John Ben Snow* Research Team in the Fall 2011.
Source : Author.

Each element of the pendulum has its own metaphorical meaning:

- *The position of the communicative contract:* The concepts of *doxa* and—hence—of *paradox* are cultural constructions (Barthes, 1988; Bourdieu, 1977; Geertz, 2007; Sodré, 2009). That is, the parameters that characterize the circumstances of "common sense" in a particular social group or socio-historical settings may not necessarily be the same for other groups or social settings. Such relationships are also related to the concept of "communicative contract" (Charaudeau, 2003) and to its position of operation in the social system. In Patrick Charaudeau's perspective, the symbolic movement from a "raw event" (interpreted by an speaker) to an event built as news (and exchanged by an addressee) is characterized by complementary processes of *transformation* (between something "to mean" to something "with meaning") and of *transaction* (between the two poles of the communicative chain, speaker and addressee). In other words, within the understanding of the symbolic exchanges that take place in communication, it can be understood that "the attributes derived from the macro-social positions occupied by individuals only become relevant in conjunction with the micro-social circumstances".[7] In addition, it is necessary that "these attributes are recognized by the addressed individuals in order to become themselves operative" (Nogueira, 2004, p. 4). Moreover, considering the mentioned metaphor, the position of the pendulum in the semio-discursive and social systems is relevant only from the understanding of the conceptions of *doxa* and *paradox* and, ultimately, from the dialogue between the news narrative and the cultural construction of everyday regularity.

- *Newsworthiness:* The concept of newsworthiness has a complex nature. When observed by a historical horizon, the concept is understood from a classic pattern of "deviance"—in short, it is considered the comprehension that an event to become newsworthy must "violate" a moral or probabilistic rule. At least two studies conducted at different historical moments can be seen as representative of this approach: the seventeenth-century work, *De Relationibus Novellis*, by the German scholar Tobias Peucer (2000),[8] and the mathematically inspired system proposed by the Danish researchers Johan Galtung and Mari Holmboe Ruge (1965). Over time, however, the concept of newsworthiness passed through a number of other refinements, which allowed for differentiation. Herbert Gans (2004),[9] for instance, argues that the existence of guiding criteria of journalistic activity are related to the ideological values shared by journalists. In the European context, Mauro Wolf (2003) and Nelson Traquina (2008) emphasize that the values involved in news selection are present throughout the entire dynamics of news production: from the selection of newsworthy events until the construction of its narrative. Pamela Shoemaker (1996), in turn, besides to different aspects of "deviance" (probabilistic, normative and social change), adds to the concept of newsworthiness other dimensions that refer to the idea of "social significance" (political, cultural, economic and public significance). Moreover, the author adds to them the notion of "complexity" (the combination of deviance and social significance dimensions as characteristics of a particular event) (Shoemaker & Cohen, 2006). Despite these representative theoretical and conceptual improvements, however, this chapter aims to understand the concept of news as a "hybrid narrative" that permeates at the same time the "uniqueness" of journalistic events and the symbolic parameters of everyday life (Faro, 2011). Thus, the concept of newsworthiness is understood in parallel to the idea of *everyday paradoxes*. Specifically, that is, in accordance with the pendulum model presented above, newsworthiness configures the "amplitude" of the angle that determines the pathway between *doxa* and its *paradoxical deviance*. Therefore, it can be deduced that the more *paradoxical* (deviant from *common sense* regularity) an event is interpreted, the more aspects of newsworthiness it will eventually have. On the other hand, the absence of newsworthiness is represented as the existence of no deviation from everyday regularity.

- *News value assigned to the event:* Every event endowed with some degree of newsworthiness receives generally a news value that determines its position in the media outlets. In an operational approach to the news selection process, such valuation can be translated into three empirically verifiable aspects: 1) journalistic prominence of the event (amount of news items about the event, filled space and the event's hierarchical position within the news); 2) sources (amount of quoted experts, space for them in providing a meaningful sense to an event and the degree of *rationality* imbricated in these experts' opinions); and 3) *attributive events* related to the event (amount of secondary events that reverberate the complexity of the *paradox* besides its initial dissonant meanings) (Koch, 1990). It is not, however, a mere quantitative issue. Although in some occasions it can be quantified, the capital that takes place in the establishment of news values is essentially symbolic (Bourdieu, 1977, 1997). Hence the relevance of its understanding based on a theoretical and conceptual Bourdieusian framework.[10] Considering the pendulum metaphor, the "news value assigned to the event" is the pendulum length. Therefore, in combination with the angle amplitude that represents the "newsworthiness", results in characterizing the "trajectory of deviance from the everyday order (deviance from common sense)".
- *Return to the hegemonic social meanings:* Also related to items previously explored, the idea of "return to hegemonic social meanings" refers directly to the process of journalistic allocation of explanatory senses to *everyday paradoxes*. They are: 1) Journalistic segmentation of reality into functional and independent units (editions, sections, episodes, etc); 2) recognition of the factual (here and now) as temporal dimension to solve everyday problems; 3) legitimation of journalistic sources based on a hegemonic backdrop entangled in everyday life; as well as 4) establishing of different levels of meaning from secondary events (attributive events) that help to dissolve the *paradoxical sense* of the original news event. It is, in sum, a process of attenuation of the dissonant senses from *doxa* and the return provided by its symbolic movement in everyday regularity. In the pendulum model, it is related to an identical angle—but on the opposite side—to the conception of newsworthiness. In this scenario, it helps to elucidate the dynamics of replacing an event by another—on the media agenda—after it has been

incorporated by a hegemonic explanatory sense and being stripped of its paradox condition.

- *Trajectory of the deviance from the everyday order:* Metaphorically, the symbolic movement between *doxa* and its *paradoxical deviance* is the total displacement conducted by the pendulum. In other words, the movement refers to deviance that an event establishes in the regularity of common sense as well as to its return, based on the assignment of an explanatory sense by the news story. Determined by the combination of the degree of newsworthiness of an event (the angle of the pendulum in the model) and by the news value received (pendulum length), this trajectory, although symbolic, is related to the frame (time and amount) of the news media coverage. From a metaphorical point of view, the trajectory of the pendulum can be completed regardless of the *everyday paradox* established on the real-historical level (a phenomenal level in Kantian perspective). Thus, a journalistic event can reach a new symbolic status once it produces potential effects of sense—at the symbolic level—beyond its reality effects (Gomes, 2009), without changing, evidently, its status in the real-historical world. A plane crash, for example, may have its *paradoxical senses* attenuated—"dissolved"—based on the explanation of its causes and, thus, eventually drops from the media agenda, but this attenuation will not change anything in its reality effects—wrecks, deaths, etc.—located on the pragmatic level (phenomenal world). Nevertheless, these same effects of meaning provided by the news will be taken, in a second step, to constitute new effects of reality. Therefore, the trajectory between *doxa* and *paradox*—and vice versa—is represented by a rhythmic movement that refers to an ordering sense characterized by modern cultural patterns of everyday regularity.

It is suggested that the relevance of the pendulum metaphor is precisely located on its didactic illustration that allows the viewing of the two stages of the news narrative construction process: the characterization of *everyday paradoxes* as news events and the "dissolution" of the same by narrative resources of journalism. Once again, it can be highlighted the relevant words of Wilson Gomes (2009, p. 15): "through the news, world ceases to be a complex of things and persons forming an existential circle to become, beyond this, a horizon".[11]

Such a horizon, however, depends on a "tacit agreement between news consumers and journalists" that "is completed by drawing the line between what is and what is worthy of mention as well as what does not exist or does not deserve attention" (Gomes, 2009, p. 15).[12] It is, therefore, a kind of "discursive contract" according to which "without people's perception, there is no event" (Sodré, 2009, p. 34).[13] There is, therefore, an important reservation: although recognizing the relationship established at the symbolic level between journalism and the attenuation of *everyday paradoxes*, this relationship depends of "discursive negotiations" between the peculiarities of the media agenda that guides the news and its symbolic "sense of community".

In this scenario, the ideas of *paradox* and consensual order (components of the metaphorical pendulum movement established by journalism) do not project themselves at reality (at phenomenal world) in a constant or unequivocal way, but, as discussed earlier, are culturally constructed from different socio-cultural variables and different "communicative contracts" (Charaudeau, 2003).

LIMITS OF FUNCTIONALISM AND DIFFERENCES WITH A CULTURALIST APPROACH

The pendulum—or, specifically, its isochronous oscillation mechanism identified by Galileo in the late sixteenth century—has been historically inserted in the functioning of several instruments to accurately measure the regularity that characterizes the modern way of life. Examples range from the classic pendulum clocks created in the mid-seventeenth century—important instruments in the formulation of a new time pattern that integrates the historical process called by Martin-Barbero (2003) as "long process of enculturation"—to the old metronomes—equipment invented in the early nineteenth century and which are essential in introducing a steady and measured pace in the musical field.

This scenario, along with the methodological shift suggested by Martin-Barbero (2003) from "media" to "cultural mediations", inspires, here, a new understanding of a journalistic way of narrating reality: moving from the idea of "mechanism" as a total theoretical and methodological approach to its understanding as a cultural pattern characterizing a way of life marked by the valorization of a typically instrumental pattern of rationality.

In this case, although the rhythmical pendulum metaphor, as suggested above, configures a substantially mechanical analogy, it is not the result of a mechanistic theoretical-methodological perspective, since it is based on an essentially culturalist approach. What the metaphor intends to explain—within this theoretical perspective—is precisely the dynamic by which news (involving the processes of selection, construction and dissemination) are intrinsically incorporated into everyday life as one among many modes of expression that diffuse themselves based on modern rationality. It is not, therefore, an understanding of journalism as an organic system, with repair functions of the social system—as it could be suggested by a functionalist point of view—but a multifaceted system of a production of meanings.

The limitations derived from organic (theoretical) and quantitative (methodological) dimensions, among other characteristics of functionalism, insert this perspective in a critical position compared to other approaches that gradually gained ground in the social sciences and particularly in the communication field. In this sense, Adelmo Genro Filho (2012) is categorical in pointing to the precariousness of functionalism for understanding journalistic practice. Within a Marxist perspective, the author outlines the concept of "knowledge" as a way of apprehending reality crossed by a number of inherent contradictions—which calls into question the concept of any "organic role" played by journalism as a way of knowledge of reality.

The recognition of the relevance of the criticism by Adelmo Genro Filho (2012) puts even more emphasis on the need to avoid a functionalist approach. For this reason, the pendulum model is meant to be a didactic element for understand the news construction and dissemination processes, in as much as it is not a simple mechanical analogy, but is rather a metaphor that substantially illustrates an established movement at the symbolic level. It is, therefore, a kind of production of meaning about (and on) an objective reality.

In this context, once again, the importance of Gramsci's concept of hegemony is useful for building a critical understanding of the practice of journalism. A significant example comes from the analysis of Stuart Hall (1977). The British thinker[14] uses the term "function" to refer to the correlation between media and ideology; however, he is not suggesting a functionalist approach. In fact, the use of the word "function", in this case, serves as a semantic resource for an eminently culturalist discussion—building here similarly on Clifford Geertz's (2007) notion of culture.

According to Hall (1977, pp. 340–341), the first "function" played by the media is "the provision and the selective construction of social knowledge, of social imagery" through which people "perceive the 'worlds', the lived realities' of others" beyond their own immediate contexts. The second "function" reflects the concept of "plurality" to disseminate an inventory of lexicons, lifestyles and ideologies through a constant process of objectifying the world. At this point, "social knowledge" selectively disseminated by media becomes "ranked and arranged within the great normative and evaluative classifications" ratified by culture. In sum, this is the way paved by the media so that people not only "know more about the world" but also "make sense of it" (Hall, 1977, p. 341). Finally, the third "function" identified by the author refers to the dynamics of "organization, orchestration and alignment of voices" that the media performs—considered that, within a hegemonic scenario, "some degree of integration and cohesion" should be socially recognized. Inside this reciprocal voices, Hall (1977, p. 342) argues, some actors exhibit higher strength, but always need the legitimacy provided by other actors—minority opinions and contrary views—a process that supports the complex dynamics of legitimacy and consensus production in society.

The description of the media "functions" presented by Stuart Hall, one of the leading exponents of British Cultural Studies, marks a clear distinction of those functions propagated by a traditional functionalist approach—such as the concepts of "narcotizing dysfunction" and "social repair". Such theoretical and conceptual formulations—and its many functionalistic branches—however, are based on a paradigm becoming hegemonic over time in the Western world—hence the recognition of its strength and dissemination.

Therefore, even if this chapter resorts to a metaphor of mechanical and rhythmic inspiration (a pendulum), the concepts of "instrumental rationality" and "everyday regularity" related to it cannot be interpreted as functional consequences of journalistic practice based on alleged social "disorders" or "damage" that need to be "fixed" within an organic system. Far from it, journalistic activity is understood as a social disseminator of rationalizations of *everyday paradoxes* precisely because it transcodes the hegemonic cultural patterns of rationality and regularity that are entangled in everyday life.

FROM THE NEWSSTANDS TO THE RECYCLE BIN: THE REPLACEMENT OF A *PARADOX* BY ANOTHER WITHIN THE EVERYDAY REGULARITY

In the heart of subjectivity that characterizes the social construction of journalistic facts, there is always an aspect of concrete objectivity that cannot be disregarded. Adelmo Genro Filho (2012) argues that a singular event necessarily requires a subjective description in a particular context to make sense as a dimension of knowledge:

> Here, the question arising is not only the problem of proper language, but mainly the epistemological approach that will preside over this language and allow its effectiveness. There is a minimum degree of objective knowledge that must be provided by the singular significance (at singular-significant), which requires a minimum of a particular context, so that the news would perform effectively as a form of knowledge. From this minimally harmonious relationship between the singular and the particular, the news can—depending on their ideological approach—become a critical understanding of reality. (Genro Filho, 2012, p. 202)[15]

The Brazilian author continues: "whenever a fact becomes journalistic news, he is seized by the angle of its uniqueness, but opening a certain range of relationships that form its particular context" (Genro Filho, 2012, p. 201).[16] As a way to systemize the theoretical and conceptual debate, the horizon of this study finds its culmination exactly on contextual relationships located ahead of the immediacy of news events. The context mentioned here, however, refers to an aesthetic-expressive level of the news narrative that, in turn, roots and is rooted (in a circular process) in cultural patterns built in the everyday experience in modernity.

In this sense, the literary critic Roberto Schwarz (2012), using an ancient formula of the Hungarian thinker György Luckács for the analysis of fictional texts, is pertinent to point out that the social aspect of a composition (a "masterpiece") is located substantially in its "form". The Brazilian author explains:

> Not that the contents are not social, but when the form works with them and organize them, or also by being inflected by them [by the contents], it configures something more general, analogous to the precedence of society over its separated contents. If the compositions matter, it is because they have an order in a revealing manner, which has some basis in the organization of the historical world. (Schwarz, 2012, p. 288)[17]

Such reasoning, coming from the literary field, is relevant for the journalistic field. The aesthetics of the journalistic way of narrating the reality (i.e., the news), in this case, matches the dynamic duo of transcoding and dissemination of a social sense of regularity modeled on the culture. In a similar perspective, Schwarz adds:

> The form—which is not obvious and that it is for literary critics to identify and study—would be an individual ordering principle, which both regulates an imaginary universe as an aspect of external reality. In varying proportions, it combines the artistic manufacturing and intuition of pre-existing social rhythms. (…) The back-and-forth requires a structured description of the two fields, as is the work of social reality, whose bonds are topics of reflection. (Schwarz, 2012, p. 48)[18]

When this perspective is interpreted in the specific field of news reporting, it finds resonance in the process of connecting everyday facts to the mass culture (Nora, 1979) in a way that an event can replace another in a symbolic movement marked by regularity. Or still, as discussed by Franco Moretti (2003) in his study about European novels, it refers to the everyday possibility of "turning the page" of a newspaper without the reader having a major scare, because rationality is embedded in the journalistic way of refracting reality. Thus, the *paradoxes* of "yesterday", once rationalized and attenuated ("dissolved"), are replaced by the news of the "today" (or of "now"), being relegated to a symbolic space that addresses to the past (or, in the case of secondhand newspapers, to the recyclable waste bin).

In this scenario, in the same way as modern society—which, in a broader perspective, deals with its daily obstacles in order to solve them in a rational sense of "domestication" (Birman, 2010)—journalism transcodes this pattern of instrumental rationality beyond the limits of its content. It permits extending it to its own aesthetic and expressive dimension: as in the metaphorical movement of a pendulum, the journalistic discourse identifies these *everyday paradoxes* as events endowed with newsworthiness; and, so—based on specific communicative contracts—"clarifies" and "dissolves" them, returning them to culturally paved *doxal senses*.

That said, it must be recognized that a set of theoretical conceptions mentioned in this chapter have no sense when viewed in a desultory point of view; that is, within the parameters that Douglas Kellner (2001) calls *"theoretical pot-pourri"*. When articulated in a broader context, however, the concepts start to set up a viable interpretation model both for complex characterization of the newsworthiness idea in journalism and for its critical understanding within the daily regularity that marks the modern way of life as a cultural pattern. Thus, Figure 5.3—prepared to guide the visualization of the main relationships between the concepts—enables a better location of the ideas that make up the study:

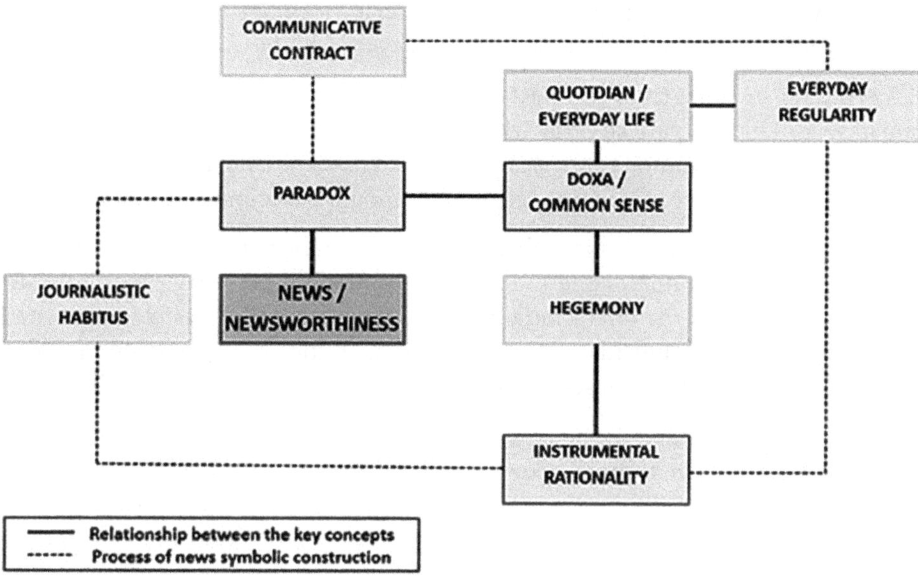

Figure 5.3: Graphic Representation of the Main Theoretical and Conceptual Relationships
Source : Author.

Once taking the assumption that the news narrative is a complex cultural construction that can be theoretically explained on the basis of a dynamic and dialectical relationship between the concepts discussed above, it is justified, for example, the absence of arrows or directional symbols in the model so that, as stated previously, all related concepts are not seen under a closed or a deterministic approach.

However, the diagram is only a kind of "draft" to visualize the theoretical and conceptual relationships mentioned—and, therefore, it has little meaning in itself. Above all, it is essential to recognize that the news narrative is a rich and multifaceted issue that only spreads socially when it finds legitimacy and support in broader cultural patterns—a problem that will, finally, be systematized in the following paragraphs:

(I) Society organizes itself around a complex of socially shared meanings and understood via the idea of *doxa*—or *common sense* in the Aristotelian conceptualization—an essential dimension for attributing meaning to everyday life.

(II) In this scenario, the notion of *paradox*, etymologically understood as something unusual in the background of *doxa*, sets a symbolic status that breaks the socially shared order. It is by their deviant nature, therefore, that the issues considered *paradoxes* receive salience in the everyday experience.

(III) In turn, the structure of *common sense* is also related to Gramsci's concept of hegemony—the dimension in which the dominant ideological aspects of society spread themselves in the ordinary practices of everyday life.

(IV) Among such hegemonic aspects is the idea of *instrumental rationality*, a parameter—or cultural pattern—for which the "controlled access" of elements that break the order of common sense is closely linked to way of life in modernity; these elements are, therefore, *paradoxical events* and should be rationally explained.

(V) This process, eminently symbolic, roots itself into the nature of the journalistic narrative, considered one of the touchstones of modern everyday experience. In this context, there is the characterization of *everyday paradoxes* as elements that, on the one hand, are liable to configure news and, on the other, are deserving of an explanation in the typical senses and procedures of instrumental rationality.

(VI) Within this aspect that guides the *ethos* of modern journalism, the news narrative can be considered, then, a particular cultural practice whose production of meaning results in the "dilution"—identification, singling and later explanation—of the *paradoxes* that break the symbolic order instituted in everyday life by common sense.

(VII) Within this explanatory key, it can be understood the ways that the news narrative uses and explores the most *paradoxical senses* of its newsworthiness criteria. In the aesthetic construction of a journalistic narrative, for example, graphics and specific analytical sections—the famous cliché-elements around the idea of "understanding the case"—present themselves as an index of a common symbolic trace: the return to the (previously intact) hegemonic consensus through a culturally accepted explanation. Similarly, "experts" from different fields—social actors legitimized as information sources—attribute their arguments, supposedly anchored in the journalistic objectivity and/or in the scientific rationality, to the "capture" of the *paradoxical sense* that disturbs the everyday regularity and, afterwards, for returning them to *doxal meanings* supported by society.

(VIII) It is understood that the linking of journalistic facts within specific news sections—targeted at particular temporal symmetries (dailies, weeklies, monthlies, etc.)—contributes to the spread, in the aesthetic-expressive plan of the journalistic narrative, of a peculiar sense of regularity and everyday ordering.

(IX) This characterization, however, has complexity and only penetrates the core of journalistic culture through the conception of *habitus* (Bourdieu, 1977, 1997), the symbolic instance that should be also understood as a privileged space for the emergence of hegemonic aspects of society inside the journalistic field.

(X) Moreover, once understood as a complex cultural construction, the idea of common sense cannot be seen as a universal conception—a position that, by analogy, also projected itself to the concept of *paradox*. Thus, in the same way that the characterization of an *everyday paradox* is related to a determined sociocultural or temporal frame/background and may not be the same in another circumstance, the symbolic practice of explaining (and "dissolving") the *paradoxical senses* of society will not be the same in different contexts. Within the journalistic practice, a happening that constitutes a newsworthy event in a given scenario, may not, in another context, even deserve attention. Therefore, as noted by Patrick Charaudeau (2003), before manifested in the world, a journalistic narrative expresses a relationship. The explanation, here, is linked to the concept of "communicative contract".

(XI) It is understood, finally, that all these processes find meaning in everyday life, a dimension that has both the common sense and the rhythm of regularity, respectively, in its intrinsic form of knowledge and its fundamental temporal dimension. In this context, the rhythmic movement of which journalism, at the same step, is active and passive parts, provides to the "ordinary dealing" with *everyday paradoxes* its own sense of regularity—a kind of symbolic "back-and-forth", as a pendulum—typical of a rational way of sociability (within the capitalistic mode of production) that instrumentally dissolves its routine unforeseen.

(XII) In short, the concept of newsworthiness is understood as related to the idea of *paradox* and its social operation only finds meaning in the regularity of everyday life. Therefore, it is a symbolic movement, with a complex nature, encoded in culture, in which all the concepts presented above appear dialectically linked.

NOTES

1. In Portuguese, "o dia conta histórias sempre iguais".
2. Originally, in Portuguese, "singularidade".
3. The conception of *doxa* (in Greek, *δοξα*) originally refers to Classical Antiquity. In a very simple way, it may be referred as "general opinion", but there is a range of complexity to be considered. According to Heidegger (2009), *doxa* is also discussed by Plato, but it is clearly and deeply understood by the Aristotelian tradition. In sum, Aristotle proposes a different approach moving beyond the opposition suggested by Plato (between *doxa*, as inferior knowledge, and *episteme*, as true way of knowledge). In an Aristotelian view, *doxa* and *episteme* are not ways of knowledge separated from each other (such as the Platonic tradition proposes), but they are related conceptions. So, *doxa* and *Episteme* are just two different kinds of knowledge. While *Episteme* is verifiable in concrete reality; *doxa*, on the other hand, is a commonly consensual knowledge. The correlation between the concept of *doxa* and the idea of common sense derives from this context.
4. The term, here, is adapted from the reflections by Franco Moretti (2003) on the literary field. The Italian author uses the idea of "bifurcation" in his analysis of European novels of the second half of the nineteenth century. Conceptually, in the literary field, the "bifurcations" can be understood

as possible unfolding of the plot, in other words, the summits and climax points found in the course of the narrative—the kiss, the death, the imprisonment, the sanctions, etc. They are operationalized on the narrative level in opposition to the "fillers". In turn, as the name suggests, the "fillers" consist of what happens between a change and another—it is therefore of the narrative fill spaces between the forks.

5. Originally, in Portuguese: "Os microaspectos do fato, como as notas, fluem ritmicamente dentro de uma 'métrica', que é a temporalidade marcada como 'o cotidiano'".
6. Originally: "Um ciclo cuja duração varia, na prática, de acordo com o valor jornalisticamente atribuído ao fato".
7. Originally, in Portuguese: "Os atributos decorrentes das posições macrossociais ocupadas pelos sujeitos só tornam-se relevantes em articulação com as circunstâncias microssociais (...). Faz-se necessário que "esses atributos sejam reconhecidos pelos sujeitos destinatários para que eles se tornem operantes" (Nogueira, 2004, p. 4).
8. The Tobias Peucer's thesis was translated to Portuguese by Paulo da Rocha Dias and published in the journal Comunicação e Sociedade (Communication and Society, in English), of the Methodist University of São Paulo. View: Peucer (2000). The historical study has also its major ideas systematized in the article "Tobias Peucer: o progenitor da Teoria do Jornalismo" (in English, "Tobias Peucer: the progenitor of Journalism Theory"), by Jorge Pedro Sousa, published in Brazil by the Federal University of Santa Catarina. View: Sousa (2004). Both approaches are used in the context of this chapter. It is important to highlighted that already in the seventeenth century Tobias Peucer outlined a series of categories on which the news, ultimately, should universally be about: things happened recently; important historical facts; issues of civic interest; unusual events; disasters; and what is happening with the distinguished persons (Sousa, 2004, p. 41).
9. The original version was published in 1979.
10. For instance, the concept of journalistic habitus is established as a fundamental key to explaining how the everyday paradoxes (events originated from expectations rupturing introduced in the regularity of common sense) are interpreted as newsworthy events in the operationalization of journalism. The idea of *habitus* is located as an indispensable part of the triad which supports the so-called "sociology of fields" by Pierre Bourdieu (1977). Next to the notions of "field" and "capital", the conception of *habitus* integrates the conceptual framework that, from the French thinker's perspective, helps to explain the intrinsic problems of the social world. In summary, the *habitus* is a key element that allows the operation of symbolic systems within the social fields—such as the journalistic field (Bourdieu, 1997). The Bourdieusian idea of *habitus* still recovers two features of the Aristotelian notion of "habit"; that is, besides being "socially constructed", refers to a knowledge related to a "calculator action of consciousness".
11. Originally, in Portuguese: "Através das notícias o mundo deixa de ser o complexo das coisas e pessoas que formam o meu círculo existencial para tornar-se, para além deste, um horizonte" (Gomes, 2009, p. 15).
12. Originally, in Portuguese: Tal horizonte, contudo, depende de um "acordo tácito entre consumidores de notícia e jornalismo" que "finda por estabelecer o limite entre o que existe e é digno de menção e o que não existe ou não merece atenção" (Gomes, 2009, p. 15).
13. Originally, in Portuguese: "Sem sujeitos de percepção, inexiste acontecimento" (Sodré, 2009, p. 34).
14. Although considered British, Stuart Hall was born in Jamaica in the period when the Caribbean island was considered colony of England.
15. Originally, in Portuguese: "Aqui entra em jogo não apenas o problema de uma linguagem adequada, mas, principalmente, o enfoque epistemológico que vai presidir essa linguagem e permitir

sua eficácia. Há um grau mínimo de conhecimento objetivo que deve ser proporcionado pela significação do singular (pelo singular-significante), que exige um mínimo de contextualização do particular, para que a notícia se realize efetivamente como forma de conhecimento. A partir dessa relação minimamente harmônica entre o singular e o particular, a notícia poderá—dependendo de sua abordagem ideológica—tornar-se uma apreensão crítica da realidade".

16. Originally, in Portuguese: "Sempre que um fato se torna notícia jornalística, ele é apreendido pelo ângulo da sua singularidade, mas abrindo um determinado leque de relações que formam o seu contexto particular".
17. Originally, in Portuguese: "Não que os conteúdos não sejam sociais, mas a forma, ao trabalhá-los e organizá-los, ou também ao ser infletida por eles, configura algo de mais geral, análogo à precedência da sociedade sobre os seus conteúdos separados. Se as obras interessam, é porque se organizam de um modo revelador, que algum fundamento tem na organização do mundo histórico".
18. Originally, in Portuguese: "A forma—que não é evidente e que cabe à crítica identificar e estudar—seria um princípio ordenador individual, que tanto regula um universo imaginário como um aspecto da realidade exterior. Em proporções variáveis, ela combina a fabricação artística e a intuição de ritmos sociais preexistentes. (...) O vaivém exige uma descrição estruturada dos dois campos, tanto da obra como da realidade social, cujas ligações são matéria de reflexão".

REFERENCES

Adorno, T. W., & Horkheimer, M. (1985). *Dialética do esclarecimento: Fragmentos filosóficos.* Rio de Janeiro: Jorge Zahar.

Barthes, R. (1988). *O rumor da língua.* São Paulo: Brasiliense.

Birman, J. (2010). Muitas felicidades?!: O imperativo de ser feliz na contemporaneidade. In J. Freire Filho (Org.). *Ser feliz hoje: reflexões sobre o imperativo da felicidade.* Rio de Janeiro: FGV.

Bourdieu, P. (1977). *Outline of a theory of practice.* Cambridge: Cambridge University Press.

Bourdieu, P. (1997). *Sobre a televisão.* Rio de Janeiro: Zahar.

Charaudeau, P. (2003). *El discurso de la información: la construcción del espejo social.* Barcelona: Gedisa Editorial.

Earley, B. (2009, spring). A large complex: Meditations on instrumental rationality and Adorno while shopping in Ikea. *Art & Research, 2*(2) http://www.artandresearch.org.uk/v2n2/earley.html.

Faro, J. S. (2011). À flor da pele: narrativas híbridas, cotidiano e comunicação. *Revista Intexto, 2*(25) 117–127.

Galtung, J., & Ruge, M. H. (1965). The structure of foreign news: The presentation of the Congo, Cuba and Cyprus crises in four Norwegian newspapers. *Journal of Peace Research, 2*(1), 64–90.

Gans, H. J. (2004) *Deciding what's news: A study of CBS Evening News, NBC Nightly News, Newsweek and Time.* Evanston, IL: Northwestern University Press.

Geertz, C. J. (2007). O Senso comum como um sistema cultural. In C. J. Geertz (Ed.), *O saber local: novos ensaios em antropologia interpretativa.* Petrópolis: Vozes.

Genro Filho, A. (2012). *O segredo da pirâmide: para uma teoria marxista do jornalismo.* Florianópolis: Insular.

Gomes, W. (2009). *Jornalismo, fatos e interesses: ensaios de teorias do jornalismo.* Florianópolis: Insular.

Hall, S. (1977). Culture, the media and the ideological effect. In J. Curran, M. Gurevitch, & J. Woollacott, (Orgs.). *Mass media and society.* London: Edward Arnold Editor e Open University Press.

Heidegger, M. (2009). *Basic concepts of Aristotelian Philosophy*. Bloomington, IN: Indiana University Press.

Kellner, D. (2001). *A cultura da mídia: estudos culturais: identidade e política entre o moderno e o pós-moderno*. Bauru: Edusc.

Koch, T. (1990). *The news as myth: Fact and context in journalism*. New York, NY: Greenwood Press.

Martin-Barbero, J. (2003). *Dos meios às mediações*. Rio de Janeiro: UFRJ.

Moretti, F. (2003). O Século sério. *Revista Novos Estudos*. Cebrap, n. 65.

Nogueira, C. M. (2004). Considerações sobre o modelo de análise do discurso de Patrick Charaudeau. *Revista Ensaio*, Universidade Federal de Minas Gerais, *6*(1) 66–71.

Nora, P. (1979), O retorno do fato. In J. Le Goff & P. Nora (Eds.), *História: novos problemas*. Rio de Janeiro: Francisco Alves Editora.

Peucer, T. (2000). Os relatos jornalísticos. *Revista Comunicação & Sociedade*. Universidade Metodista de São Paulo, n. 33.

Schudson, M. (1978). *Discovering the news: A social history of American newspapers*. New York, NY: Basic Books.

Schwarz, R. (2012). *Martinha versus Lucrécia: ensaios e entrevistas*. São Paulo: Companhia das Letras.

Shoemaker, P. J. (1996). Hardwired for news: Using biological and cultural evolution to explain the surveillance function. *Journal of Communication*, *46*(3), 32–47.

Shoemaker, P. J., & Cohen, A. (2006). *News around the world: Practitioners, content, and the public*. New York, NY: Routledge.

Sodré, M. (2009). *A narração do fato: notas para uma teoria do acontecimento*. Petrópolis: Vozes.

Sousa, J. P. A. S. (2004). Tobias Peucer: Progenitor da teoria do jornalismo. *Estudos em jornalismo e mídia*, *1*(2).

Traquina, N. (2008). *Teorias do jornalismo: A tribo jornalística / uma comunidade interpretativa internacional*. Florianópolis: Insular.

White, D. M. (1950). The gatekeeper: A case study in the selection of news. *Journalism Quarterly*, *27*(4), 383–390.

Wolf, M. (2003). *Teorias da comunicação*. Lisbon: Editorial Presença.

CHAPTER SIX

Deviance, Social Significance, AND International Public Relations

A Synthesized View of Influencing Factors on National Image in News

SUMAN LEE*

INTRODUCTION

National image is a set of attitudes and opinions people of one nation have toward other nations. This evaluation or judgment is important for both government and business leaders. For businesses, a positive and favorable national image can accelerate business interests because corporations representing a favored country are positively perceived by foreign consumers. For governments, a foreign public's thoughts and attitudes are important factors in making policy decisions because governments in today's world need to communicate with, not only other countries' governments, but also their publics.

Mass media play a significant role in forming a picture of the world (Lippmann, 1922). For most people, mass media are the major sources of information about other countries and world events. Kunczik (1997) mentioned that "mass media influence the way a country's people form their images of the people and govern-

* Suman Lee is Associate Professor in the Greenlee School of Journalism and Communication at Iowa State University. Email: smlee@iastate.edu.

ments of other countries, because it is the mass media that disseminate the greater part of the information about foreign countries" (p. 7).

International public relations scholars believe that public relations by other countries in a target country needs to be examined as an important factor to affect news coverage of those nations (Kunczik, 1997; Lee, 2007; Manheim & Albritton, 1984). Many governments and corporations hire public relations firms to promote their national image in a target country's media (Lee, 2006). However, these studies mainly focus on the influence of strategic public relations on news content and tend to exaggerate its effect by neglecting the perspectives of news editors and reporters.

The purpose of this chapter is to extend international public relations scholarship by integrating the newsworthiness concept (deviance and social significance) of world events and country characteristics in the world system. By doing so, this study will expand our understanding about influencing factors on national image in news.

NATIONAL IMAGE AND NEWS

According to Nimmo and Savage (1976), image is defined as "a human construct imposed on an array of perceived attributes projected by an object, event, or person" (p. 8). This definition makes a very important distinction between the sender's projected image and the receiver's perceived image, which are not necessarily identical. Applying nation as an object of image, national image can be defined as perceived or projected attributes toward a nation. For example, South Korea launched a national image campaign called "Dynamic Korea" targeting tourists overseas. The projected images and meanings of "dynamic" are fast-growing, innovative, and exciting as a tourist destination. Many foreign tourists, however, associate this campaign slogan with violent demonstrations against the government, safety concern in relation to North Korea, and terrible traffic conditions. This shows a significant gap between projected and perceived images.

Smith (1973) also indicated that most people develop national image toward other nations without firsthand contact with the image object and that they usually have mass media channels as sources of information. He tested the impact of shortwave broadcasting of the Soviet Union (Radio Moscow) on the change of favorability toward the Soviet Union among American people. He found that national images are highly vulnerable to the portrayal of mass media because many respondents changed their original perceptions toward the Soviet Union after listening to the Radio Moscow. North Korea is a mysteriously closed country to the global society. Most people form their perception and image of North Korea depending on major global news outlets, such as BBC, CNN and the New York Times. The frequently covered stories about North Korea are nuclear threats, missile launch tests, poverty, dictatorship, and conflicts with the U.S., South Korea, and Japan.

Manheim and Albritton (1984) identified two dimensions of national image portrayed in the news, visibility and valence. Visibility refers to "the amount of media coverage that the country receives and valence refers to the degree to which the content that is available reflects either favorably or unfavorably on the country" (p. 645). Unfavorable references include mention of unreliability, untrustworthiness, weakness, instability, retreat, and inefficiency on the part of a given country. Favorable references include mention of progress, prosperity, resources, strength, stability, and trustworthiness on the part of a given country. Neutral references included neither positive nor negative mention about a given country.

Based on a combination of visibility and valence in the news, Manheim and Albritton (1984) categorized four possible national image states. First, a country's image is in crisis when it gets a high visibility from a target country's media but the coverage is mostly negative. Second, a country's image is in mitigation from crisis when it gets a low visibility from a target country's media but the coverage is still negative. Third, a country's image can be improved from the previous state when the valence of coverage transforms into positive while maintaining a low visibility. Lastly, a country enjoys its ideal state when visibility is high and valence is positive. For example, North Korea is a country with high visibility from the U.S. news media and its coverage is mostly negative (e.g., nuclear threat). Mexico is a country with relatively low visibility from the U.S. news media and negative valence (e.g., illegal immigration, drug and gun trafficking). News about Sweden is rare (low visibility) in the U.S. but the stories are positive in general (e.g., quality of life and tourist destination). Japan is a country with high visibility and positive valence (strongly alliance to the U.S. and economic partnership) in the U.S. news media.

Whenever possible, a country would like to build or move toward an ideal state of national image (high visibility and positive valence) in a target country's news media. Manheim and Albritton (1984) suggested that public relations intervention facilitates this directional change of national image. Countries under crisis suffering from negative media coverage and high visibility often need to first make their visibility lower (moving to crisis mitigation), make efforts to convert valence from negative to positive (moving to improved image), and finally increase visibility (ideal image).

In sum, national image is people's perception toward a country as well as the attributes projected by a country. A perceived national image is not always the same as a projected one. International news is a primary source of information from which persons form a national image in their minds. Visibility and valence are two dimensions of national image in news and public relations that play a role in changing direction of national image in news by reducing negative visibility and increasing positive valence.

PUBLIC RELATIONS INFLUENCE ON NEWS

In many studies on media sociology, scholars have identified a number of factors influencing the media content. Among them, Shoemaker and her colleagues categorized five levels of influence on media content in a hierarchical model (Shoemaker, 1991; Shoemaker & Reese, 2014). These levels include: (1) social systems (e.g., societal-level ideologies); (2) social institutions (e.g., economic environment in which the media operate and other cultural and national variables); (3) organizations (e.g., political endorsements, editorial positions, and corporate policies); (4) media routines (e.g., gatekeeping, beat system, and pack journalism); and (5) individuals (e.g., media professionals' personal attitudes). According to Shoemaker and Reese (2014), public relations efforts have significant influences on media content at the social institutions level. Manheim (1987) also argued that external influences weigh on decisions to select or discard as items for a media agenda; among those influences, strategic public relations of news sources played a great part in controlling the flow of information. For example, when Samsung recalled millions of Galaxy Note 7 mobile phones due to heated battery explosions, overall news coverage was negative and concerned about the future of Samsung. There was, however, a stream of positive news about Samsung's quick decision of a preemptive global recall, which put consumer safety as the top priority even in the face of billions in monetary losses. This story was believed to be the message Samsung's public relations team wanted to promote through international news media.

Not only is media coverage a cost-effective way to reach the public for the organizations, but also public relations efforts, such as distribution of press releases, help journalist find news items and fill space with limited time and labor resources (Shoemaker, 1991). Shoemaker (1991) explains that public relations affects media content, either directly by disseminating press releases to the media and making journalists support the organizations' position, or indirectly by listing the organization-related issues on the public agenda through the media. Public relations sometimes creates pseudo-events, such as demonstrations and protests, to gain media attention, and eventually public attention, and to control media content toward the direction the organizations intended (Shoemaker, 1991; Shoemaker & Reese, 2014). Manheim and Albritton (1984) summarized many services that public relations firms provide for foreign clients as follows:

> The preparation of press kits, direct mailings, newsletters, and brochures is prominent among the services provided under public relations contracts. More important, however, public relations firms also routinely counsel their international clients' embassy personnel on how to talk about such problems as terrorism or human rights, schedule and conduct field trips for the press, organize visits with editors and lunches with business groups, and conduct financial seminars dealing with opportunities offered by the countries…Perhaps one of

> the most important services such firms offer is to provide easier access to officials of the government in question for American reporters. (p. 645)

Despite its significant influence on the flow of news, however, scholars have paid less attention to the role of public relations compared to other influential factors previously identified. Especially, in terms of international news, the effect of public relations was less regarded as an influential factor on media content. Therefore, some scholars have tried to empirically show the evidence of public relations' influence on media content. The results are sometimes contradictory; Albritton and Manheim (1983) found that a public relations campaign improved Rhodesia's image in the U.S. press, whereas Stocking (1985) concluded that news value was a more powerful feature to make an issue appear in the media coverage.

According to Manheim and Albritton (1984), however, the number of public relations contracts on behalf of foreign governments noticeably increased in the U.S. and those contracts mostly targeted fostering a positive image in the U.S. news media. They tested the effect of public relations intervention on media coverage. They found the improvement of national image in media portrayals before and after signing public relations contracts. They found that public relations efforts can change how the countries are portrayed in the media of a target country, particularly in U.S. news coverage. For example, this study showed a decrease of news visibility and an increase of positive news about Argentina in the New York Times over time. This change of national image in news occurred before and after Argentina's public relations intervention in the U.S.

Recent empirical studies show somewhat limited effect of international public relations on news content of foreign news media (Lee, 2007; Yoon, 2005). Yoon (2005) summarized that the previous studies about how public relations influences news content could be grouped into two big categories: (1) acceptance or rejection of sources' news releases and how they are utilized; (2) journalists' perceptions of public relations and practitioners and how these perceptions affect their news products. It is widely supported by previous studies that organizations can build legitimacy as a news source, and therefore, can garner more attention from the media by steadily providing the media with information they generate (Yoon, 2005). Lee (2007) found that the more public relations contracts the countries had with PR agencies in the US, the more coverage the countries received at U.S. newspapers. He also found that the number of public relations contracts was positively related to the prominence of media coverage in the U.S. Public relations turned out to be a significant factor to explain the prominence the countries received in the U.S. newspapers after controlling other factors. He concluded that public relations might be more associated with the quantity of the prominence (length and position of news articles) whereas the quality of the coverage is influenced by newsworthiness. It seems relatively more plausible that public relations contributes to increasing the prominence of media coverage rather than the valence, because the change of valence requires more efforts over a long period of time (Lee, 2007).

Public relations has been identified as an influencing factor that affects news content. Governments conduct a variety of international public relations activities to influence foreign news coverage toward their countries. Much empirical evidence supports public relations' influence. However, people who emphasize journalistic objectivity and autonomy in the process of news production see public relations influence in conflict with news value itself. Thus, the newsworthiness concept needs to be explained along with public relations' influence.

INTERNATIONAL NEWSWORTHINESS

Since the 1960s, many studies have explored the characteristics of international news coverage. Researchers generally agree that there have been two perspectives in this line of research—gatekeeper and logistical (Ahern, 1984; Chang, Shoemaker, & Brendlinger, 1987; Golan & Bakker, 2003; Hjarvard, 2002; Wu, 1998). The gatekeeper perspective is particularly concerned about the social psychology of news professionals and how these elements affect the process of selecting news items. The logistical perspective is interested in socio-economic characteristics and physical logistics of news processing, focusing on macro-level systematic factors. Based on these approaches, a great number of variables have been identified and tested.

Galtung and Ruge (1965; Galtung, 1971; Ostgaard, 1965) argue that the economic, social, political, and geographic factors of a nation influence the coverage one country receives in another country's news media. This approach sees the world as a global system consisting of interacting nations structured into a center-peripheral scheme. This approach explains that international news production is mainly led by a few global media, such as BBC, CNN, AP, and Reuters, and these western media (the center) generate and distribute international news, filtered by their own interests and biases, to the third world (the periphery). This approach implicitly assumes that a western-dominated paradigm functions as the frame of international news. This approach has much empirical support (Adams, 1986; Chang, 1998; Hicks & Gordon, 1974; Kariel & Rosenvall, 1984; Nnaemeka & Richstad, 1980).

A structural theory approach also identifies other systemic factors that influence international news flow: (1) national traits, (2) interactions and relatedness, and (3) logistics of news gathering and distribution. These systemic factors influence the amount and content of international news and determine the topic areas of international news available to gatekeepers (Wu, 2000).

Ostgaard (1965) identified two factors to influence the structure and flow of news¾external factors such as political and economic factors and internal factors, particularly the newsworthiness of the event. Galtung and Ruge (1965) suggested

12 factors to affect the newsworthiness of international events: frequency, threshold (absolute intensity and intensity increase), unambiguity, meaningfulness (cultural proximity and relevance), consonance (predictability and demand), unexpectedness (unpredictability and scarcity), continuity, composition, reference to elite nations, reference to elite people, reference to persons, and reference to something negative. Galtung and Ruge (1965) differentiated culture-free and culture-bound factors, and identified culture-bound factors (reference to elite nations, reference to elite people, reference to persons, and reference to something negative) relevant for the center nations of the world system.

Many empirical studies have been conducted based on this theory. For example, Shoemaker, Danielian, and Brendlinger (1991) identified communication constraints as determinants of international news coverage. Communication constraints are defined as "characteristics of the event country that may hinder (or help) communication about newsworthy events to the United States" (p. 785). They identified six indicators—proximity, language similarity, literacy rate, newspaper, radio, and television diffusion. Countries that are far from the U.S. that have limited communication media, and that have fewer persons who can speak English will be less likely covered by the U.S. media because of these communication hindrances.

There have been many different ways to explain why some countries, rather than others, are covered more prominently or favorably by international news media. However, three main factors emerge: (1) power of international politics (e.g., central vs. peripheral world system), (2) characteristics of a news event itself (e.g., frequency and unexpectedness), and (3) communication constraints (e.g., proximity and language similarity). Some of these factors, however, conceptually overlap and are not clearly distinguished from each other.

DEVIANCE AND SOCIAL SIGNIFICANCE

Shoemaker and her colleagues (Shoemaker, 1996; Chang et al., 1987; Shoemaker & Cohen, 2006; Shoemaker et al., 1991) made a significant contribution by rearranging multiple indicators addressed above into a theoretically robust newsworthiness model based on two main constructs—deviance and social significance. This model makes it possible to synthesize an event-oriented approach (deviance) and a country-oriented approach (social significance) into a single theoretical model.

Deviance refers to news items that are unusual and that are not considered normal by socially accepted values and beliefs. However, this concept includes good news as well as bad news. The deviance construct has three components—statistical deviance, potential for social change deviance, and normative deviance. Statistical deviance refers to the likelihood of a news event actually happening, statistically speaking the difference from the mean. Potential for social change deviance refers to an event's potential to threaten or change the status quo in a city, region, country or the international system. Normative deviance refers to a behavior, attitude, or opinion that violates or breaks a social collective's existing norms, rules, or laws (Shoemaker, 1984).

Deviance can be applied to a country as well as to a news event. For example, in the eyes of the U.S. media, North Korea has been regarded as a deviant country and this perception has influenced its coverage. North Korea has been portrayed for decades as a bizarre and abnormal country: as extremely closed society, cult-like obedience to a dictator, and excessive military spending (more than 30% of GDP), and nuclear threats to neighboring countries.

> Social significance refers to the degree to which a news item is important to a society. Shoemaker et al. (1991) found that events of high deviance and high social significance received the most prominent coverage. Social significance has three dimensions¾economic significance, political significance, and cultural significance (Shoemaker et al., 1991). These three dimensions are very useful in categorizing many predictors to determine international news coverage, particularly, country-related variables.

Economic significance is defined as "the business-dominated links" (Shoemaker et al., 1991, p. 784) between two countries. The indicators are gross domestic product, direct investment, exports, and imports. The magnitude of economic interaction between countries is one of the powerful factors to predict the amount of media coverage in a target country's news (Ahern, 1984; Dupree, 1971; Kariel & Rosenvall, 1984). This predictor is important because "economic interest propels people to learn about those countries that are more economically related than others that are not" (Wu, 1998, p. 499).

Political significance is defined as "government-dominated links" (Shoemaker et al., 1991, p. 785) between two countries. The indicators are, for example, U.S. military presence, military alliance with the U.S., and economic aid from the U.S. Countries under the same political camp or ideological group are likely to interact more frequently; therefore, their media are more likely to cover their congenial partners instead of their incongruent counterparts (Wu, 1998). Although a rigid political line-up among nations was dissociated after the Cold War, political significance functions as an important factor to catch media attention because the media cannot ignore the political importance of other nations in terms of their "national interest" to the U.S.

Cultural significance is defined as "a function of similarities among the people of the two countries" (Shoemaker et al., 1991, p. 785). For example, countries with similar cultural backgrounds, based on such things as religion and ethnicity, can communicate more effectively than with culturally heterogeneous counterparts. Mass media definitely have a preference for covering culturally similar countries.

Shoemaker's deviance and social significance model is a synthesized and parsimonious conceptual framework to rearrange multiple factors of international newsworthiness. This model can be applied to explain national image in news.

CONCLUSION

Based on the literature review, national image in a target country's news media is explained by international public relations, newsworthiness, deviance and social significance. Especially the concept of newsworthiness, represented by deviance and social significance, has made a great contribution to reconsidering the influence of international public relations on news. There are several points to highlight.

First, public relations influence on news needs to be understood as a relationship building process with news media. Public relations does not intend to manipulate or twist reality to a client country's favor. A widely accepted definition of public relations is "the management function that establishes and maintains mutually beneficial relationships between an organization and the publics on whom its success and failure depends" (Cutlip, Center, & Broom, 2000, p. 6). From this definition of public relations, mutuality is a core meaning of public relations and therefore, media relations as a specific function of public relations is not an exception. A primary goal of international public relations targeting foreign news coverage is to build and maintain mutually beneficial relationships between a country and a target country's news media. It is not a secretive spin-doctoring or one-way persuasion but a reciprocal relationship management.

Second, like public relations, deviance and social significance highlight a "relational interaction" between a country and a target country's media. Countries with high deviance (either negatively or positively) and social significance (political, economic, and cultural importance) will receive prominent news coverage and relative valence in a target country's news media. This axiom provides valuable strategic implications when public relations professionals work for a client country. Deviance and social significance in a target country's news media are effective evaluation criteria to measure current national image of a client country. Based on this evaluation, public relations strategies and tactics can be planned and executed for improvement. For example, Japan's history of conflict with its neighboring countries, such as China and South Korea, has been viewed as deviant foreign policy. This, of course, is against the norm of international community in as much as Japan has tried to deny or downplay harms and pains during World War II. Germany has been frequently compared with Japan and praised as a responsible country to honestly face her shameful past. Japan is a politically, economically, and culturally significant country to the U.S. Japan is a long time U.S. ally, a top trading partner, and a country that shares similar cultural values, such as democracy and freedom. Considering Japan's national image in the U.S. and news media, assessing the current image of Japan from a deviance and social significance perspective is a good start. From this assessment, future public relations plans can be formulated.

Third, deviance and social significance remind public relations professionals of the importance of newsworthiness in public relations practice. A country's national image depends on how international public relations can generate politically, economically, and culturally significant newsworthy events and stories that a target country's news media would like to cover prominently and positively.

Lastly, international public relations effort needs to be consistent and effective over time. National image is not built over night and it takes a long time. To manage a crisis situation or to change direction of current national image, deviance and social significance of newsworthiness can provide long-term public relations strategies to guide many tactical activities and events. For example, a longitudinal study could test causal relationships between public relations expenditures and news coverage (prominence and valence) over time using a time-series analysis. This study could show whether public relations expenditures can influence news coverage immediately or gradually in time and also whether current news coverage can influence future public relations expenditures. The former effect sees news content as a consequence of international public relations and the latter sees news as a baseline for future adjustment of public relations. Both directions of causality can happen in reality.

REFERENCES

Albritton, R. B., & Manheim, J. B. (1983). News of Rhodesia: The impact of a public relations campaign. *Journalism Quarterly, 60,* 622–628.

Adams, W. C. (1986). Whose lives count? TV coverage of natural disaster. *Journal of Communication, 36,* 113–122.

Ahern, T. J. (1984). Determinants of foreign coverage in newspaper. In R. L. Stevenson & D. L. Shaw (Eds.), *Foreign news and the new world information order.* Ames, IA: Iowa State University Press.

Chang, T. (1998). All countries not created equal to be news: World system and international communication. *Communication Research, 25,* 528–563.

Chang, T. K., Shoemaker, P. J., & Brendlinger, N. (1987). Determinants of international news coverage in the U.S. media. *Communication Research, 14,* 396–414.

Cutlip, S. M., Center, A. H., & Broom, G. M. (2000). *Effective public relations* (8th ed.). Upper Saddle River, NJ: Prentice Hall.

Dupree, J. D. (1971). International communication: View from a window on the world. *Gazette, 17,* 224–235.

Galtung, J. (1971). A structural theory of imperialism. *Journal of Peace Research, 8,* 81–118.

Galtung, J., & Ruge, M. H. (1965). The structure of foreign news: The presentation of the Congo, Cuba and Cyprus crises in four Norwegian newspapers. *Journal of Peace Research, 2*(1), 64–90.

Golan, G., & Bakker, R. (2003, August). *The determinants of international news coverage: A contextual approach.* Paper presented at the meeting of the Association for Education in Journalism and Mass Communication, Kansas City, MO.

Hjarvard, S. (2002). The study of international news. In K. B. Jensen (Ed.), *A handbook of media and communication research: Qualitative and quantitative methodologies* (pp. 91–97). New York, NY: Routledge.

Hicks, R. G., & Gordon, A. (1974). Foreign news content in Israeli and US newspapers. *Journalism Quarterly, 51,* 639–644.

Kariel, H. G., & Rosenvall, L. A. (1984). Factors influencing international news flow. *Journalism Quarterly, 61,* 509–516.

Kunczik, M. (1997). *Images of nations and international public relations.* Mahwah, NJ: Lawrence Erlbaum.

Lee, S. (2006). An analysis of other countries' international public relations in the US. *Public Relations Review, 32,* 97–103.

Lee, S. (2007). International public relations as a predictor of prominence of US news coverage. *Public Relations Review, 33,* 158–165.

Lippmann, W. (1922). *Public opinion.* New York, NY: Macmillan.

Manheim, J. B. (1987). A model of agenda dynamics. In M. McLaughlin (Ed.), *Communication Year-Book Vol. 10* (pp. 499–516). Beverly Hills, CA: Sage.

Manheim, J. B., & Albritton, R. B. (1984). Changing national images: International public relations and media agenda setting. *The American Political Science Review, 78,* 641–657.

Nnaemeka, T., & Richstad, J. (1980). Structured relations and foreign news flow in the pacific region. *Gazette, 26,* 235–258.

Nimmo, D., & Savage, R. L. (1976). *Candidates and their images: Concepts, methods and findings.* Pacific Palisades: Goodyear.

Ostgaard, E. (1965). Factors influencing the flow of news. *Journal of Peace Research, 2,* 39–63.

Shoemaker, P. J. (1984). Media treatment of deviant political groups. *Journalism Quarterly, 61,* 66–75, 82.

Shoemaker, P. J. (1991). *Gatekeeping.* Newbury Park, CA: Sage.

Shoemaker, P. J. (1996). Hardwired for news: Using biological and cultural evolution to explain the surveillance function. *Journal of Communication, 46*(3), 32–47.

Shoemaker, P. J., & Cohen, A. A. (2006). *News around the world: Content, practitioners, and the public.* New York, NY: Routledge.

Shoemaker, P. J., Danielian, L. H., & Brendlinger, N. (1991). Deviant acts, risky business and U.S. interests: The newsworthiness of world events. *Journalism Quarterly, 68*(4), 781–795.

Shoemaker, P. J., & Reese, S. D. (2014). *Mediating the message in the 21th century: A media sociology perspective* (3rd ed.). New York, NY: Routledge.

Smith, D. D. (1973). Mass communications and international image change. *The Journal of Conflict Resolution, 17,* 115–129.

Stocking, S. H. (1985). Effect of public relations efforts on media visibility of organizations. *Journalism Quarterly, 62*(2), 358–450.

Wu, H. D. (1998). Investigating the determinants of international news flow: A meta-analysis. *Gazette, 60,* 493–512.

Wu, H. D. (2000). Systemic determinants of international news coverage: A comparison of 38 countries. *Journal of Communication, 50,* 110–130.

Yoon, Y. (2005). Legitimacy, public relations, and media access: Proposing and testing a media access model. *Communication Research, 32*(6), 762–793.

CHAPTER SEVEN

Communication Research as a "Great Crossroads"

Bridging Fields of Social Science

DOMINIC L. LASORSA*

INTRODUCTION

In 1959, Wilbur Schramm (1959, p. 6) described the field of communication research as "a great crossroads" where those studying economics, political science, psychology, sociology and other social sciences could advance their understanding of consumption, voting, attitudes, community and other core social science concepts by considering pertinent communication processes. Social scientists then and now have made notable forays into communication research. Still, few social scientists outside of communication schools have shown much interest in the processes and effects of communication. In fact, Schramm's description of communication research as "a great crossroads" was written in response to Bernard Berelson's (1959, p. 1) claim that "communication research … is withering away". More than anything else, Berelson faulted communication research for its almost exclusive investigation of short-term persuasion effects which, after all, rarely are robust. It is fair to say that in the intervening years since 1959, communication research has expanded its concerns. Yet, at the same time, it also is still fair to say that the attitudes of many social scientists toward communication research has not changed much. In some ways it is curious that other social sciences still don't appear to regard communication as particularly important in their own investigations. Communication

* Dominic L. Lasorsa is Associate Professor in the School of Journalism at the University of Texas at Austin. Email: lasorsa@austin.utexas.edu.

patterns among humans are diverse, with persons differing in many ways regarding how they communicate. Whether one is studying a person's buying habits, political participation, attitude change or community life, it is likely that one or more communication patterns may be implicated in the outcome obtained. Humans differ in how outspoken or reticent they are, in what mass media they use, how often and for what purposes. These and other differences in one's communication patterns could affect economies, politics, minds and societies, and aspects of them. Communication cuts across all these fields and their products. Here we have this perfectly good crossroads but few of our adjoining neighbors seem much interested. They largely continue to ignore the role of communication in the processes they study. This is particularly curious today because recent developments in communication technology have revolutionized the lives of most people and thus have affected their consumption, voting, attitudes, community and other aspects of their social lives that social scientists have been studying for many years.

A crossroads, though, is a two-way street, so to speak. If even in these times of great communication advancements most social scientists continue to stay clear of the field of communication research that does not mean that communication researchers have been staying clear of adjoining fields. Indeed, within communication schools, scholars have been finding the great crossroads to be a fertile field that allows them to make productive forays into neighboring terrain. Among the notable scholars who have shown the value of exploring the communicative aspects of the central concerns of social science is Pam Shoemaker. My own research has drawn inspiration from Shoemaker's willingness to hunt far and wide for a good idea, her ability to make connections between key concepts in different fields, and her integrative approach to communication research in which she explores both the factors involved in the construction of media products and also the effects of media products (Shoemaker & Cohen, 2006; Shoemaker & Reese, 1996; Shoemaker, Tankard, & Lasorsa, 2004; Shoemaker & Vos, 2009).

MEDIA FRAMING THEORY

Media framing theory offers good examples of current communication research that bridges social science disciplines. Reese (2007, p. 148) speculated that "the most interesting happens at the edges of disciplines" where scholars bump into those at the periphery of neighboring disciplines. Speaking of communication research, Reese said the framing concept provides a model also "that bridges parts of the field that need to be in touch with each other: quantitative and qualitative, empirical and interpretive, psychological and sociological, and academic and professional". For example, Yang's (2015) aptly labeled cognitive-sociological model of stereotypes is built upon the psychological concepts of framing and stereotyping, and the sociological concept of social distance. Yang builds upon media effects studies which suggest that stereotypical media frames can activate negative cognitive/affective responses in audiences, coupled with studies of media frame construction which suggest that socially disadvantaged groups are frequently subjected to negative media framing. As Yang (2015, p. 254) said, "little effort has been made to bridge findings from these 2 approaches and explain the mechanism through which these activated responses further influence people's social interaction patterns". Yang's model explains the following relationship: (a) stereotypical frames can be classified into different genres according to their possible cognitive/affective effects; (b) responses activated by stereotypical frames are positively related to people's willingness to keep social distance in their minds; and (c) there is a negative relationship between social distance and the changing of people's stereotypical attitudes. The three pairs of relationships include message features, cognitive/affective effects, and social effects. One particularly notable contribution of this cognitive-sociological model of stereotypes is its identification of five distinct genres of stereotyping frames, each with its own unique effect. These media stereotyping frame genres are exhaustive and mutually exclusive, and general enough to account for practically all instances of stereotypical media content. Thus, anyone studying any important social science concept with which media stereotyping might be implicated, from attitudes to voting, is likely to benefit from considering how an integrative model of stereotyping like this one might guide one's research.

Another example of media framing theory bridging social science disciplines in an even grander way comes from Matthes (2012, p. 247) who noted that "one of the strengths of framing research has been to bridge several research areas in mass communication, such as the origin, journalistic production, content, and effects of news". Matthes proposed a model of the entire framing process, including frame construction, frame building and frame setting. The model consists of political actors, media actors and citizen actors, each of which involves decisions and processes within politics, the media and the audience, respectively. Each of these three sets of actors is directly connected to the other two so that a complete investigation of the media framing process involves three sets of analyses: the media actors-citizen actors relationship, the political actors-citizen actors relationship, and the political actors-media actors relationship. Matthes identifies these analyses as the analysis of media use and media effects, the analysis of direct and indirect effects on decision makers, and the input-output analysis between political actors (PR) and media actors (news). The special value of an integrative model like that of Matthes resides in its ability to make up for deficiencies in models that ignore one or more of the basic parts of the media framing process. For example, research that consists only of an analysis of media content enlightens us little about the influence of political actors on the construction of frames. Similarly, research that consists only of an analysis of the political input underestimates the effect of journalistic autonomy on frame building. In Matthes' model, each of the three sets of actors interact with and affect each of the other two sets. As Matthes (2012, p. 248) put it, "the intentional strategies of politicians and media actors and the reactions of the citizens need to be studied with an integrated approach".

In my own recent research, I also have attempted to bridge (a) the study of the construction of media frames and (b) the effect of media frames on public attitudes, with a special emphasis upon the study of media framing and attitude change over time. In one recent study, my colleagues and I examined how two major New York daily newspapers with distinctly different ideological orientations framed the issue of same-sex marriage over 17 years (Lasorsa, Suk, & Fadnis, 2015a). In the late 1990s and early 2000s, both the ideologically conservative *New York Post* and the ideologically liberal *New York Times* framed same-sex marriage primarily in terms of morality but over time both newspapers, but especially the *Times,* gradually shifted their framing of the issue from a predominantly morality frame to a predominantly equality frame. Even in the late 2000s and well into the 2010s, the *Post* continued to frame the issue of same-sex marriage in terms of morality more than did the *Times* and, interestingly, the morality framing of the same-sex marriage issue in the *Post* consistently increased in election years.

Of course, without studying the effect of media framing on audiences one may only speculate about possible effects. Consequently, we also examined the connection between changes in how the media framed the issue of same-sex marriage over time and changes in public attitudes over the same time as measured by public opinion polls (Lasorsa, Suk, & Fadnis, 2015b). As expected, time-series analyses revealed that changes in the framing of same-sex marriage in the *New York Times* between 1998 and 2014 preceded changes in public attitudes. In sharp contrast, however, changes in the *New York Post's* framing of the same-sex issue did not precede changes in public attitudes, as expected, but actually seemed to follow public attitudes.

While these correlational and time-order findings suggest that media framing has the potential under certain specific conditions to influence public attitudes, it is possible that one or more other factors is responsible for the relationships. In fact, a number of alternative explanations have been given for changes in attitudes toward same-sex marriage, including shifts in *age cohorts* (younger people disproportionately favoring same-sex marriage) (Baunach, 2011), *jurisprudence* (courts and other deliberative bodies increasingly judging same-sex marriage bans as discriminatory) (Machacek & Fulco, 2004), *social visibility* (gays, lesbians, bisexuals and transgendered individuals becoming more active publicly) (Gilgoff, 2003; Peters, 2009), *personal contact* (people getting to know more gay people personally) (Allport, 1979; Herek & Glunt, 1993; Merino, 2013), and *entertainment portrayals* (with negative pop culture representations being replaced with more positive ones) (Gross, 2001; Horton & Wohl, 1956; Schiappa, Gregg, & Hewes, 2005). It is possible that all of these varied factors, plus media framing, have contributed uniquely to the observed changes in same-sex marriage attitudes. By cutting across disciplinary boundaries, by drawing directly upon research conducted in a variety of social science disciplines, including law, popular culture, psychology and sociology, it is possible to construct an integrated model of media framing that addresses systematically a rich array of predictors of attitude change.

This begs the question: If interdisciplinary research is so fertile, why don't we see more of it? One reason why research that bridges social science disciplines is less prolific may be the movement toward increasingly focused journals that cater to specific disciplines. Most of the factors mentioned earlier as predictors of changes in attitude toward same-sex marriage were identified in journals outside the field of communication, including *Psychiatry*, the *Journal of Sex Research*, and the *Journal of Church and State*. Building intriguing social science theory may benefit from looking beyond one's own backyard.

CIVIC ENGAGEMENT

Another example of an important social outcome which many social scientists apparently have assumed to have little to do with communication is civic engagement. Scholars in a variety of fields have been working long and hard to determine the causes of civic engagement (Bourdieu, 1986; Gil de Zuniga, 2015). Social capital theory maintains that people hold to a "norm of reciprocity" which encourages a person to help others, trusting that they will reciprocate if the need arises. In this way, "social capital" accrues. According to social capital theory, social interaction leads to social trust which leads to social capital which leads to civic engagement (Coleman, 1988; Wellman, 1990).

Social scientists have theorized that social interactions with certain particular properties are more likely to stimulate civic engagement than other social interactions. Specifically, formal social ties are expected to encourage civic engagement. Formal social ties have been conceptualized in a variety of ways with movement in recent years toward a concept of associations with public spaces where people may interact, such as a library, and also voluntary, active associations with such public institutions. This view discounts both mandatory association membership (e.g., labor unions) and voluntary but passive ("checkbook") association membership. Formal social ties such as active voluntary associational memberships and recurrent excursions to public institutions provide a "public sphere" where socializing is likely to happen, where opportunity to build social trust is likely to occur, where capital is likely to be built, and where civic engagement is likely to ensue (Baumgartner & Walker, 1988; Putnam, 1993, 2000).

Additionally, social scientists have theorized that less formal social ties also may contribute to civic engagement. Unlike formal social ties, informal social ties are less rigidly structured and do not require public institutional structures at all. An informal social tie consists of an individual's personal association with another person, and the sum of such associations make up one's interpersonal network. Social scientists further have theorized that certain characteristics of one's interpersonal network contribute more than others to civic engagement, including the size and diversity of one's interpersonal network (Fischer, 1982; Rojas, Shah, & Friedland, 2011).

Most models of civic engagement are built on the same relatively few variables. Controls include standard demographic variables such as age, gender, education and income, and traditional political predispositions such as political interest, knowledge, efficacy and ideology. Then over and above the influence of those variables, both formal social ties and informal social ties are explored for their contributions to civic engagement (Edelstein & Larsen, 1960; Jeffres, Dobos, & Lee, 1988; McLeod et al., 1996, 1999; McLeod & McDonald, 1985; Robinson & Wilkinson, 1995; Stamm, 1985).

Having established what they believed to be the basic parameters of the process of civic engagement, social scientists in recent years have focused much of their attention on refining the conceptualizations and measurements of the key concepts, including formal social ties, informal social ties, and civic engagement itself (Diez de Ulzurrun, 2002). Even today the very definition of civic engagement is hotly contested. As Vraga (2015, p. 1007) recently pointed out in her review of a new anthology on civic engagement research, "Scholars…offer competing definitions of what it means to be civically engaged, ranging from more traditional definitions of political participation and consumption habits, to engagement in civic organizations and volunteerism, to emerging conceptualizations of being a 'good person'…as a form of civic engagement". And interest has anything but diminished. In the four years between 2011 and 2015, more than 30 articles in The American Scientist alone mentioned social capital. Predictably, though, very few articles in that premiere journal and others have gone beyond the basic models to consider the role of communication in generating social capital and encouraging civic engagement. Also predictably, advancements in this area have occurred not because of the work of social scientists in other disciplines recognizing the importance of communication in generating social capital but mainly because communication researchers have drawn social capital theory to their great crossroads, and are staking a claim on it. A number of such forays into social capital territory have yielded promising results. Two notable examples include the work of Sandra Ball-Rokeach and her colleagues on communication infrastructure theory (e.g., Kim & Ball-Rokeach, 2006) and the work of Hernando Rojas and his colleagues on a communicative approach to social capital (e.g., Rojas et al., 2011). For the sake of convenience, such work that gives a critical role to communication ties in the production of civic engagement has been labeled "communicative social capital" (Ginman, 2003).

COMMUNICATION INFRASTRUCTURE

In an effort to understand better why communities differ in the extent to which their residents are civically engaged, communication infrastructure theory maintains that communities differ in the communication resources that fuel civic engagement. Specifically, if key community storytellers encourage community members to talk about the community then that increases these members' sense of belonging to the community, their collective efficacy, and their participation in civic activities (Kim & Ball-Rokeach, 2006). A community's communication infrastructure is comprised of a communication action context, that is, a neighborhood resource that promotes communication between residents, such as safe streets, parks, libraries, schools, transportation, health care resources, and ethnic and cultural diversity, and a neighborhood storytelling network which is set in that communication action context. Kim and Ball-Rokeach (2006, p. 178) conceptualized a neighborhood storytelling network as consisting of "everyday conversations and neighborhood stories that people, media, and grassroots organizations create and disseminate" about the community. They said what is unique in the CIT approach is that it focuses not only on the strength of each community storyteller but also on the value added when they form a storytelling network. Kim and Ball-Rokeach (2006, p. 181) said, "One important criterion in the measurement of the quality of a storytelling network is the level of integration of the communicative actions of the three community storytellers—local media, community organizations, and residents. In an ideal community, meso-and micro-storytellers form an integrated network where each storyteller stimulates the others to talk about the local community". The theory holds that in a community with an integrated storytelling network, people are informed about what is happening in their local neighborhood and talk about neighborhood issues and events with their neighbors and do so in a way that motivates participation in community-building activities.

COMMUNICATIVE INTEGRATION

Another theory that gives communication a crucial integration role in stimulating civic engagement was proposed by Rojas et al. (2011, p. 690) who said, "We view communication as the fundamental source of societal integration, contending that integration that occurs at the system level via news media consumption and at the individual level via interpersonal discussion is amplified through formal and informal ties at the community level". Besides the communication ties associated with news exposure, news attention and interpersonal offline and online communication, Rojas et al. (2011) proposed one additional communication tie that may create social capital and stimulate civic engagement. They maintained that whether offline or online, communication in which one's intention is to share meaning and come to an understanding, as opposed to an interaction in which one's intention is to persuade another person, is likely to accrue social capital and thereby induce civic engagement. This echoes Laden's (2012, p. 26) sentiment:

> Engagement...is not merely a matter of being active, of deploying the rhetorical and cognitive skills necessary to make your case and press your point. To engage with others requires that we hear what they have to say, that we make space in our interaction for them to respond fully and genuinely, and that we are fully responsive to their responses and proposals.

Conversely, one might argue that what crystalizes political discussion is possessing a point of view and actively espousing it, in a competitive marketplace of ideas clamoring for attention and approval (Brader, 2005).

Above and beyond the influences of social ties, news use, and political talk on civic engagement, Rojas and colleagues (2011) theorize that the social-by-personal-level interplay further encourages civic engagement. The theory distinguishes between the extent of news use and political talk and the orientation toward the consumption and conversation. Specifically, communication ties—news attention and exposure along with conversational frequency and orientation toward conversational understanding—are theorized to interact with the formal and informal social ties—associational membership and interpersonal network size—to foster civic engagement. Rojas et al. (2011, p. 695) said:

> Communicative social capital, then, is conceptualized as both a structural feature embedded in social ties and a resource of the individual comprised of information flows, with the interactions among these elements producing a range of pathways to participation and the reconstruction of social capital.

They found that news exposure and news attention along with conversational frequency and orientation toward conversational understanding interacted with associational membership and network size to foster civic engagement.

ONLINE PERSONAL COMMUNICATION

Certain types of association memberships have been found to be particularly effective at generating social capital, namely, voluntary as opposed to mandatory associations, and also face-to-face active membership as opposed to passive "checkbook" membership (Putnam, 2000). New communication technologies, however, have made possible new forms of association (Thompson, 1995), such as participating in a virtual community (Matei & Ball-Rokeach, 2002) or taking part in global civil society (Teheranian, 1999). In their work to advance communication infrastructure theory, Ognyanova and colleagues (2013, p. 2448) concluded that "online platforms and activities…should be incorporated into this theory as a mode of participation complementing more traditional indicators of civic engagement" and they highlighted "the importance of studying a range of goal-oriented digital forms of engaging with local issues". Johansen and Givskov (2014, p. 2) proposed that the role of media in civic engagement may be considered from three related but distinct perspectives: "media at the official, political level of communication, civic and often oppositional communication through and with digital media, and media and communication in culture and everyday life in different arenas such as museums, documentary film, and gaming culture".

We agree that in today's world of smart phones and social media, some of the benefits of interpersonal communication may be acquired online and digitally. In a relatively short time, we have experienced remarkable advancements in the ability of one to engage in what seems like a rather natural conversation with others and as new communication technologies are developed we can expect "online talk" to serve as a reasonable surrogate for face-to-face communication and communication via other traditional means of communication such as telephones. Some people, in fact, might use the Internet, smart phones and other online media devices and services primarily to stay in touch with relatives, to chat with friends, to check with neighbors, and otherwise to converse with others they know. We might label this "personal" use of online communication technologies as *online talk.*

These communication technologies, of course, possess many other functions, often having to do with convenience, such as obtaining information on topics of interest, seeking amusement, paying bills, making purchases, and the like. Some people might use the Internet, smart phones and other online media devices and services primarily for these other reasons. We might label these "impersonal" uses of online communication technologies as *online surfing.*

The reason we make this particular distinction is that we think that these major two reasons for going online—online talking versus online surfing—have different effects on civic engagement. Specifically, we propose that those who go online mainly for non-personal reasons, essentially to surf for information, amusement or convenience, will generate *less* civic engagement through their use of the Internet and other online services, whereas those who go online mainly for personal reasons, essentially to talk online with those they know, will generate *more* civic engagement through their use of the Internet.

We reason that if one's attention is turned to entertainment and popular culture and other mediated content that permeates and pervades the Internet and the World Wide Web then one may have less interest in or time, energy or other resources to cultivate social ties, generate social capital, and engage civilly. On the other hand, if one uses these means of communication as merely another tool for talking to others whom one knows via email, messaging and so forth then this online talk use of these online communication tools may lead to more civic engagement, just as talking to others offline is expected to increase the likelihood of civic engagement. To put it simply, online surfing distracts us from civic engagement while online talking focuses us on civic engagement. Therefore, we propose that the extent to which one goes online to talk positively affects civic engagement while the extent to which one goes online to surf negatively affects civic engagement. At least, that's the theory.

COMMUNICATION INTENT

We are preliminarily exploring these ideas about the role of communication ties in the advancement of social capital and civic engagement by analyzing data from the 2012 General Social Survey. Sixteen items from this national survey were combined to form an index of *civic engagement*. These items measured whether one voted in the last presidential election, and how often in the past 12 months one donated blood, gave food or money to a homeless person, returned money to a cashier after getting too much change, allowed a stranger to go ahead in line, did volunteer work for a charity, gave money to a charity, offered a seat on a bus or in a public place to a stranger, housesat for a neighbor, carried a stranger's belongings, gave directions to a stranger, let someone not well known borrow a valuable item, helped someone outside the household with housework or shopping, lent quite a bit of money to another person, spent time talking with someone who was a bit down or depressed, and helped someone find a job.

Our theoretical model of civic engagement included four established demographic control variables—*gender*, *age*, *education* and *income*—and four measures of political predispositions conventionally included in such models: *political interest*, *political ideology*, *political knowledge*, and *political efficacy*. *Social trust* also was measured with a conventional survey question.

Formal social ties were measured with an index that asked how often in the past year one visited a variety of public institutions, including an art museum, natural history museum, zoo, aquarium, and science museum. Informal social ties were measured across three dimensions of a person's interpersonal network. *Network size* was measured in terms of a four-item index asking how often one spends social evenings with a variety of other persons, including relatives, persons living in one's neighborhood, persons living outside one's neighborhood, and socializing at a bar or tavern, ranging from almost daily, several times a week, several times a month, once a month, several times a year, yearly and never. *Network diversity* was measured in terms of the racial characteristics of one's neighborhood. *Network proximity* was measured with a four-item index accounting for one's socializing orientation in terms of being oriented *within* the immediate neighborhood (that is, socializing primarily with those in close proximity) or extending *beyond* the immediate neighborhood (that is, socializing primarily with those further away).

News exposure was measured in terms of how often in a week one reads a newspaper. *Online surfing* was measured with a five-item index assessing how much time one spends online in a week seeking amusement and browsing the web without the specific intention of communicating with other persons who one knows. *Online talk* was measured with a four-item index assessing how much time one spends online with the intention of communicating with others one knows, as opposed to surfing the web for amusement and general surfing. *Orientation to understanding* was measured with a three-item index combining two items that asked about how important was wanting to gain knowledge or learn something new in one's decision to engage in two civic activities, and one item asking how important it is to listen to people who are different from oneself, even when one disagrees with them, because one still wants to understand them.

In an effort to replicate the community level-interpersonal level cross-level interaction affects proposed by Rojas et al. (2011), eight two-way multiplicative interaction terms were created from one of the two measures of social ties—associational membership or interpersonal network size—and one of the four measures of communication— news exposure, online surfing, online talk, and orientation to understanding. All variables used to construct the interaction terms were standardized before the interaction terms were created (Eveland, 1997). These eight interaction terms are (a) associational membership and news exposure; (b) associational membership and online surfing; (c) network size and news exposure; (d) network size and online surfing; (e) associational membership and online talk; (f) associational membership and an orientation toward reaching understanding; (g) network size and online talk; and (h) network size and an orientation toward reaching understanding. Due to the high correlations between each of the four pairs of two-way interaction terms, we ran four separate analyses each with one of the four pairs of interaction terms. To test these four models of civic engagement, we ran four ordinary least squares linear hierarchical regression analyses.

PRELIMINARY RESULTS

We proposed that communication ties advance formal and informal social ties, thereby contributing to the generation of social capital, which promotes civic engagement. We found considerable support for this proposition. With the exception of the control variables not expected to affect civic engagement, all of the predictor variables in the model were statistically significant contributors to civic engagement.

In other words, all of the formal and informal social ties predicted civic engagement, as did all of the communication ties. Our hypothesis regarding social trust also was supported. Social trust was a positive predictor of civic engagement. Most interesting, though, were the findings supporting our expectations about the differential communicative effects of online talking and online surfing on civic engagement. Online talking appears to work similarly to offline talk, encouraging civic engagement, whereas online surfing appears to distract one away from civic engagement.

However, not all of the statistically significant relationships we found were in the hypothesized direction. Civic engagement was positively correlated, as expected, with political efficacy and perceived political knowledge, but it was negatively correlated with political interest. We expected that the political activities associated with some forms of civic engagement would make civic engagement correlate positively with political interest. In looking for an explanation for this unexpected finding, we noted that our measure of civic engagement was heavily weighted in favor of apolitical civic engagement. Further, when we split the civic engagement scale into its political and apolitical components, we found that political participation and non-political civic engagement were negatively correlated, as well. Perhaps future research should give greater attention to the extent to which political and non-political activities constitute civic engagement and the theoretical possibility that some individuals may be largely engaged in one or the other but not both forms of engagement.

Interestingly, orientation to understanding, that is, communicating with the intent to come to an understanding with others, was negatively correlated with civic engagement. We found that strategic communication, notably trying to persuade others, predicted civic engagement, contrary to what Rojas et al. (2011) found. We expect that this may be due to the different ways orientation to understanding was measured. We measured the concept in terms of one's orientation to learn and gain knowledge, and to listen to others who are different in order to understand them better. Rojas et al. (2011) measured the concept in terms of protection for the rights of others and political conversation as a mechanism to promote solidarity. Future research might investigate this intriguing concept more fully, focusing in particular on refining the measurement to reflect as well as possible the conceptualization and its rationale.

The current study did not find support for the proposition that interactions between the social level and interpersonal level through the interplay of social ties and communication ties would contribute to civic engagement over and above the contributions of each individual tie. Rojas et al. (2011) offer empirical evidence that communication ties, specifically news attention and exposure along with conversational frequency and orientation toward conversational understanding, interact with associational membership and network size to foster civic engagement. We did not find statistically significant the interactions between each type of social tie (association membership and interpersonal network size) and each type of communication tie (news exposure and online talk). This difference in the two studies' findings could be due to any of a number of reasons, including the different ways communication ties were operationalized, and differences between the two places where the studies were conducted (Colombia and the U.S.). The difference in the two studies' findings regarding interactions indicates an intriguing area of exploration for future research.

Despite the fact that some of our measurements are quite weak, my colleagues and I found the results of this exploratory study promising enough to encourage us to plan a full investigation with more suitable data. In particular, we were gratified to find that our primary theoretical proposition, namely, that online talking and online surfing would have completely different effects on civic engagement, performed as hypothesized. My colleagues and I are eager to give this hypothesis and our model of civic engagement generally a more rigorous empirical test.

CONCLUSION

I opened this article with a reference to Wilbur Schramm's response to Bernard Berelson's (1959, p. 1) claim that communication research was "withering away". In their perceptive essay on why sociology has continued to abandon communication research, Jefferson Pooley and Elihu Katz (2008) described how some early communication scholars reacted in a positive way to those abandoning the study of communication. Wilbur Schramm, for instance, figured that if sociologists and other social scientists were going to take their balls and go home then he would simply have to construct his own ballfields. Pooley and Katz (2008, p. 773) singled out Schramm as the Johnny Appleseed of communication research:

> Berelson's death sentence struck Schramm as premature because his communication research—the sort establishing itself within professional schools of journalism across the U.S. Midwest and beyond—was just getting started. By 1959, Schramm had labored for over 15 years to seed journalism schools with Ph.D. programs in "mass communication" and with gathering success. Conferences, institutes, book-length readers, doctoral tracks, symposia: all of it "social capital" in Oakes and Vidich's (1999) sense, invested with the intent to institutionalize the young field.

Given my interest in social capital, I find it appealing to think of Wilbur Schramm as providing an excellent example of social capital at work. I don't know if Wilbur Schramm would have been pleased to be called a "social capitalist" and I don't know if Pam Shoemaker wants to be remembered that way. But in my mind they are both excellent examples of communication researchers who have been premiere generators of social capital and who, beyond the great value of their own personal research, will be remembered fondly for their efforts to get others to want to engage civilly in communication research.

REFERENCES

Allport, G. W. (1979). *The nature of prejudice*. New York, NY: Basic Books.

Baumgartner, F. R., & Walker, J. L. (1988). Survey research and membership in voluntary associations. *American Journal of Political Science, 32*, 908–928.

Baunach, D. M. (2011). Decomposing trends in attitudes toward gay marriage, 1988–2006. *Social Science Quarterly, 92*(2), 346–363.

Berelson, B. (1959). The state of communication research. *Public Opinion Quarterly, 23*, 1–2.

Brader, T. (2005). Striking a responsive chord: How political ads motivate and persuade voters by appealing to emotions. *American Journal of Political Science, 49*(2), 388–405.

Bourdieu, P. (1986). The forms of capital. In J. Richardson (Ed.), *Handbook of theory and research for the sociology of education* (pp. 241–258). New York, NY: Greenwood Press.

Coleman, J. S. (1988). Social capital in the creation of human capital. *American Journal of Sociology, 94*, 95–120.

Diez de Ulzurrun, L. M. (2002). Associational membership and social capital in comparative perspective: A note on the problems of measurement. *Politics & Society, 30*, 497–523.

Edelstein, A. S., & Larsen, O. N. (1960). The weekly press' contribution to a sense of urban community. *Journalism Quarterly, 37*, 489–498.

Eveland, W. P. (1997). Interactions and nonlinearity in mass communication: Connecting theory and methodology. *Journalism & Mass Communication Quarterly, 97*(2), 400–416.

Fischer, C. S. (1982). *To dwell among friends: Personal networks in town and city*. Chicago, IL: University of Chicago Press.

Gil de Zuniga, H. (2015). *New technologies and civic engagement: New agendas in communication*. New York, NY: Routledge.

Gilgoff, D. (2003, August 25). Gays force the issue. *U.S. News & World Report*.

Ginman, M. (2003). Social capital as a communicative paradigm. *Health Informatics Journal, 9*(1), 57–64.

Gross, L. P. (2001) *Up from invisibility: Lesbians, gay men, and the media in America*. New York, NY: Columbia University Press.

Herek, G. H., & Glunt, E. K. (1993). Interpersonal contact and heterosexuals' attitudes toward gay men: Results from a national survey. *Journal of Sex Research, 30*(3), 239–244.

Horton, D., & Wohl, R. R. (1956). Mass communication and para-social interaction: Observations on intimacy at a distance. *Psychiatry, 19*(3), 215–229.

Jeffres, L. W., Dobos, J., & Lee, J.-W. (1988). Media use and community ties. *Journalism Quarterly, 65*, 575–581.

Johansen, S. L., & Givskov, C. (2014). Media and civic engagement. *MedieKultur, 56*, 1–4.

Kim, Y. C., & Ball-Rokeach, S. J. (2006). Civic engagement from a communication infrastructure perspective. *Communication Theory, 16*(2), 173–197.

Laden, A. S. (2012). Taking the engagement in civic engagement seriously. Published by the University of Illinois at Chicago (UIC) Institute on Politics and Civic Engagement. Retrieved from http://www.uic.edu/cuppa/ipce/interior/TakingCivicEngagementSeriouslyFinalFY12.pdf.

Lasorsa, D., Suk, J., & Fadnis, D. (2015a, August). *The role of ideology in media framing of same-sex marriage, 1998–2014*. Paper presented to the Association for Education in Journalism and Mass Communication, San Francisco, CA.

Lasorsa, D., Suk, J., & Fadnis, D. (2015b, August). *Media framing of same-sex marriage and attitude change: A time-series analysis.* Paper presented to the Association for Education in Journalism and Mass Communication, San Francisco, CA.

Machacek, D. W., & Fulco, A. (2004). The courts and public discourse: The case of gay marriage. *Journal of Church and State, 46*, 767–785.

Matei, S., & Ball-Rokeach, S. J. (2002). Belonging across geographic and Internet spaces: Ethnic area variations. In B. Wellman & C. Haythornthwaite (Eds.), *The internet in everyday life* (pp. 404–430). Oxford: Blackwell.

Matthes, J. (2012). Framing politics: An integrative approach. *American Behavioral Scientist, 56*(3), 247–259.

McLeod, J. M., Daily, K., Guo, Z., Eveland, W. P., Jr., Bayer, J., & Yang, S. (1996). Community integration, local media use, and democratic processes. *Communication Research, 23*, 463–487.

McLeod, J. M., & McDonald, D. G. (1985). Beyond simple exposure: Media orientations and their impact on political processes. *Communication Research, 12*, 3–33.

McLeod, J. M., Scheufele, D., Moy, P., Horowitz, E. M., Holbert, R. L., & Zhang, W. (1999). Understanding deliberation: The effects of discussion networks on participation in a public forum. *Communication Research, 26*, 743–774.

Merino, S. M. (2013). Contact with gays and lesbians and same-sex marriage support: The moderating role of social context. *Social Science Research, 42*(4), 1156–1166.

Oakes, G., & Vidich, A. (1999). *Collaboration, reputation, and ethics in American academic life: Hans H. Gerth and C. Wright Mills.* Urbana, IL: University of Illinois Press.

Ognyanova, K., Chen, N. N., Ball-Rokeach, S., An, Z., Son, M., Parks, M., & Gerson, D. (2013). Online participation in a community context: Civic engagement and connections to local communication resources. *International Journal of Communication, 7*, 2433–2456.

Peters, J. W. (2009, October 11). Gay rights marchers press cause in Washington. *The New York Times.* Retrieved from http://www.nytimes.com/2009/10/12/us/politics/12protest.html

Pooley, J., & Katz, E. (2008). Further notes on why American sociology abandoned mass communication research. *Journal of Communication, 58*(4), 767–786.

Putnam, R. D. (1993). *Making democracy work: Civic traditions in modern Italy.* Princeton, NJ: Princeton University Press.

Putnam, R. D. (2000). *Bowling alone: The collapse and revival of American community.* New York, NY: Simon & Schuster.

Reese, S. D. (2007). The framing project: A bridging model for media research revisited. *Journal of Communication, 57*, 148–154.

Robinson, D., & Wilkinson, D. (1995). Sense of community in a remote mining town: Validating a neighborhood cohesion scale. *American Journal of Community Psychology, 23*, 137–148.

Rojas, H., Shah, D., & Friedland, L. A. (2011). A communicative approach to social capital. *Journal of Communication, 61*, 689–712.

Schiappa, E., Gregg, P. B., & Hewes, D. E. (2005). The parasocial contact hypothesis. *Communication Monographs, 72*(1), 92–115.

Schramm, W. (1959). Comments by Wilbur Schramm. *Public Opinion Quarterly, 23*, 6–9.

Shoemaker, P. J., & Cohen, A. A. (2006). *News around the world: Practitioners, content, and the public.* New York, NY: Routledge.

Shoemaker, P. J., & Reese, S. D. (1996). *Mediating the message: Theories of influences on mass media content.* White Plains, NY: Longman.

Shoemaker, P. J., Tankard, J. W., & Lasorsa, D. L. (2004). *How to build social science theories.* Thousand Oaks, CA: Sage.

Shoemaker, P. J., & Vos, T. P. (2009). *Gatekeeping theory.* New York, NY: Routledge.

Stamm, K. R. (1985). *Newspaper use and community ties: Toward a dynamic theory.* Norwood, NJ: Ablex.

Teheranian, M. (1999). *Global communication and world politics: Domination, development, and discourse.* Boulder, CO: Lynne Rienner.

Thompson, J. B. (1995). *The media and modernity: A social theory of the media.* Stanford, CA: Stanford University Press.

Vraga, E. K. (2015). Book review: New technologies and civic engagement: New agendas in communication. *Journalism & Mass Communication Quarterly, 92*(4), 1007–1009.

Wellman, B. (1990). Different strokes for different folks: Community ties and social support. *American Journal of Sociology, 96*, 558–588.

Yang, A. (2015). Building a cognitive-sociological model of stereotypes: Stereotypical frames, social distance and framing effects. *Howard Journal of Communications, 26*(3), 254–274.

CHAPTER EIGHT

Mediating THE Digital Message

Agenda-Setting Theory in Modern Russian Media

ELENA VARTANOVA*

INTRODUCTION

The Internet has dramatically changed the media environment, media industry and professional practices of the field. In recent decades the rise of digital media has become the mostly debated issue among media scholars (Flew, 2014; Manovich, 2001). Among questions in this area of inquiry are the nature of new media as compared to the old ones (Kung, Picard, & Towse, 2008); the emergence of the new public sphere (Fenton, 2009); changing newsrooms practices and roles of professionals and amateurs; new economics of digital news (Doctor, 2010); and new understanding of information, knowledge and literacy, and digital media consumption (Frau-Meigs, 2007).

Besides theorizing about these new phenomena, there still exists a need to compare them with traditional research paradigms and create a common theoretical ground for the contemporary controversial media reality. Hence, fundamental theories to explain media phenomena require re-conceptualization. The framing of news in relation to gatekeeping and agenda-setting should be among the first reconsidered.

* Elena Vartanova is Full Professor of Media Theory and Media Economics and Dean and Chair of the Faculty of Journalism, Lomonosov Moscow State University. Email: evarta@mail.ru.

THEORETICAL APPROACHES TO NEWS IN RUSSIAN MEDIA STUDIES

The theorizing about news in Western European and North American journalism studies has a long tradition and focused on its relation to reality, and its potential influence on the audience (Atwood & de Beer, 2001; Lasswell, 1927). In the 20th century foreign scholars described basic features of news as a product of journalistic professional activity and identified relations between reality and facts. These endeavors included the process of making/representing news by newsroom professionals and the construction of reality presented for the audience, including the role of journalists in making news (McCombs, Shaw, & Weaver, 1997; Schudson, 2002; Tuchman, 1978).

One of the most influential concepts in the area has been agenda-setting (McCombs & Shaw, 1972) and Shoemaker and Reese's (1996, 2014) subsequent model that identified a hierarchical variety of influences in the gatekeeping process, thus stressing impacts of different factors on media content production including the agenda-setting process. Thus, they have pointed to a complex nature of media content production which has become very useful for a contemporary understanding of the news gathering, writing, dissemination and selection by audiences in the context of modern digital transformations.

Generally speaking, journalism as a profession could be theorized through a few important concepts among which the gatekeeping, agenda-setting and mediating reality should be considered the key ones. The gatekeeping concept is extremely relevant to the social and professional goals of journalism as well as to activities of media companies, newsrooms, industry professionals and journalists, since media content is a result of their professional efforts. Certainly, gatekeeping is being realized not only by journalists, and Shoemaker and Reese have profoundly described major forces of influences, but journalists themselves are traditionally very much involved in the process (Shoemaker & Reese, 2014).

On the other hand, the agenda-setting process being at the same time a multistakeholder process and a result of journalists' professional activity may be considered an essential outcome of gatekeeping, thus mediating to society news about reality. Gatekeeping in fact is an essential process within media production and results in the news agenda, produced by formal and informal industrial and organizational routines. In theories of journalism, gatekeeping and agenda-setting as scholarly concepts are closely intertwined, since they analyze different but inter-dependent stages of journalistic news production.

The Russian school of studying the news made a different and nationally determined contribution to the Western theory of news. Based upon philologically and philosophically oriented press theory, Soviet researchers underlined the importance of transforming information about reality into news, the need to develop it, systematize it, and make it more exact and accurate. However, in some cases that also pointed to the need to destroy and devaluate it, which suggests an analogy with gate-keeping analysis (Gorokhov, 1984; Pelt, 1980). Texts of the news were supposed to be original and unusual, accessible and decodable as well as significant for the audience. Comprehensiveness and truth as defined by Soviet press theory were considered the pivot of journalistic activity. Facts should be checked before publication of the news therefore the speed of its distribution was subordinate to its accuracy (Gorokhov, 1975; Grabelnikov, 1987; Lazutina, 2000; Pelt, 1980).

The approach to news, as developed by Soviet media studies, was widely based on the concept of information, which stimulated a discussion about the theory of news among many Russian researchers. For instance, one of the first scholars to explore the concept of news was Vladimir Pelt who argued that "journalistic information…explains events and facts, that is, it comments, interprets information (about reality—E.V.)" (Pelt, 1980, p. 63). In the Soviet period journalism research made an important link between news and opinion writing. Value judgments, a tendency to advocate journalists' right to express their personal opinions, a striving to "educate" and "lift up" the audience, and partisan journalists' comments though based on real facts became essential features of journalistic news products, thus theoretically legitimizing the opinion polarization of the Russian news media (Prokhorov, 2011; Uchenova, 2009).

Consequently, the theoretical boundaries between neutral and opinionated reporting, and between journalism and propaganda have been blurred; Soviet press theory has created foundations for a hybrid model of news and ideologically determined/polarized journalism. Opinion writing, or in Russian terms "publicistika", has been and still is considered to be the journalists' highest professional achievement, the result of their creativity and writing talent (Lashchuk, 2013; Lazutina, 2000; Nakoriakova, 2009).

After 1991 when Russian media studies began an uneasy process of de-Sovietization, and scholars imported a great deal from Western theory. This was particularly true for the agenda-setting concept which became very popular among researchers. The agenda-setting mechanisms have been considered in the context of Russian socio-cultural development both as an effect and a constant process; in its interrelations with framing and salience (Kazakov, 2015); through structural and constructivist approach to agenda-setting processes (Fotieva, 2014; Frolova, 2009); and in its regional aspects (Fokina, 2012). Some scholars pointed out the concept's new role to theorizing public relations with five new tasks for media relations including influence of PR on journalism through "news sources", through "construction of format", through mediation between journalists and newsmakers, by correction negative media coverage and by influencing "journalists' expectations" (Sharkova, 2013).

DIGITAL MEDIA AND NEW THEORETICAL ASPECTS OF AGENDA-SETTING

The dual transition of the Russian media, that of the social transformation and technological revolution, forced scholars to reconsider the concept of news. The particular interest strived from the fact that processes of its production and distribution in a new digital environment involved an increased number of actors both professional (e.g., journalists, advertisers, PR specialists) and non-professional (e.g., bloggers, Internet and social networks users) who set the news agendas. Their roles have been transformed and their influences diversified.

Russian researchers have identified new conditions of making, disseminating and developing news in digital media (Dunas, Gureeva, Tkacheva, & Vartanov, 2016), as well as of the nature of the news provision in the domestic context pointing to an increased influence of new media on the Russian media system (Gureeva, 2015); new role of audiences in consuming, sourcing, producing and disseminating of news; growing gaps in generational media cultures (Kulchitskaya, 2014; Vartanova, Tolokonnikova, & Cherevko, 2014); and in diversification of news sources and agendas (Tolokonnikova & Cherevko, 2016).

Interactivity helped to facilitate re-examination of traditional relations of news producers, journalists and audience, resulting in news production decentralization, de-hierarchization and de-monopolization. For the audience it is easier to bypass journalists as monopolist producers of news and news agendas although new outcomes of the process are both positive (increased speed, sources' accessibility, audience's involvement in the production process) and negative (deskilling, unreliability, manipulation) (Balmaeva & Lukina, 2016; Lukina, 2010).

Together with structural changes, media have altered their nature. For instance, news agencies now directly access audiences, providing news on the consumer's first demand, becoming competitors for press and audio-visual media (Vartanova, 2014). On the other hand, any individual may represent an analogue of the news agency. The classical model of the information agenda is complemented with the alternative or parallel agenda models, actively involving users' new production and active dissemination (Vartanova, 2014).

The Internet in Russia has strengthened the tradition of polarized journalism causing gaps in the news agenda. Many non-professional bloggers with no understanding of journalistic standards compete with professionally designed media content functioning as an alternative not only to conventional media (Oushkin, 2014).

Nonetheless, news gets a new life cycle on the Internet. Researchers have indicated the possibility of building a mathematical diffusion model that would account for the whole range of new influences over the news in the digital media (Gubanov, Novikov, & Chkhartishvili, 2010). A recent empirical study by Russian scholars used mathematic methods to model a digital news' life cycle. This study argued that building a news agenda is more than a spontaneous result of professional efforts of journalists, but also a result of spin-doctoring, newsjacking, or botting, thus becoming a mathematically constructed action. In the new media, scholars underline, external forces could construct the remediation of old news many times (Dunas at al., 2016, pp. 10–11).

Another key issue is trust in news in digital media. A study of trust as a psychological phenomenon in the modern Russian society, its psychological mechanisms, the impact of new information technologies as represented in sociological surveys of trust in media, and psychology of virtual reality could be found in the works by psychologists (Zinchenko, 2009, 2011). On the other hand, audience trust in media is related to the increased impact of the blogosphere where basic standards of journalism are being transformed or are missing entirely. As a result, parallel or alternative agendas set by non-professionals can guarantee neither accuracy nor impartiality in covering events, and audiences do not trust professional media and/or trust non-professional content (Gavrilov & Tolmach, 2014).

Therefore, the debate on agenda-setting in new media has more than academic importance for the Russian media. Actually, it is intended to explain one of the most influential tendencies in the media system, that of the rise of the Internet.

RUSSIAN INTERNET AS NEWS MEDIA

The Russian Internet blossomed in the mid-1990s with the number of users almost doubling each year. In 2015, the number of Russians who used the Internet at least once a month was about 74% of the adult population, or 46.9 million people, and almost 44.6 million people (71%) went online once a week. As elsewhere in the world, the Internet penetration firstly grew in industrial cities, especially in Moscow (76% use the Internet at least once a week), St. Petersburg (75%) and regional centers.

In the 2010s increased diffusion of broadband and mobile telephony has decreased the territorial inequality of Russian regions in term of access to the Internet. Still the large cities demonstrate both the higher level of computer penetration and internet daily usage (79% and 60% in comparison with 73% and 49% in regional cities, 69% and 47% in district centers/urban villages, 58% and 37% in the villages. Still, the digital divide marked by various indicators of access to technologies and communication networks to lifestyle and digital literacy remains a serious problem for Russia.

In terms of devices being used for Internet access in different Russian regions, mobile ones such as phones and tablets are becoming quite popular. In 2015 almost 26.7 million users went online via mobile Internet every day. And Moscow is not the leader here since the broadband Internet is widespread in the capital. The most noticeable share of mobile users compared to other Russian regions is in the North

Caucasus and the Far East where the most significant shares of the population use smartphones or tablets to connect to the Internet (60% and 59% vs. 50% in the Central Federal region).

Younger Russians spend much more time on the Internet than their parents, but Internet use by the older age groups is also growing steadily. A recent sociological survey (2015) revealed that the maximum time spent online per day—153 minutes—has been shown among the youngest audience group (12–17 years old), while older users spend less time: 18–24 years old (135 minutes), 25–34 (116 minutes), 35–44 (126 minutes), 45–54 (132 minutes) (TNS Web Index, July 2015).

In the Russian media system, the Internet has become a universal media space with a huge volume of content distributed and high level of use by urban residents who represent the educated: the most active, relatively well-to-do and comparatively young segments of the Russian society. These are school children, university students, and professionals who are involved into the digital economy. In Russian cities with the population over one million, about 70% of youngsters under age 22 are digital natives. Major political parties and official state agencies also operate numerous sites, but a diversity of political and cultural views is created by the Internet presence of many oppositional views. It is also indicative that online media, especially social networks, have shown their mobilization capacities becoming instruments for organization and coordination protest activities in Moscow and some large industrial centers (Trenin et al., 2012).

In the 2010s, new issues in regards to online content regulation and provision have emerged. Recent laws to regulate various aspects of content supply and ethical standards of online news and communication have reflected a manifest concern of both legislators and politicians (criticism and investigation) and the audiences (low level of quality and ethics). Social networks put forward many conflictual issues such as "reputation wars", information overload, and competition of journalists with bloggers. Copyright issues, protection of minors and terrorism coverage are coming to the heart of the debate between professional and non-professional authors.

With its increasing penetration, the Internet currently has become the most serious challenger to traditional media. The Russian Internet monthly audience is about 52% of the adult population; about two thirds are represented by daily users. Although the television remains the main mass medium in Russia with the average time of watching it about 4 hours 4 minutes daily in 2014 (the audience is older than 4 years old) the Internet is challenging the traditional media hierarchy (FAPMC, 2016).

Media companies have been active in moving online since the early days of the Internet in Russia, and in addition a huge number of professional and amateur content projects on the Internet have established themselves as online media. In 2014 on the Runet (Russian language segment of the Internet) there existed more than 5 million sites in Russian language. Among them over 6,000 sites declared themselves as online media, of which 4,600 have been officially registered by the RKN as media companies (Lukina, 2010).

Several popular offline dailies, like the Nezavisimaya Gazeta, were already exploring the Internet in 1994. The first online media projects were started by literary critics and writers who launched the Russkii Zhurnal. Currently the most popular online news media are Lenta.ru, KP.ru, Gazeta.ru, RG.ru, NEWSru.com, LifeNews.ru. In addition to online media, a very influential role over news distribution and even production is played by social media, which include the blogosphere, social networks (e.g., VKontakte.ru and Odnoklassniki.ru of the Russian origin together with the Facebook), microblogs (e.g., Twitter, Instagram) and the like. As of 2015, RUnet comprised 194 million blogs, 34 million of which were regularly updated (minimum 1 post per month). In 2015, social networks in Russia became one of the most popular Internet resources (26% of all audience consider them as N 1 Internet resource). Also, search engines (e.g., the Russian language Yandex and the global Google) and mail services (e.g., Mail.ru) began to play a role in news provision and shaping the news agenda.

Russians still trust television. As far as the national audience is concerned, about one quarter (25%) consider television the most trustworthy source of information while online news sites are considered the most trustworthy by 19% of Russians. No more tha 10% do not have clear opinion. The situation slightly differs among Muscovites: for 26% of them it is online news sites which are considered the most trustworthy sources of news, while 22% consider TV and 15% do not have an opinion (FOM, 2015).

Undoubtedly, Russian media reality does not differ much from the practice of many other national media. In the context of multi-platformity and increasing content supply, the audience feels more freedom in content selection. Dissatisfaction with traditional journalism and conventional media may lead the audience to turn away from them in favor of those media that will more readily meet its demands. As media technologies develop, the processes of social transformation are starting to gain momentum due to the development of digital information and communication technologies changing media structures, media typology and mostly media consumption.

ONLINE NEWS CONSUMPTION AMONG RUSSIAN JOURNALISM STUDENTS

The new media realities are increasingly reflected in empirical evidence. The first stage of an on-going survey conducted at the Faculty of Journalism aimed to identify the main features of media consumption among journalism students. The importance of this target group is explained by its future role in maintaining journalistic standards and creating professional news agendas for tomorrow's media. While scholars have argued that the agenda-setting process has become multi-faceted and multi-layered, there still remain a core understanding that journalists have a crucial role in shaping news agendas (McQuail, 2013). In addition, this group is rather illustrative because it shows the new patterns of audience behavior that combines passive and active media use.

The first stage of the study was conducted during two weeks from 24 February 2015 till 9 March 2015 and was based on a qualitative method—diary study (Tolokonnikova & Cherevko, 2016). Firstly, 40 students aged 17–22 indicated in news diaries which media they consume to get the news. They were also asked to provide the schedule of their daily personal media consumption by fixing all visited online news sites, hours and duration of visits, titles and topics of news consumed. They also mentioned how many links they used to get into the depth of news pointing to the order of links. Secondly, students were asked to write qualitative reports to describe personal environments of their media consumption, their news priorities and the conditions for news reliability as well as sources of trustworthy information. This article provides the preliminary results of the qualitative analysis of the most complete students diaries.

It should be noted that the complexity of socio-cultural and individual factors that influence media consumption patterns do not allow for broad conclusions and re-definitions of the agenda-setting concepts and mechanisms; however, the results below have distinguished and identified the emerging and transforming practices of news consumption, which in turn provides new approaches to the agenda-setting processes among this group of future media professionals.

The empirical data show that Russian journalism students widely use the Internet to get news. During the two weeks of the study, the respondents viewed 2,693 news sites, and social networks significantly dominated the news consumption process. Students read 1,522 news items (57% from the whole number), while 1,080 news items were taken from Internet news sites or their mobile applications.

Students' news consumption via the Internet happens throughout the day with interruptions only for sleeping. A non-significant decline of this was tracked only during weekends and holidays. This creates a serious task for the new media sources: in order to satisfy the needs of the contemporary audience they should provide content in a 24/7 regime. Students actively use the social networks as news sources: During the period of the study respondents read more news in social media as compared to sites of online media.

Among the sites most viewed by respondents was the Russian social network VKontakte (VK). With a monthly audience of 47 million people, it has been ranked in first place, leaving far behind such popular Russian search engines as Yandex.ru and Mail.ru. Nearly 76% of respondents visited VK for getting news, while the main page of the search engine Yandex was visited by 60%, and Mail.ru by 46%.

This finding shows that VK appears to be the leader in agenda-setting among students. During the two weeks, the respondents read 266 news items in VK, which comprise 40% of all the news materials consumed by them. This figure is twice as large as those for other social media.

The second most popular social network in Russia Odnoklassniki (OK), which has a monthly audience of 34 million people, was not even mentioned in the diaries and reports of our respondents. This finding reflects the trend of audience segmentation by different social networks. Currently OR is a social media predominantly used by middle aged and elderly aged people, as well as people living outside capital regions.

Globally the most popular social network is Facebook, which in Russia is ranked as the third most popular social medium (its monthly audience is 21 million users) . The core of the audience (70%) is 25–44 years of age, and Moscow is the region where the majority of its users live. The number of active Facebook users in the capital of Russia is twice as large as the same parameters for other TOP-10 regions altogether. Facebook is included in the list of information sources of Russian students, but its share is quite small due to a low demand among the representatives of this age group.

Twitter has a much bigger influence on the respondents. During the two weeks, students read 109 news items on Twitter, and this comprised one-third of all news materials consumed by them though social networks. The role of Instagram as a news source was very small. Although the number of subscribers to Twitter is quite large, student reports show that in their news feed on Instagram there are more personal messages than newsworthy topics.

The respondents also consumed news from Internet news sites. For the two weeks of the study, the respondents read 270 news items in online media, which they accessed directly, not using social network links. The list of the most viewed sites includes online newspapers (Lenta.ru, Gazeta.ru, Meduza, etc.), online versions of print dailies and weeklies (Izvestia, Kommersant, Russky reportyor, etc.), and news agencies (RIA Novosty, Interfax, Newsru.com). Among the top 10 sites there are also online versions of TV channels (LifeNews, RT, Dozhd), where the respondents viewed video materials.

The empirical data shows that in every second case users continued to stay online in order to go to further content on the Internet. While reading news on social networks, users most actively switched to other sites following the links (70% of the cases). Following the third link was aimed at getting a more detailed image of a news event, but happened only in 21% of the cases. Only 4% of the news stories viewed on the social networks provoked the user to read at least three items on other sites.

The situation is similar for online media. Having read an article in online media, 33% of users followed the links, which redirected them to other materials, expanding the news item or giving more details about the initial event. Every second user goes further following the third link and after that only 1/3 of the remaining users follow a 4th redirection—representing only 5% of those who read the initial news item. This phenomenon undoubtedly warrants further exploration.

Respondents' attention is attracted not by specific news sites, but by specific events, materials and headlines. Having read a text, users were not inclined to consume all content of the media outlet. On the contrary, after reading a particular topic they created a new information request, went back to the social networks, or stopped reading. It is obvious that the agenda of the personal news feeds in the social networks defined the attention of respondents and influenced the depth of news consumption.

Results of the study indicate that Twitter is the most rapid source of news and in some respects remains a regulator of a personal news agenda, which is controlled by users. On the other hand, the most popular media sources on the Internet are professional media—such as Kommersant, Gazeta.ru, Meduza, etc. This is demonstrated by the number of direct clicks and by the number of redirections from social media sites (see Table 8.1).

Table 8.1: Top Online Media Sites

Title	Number of visits	The number of links (redirections) to the news sites from social networks
Kommersant	188	32
Meduza	108	94
RIA Novosti	64	104
Gazeta.ru	20	136
LifeNews	20	40
RT	20	44
Dozhd	16	76
Village	16	56
Snob	16	28

The ranking of professional media sites that the users visited via links from the social networks is a bit different compared to the list of media visited by students directly. In the list of the online newspapers Kommersant has moved to the end of the list, while Gazeta.ru, on the contrary, ranked first. Among the news agencies the top one was obviously RIA Novosti. This may be explained by the limited activities of other news agencies on social media. The place of Meduza was quite stable: the site was quite popular itself, as well as the links to it via social networks. It demonstrates that mass media with politically alternative content such as Meduza provoked greater interest among respondents. Still, students' demand for quality information was not fully satisfied by the user generated content (UGC).

Respondents' trust in professional news might be explained by the professional standards of journalism such as topicality, credibility, provision of background details and context of the stories. Results of the survey demonstrated that students have an active position in terms of online news selection and use which have been defined by them independently. On the other hand, the majority of students do not go deeper into the news than two links, and the depth of news consumption to a large extent correlates with news topic. Among the topics that provoked users to follow several links, were those that demanded a deeper understanding of the news such as international events (Ukraine, Syria, migrants), emergency situations (Russian politician Nemtsov's murder), and legal topics related to news.

Social networks allow students to consume news in a background mode and help them regularly follow their personalized news agendas. Users quite actively re-direct their demand from social networks to online media, but then they usually go back to social media' news feeds and continue to follow them. Even the most popular online media were visited by respondents only 2–3 times a day while they followed social media consistently throughout the day. In most cases students viewed the site in order to read some specific material, rather than take a glimpse at the overall news agenda.

Thus, the main result of the study might be formulated as following. Journalism students have shown different levels of interest to social and online media with social media as a leader and a major driver of the agenda-setting process, while the individual agendas are becoming increasingly personalized.

CONCLUSION

In many respects a modern citizen in a digital society—as a professional, consumer, or member of a community—becomes crucially dependent on digital media. In this context a hypothesis that social networks are central for media consumption of audiences needs to be further elaborated. Moreover, the results of the survey have revealed that social networks have become a hybrid medium that combine both professional content, journalistic news agendas with individual, often non-professional and quite subjective agendas.

As Shoemaker and Reese stated, "we are in a time of a great social change with mediated communication at the heart of the change" (Shoemaker & Reese, 2014, p. 239). The reality of new media characterized by the rise of active audiences and their new roles in building their news agendas requires further substantial empirical research though it is clear that an audience has become a new factor that influences media content.

The fact that social media create personal news agendas based on individual preferences and news demand, changes not only the production and distribution of news by professional news rooms, but also the traditional theoretic understanding of the agenda-setting process, its players, filters and barriers. The implications for young journalists are quite striking, both as consumers and producers of the news agenda. The new role and impact of audience on agenda-setting in digital media warrants further conceptualization.

REFERENCES

Atwood, R., & de Beer, A. (2001). The roots of academic news research: Tobias Peuser's De relationibus movellis. *Journalism Studies, 2*(4), 485–496.

Balmaeva, S., & Lukina, M. (2016*). Kak novye media izmenili zhurnalistiku (2012–2016)* [How new media changed the journalism (2012–2016)]. Ekaterinburg: Gumanitarnyi universitet.

Doctor, K. (2010). *Newsonomics: Twelve trends that will shape the news you get.* New York, NY: St-Martins Press.

Dunas, D., Gureeva, A., Tkacheva, N., & Vartanov, S. (2016). K voprosu o teoreticheskom poniman,ii novostei v tcifrovuiu epokhu: transformatciia struktury, sil vliianiia, zhiznennogo tcikla [On the question of the theoretical understanding of news in the digital era: The transformation of the structure, the influence of the forces and the life cycle]. *Vestnik Moskovskogo Universiteta, seriya 10, Zhurnalistika* (Bulletin of the Moscow State University, Series 10, Journalism), *3*, 3–16.

FAPMC. (2016). Televidenije v Rossii. Sostojaniye, tendencii I perspektivy razvitija [Television in Russia. Current state, trends and prospects for development]. *Report of the Federal Agency for Press and Mass Communications*. Retrieved from http://fapmc.ru/rospechat/activities/reports/2016/television-in-russia.html

Fenton, N. (2009). *New media, old news: Journalism and democracy in the digital age.* London: Sage.

Flew, T. (2014). *New media.* Oxford: Oxford University Press.

Fokina, O. (2012). Regionalnaia povestka obshcherossiiskoi periodiki: teoreticheskaia i empiricheskaia modeli [Regional agenda of nationwide periodicals: Theoretical and empirical models]. *Voprosy teorii i praktiki zhurnalistiki* (Issues of the Theory and Practice of Journalism), *2*, 124–130.

FOM. (2015). Doverie rossijskim SMI [Trust to Russian Mass Media]. *Opinion poll.* Retrieved from http://fom.ru/SMI-i-internet/12140.

Fotieva, I. V. (2014). Problema konstruirovaniia realnosti v SMI: filosofskii rakurs rassmotreniia [The problem of constructing of reality in the media: A philosophical aspect]. *Izvestiia Altaiskogo gosudarstvennogo universiteta* (News of Altai State University), *2*, 215–217.

Frau-Meigs, D. (2007). *Media education. A kit for teachers, students, parents and professionals.* Paris: UNESCO.

Frolova, T. I. (2009). Dinamika strategii v sotcialnom mediadiskurse [Dynamic of strategies in social media discourse]. *Vestnik Moskovskogo Universiteta, seriya 10, Zhurnalistika* [Bulletin of the Moscow State University, Series 10, Journalism], *5*, 94–116.

Gavrilov, K. A., & Tolmach, A. D. (2014). Kto vinovat: content-analiz blogov o terakte v Domodedovo [Whose fault is it: The content analysis of blogs on terrorist attack in Domodedovo]. *Socis, 2*, 81–88.

Gorokhov, V. M. (1975). *Zakonomernosti publitcisticheskogo tvorchestva* [Laws of journalistic creativity]. Moscow: Mysl.

Gorokhov, V. M. (1984). *Osnovy zhurnalistskogo masterstva* [The basics of journalistic skills]. Moscow: Moscow State University Press.

Grabelnikov, A. A. (1987). *Organizatsiya I proizvodstvo zhurnalistskikh tekstov* [The organisation and production of journalism texts]. Moscow: Globus.

Gubanov, D. A., Novikov, D. A., & Chkhartishvili, A. G. (2010). *Sotsialnye seti: modeli informatsionnogo vliyaniya, upravleniya I protivoborstva* [Social networks: Models of information influence, management and confrontation]. Moscow: FIZMATLIT.

Gureeva, A. N. (2015). Sotsialnye seti v sostave sovremennykh mediakommunikatsij rossijskogo vuza [Social networks in the structure of modern media communications of Russian higher schools]. *Vestnik Moskovskogo universiteta. Ser. 10. Zhurnalistika, 6*, 146–160.

Kazakov, A. A. (2015). Freiming mediatekstov kak instrument vozdeistviia na auditoriiu obzor rasprostranennykh traktovok [Framing in media stories as a tool of influence on the audience: Review of widely spread interpretations]. *Izvestiia Saratovskogo universiteta. Novaia seriia. Seriia: Sotciologiia Politologiia* (News of Saratov University. New series. Series: Sociology. Political science), *1*, 111–119.

Kulchitskaya, D. Y. (2014). Psychological prerequisites and effects of using multimedia content in the mass media. *Psychology in Russia: State of the Art, 7*(4), 88–97.

Kung, L., Picard, R. G., &Towse, R. (Eds.). (2008). *The internet and the mass media*. London: Sage.

Lashchuk, O. (2013). *Reraiterskie novostnye soobshcheniia: sozdanie i redaktirovani* [Re-writing of news: Creating and editing]. Moscow: Media Mir.

Lasswell, H. (1927). *Propaganda techniques in the first world war.* New York, NY: Alfred Knopf.

Lazutina, G. V. (2000). *Osnovy tvorcheskoi deiatelnosti zhurnalista* [Fundamentals of creative activity of journalists]. Moscow: Aspekt Press.

Lukina, M. (Ed.). (2010). *Internet-SMI: teoriia i praktika* [Online media: theory and practice]. Moscow: Aspect Press.

Manovich, L. (2001). *The language of new media*. New York, NY: MIT Press.

McCombs, M., & Shaw, D. L. (1972). The agenda-setting function of mass media. *Public Opinion Quarterly, 36*(2), 176–187.

McCombs, M., Shaw, D. L.,& Weaver, D. (Eds.). (1997). *Communication and democracy: Exploring the intellectual frontiers in agenda-setting theory.* Mahwah, NJ: Lawrence Erlbaum Associates.

McQuail, D. (2013). *Journalism and society*. London: SAGE Publications.

Nakoriakova, K. (2009). *Literaturnoe redaktirovanie* [Literary editing]. Moscow: IKAR.

Oushkin, S. G. (2014). Polzovaelskie kommentarii k protestnym akcijam v russkojazychnom segmente YouTube [Users comments to protest activities on the Russian segment of YouTube]. *Socis, 6*, 127–133.

Pelt, V. D. (1980). *Informatsya v gazette* [Information in a newspaper]. Moscow: Moscow State University Press.

Prokhorov, E. P. (2011). *Vvedenie v teoriiu zhurnalistiki* [Introduction to journalism theory]. Moscow: Aspekt Press.

Schudson M. (2002). *The sociology of news*. New York, NY: Norton.

Sharkova, I. V. (2013). Metodika issledovaniia povestki dnia s tceliu upravleniia imidzhem regiona [Research methodology of agenda in order to manage the image of the region]. *Innovatcionnaia ekonomika i obshchestvo* [Innovative Economy and Society], *1*, 106–110.

Shoemaker, P. J., & Reese, S. D. (1996). *Mediating the message: Theories of influences on mass media content* (2nd ed.). White Plains, NY: Longman.

Shoemaker, P. J., & Reese, S. D. (2014). *Mediating the message in the 21st century: A media sociology perspective* (3rd ed.). New York, NY: Routledge.

Tolokonnikova, A., & Cherevko, T. (2016). Potreblenie novostnoi informatcii v Internete studentami MGU imeni M. V. Lomonosova [News media consumption online: Case study of students at Lomonosov Moscow State University]. *Vestnik Moskovskogo Universiteta, seriya 10, Zhurnalistika*[Bulletin of the Moscow State University, Series 10, Journalism], *4*, 160–179.

Trenin, D., Arbatov, A., Lipman, M., Malashenko, A., Petrov, N., Ryabov, A., & Shevtsova, L. (2012). *The Russian awakening. A Joint paper by the Carnegie Moscow Center.* Moscow: Carnegie Moscow Center.

Tuchman, G. (1978). *Making news: A study in the contraction of reality*. New York, NY: Free Press.

Uchenova, V. V. (2009). *Tri grani teorii zhurnalistiki* [Three facets of journalism theory]. Moscow: Aspect Press.

Vartanova, E. (2014). Media in digital society: Challenges of active audiences. *Global Media Journal, 2*(2), 16–27.

Vartanova, E. L., Tolokonnikova, A. V., & Cherevko, T. S. (2014). The information security of children: Self-regulatory approaches. *Psychology in Russia: State of the Art, 7*(3), 136–145.

Zinchenko, Y. P. (2009). Mass media as an effective tool for prevention of socio-psychological factors in the development of terrorism. *Psychology in Russia: State of the Art, 2*, 459–476.

Zinchenko, Y. P. (2011). *Psikhologiia virtualnoi realnosti* [The virtual reality psychology]. Moscow: Moscow State University Press.

The Empirical Landscape in a Transitional Age

CHAPTER NINE

The World THROUGH THE Eyes OF THE *New York Times* AND *People's Daily*

A Network Agenda-Setting Analysis of Psychological Geography

MAXWELL MCCOMBS*, PEI ZHENG†, AND PARO PAIN‡

Walter Lippmann metaphorically described the news media as "a searchlight that moves restlessly about, bringing one episode and then another out of darkness". As a consequence of this restlessness, many situations are highlighted at least briefly, but others never appear at all in the news. This is true for a wide variety of topics, even more so for the amount of attention paid to countries around the world. Put another way, the geographic agenda of the news is a highly stratified map of the world with numerous omissions. In turn, agenda-setting theory suggests that the cognitive maps of world held by the public reflect this fragmented and incomplete geography of the world presented by the news media.

Lippmann (1922) is the intellectual father of agenda-setting, and the title of his opening chapter in *Public Opinion,* "The World Outside and the Pictures in our Heads", succinctly summarizes the agenda-setting idea even though Lippmann did not use that phrase. His thesis is that the news media, our windows to the vast world beyond direct experience, determine our cognitive maps of that world.

* Maxwell McCombs is the Jesse H. Jones Centennial Chair in Communication Emeritus in the School of Journalism at the University of Texas at Austin. Email: maxmccombs@utexas.edu.

† Pei Zheng is Assistant Professor in the Roy H. Park School of Communications at Ithaca College. Email: pei.cindy.zheng@gmail.com.

‡ Paromita Pain is a doctoral student in the School of Journalism at the University of Texas at Austin. Email: paromita.pain@gmail.com.

> There is a famous *New Yorker* magazine cover parodying Manhattan residents' view of the United States. This drawing is dominated by a very large New York City and a rather large California on the other side of the country. All the states in between are squeezed tightly together and barely exist. There is a similar drawing of the Texan's view of the United States, which, of course, is dominated by a huge Texas with forty-seven tiny states squeezed around the edges. Neither of these psychological maps of the United States bears much resemblance to the geographer's map that you studied in school, but both—albeit exaggerated—are viable psychological maps of the United States. (McCombs, 2014, p. 25)

Our focus here is a comparison of the geographic maps of the world sketched by the international news coverage of the *People's Daily* and the *New York Times*, major newspapers in countries that are culturally and politically very different.

INTERNATIONAL NEWS

In general, transnational media studies are grounded in two distinct perspectives on how journalists in different countries cover international issues. One side of the story has highlighted the role of globalization in journalism, arguing that contemporary news coverage tends to embrace a global perspective, which extends beyond viewpoints aligned with the country and region where the event has occurred or the news organization is located (Beck, 2005; Berglez, 2008; Shoemaker & Cohen, 2006).

Others, however, have argued that news coverage in different countries and regions can be significantly different due to differences in culture as well as their governments' political stance regarding an issue and that journalists localize or "domesticate" international news in order to make it more relevant to their national audience (Clausen, 2004; Hafez, 2007). Cottle (2009, p. 34) notes the recent emergence of these latter perspectives that "exhibit a more theoretically circumspect or cautious stance towards claims of an emergent global public sphere…Studies of world news audiences also suggest that 'varied local cultures manifest themselves in the interpretation of foreign as well as domestic news' and that 'culture shines through' in processes of news reception" (Jensen, 2003, p. 190).

Both the disparate attention by Western news media to different parts of the world—the international version of the New York and Texas maps described in the introduction—as well as variations across countries—the focus of this study—have been extensively documented. The GDELT project at Oxford University (Global Database of Events, Language and Tone) has monitored international news flow since 1979 and produced numerous reports and papers, including, for example, maps of the world as it would look if the size of countries was based on the number of times *The Guardian* covered them. Needless to say, these maps look considerably different from the maps of physical geography.

In line with the focus of this study, a recent paper from GDELT, "Mapping Greece through the Eyes of the World", illustrates the disparity of geographic attention to a major event, the economic crisis in Greece (Hunnig, 2015). In the international news coverage of U.S. news media from July 13 to 18, 2015, 2.37% concerned Greece. The coverage in China was similar, 2.34%. However, coverage of Greece was much lower in Japan (1.17%) and Australia (1.92%). Not surprisingly, coverage of Greece was much high in Western Europe: Spain—3.53%; France—5.09%; and Germany—6.15%.

Differences in how a particular event is covered in the news of various countries also is documented in Guo et al.'s (2015) comparison of the attribute agenda in the news coverage of the Iraq War in the newspapers of China, Taiwan, Poland and the U.S. The major factor explaining a high degree of similarity or dissimilarity between these various countries was their political stance in regard to the war.

THE MEDIA AGENDA

In line with Guo et al.'s (2015) comparative research, this study's examination of the geography of international news coverage in the major newspapers of China and the U.S. is grounded in agenda-setting theory. At the core of the theory is the media agenda-public agenda dyad and the empirically well-established influence of the media agenda on the public's perception of the most important issues of the day. In recent years, this agenda-setting influence of the media has been extended to the salience among the public of a wide variety of other elements in the news, including public figures, corporate reputations, and cultural activities. This study contributes to this trend, examining the salience of countries around the world in the news coverage of two newspapers published in distinctly different countries, China and the U.S.

From the viewpoint of agenda-setting theory, findings in line with the perspective of limited globalization and distinct differences among countries are more interesting. Such findings suggest distinct agenda-setting effects on the psychological geography of the public from country to country rather than global, rather homogenous, agenda-setting effects across countries. Our key hypothesis is that the geography of the world presented on the front pages of the *People's Daily* and the *New York Times* will exhibit only a moderate degree of correspondence. In agenda-setting terms, this is an assertion that the priority of attention to countries around the world in these two newspapers will exhibit a modest correlation at best.

Further analysis grounded in a new aspect of agenda-setting theory, network agenda-setting, will bring us closer to an actual map of this news coverage. Moving beyond the transfer of salience of individual countries, network agenda-setting examines the extent to which the news media can transfer the salience of an integrated image, a more comprehensive picture that is a map of the world as presented in the news coverage. In traditional agenda-setting research, the elements investigated are discrete objects—in this study, individual countries. That is, objects are disaggregated from their larger context—in this study, total international news coverage—and rank-ordered according to the frequency of their individual appearance in the news. However, in the international news coverage over any period of time, many of these countries are bundled together in the news package. Network agenda-setting theorizes that the salience of these bundled relationships among countries—their appearance in the news during the same time period—are also transferred from the news media to the public.

Theoretically central to this perspective is an associative network model of memory. Rather than conceptualizing our mental representations as a hierarchical or linear structure as implied in the traditional understanding of agenda-setting theory, this associative network model holds that representation operates pictorially, diagrammatically, or cartographically (Braddon-Mitchell & Jackson, 2007; Cummins, 1996). In this network model, individuals' cognitive representations are presented as a network-like structure where each element is connected to numerous other elements, a cognitive structure that corresponds, for example, to the simultaneous appearance of countries over a period of time in international news coverage. An extensive introduction to this new aspect of agenda-setting theory and more than a dozen empirical investigations from Asia, North America, and Europe are presented in *The Power of Information Networks* (Guo & McCombs, 2015).

The new study reported here is focused on the first element of the media agenda-public agenda dyad. Until we know something about the nature of the psychological maps in the newspapers of various countries—whether they are very similar or quite dissimilar—a sound comparative hypothesis about the effects of these agendas on the publics of these countries cannot be framed. For the opening gambit of this exploration of the psychological geography of the media and the public, we employ a "contrast of opposites" strategy, comparing the newspapers of two culturally and politically distinct countries. Our comparisons are guided by a hypothesis and a research question:

Hypothesis: The priorities of the *People's Daily* and the *New York Times* in their attention to countries around the world as reflected in their international news coverage have a low to moderate degree of correspondence.

Research Question: How frequently are various pairs of countries linked in the news coverage? That is, over a specified period of time (i.e., a week) how frequently does a particular pair of countries appear in the news?

From this network analysis of the international news coverage of the *People's Daily* and the *New York Times*, additional questions can be posed. For example, which countries are in the core of the network of coverage? Which are at the periphery?

PREVIOUS RESEARCH ON PSYCHOLOGICAL GEOGRAPHY

Research on psychological geography covers a vast array of cognitive representations of the world around us (Downs & Stea, 1977; Gillis, 2010; Kitchin, 2002). Our interest is specifically those geographic aspects of the geography of the world presented in the news media and its impact on the public—in other words, the versions of geography found on the media agenda and the public agenda.

We are encouraged to pursue this preface to a fuller study of psychological geography by existing evidence in the research literature. Wanta, Golan, and Lee (2004) combined a content analysis of network newscasts in the U.S. and a national poll to determine if coverage of foreign nations had an agenda-setting influence on the public. They found that the more media coverage a nation received, the more likely respondents were to think the nation was vitally important to U.S. interests, evidence supporting their agenda-setting hypothesis. Furthermore, the more negative coverage a nation received, the more likely respondents were to think negatively about the nation, supporting the second level of agenda setting. Positive coverage of a nation had no influence on public perceptions.

Generalizing from his analysis of the recent news coverage of Greece that was discussed above, Hunnig (2015) asserted that "the geography of reporting… influences the ways in which we perceive the world".

Once these geographic agendas in the news have been mapped, future research can extend to the impact of these agendas on the respective public agendas and further explicate the process of gatekeeping and its implications for our views of the world. This is, of course, the theoretical area richly explored by Pamela Shoemaker in numerous papers and three key books: *Gatekeeping* (Shoemaker, 1991), *News around the World: Content, Practitioners, and the Public* (Shoemaker & Cohen, 2006), and *Gatekeeping Theory* (Shoemaker & Vos, 2009).

METHOD

Dataset

To test the hypothesis and answer the research question, two flagship daily newspapers were the subjects of the content analysis and network analysis, the *New York Times* from the United States, and the *People's Daily* from Mainland China. The *New York Times* is a major publication in the United States, whose agenda-setting role has been extensively documented (McCombs, 2014). The *People's Daily* is Mainland China's official newspaper, the organ of the Central Committee of the Chinese Communist Party (Zhou & Moy, 2007). The international news on the front page of both newspapers in the past year, 2014, were coded. Two coders who analyzed the *New York Times* are graduate students who are fluent in English. Two coders who analyzed the *People's Daily* were graduate students whose native language is Chinese. The coders attended training sessions and tested the codebook before an initial inter-coder reliability assessment was conducted on 10% of the news articles.

Content Analysis

The unit of analysis was international news article on the front page. In each article, we coded up to two countries where the international news story took place or that the news issue focused on. In both newspapers, we excluded the news that only showed the lead on the front page. Therefore, on average, there are two to five international news articles on the front page per day for a single newspaper, adding up to 779 international news articles in the *People's Daily* and 1,168 articles in the *New York Times* during 2014. From the 1,447 news articles, we identified 119 countries.

Network Analysis

Network analysis (Guo, 2012; Hanneman & Riddle, 2005; Wasserman & Faust, 1994) was employed to examine the attribute agendas of the international news selected by the two newspapers. The first step was to create a matrix of countries to represent the network agenda of each newspaper. The entry in each cell is the numerical value that represents the level of interrelationship between two corresponding elements. Since network analysis in this study focused on the analysis of connections among countries, therefore, each newspaper's matrix is composed of symmetrical rows and columns with the names of countries. The matrices for media agenda networks are constructed according to the interrelationships between the elements found in the media messages. As mentioned before, there are two ways to numerically describe the interrelationships between a pair of elements in a network. One way of calculation is based on the frequency of two elements' co-occurrence in the same coding unit. The more frequently the two items co-occur across coding units, the stronger their connection.

For illustration purposes, Table 9.1 provides an excerpt of the matrix that represents a newspaper's network attribute agenda. Each cell in the matrix reports the number of times the two countries were mentioned during the same week. For example, the cell corresponding to A and B is 50, which means that country A and country B were mentioned together during the same week in 50 out of 1,194 newspaper articles analyzed in the study. Likewise, the cell that represents the interrelationship between A and C is 0, meaning that country A and country C were never mentioned together during the same week.

Table 9.1: A Sample Network Analysis Matrix

	A	B	C
A	N/A	20	0
B	20	N/A	10
C	0	10	N/A

In order to answer the research question that consider the degree of similarity or dissimilarity among the two newspapers' network agendas, we used the Quadratic Assignment Procedure (QAP), a statistical tool that compares matrices, to calculate the correlations among the international news networks of the *People's Daily* and the *New York Times*.

Moreover, to explore which country is most important in the news coverage of each country, we calculated both the frequency and degree centrality of each country in the news coverage. In network analysis, degree centrality refers to the number of ties that a node has to connect with other nodes (Wasserman & Faust, 1994). In the analysis here, the nodes are countries. Therefore, the more connections the country has with other countries, the more central it is in the network.

RESULTS

The editors of the *New York Times* and the *People's Daily* cast their international surveillance nets very broadly. Across 2014 they ran news stories about more than 100 countries. However, many of these countries are covered only infrequently. Zooming in for a close look at the international coverage of these two newspapers, we see in Table 9.2 that the coverage of the top 10 countries in each newspaper is just short of half the total international coverage for the year. Regarding this intensive coverage, the *New York Times* and the *People's Daily* share a sharp focus on five countries—Russia, Ukraine, Syria, Afghanistan and India—although the *New York Times* devoted somewhat more of its international coverage to these nations than did the *People's Daily*. Needless to say, both newspapers paid major attention to the home country of the other. Some 17.2% of the *People's Daily* international coverage was on the United States. The *New York Times* devoted 5.0% of its international coverage to China.

Table 9.2: Top 10 Countries in the *New York Times* and *People's Daily* News Coverage

New York Times		*People's Daily*	
Russia	9.3%	United States	17.2%
Ukraine	7.6%	**Russia**	5.6%
Iraq	5.7%	E.U./Europe	4.2%
China	5.0%	**Syria**	4.2%
Afghanistan	4.8%	Japan	3.9%
Syria	4.6%	Germany	3.9%
Israel	3.7%	**Ukraine**	3.4%
Iran	2.4%	United Kingdom	2.6%
India	2.3%	**Afghanistan**	2.4%
Palestine	2.2%	**India**	2.4%
% of Total Coverage	47.6%	% of Total Coverage	49.6
Total Coverage:	N=1518	Total Coverage:	N=963

Zooming out for a broader look at the focus of the international coverage in these newspapers, Table 9.3 shows the distribution of the total international coverage in each newspaper by major geographic regions. Overall, there is a high degree of similarity in their regional coverage. Both newspapers pay considerable attention to Asia, accounting for nearly half of the coverage when the coverage of the top countries listed in Table 9.2 is augmented with the coverage of numerous other countries across Asia. The two newspaper also show a similar pattern of attention to Europe, devoting just over a quarter of their international news coverage to Europe. Attention to all other parts of the world ranks much lower in both newspapers. Africa receives less than 10% of the coverage in either newspaper; Latin America, less than 5%. To a considerable degree these patterns reflect similar news values by American and Chinese journalists. Across 2014, there were major news events in both Asia and Europe that attracted major attention by all news organizations.

Table 9.3: *People's Daily* and *New York Times* Coverage by Region

		People's Daily %	*The New York Times* %
Africa	Africa	6.7	9.6
Australia	Australia	1.2	0.3
Asia	Middle East/North Africa	16.0	21.3
	Central Asia	2.7	6.0
	East Asia	12.4	7.4
	South/South East Asia	10.8	10.8

		People's Daily %	*The New York Times* %
Europe	East Europe	7.7	16.7
	EU & UK	19.0	11.0
America	Latin America	4.0	3.9
	North America (U.S. and Canada)	16.9	11.1
No specific region	International	1.7	0.0
	Others	0.9	1.8
Total		100.0	100.0

Table 9.4 presents the complete details of the content analysis of the international coverage of the *New York Times* and *People's Daily*, an alphabetical list of all the countries receiving attention on the front pages of either or both countries. Although the top ten countries account for nearly half of the *New York Times*' and *People's Daily* international coverage, another hundred countries received some coverage.

Table 9.4: Frequency of Mentions for Each Country in the *People's Daily* and *New York Times*

	People's Daily	*New York Times*	**Total**
Afghanistan	23	73	96
Algeria	1	0	1
Argentina	2	5	7
Australia	11	6	17
Bahrain	1	1	2
Bangladesh	2	2	4
Belgium	4	4	8
Bolivia	0	1	1
Brazil	11	13	24
Brussels	0	1	1
Bulgaria	0	1	1
Burkina Faso	0	1	1
Cambodia	2	2	4
Canada	4	7	11
Central African Republic	3	0	3
China	N/A	76	76

	People's Daily	*New York Times*	**Total**
Columbia	1	1	2
Costa Rica	0	2	2
Crimea	0	9	9
Croatia	2	0	2
Cuba	5	12	17
Curaçao	0	1	1
Czech Republic	3	1	4
Denmark	1	0	1
Dominican republic	0	1	1
DR Congo	2	1	3
Dubai	0	1	1
Ecuador	2	2	4
Egypt	14	26	40
Ethiopia	1	0	1
France	20	16	36
Georgia	0	1	1
Germany	38	20	58
Greece	2	6	8
Guinea	2	5	7
Haiti	0	1	1
Havana	0	3	3
Honduras	0	3	3
Hong Kong	0	22	22
Hungary	2	1	3
India	23	35	58
Indonesia	7	5	12
Iran	10	37	47
Iraq	16	87	103
Ireland	1	5	6
Israel	11	56	67
Italy	6	17	23
Japan	38	23	61
Jordon	0	4	4

	People's Daily	*New York Times*	**Total**
Kabul	0	1	1
Kazakhstan	3	0	3
Kenya	1	5	6
Kurdistan	0	1	1
Laos	1	0	1
Liberia	2	19	21
Libya	6	24	30
Malaysia	3	17	20
Maldives	1	0	1
Malta	0	1	1
Mexico	5	12	17
Mongolia	1	0	1
Myanmar	1	7	8
Nepal	2	2	4
Netherlands	1	5	6
New Zealand	2	0	2
Nicaragua	0	1	1
Nigeria	3	20	23
North Korea	2	10	12
Norway	1	2	3
Pakistan	16	12	28
Palestine	6	34	40
Panama	1	0	1
Peru	1	1	2
Philippines	5	4	9
Poland	2	1	3
Portugal	0	1	1
Puerto Rico	0	2	2
Qatar	0	6	6
Republic of Kosovo	1	1	2
Republic of Lebanon	2	9	11
Republic of Mali	3	4	7
Romania	3	1	4

	People's Daily	*New York Times*	**Total**
Russia	54	141	195
Rwanda	4	0	4
Saudi Arabia	6	3	9
Scotland	0	7	7
Senegal	0	1	1
Serbia	4	0	4
Sierra Leone	3	10	13
Singapore	1	0	1
Slovakia	0	1	1
Somalia	2	1	3
South Africa	12	4	16
South Korea	22	13	35
Spain	7	8	15
Sri Lanka	3	0	3
Sudan	5	4	9
Sweden	0	2	2
Switzerland	3	3	6
Syria	39	70	109
Tajikistan	1	0	1
Thailand	19	8	27
Tunisia	1	5	6
Turkey	4	27	31
Uganda	3	1	4
UK	25	19	44
Ukraine	33	116	149
Uruguay	0	2	2
USA	166	N/A	166
Vatican	0	2	2
Venezuela	2	1	3
Vietnam	2	8	10
Yemen	1	8	9
	963	1518	2481

NETWORK ANALYSIS

Returning to Lippmann's phrase in the opening chapter of *Public Opinion*, "the pictures in our heads", we now turn to examining the "map" or "geographic picture" of the world presented by these two newspapers. Table 9.2 highlighted the dominant countries in these maps, and much like the satirical maps of the United States cited earlier for New Yorkers and Texans, the map suggested by Table 9.2 bears faint resemblance to the geographer's map of the world. For example, three small countries—Afghanistan, Syria and Ukraine—received significant attention alongside very large countries, India, Russia, China and the United States. Table 9.4 cataloged all the countries covered in 2014 by these newspapers, but does little to bring these psychological maps of the world into context.

To better see these geographic pictures presented by the media more clearly, we turn to network analysis, which is the latest addition to agenda setting theory (Guo & McCombs, 2015). Here the concept of network agenda setting is focused on a comparison of the geographic agendas of the *New York Times* and the *People's Daily*, a more detailed investigation of the similarity of these two media agendas. The application of network analysis here enables us to see maps of the world constructed on the basis of the strength of the links or associations between the home country of each newspaper and its international coverage as well as the frequency of association between all the countries in the daily presentations of the news. In journalistic terms, this analysis will show the degree of similarity in these two newspapers' news judgments as they construct each day's international agenda.

A key statistic in network analysis is degree centrality, which measures the frequency with which each country appears with every other country in the news reports during the same week across the entire year of 2014. Although degree centrality and sheer frequency of appearance are correlated, the patterns resulting from the two measures are far from identical. A country may appear with some frequency, but not necessarily coincide with news about other countries. A striking example of the difference between the two measures was found in Guo et al.'s (2015) network analysis of the attributes of the Iraq War in the *New York Times*. Although the paper ran numerous stories about "weapons of mass destruction", these stories and other stories on the same day seldom discussed other aspects of the war. In the network analysis WSD was not central to the coverage, but rather was on the periphery.

First let's look at the graphics produced by the computer from these centrality scores. To keep these graphics reasonably legible and readable, the networks were constructed from the top 20 countries in each newspaper's international coverage. Figure 9.1 displays the geographic network of the *New York Times*. Russia is in close proximity to the U.S. in this map, and China, Ukraine and Afghanistan are close by. On the other hand, South Korea, Turkey, and the United Kingdom are on the periphery of the network. When they appear on the front page of the *New York Times*, there typically is little other international news on the front page. In contrast, Russia, China, Ukraine and Afghanistan often appear together on the front page.

Figure 9.2 displays the geographic network of the *People's Daily.* Here the U.S., Russia, and Germany are near the center of the network. The centrality of the U.S. and Russia seems obvious, given the events of 2014. But the centrality of Germany is less obvious and suggests a closer look its coverage in the *People's Daily*. Network analysis is particularly useful in turning up unexpected relationships. On the periphery of the *People's Daily* international coverage network are Libya, Palestine and Turkey.

Obviously, there are similarities in the international news focus of these two newspapers, but at the same time there are many differences. The degree of correspondence between them is best summed by the QAP correlation for the two networks, 0.529, a mid-level degree of correspondence.

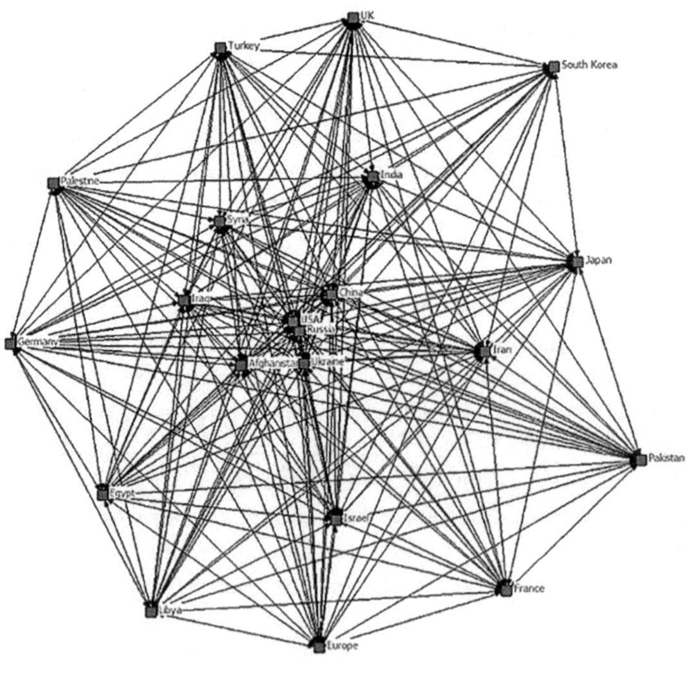

Figure 9.1: Geographic Network of the *New York Times*

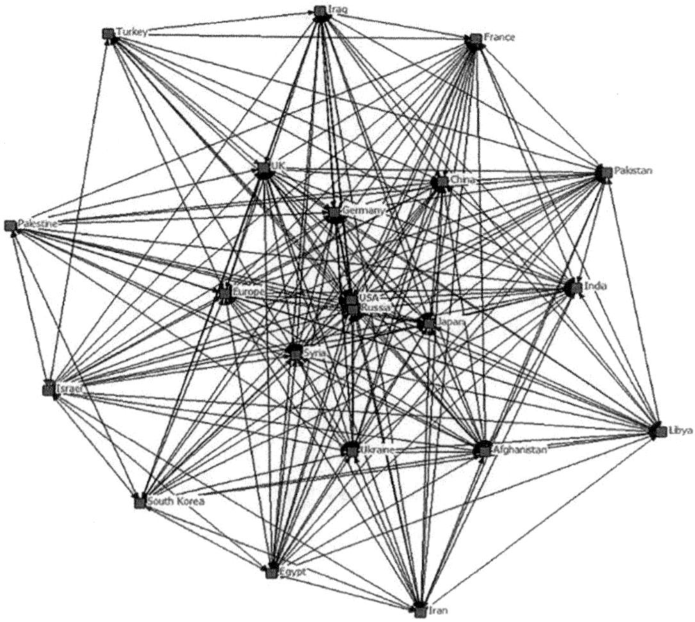

Figure 9.2: Geographic Network of the *People's Daily*

The entire set of centrality scores for each newspaper is presented in Tables 9.5 and 9.6. As noted previously, these are precise measures of how central each of these countries is in the total international coverage of the newspaper. In turn, these measures can be used for subsequent analysis of the various factors that influence a newspaper coverage of a particular country. For example, such factors as its political relationship or past and current involvement with the country, its economic links via foreign trade, and its regional proximity.

Table 9.5: Centrality Scores for the Top 20 Countries in the *New York Times* International Coverage

	Country	Degree of Centrality	Normalized Degree of Centrality
1	USA	450.000	22.500
2	Russia	397.000	19.850
3	China	348.000	17.400
4	Ukraine	347.000	17.350
5	Afghanistan	330.000	16.500
6	Iraq	300.000	15.000

	Country	Degree of Centrality	Normalized Degree of Centrality
7	Syria	280.000	14.000
8	India	247.000	12.350
9	Iran	223.000	11.150
10	Israel	221.000	11.050
11	Egypt	188.000	9.400
12	Turkey	170.000	8.500
13	Palestine	166.000	8.300
14	Japan	162.000	8.100
15	Germany	159.000	7.950
16	UK	153.000	7.650
17	Europe	149.000	7.450
18	Libya	133.000	6.650
19	France	110.000	5.500
20	South Korea	75.000	3.750
21	Pakistan	74.000	3.700

Table 9.6: Centrality Scores for the Top 20 Countries in the *People's Daily* International Coverage

	Country	Degree of Centrality	Normalized Degree of Centrality
1	USA	320.000	16.000
2	Russia	235.000	11.750
3	Syria	198.000	9.900
4	Germany	194.000	9.700
5	Japan	193.000	9.650
6	Europe	179. 000	8.950
7	Ukraine	166.000	8.300
8	UK	165.000	8.250
9	China	161. 000	8.050
10	Afghanistan	140.000	7.000
11	India	127.000	6.350
12	Pakistan	107.000	5.350
13	Egypt	98.000	4.900

	Country	Degree of Centrality	Normalized Degree of Centrality
14	France	96.000	4.800
15	South Korea	95.000	4.750
16	Iraq	92.000	4.600
17	Israel	72.000	3.600
18	Iran	67.000	3.350
19	Libya	52.000	2.600
20	Palestine	39.000	1.950
21	Turkey	24.000	1.200

CONCLUSION

The continuing evolution of agenda-setting theory in the years since the Chapel Hill study (McCombs & Shaw, 1972) is a continual explication of exactly which aspects of news reports impact public opinion. The initial research, now refereed to first level agenda setting, identified the objects of attention that impact public opinion. The second level of agenda setting, attribute agenda setting, revealed the role of the attributes of these objects in shaping public opinion. Theoretically and analytically, first and second-level agenda setting treat objects and their attributes as separate and distinct disaggregated elements.

The hypothesis for first and second level agenda setting effects is that these discrete elements that are salient in the news tend to become salience among the public. Of course, in reality objects and their attributes are bundled together in media messages and in public thought and conversation. Network agenda setting considers the gestalt presented by the news, the bundle of elements. Considering this bundle as a whole adds context to the examination of which elements in the news result in agenda setting effects. Third level agenda setting also test a much bolder and stronger hypothesis about agenda setting effects, namely that the salience of the associations between the objects and/or attributes in the media network agenda creates a similar network of elements among the public.

The research reported here is an early investigation of the geographic network agenda presented by two major newspapers, the *New York Times* and the *People's Daily*, an examination of the extent to which these two media present a common geography in their news reports. Does a global perspective guide international coverage, so that newspapers around the world have similar patterns of coverage? Or is the international coverage of a newspaper strongly influenced by local factors? In the language of standardized tests, our findings indicate that the correct answer is "All of the above". The modest correlation between the networks of the *New York Times* and the *People's Daily*, 0.529, suggests a degree of globalization and commonality in news values. On the other hand, there are clear differences in the international coverage of the two newspapers.

From the viewpoint of agenda-setting theory, clear differences among countries are more interesting. Such findings suggest distinct agenda-setting effects on the psychological geography of the public from country to country rather than global, rather homogenous, agenda-setting effects across countries. And these differences invite further research into the factors that determine the degree of centrality that exist for various countries in the international coverage of a particular newspaper.

The future is promising and intriguing for research into the elements of the media agenda, the factors that influence the salience of those factors, and the subsequent influence of the media agenda on public opinion.

REFERENCES

Beck, U. (2005). *Power in the global age.* Cambridge: Polity Press.

Berglez, P. (2008). What is global journalism? Theoretical and empirical conceptualizations. *Journalism Studies, 9*(6), 845–858.

Braddon-Mitchell, D., & Jackson, F. (2007). *Philosophy of mind and cognition* (2nd ed.). Cambridge, MA: Blackwell.

Clausen, L. (2004). *Global news production.* Copenhagen: Copenhagen Business School Press.

Cottle, S. (2009). Journalism and globalization. In K. Wahl-Jorgensen & T. Hanitzsch (Eds.), *The handbook of journalism studies* (pp. 341–356). New York, NY: Routledge.

Cummins, R. (1996). *Representations, targets, and attitudes.* Cambridge, MA: MIT Press.

Downs, R. M., & Stea, D. (1977). *Maps in minds: Reflections on cognitive mapping.* New York, NY: Harper Collins.

Gillis, J. R. (2010). *Islands of the mind: How the human imagination created the Atlantic world.* New York, NY: Palgrave Macmillan.

Guo, L. (2012). The application of social network analysis in agenda setting research: A methodological exploration. *Journal of Broadcasting & Electronic Media, 56*(4), 616–631.

Guo, L., Chen, Y. N. K., Vu, H., Wang, Q., Aksamit, R., Guzek, D., … McCombs, M. (2015). Coverage of the Iraq War in the United States, Mainland China, Taiwan and Poland: A transnational network agenda-setting study. *Journalism Studies, 16*(3), 343–362.

Guo, L., & McCombs, M. (2015). *The power of information networks.* New York, NY: Routledge.

Hafez, K. (2007). *The myth of media globalization.* Cambridge: Polity Press.

Hanneman, R. A., & Riddle, M. (2005). *Introduction to social network methods* (published in digital form at http://faculty.ucr.edu/hanneman/). Riverside, CA: University of California, Riverside.

Hunnig, B. (2015). Mapping Greece through the eyes of the world. Oxford: Global Database of Events, Language and Tone. Gdeltproject.org

Jensen, K. B. (2003). *News of the world: World cultures look at television news.* London: Routledge.

Kitchin, R. (2002). *The cognition of geographic space.* London: I.B. Tauris.

Lippmann, W. (1922). *Public opinion.* New York, NY: Macmillan.

McCombs, M. (2014). *Setting the agenda: The mass media and public opinion* (2nd ed.). Cambridge: Polity Press.

McCombs, M., & Shaw, D. L. (1972). The agenda-setting function of mass media. *Public Opinion Quarterly, 36*(2), 176–187.

Shoemaker, P. J. (1991). *Gatekeeping*. Newbury Park, CA: Sage.

Shoemaker, P. J., & Cohen, A. A. (2006). *News around the world: Content, practitioners, and the public.* New York, NY: Routledge.

Shoemaker, P. J., & Vos, T. P. (2009). *Gatekeeping theory*. New York, NY: Routledge.

Wanta, W., Golan, G., & Lee, C. (2004). Agenda setting and international news: Media influence on public perceptions of foreign nations. *Journalism & Mass Communication Quarterly, 81*(2), 364–377.

Wasserman, S., & Faust, K. (1994). *Social network analysis: Methods and applications.* Cambridge: Cambridge University Press.

Zhou, Y., & Moy, P. (2007). Parsing framing processes: The interplay between online public opinion and media coverage. *Journal of Communication, 57*(1), 79–98.

CHAPTER TEN

Geographical Difference in Media Effects on Political Discussion in China

Economy, Cultural Characteristics and Social Trust

DI ZHANG*, SHUYA PAN†, AND XIULI WANG‡

Political discussion, defined as informal conversation about public affairs among citizens (Eveland, Morey, & Hutchens, 2011), plays an important role in the democratic process because it can help people reflect upon political messages received from media, raise awareness of problems impacting communities and stimulate one's interests in political participation (Mutz, 2006; Shah et al., 2007). It can be an information source comparable to newspapers and television, and it can be a deliberation venue where people discuss public issues after exposure to information from media sources (e.g., Carpini, Cook, & Jacobs, 2004; McLeod, Scheufele, & Moy, 1999); it thus functions as a crucial mediator between informational use of media, which refers to exposure to public affairs content on media in this study, and participation in civic activities such as voting and protests (Shah et al., 2007).

* Di Zhang is Associate Professor in the School of Journalism and Communication at Renmin University of China. Email: zhangdi204@gmail.com.

† Shuya Pan is Assistant Professor in the School of Journalism and Communication at Renmin University of China. Email: shuya.pan@gmail.com.

‡ Xiuli Wang is Associate Professor in the School of Journalism and Communication at Peking University. Email: xiuli.wang@pku.edu.cn.

This study treats political discussion as an outcome of media exposure instead of as an information stimulus.

Due to its significance, scholars have conducted numerous studies to uncover the factors that stimulate political discussion. One line of such inquiry focused on individual-level factors and micro-psychological processes such as demographics, political efficacy and media use (Shah, Rojas, & Cho, 2008); and the other examined contextual influences such as macro-level social capital, culture and other characteristics of the context in which people are nested. In contrast with the former, the contextual factor-focused research has been relatively lacking (Shah et al., 2008). The present study examines how contextual factors moderate the effects of informational media use on political discussion in China. Specifically, this study is most interested in the cultural characteristics of a region (contextual factors) because they are related to one's expressive behaviors, as in the case of spiral of silence (Scheufle & Moy, 2000).

Furthermore, media effects and civic activities is an important topic in Chinese communication scholarship. However, most such studies are based on data collected in major Chinese metropolitan areas, and nationally representative studies are rare. This study, based on a nationally representative secondary dataset and a multilevel design, can present a more comprehensive and in-depth understanding of Chinese political communication.

THEORETICAL FRAMEWORK

Media Effects on Political Discussion

Unlike formal and rule-bound political deliberation, political discussion is informal and commonly takes place within one's interpersonal social network (Eveland et al., 2011). People who discuss public affairs more frequently are exposed to more diverse political perspectives, which in turn increases their interest in politics, their opinion quality, and their social tolerance (Mutz, 2002). Although it can be motivated by individual impression and identity management, relationship management and development and enjoyment, most political communication scholars explore the reasons for discussing public affairs within the framework of citizenship (Eveland et al., 2011). As most studies have, this research chooses to approach the topic from the perspective of civic responsibility. Mass media such as newspapers commonly cover political, economic and social issues of high public significance (Shoemaker & Reese, 2014). Exposure to public affairs on media has the potential to help people gain political knowledge, create awareness of issues and opinions otherwise unavailable in interpersonal channels (e.g., Mutz & Martin, 2001), and organize their thoughts on public issues impacting communities (Shah et al., 2008). Moreover, it provides the basis for political discussion among citizens (McLeod, Bybee, & Durall, 1979) since media have agenda setting, priming and framing effects. Using surveys and experimental designs, political scientists and communication scholars have consistently documented the positive effects of informational media use on people's political discussion (e.g., Mondak, 1995; Pan, Shen, Paek, & Sun, 2006; Shah, Cho, Eveland, & Kwak, 2005). Plus, studies on Chinese political communication have found positive effects of media on promoting political discussion (e.g., Chan & Zhou, 2011; Pan, Jing, Yan, & Zheng, 2010). Therefore, the following hypothesis is proposed:

> H1: The more often people in China consume public affairs media content, the more frequently they discuss public affairs with others.

Contextual Effects on Political Discussion

In addition to media effects on political discussion, previous studies suggest that one's pre-exposure subjective orientations such as educational level, family income and political efficacy directly influence political engagement (Shah et al., 2007). Moreover, according to the Orientation-Stimulus-Orientation-Response (O-S-O-R) model, social, cultural and psychological factors moderate media effects on political engagement (Shah et al., 2007). Among these variables, scholars have begun to explore how the context in which an individual is immersed exerts influence on political engagement (e.g., Cho & McLeod, 2007; Shah et al., 2008). Communication scholars have long called for a multilevel approach, and emphasized the existing communication literature lacks such studies (Pan & McLeod, 1991). According to Pan and McLeod (1991), there exist two types of mechanisms in how contexts influence individuals—coercion and internalization. In terms of coercion, contextual factors actually force individuals to act in certain manners by, for instance, creating or limiting opportunities for certain activities (McLeod, Kosicki, & McLeod, 2010). In regards to internalization, societal influences such as cultures and norms of a given region or group can shape one's worldviews and behaviors through his or her integration of the societal values into his or her own identity or value system. For instance, Hofstede (2001) vividly describes culture as collective mental programming, and people nested in a specific culture can be programmed into particular tendencies in similar contexts, which are permanent and transferable.

Although not many studies examine how context influences media influences on political discussion, previous research that focuses on political learning and political participation can shed light on this topic. Scholars have documented that local contextual characteristics such as residential stability (Kang & Kwak, 2003), the level of political campaign (Liu, 2012), community connectedness (Shah, Mcleod, & Yoon, 2001) and local network heterogeneity (Kim & Ball-Rokeach, 2006; Kwak, Williams, Wang, & Lee, 2005) moderate the effects of informational media use on political engagement. The present study attempts to explore this topic further by examining the effects of three categories of contextual characteristics: the level of economic development, local cultural values (e.g., individualism-collectivism) and the level of macro-level social trust.

Economic Development

Scholars in comparative politics have long argued that economic development is closely tied to political liberation (Lipset, 1959). According to Dahl (1989), economic development can intensify public demands for democracy because the increasing economic benefits to the masses normally spread democratic aspirations to a wider range of people. Generally, economic development increases citizens' stakes in the political system, and they are more motivated to participate in politics to compete for interests and to get involved in the decision making process of the government (Weiner, 1971). Economic development can also increase the education and income level of an area, which are essential resources for interpersonal political discussions (Nie, Powell, & Prewitt, 1969).

However, the moderating effects of the macro-level economy on the relationship between informational use of media and concepts such as political deliberation and political knowledge acquisition have not been fully explored. The exception is Shen (2009) who found that in the United States the positive association between newspaper use and political learning becomes weaker as the economy declines, while the reversed pattern applies to television use. Although little such research can be found, it is plausible to argue that economic progress will amplify media effects on political discussion. Economic development commonly has liberalization effects, and accordingly people have better awareness of their civic duties, thus becoming more responsive to public affairs content on media. Based on the reasoning above, the following hypotheses are proposed:

> H2a: People in areas of higher economic development will be more likely to discuss public affairs than those in areas of lower economic development.
> H2b: The relationship between informational use of media and political discussion will be stronger in areas of higher economic development than those in areas of lower economic development.

Cultural Characteristics

One definition of culture is as a set of solutions that help people to handle problems, and assigns meanings to specific situations (Matsumoto, 2007). As suggested by research on the spiral of silence, cultural traditions such as the individualism-collectivism dimension are believed to have an influence on the ways people express their political opinions (e.g., Huang, 2005). Hofstede mainly proposed four cultural dimensions including power distance, individualism-collectivism, masculinity-femininity and uncertainty avoidance, which prove related to political discussion or other forms of political participation (Hofstede, 2001). Although scholars often use these dimensions to explain cultural differences between countries, research suggests that different regions within a country may also differ in culture. For instance, with respect to the individualism-collectivism dimension, "Red" states vary from "Blue" states in the United States (Vandello & Cohen, 1999), while northern China differs from southern parts of the country (Talhelm et al., 2014).

The individualism-collectivism dimension, which is highly related to one's expressive behavior, refers to the degree to which individuals are integrated into groups, and describes one's relationship to the collective and others (Hofstede, 2001).[1] In individualistic societies, people prioritize individual desires and interests over those of groups, and stress self-independence. In more individualistic cultures, people are more willing to express their political opinions even under the circumstances that their opinions are in minority (Huang, 2005). However, the motivations for people to participate in politics may come from self-interests instead of common good (Janda, Berry, & Goldman, 2008). Thus, there exists the possibility that individualistic regions may see a lower level of media influence on political discussion because public issues covered by media, in most cases, are of public concern instead of personal gains and loss. Therefore, the following hypotheses are proposed:

> H3a: People in areas of higher individualism will be more willing to discuss public affairs than those in areas of lower individualism.
> H3b: The relationship between informational use of media and political discussion will be stronger in areas with lower individualism than those of higher individualism.

Masculinity-femininity is related to the division of emotional roles between males and females and the literature suggests that in feminine cultures people are more likely to spend time discussing public affairs (Hofstede, 2001). Since people in highly masculine cultures are more ego-oriented (Hofstede, 2001), it is logical that people in such cultures, as those in cultures of high individualism, care more about their personal interests, thus decreasing media impact on political discussion.

> H4a: People in areas of higher femininity will be more willing to discuss public affairs than those in areas of lower femininity.
> H4b: The relationship between informational use of media and political discussion will be stronger in areas of higher femininity than those of lower femininity.

The uncertainty avoidance dimension refers to the degree of stress in a society in the face of an unknown future (Hofstede, 2001). Although no previous research clearly identified uncertainty avoidance as a factor that influences political expressive behaviors, the literature supplies evidence of its relations to civic participation.

According to Almond and Verba (1963), people in cultures of high uncertainty avoidance were less likely to participate in the local political decision-making process. Therefore, the following hypotheses are proposed:

> H5a: People in areas of higher uncertainty avoidance will be less willing to discuss public affairs than those in areas of lower uncertainty avoidance.
> H5b: The relationship between informational use of media and political discussion will be stronger in areas of lower uncertainty avoidance than those of higher uncertainty avoidance.

Power distance refers to the extent to which ordinary people accept the unequal power distribution structure of a society (Hofstede, 2001). The literature suggests that power distance is negatively correlated with the frequency of political discussion (Inglehart, 1990). Thus, the following hypotheses are proposed:

> H6a: People in areas of lower power distance will be more willing to discuss public affairs than those in areas of higher power distance.
> H6b: The relationship between informational use of media and political discussion will be stronger in areas of lower power distance than those of higher power distance.

Social Trust

Social trust is a key concept in the field of sociology and is believed to be an important element of a healthy society. Social trust refers to one's trust towards generalized others instead of the government or other institutions (Delhey & Newton, 2005; Putnam, 1995, 2000). As an outcome, social trust is high in countries of high ethnic homogeneity, good government, high salary and high income equality (Delhey & Newton, 2005). As a predictor, social trust can empower community members to be actively involved in community affairs and to achieve shared objectives (Putnam, 2000). A less trusting atmosphere will lead people to retract from civic life and social ties (Brehm & Rahn, 1997; Putnam, 1993; Scheufele & Shah, 2000). Thus, active political discussion depends heavily on the general level of social trust in an area. Regarding how social trust in an area may moderate media effects on political discussion, it is believed that a high level of social trust can create a pro-civic environment and produce more close social ties so that people in the area would be more willing to discuss public affairs they see in the media. Although the literature does not contain studies that have already tested the prediction in this study, Shah et al. (2001) found that the degree of connectedness of a community positively interacts with newspaper reading in predicting civic participation, but it should be noted that the interaction term is only marginally statistically significant. Therefore, the following hypotheses are posited:

> H7a: People in areas of higher social trust will be more likely to discuss public affairs than those in areas of lower social trust.

H7b: The relationship between informational use of media and political discussion will be stronger in areas of higher social trust than those in areas of lower social trust.

METHODS

Data Sources and Sampling

The multilevel approach of the study means that the data used has both individual and contextual levels. The individual-level data (level-1) comes from China General Social Survey (CGSS), which is a Chinese initiative modeled after the US General Social Survey, and was jointly launched by a group of sociology departments at several Chinese universities in 2003. The national survey, which was conducted initially every other year and annually since 2010, intends to collect information about the relationship between social structure and quality of life in urban and rural China, and how it changes over time (Bian & Li, 2012). CGSS adopted a multi-stage stratified sampling scheme with unequal probabilities, and covered all of the 31 provinces/ autonomous regions/municipalities (all referred as provinces afterwards in this section) in the Chinese mainland. Specifically, this study was mainly based on CGSS 2010, which randomly sampled 100 districts/counties in provinces plus Beijing, Shanghai, Tianjin, Guangzhou and Shenzhen as the first-level sampling units. Within each first-level sampling unit, CGSS 2010 randomly sampled 25 residential communities, within which four households were randomly chosen. CGSS 2010 then randomly selected one member in the household selected in the previous step. The sampling scheme in Beijing, Shanghai, Tianjin, Guangzhou and Shenzhen, the five major metropolitan areas in China, differed slightly in the second step, with the CGSS team randomly sampling 80 residential communities in each city. Weighing the population of each province and the ratio of urban and rural population, CGSS 2010 face-to-face interviewed 11,783 Chinese people across the mainland.

The contextual level (level-2) data comes from CGSS 2010 (social trust) and 2008 (cultural characteristics) plus macro-level data published by the National Bureau of Statistics of China (economic development). In regards to the survey data, the researchers averaged individual responses to survey items for each level-2 unit. The cultural dimensions were not measured in CGSS 2010 but in 2008, which is the immediate previous national survey designed by the same team but answered by different respondents. Generally, people do not change their values and worldviews regularly (Bandura, 2008), so it is reasonably assumed that people's answers related to cultural values are unlikely to change greatly from 2008 to 2010, which ensures the validity of using CGSS 2008.

Since urban and rural areas in China differ economically and culturally, the level-2 unit in this study is a single urban/rural region instead of a single province. Operationally, the researchers divided a province into two parts—rural and urban. Thus, this study has 62 level-2 units.[2] However, developed provinces such as Beijing and Shanghai do not have rural areas, and CGSS 2008 did not survey the respondents in Tibet, Hainan and Qinghai provinces for their attitudes towards the four cultural dimensions. Thus, the actual size of the level-2 units dropped to 50. Accordingly, this effectively reduced the level-1 units in analysis from 11,783 to 10,728. The sample size for each level-2 unit (group) ranges from 25 to 512. For studies interested in testing cross-level interactions, which is the case in this study, the sample sizes at first and second levels meet the 50/20 rule (Kreft, 1996), meaning that the number of level-2 units and the sample size for each level-2 unit should reach 50 and 20 respectively (Hox, 2002); therefore, this study meets the 50/20 rule.

Individual-Level Variables

Political discussion, the dependent variable, was measured on a 5-point "never" to "always" scale by asking the respondents "over the past one year, how often did you discuss public affairs with others? (*M*=2.22, *SD*=1.04)". *Informational use of media*, a key predictor variable, was measured by a question of "over the past one year, how often did you consume public affairs' content in newspapers, magazines and books?"[3] Similar to political discussion, it was assessed by a 5-point "never" to "always" scale (*M* = 2.24, *SD* = 1.43).

The sample consists of 5,157 males and 5,571 females. The average age of the respondents in the sample was 47.15 with standard deviation of 15.67. The respondents were asked "Compared with peers, how was your family income where you reside?", which was measured on a 5-point scale (*M* = 2.61, *SD* = .77). The educational level, which was originally measured using a 1 to 13 scale, was recoded into a 7-point scale ranging from no schooling to graduate and above, and averaged 3.13 with standard deviation of 1.41, meaning that a typical respondent completed junior high school. Political efficacy was assessed on a 5-point Likert scale by 9 items. Among them, four questions measured internal political efficacy, and asked the respondents to what extent they are able to understand the works of the government, participate in public affairs, handle the jobs of government officials and discuss public affairs with others. They formed a 4-to-20 additive index (Cronbach's a = .70) (*M* = 10.79, *SD* = 3.27). The rest evaluated external political efficacy, and asked the respondents to what extent they can influence the political decision making process and have their voices heard by government officials, and the degree to which the respondents felt that the government cared about one's voice and paid attention to their opinions. They formed a 5-to-25 additive index (Cronbach's a = .71) (M = 13.10, SD = 3.27).

Contextual-Level Variables

The researchers measured cultural characteristics of each of the 50 regions using Hofstede's cultural dimensions theory. The four primary dimensions included power distance (PDI; M = 5.81, SD = .59), individualism (IDV; M = 5.61, SD = .63), uncertainty avoidance (UAI; M = 7.24, SD = 1.23) and femininity (FEM; M = 4.81, SD = .76), each of which was measured by two seven-point items[4] in CGSS 2008.[5] High scores on these scales suggest low power distance, high individualism, low fear of uncertainty and high femininity, while low scores suggest otherwise. The two items for each dimension were summed up to form additive indexes (Cronbach's a for PDI, IDV, UAI and MAS are .60, .90, .94 and .85 respectively; other than PDI, the indexes are very reliable).

Measures of macro-level social trust for each of the 50 regions were also included. As a cultural characteristic, macro-level social trust is an aggregation of individual responses in CGSS 2010. It was measured by a single item which asked to what extent one agrees that most people in the society are trustworthy (M=3.21, SD=.21), which is often used in sociology and political studies surveys.

This study did not measure the economic development for each of the 50 regions using gross domestic product (GDP) because the Chinese government only makes available GDP for each province, and does not separate it for rural and urban areas. However, the National Bureau of Statistics makes readily available the average annual net income (in Chinese RMB yuan) for urban and rural residents for each province (M=11,499.93, SD=6,758.66), which serve as a proxy for GDP for each region analyzed in the study.

Data Analysis Procedures

To analyze the data, the researchers used multilevel modeling (MLM), which is specialized in handling data with a hierarchical structure. The model building process followed the approach recommended by Hox (2002); it started with the simplest model, individual-level predictors and fixed effects, and proceeded to more complex model, contextual-level predictors, random effects, and cross-level interactions.

RESULTS

Descriptive Statistics

Table 10.1 presents zero-order correlations among political discussion, informational use of media and other control variables. Political discussion and media exposure to public affairs are strongly correlated, and political discussion is moderately positively correlated with education and internal political efficacy. Political discussion is weakly correlated with other control variables.

Table 10.1: Zero Order Correlations among Individual Political Discussion and Level-1 Predictors

	1	*2*	*3*	*4*	*5*	*6*	*7*
Political Discussion	.63[c]	-.15[c]	.44[c]	.17[c]	.39[c]	.16[c]	-.01
Media (1)		-.12[c]	.55[c]	.20[c]	.38[c]	.16[c]	-.03[c]
Age (2)			-.41[c]	-.09[c]	-.15[c]	-.05[c]	.14[c]
Education (3)				.23[c]	.40[c]	.12[c]	-.07[c]
Income (4)					.19[c]	.14[c]	.04[c]
Internal Pol. Efficacy (5)						.30[c]	-.01
External Pol. Efficacy (6)							.07[c]
Trust (7)							

Note: a: $p < .05$; b: $p < .01$; c: $p < .001$

Table 10.2 displays zero order correlations for the regression coefficient of media effects on political discussion for each region, aggregate political discussion for each region and level-2 predictors. The media coefficient is significantly negatively correlated with individualism, while it is not related to other contextual characteristics. Political discussion is positively correlated with femininity, individualism and average net income level of a region, while it forms a negative association with average social trust of a region. It should be also noted that femininity and individualism form positive correlations with income level, while social trust has a negative association with income level.

Table 10.2: Zero Order Correlations among Regional Media Coefficients, Group Mean Political Discussion and Level-2 Predictors

	1	*2*	*3*	*4*	*5*	*6*	*7*
Reg. coefficient of media effects for regions	-.25	-.20	.19	.00	-.37[b]	-.22	-.22
Political discussion (1)		.25	-.17	.48[c]	.37[b]	-.49[c]	.83[c]
PDI (2)			-.16	.17	.30[a]	-.14	.26
UAI (3)				-.06	.04	.03	-.28
FEM (4)					.52[c]	-.26	.60[c]
IDV (5)						-.19	.44[b]
Trust (6)							-.48[c]
Income (Econ) (7)							

Note: a: $p < .05$; b: $p < .01$; c: $p < .001$

Hypothesis Testing

The results of the null model (Model 1 in Table 10.3) are used to compute intra-class correlation (ICC; ICC= $\frac{Intercept}{Intercept+Residual}$), which is used to assess if the variance in the dependent variable attributed to contextual variables is large enough to analyze using MLM. In this study, ICC is 7%, meaning that 7% of the variance in political discussion is attributed to the difference between regions. Normally, in social science, it is worthwhile to pursue MLM if ICC is above 5% (Snijders, 2012).

The log likelihood ratio test in Table 10.3 suggests that in comparison with the null model, Model 2 in Table 10.3 has a better fit. Male respondents who are younger, richer and better educated are more likely to discuss public affairs than are others. People of higher internal political efficacy are more likely to discuss politics with others. However, external political efficacy and social trust are not important predictors of political discussion.

Table 10.3: Parameter Estimates for Multilevel Model of Political Discussion

	Model 1		Model 2		Model 3		Model 4	
	Est.	SE	Est.	SE	Est.	SE	Est.	SE
Fixed effects								
Intercept	2.155[c]	.041	2.078[c]	.057	2.078[c]	.062	2.078[c]	.693
Gender(1=male)			.207[c]	.016	.205[c]	.016	.204[c]	.016
Age			-.003[c]	.001	-.002[c]	.001	-.002[c]	.001
Perceived Income Level			.024[a]	.010	.024[a]	.010	.023[a]	.010

	Model 1		Model 2		Model 3		Model 4	
	Est.	SE	Est.	SE	Est.	SE	Est.	SE
Education			.053[c]	.008	.054[c]	.008	.055[c]	.008
Internal Pol. Efficacy			.044[c]	.003	.044[c]	.003	.044[c]	.003
External Pol. Efficacy			.004[a]	.002	.004	.002	.004	.002
Individual Social Trust			.014	.007	.014[a]	.007	.013	.007
Media Exposure to Public affairs (Media)			.435[c]	.008	.441[c]	.013	.483[c]	.224
Average Regional Income (Econ)							.008	.037
Individualism (IDV)							-.047	.034
Femininity (FEM)							.007	.031
Social Trust (SOC)							.035	.101
Media x Income							-.047[a]	.021
Media x IDV							-.070[c]	.020
Media x FEM							.054[b]	.018
Media x SOC							-.138[a]	.062
Variance component								
Level-1								
WP (Residual)	.994[c]	.014	.604[c]	.008	.599[c]	.008	.598[c]	.008
Level-2								
Intercept	.077[c]	.016	.013[c]	.004	.040[c]	.012	.029[b]	.009
Media x Intercept					-.012[b]	.004	-.007[a]	.003
Media					.005[c]	.002	.003[b]	.001
Deviance (# parameters)	30518[c] (3)		25107.7[c] (11)		25066.2[c] (13)		25044.4[c] (21)	
Deviance test			5410.3		41.5		21.8	

According to models 2, 3 and 4 in Table 10.3, exposure to public affairs content on media is positively associated with political discussion. Therefore, H1 is supported. The bivariate correlation in Table 10.2 suggests that people in areas with higher level of average income per capita report higher level of political discussion, but Table 10.3 exhibits that when controlling for other individual and contextual predictors, it loses significance. Thus, H2a is not supported.

Table 10.2 suggests that two cultural characteristics—femininity and individualism—are associated with the level of political discussion positively. However, according to Table 10.3, when controlling for other variables, their coefficients lose their significance. H3a and H4a are not supported. The coefficients of uncertainty avoidance and power distance to be associated with political discussion are not statistically significant, and their interaction terms with media exposure are not, either. H5a, H5a, H6a and H6b are not supported. To keep the model parsimonious, the researchers dropped the variables out of the model so that they do not appear in Table 10.3.

Although social trust negatively correlates with political discussion, Table 10.3 reveals that macro-level social trust is not related to political discussion. Thus, H4a is not supported.

Models 3 and 4 in Table 10.3 present the test results regarding the moderating effects of contextual level variables. Model 3 allows the regression coefficients of media effects to vary between regions. The likelihood ratio test suggests that Model 3 is better than Model 2 in constraining random effects to zero, which means that it is worthwhile to further inspect the exact contextual predictors which can explain the variation in media effects coefficients. In Model 4, the researchers added interaction terms. The variance in media coefficient in the variance component part of the table in Model 4 decreases almost by half in comparison with Model 3. Moreover, the likelihood ratio test for Model 4 and Model 3 is statistically significant, suggesting that Model 4 has a better fit.

In Table 10.3, although average regional net income level is not statistically significant, the interaction term of net income level and media is statistically significant and negative. However, the results suggest that the direction is opposite the expectation. Although H2b is not supported, its implications will be discussed below.

According to Table 10.3, the coefficients for the interaction terms of individualism and femininity are statistically significant. Also, the directions of their signs are in line with our expectation. H3b and H4b are supported.

Table 10.3 suggests that the coefficient for the interaction term of social trust is negative and statistically significant. In other words, in areas of higher social trust, the relationship between informational use of media and political discussion becomes lower. Thus, H7b is not supported, but this finding will be discussed below.

DISCUSSION

This study uses nationally representative secondary data to examine how Chinese people's informational use of media influences political discussion, and to what extent a group of contextual level variables –economic development, cultural characteristics and social trust—moderate media effects on political conversation among citizens. This study adds to the literature of Chinese political communication, and, more importantly, contributes to our understanding of how contextual characteristics of a region moderate media effects on civic engagement.

In regards to media's direct effects, this study finds that informational use of media and internal and external political efficacy are positively associated with political discussion. Such results are consistent with previous studies conducted in Shanghai and other metropolitan Chinese cities (Chan & Zhou, 2011), so this study expands our knowledge of Chinese political communication from a few major Chinese cities to the entire country.

More importantly, this study explores the macroscopic differences between regions in political conversation and media effects on political discussion in the Chinese mainland. With more than 30 years of economic reforms and opening-up, different regions in China exhibit different levels of economic development, which is operationalized in this study as average income level. Although China is a country dominated by the Han ethnicity and deemed as a collectivistic culture (which is usually the case in cross-national comparative studies), cultural psychology research finds that China is not as culturally unified as it thought to be (Talhelm et al., 2014). This study finds that economic development, cultural characteristics and macro-level social trust in a given region do not have direct effects on the frequency of political discussion at the individual level. Such results are generally consistent with Shen and Liang (2014). They found that none of cross-national cultural dimensions directly predict online discussion frequency, and discovered that macro-societal self-expression, value orientation and democratic systems are predictors. Similar arguments can be made here: the level of local government's responsiveness to Chinese people's concerns and requests could play a more important role than culture, economy and social trust in directly predicting political discussion, which is, however, not measured in the secondary CGSS data.

Individualism, Femininity and Economic Development

Despite no direct effects, these three categories of contextual factors do influence the strength of media effects on political discussion. As expected, regions of lower individualism and higher femininity see stronger positive media effects on political discussion. But the direction of some interaction terms are not in line with our prediction: higher economic development and macro-level social trust are associated with lower strength of media effects.

Since no direct contextual effects of cultural characteristics on political discussion were observed, the researchers attribute cultural influences on conversation of public affairs to the ways people look at media content within a region. Such a notion is different from comparative spiral of silence studies, which mainly explain the difference in effect size from the perspective of how individualism-collectivism constrains one's expressive behaviors. Journalists' decision-making processes rely on their judgments of newsworthiness of the events; the most important criterion is the level of the event's public significance (Shoemaker & Reese, 2014). In other words, most events that public media cover do not necessarily bear direct relations to one's specific personal interests. Therefore, it is highly likely that people residing in regions of high individualism fail to link media coverage of public issues to their own personal interests, which further minimizes media's role as a catalyst for political discussion. This is largely consistent with the political culture literature which has found that people in individualistic political cultures participate in politics to advance personal interests instead of achieving the collective good (Janda et al., 2008). But, this does not mean that people in more individualistic cultures tend to discuss public affairs less. When they see their own interests at stake, they might be even more active.

Similar arguments can be made to explain why regions of high femininity see stronger media effects on political discussion. People living in feminine culture have the tendencies to care more about others, and the collective good, which in turn render them more responsive to mass media messages of public significance. Therefore, these results contribute to the literature by finding that cultural characteristics do not necessarily directly impact political expressive behaviors, but they can exert their influences in a subtler manner by moderating the relationship between political discussion and its antecedents.

This study finds a negative influence of economic development on media effects while controlling for other factors, which overthrows the researchers' initial speculation of a positive one. The initial prediction was grounded in the theory that a better economy is linked with better education, well-established local information structure and political liberalization. Giving a second thought to the research design, the researchers felt that the results of the analysis may not reflect the educational and political dimensions of economic development because educational level and political efficacy were controlled at the individual level. Therefore, economic development here may reflect the characteristics of the local information structure and culture. Economic development can completely change the communication infrastructure of a society because people afford more media channel choices. In a media-rich environment, people do not necessarily rely on mass media alone, and internet applications in these areas can be more important activators of political discussion.

Power distance does not predict political discussion in the model probably because as Table 10.2 suggests, it is significantly related to individualism, thus losing statistical significance. In regards to uncertainty avoidance and expressive behaviors, previous literature, in fact, does not provide a confirmed relationship, and this study can further remind other scholars that informal political talks differ from other civic activities in nature.

Social Trust

The most interesting finding in this study concerns the influence of societal level social trust: high macro-level social trust is associated with low media effects on political discussion, which is unexpected. However, the lack of a positive correlation between macro-level social trust and aggregate political discussion in Table 10.2 and the positive correlation between them at the individual level in Table 10.1, remind us that the negative sign of the interaction coefficient can be possibly attributed to the unique post-Communist nature of China. Since the collapse of the Communist empire in Eastern Europe, political scientists have discovered a negative association between aggregate social trust (macro-level) and civic engagement, and a positive one at individual level (Dowley & Silver, 2002; Letki & Evans, 2005), which are very different from the pattern found in North America and Western Europe. Although it is commonly believed that social trust was scarce in Communist countries, nationals residing in them needed social trust more than their counterparts in established democracies because family members and friends in their interpersonal networks were the only people they could count on in a society where the government often failed the citizens (Dowley & Silver, 2002). When the Communist rule ended and democratization and marketization began, people's relations were not as close as before because the external pressure on people to cluster together disappeared. It can be seen that the social trust in these countries was more a need for personal survival than something related to the collective good. Social trust can also be cultivated in long term experience of democracy because the well-established legal system and strict enforcement of laws ensure that violators of contracts, formal or informal, will be punished (Muller & Seligson, 1994). However, these post-Communist countries began building democratic systems less than 30 years ago, which is not long; the system-driven social trust was not fully present yet. Therefore, the social trust, if any in these post-Communist societies, comes from personal survival needs, and is inherently different from that in established democracies, which explains why social trust in these countries is not often positively related to civic engagement. China is comparable to these Eastern European countries because China has been long a Communist country with a history of political repression. Admittedly, the Communist Party's ruling style has greatly changed from the past, and China has effectively liberalized its political system. However, democratic systems do not yet exist in China. Thus, the social trust in China quite possibly comes from external pressure for personal survival in an undemocratic system. In other words, a high level of social trust in this study merely indicates that a particular Chinese region is not liberalized enough; such a context may lower people's willingness to express their opinions in fear of reprisal even though they encounter media messages of public significance.

Conclusion

This study adds to our understanding of how the strength of media effects on political discussion is contingent upon contextual characteristics including economic development, culture and social trust. Contextual factors may not always exert direct influence on the civic engagement outcome variables such as political conversation, learning and participation; rather they function more as moderators. A second important discovery is that cultural norms, through internalization of the way that people look at media content, influence media effects; culture plays a vital role in civic engagement. Finally, the study finds that macro-societal social trust can possibly function differently in various nations when interacting with media to influence political discussion because social trust can originate from different sources.

NOTES

1. The researchers acknowledge that in some other scholars' perspectives, individualism and collectivism are two orthogonal concepts. However, this study chooses to treat them as the extremes of a single concept for practical and theoretical grounds. The data collectors treated collectivism and individualism as bipolar, thus designing the questionnaire reflecting their views. Moreover, Hofstede (2001) wrote that collectivism and individualism can be treated as two separate concepts at individual level, while it is inappropriate to do so at aggregate level. Since this study approaches them at contextual level, the researchers' choice here is theoretically viable.
2. Chinese mainland has 31 provinces.
3. Although these two concepts are measured using single items, measurements are valid in terms of their predicative validity. The manner of political discussion's association with exposure to public affairs on media and other individual level control variables follow similar patterns with Chan and Zhou (2011), which was conducted in Shanghai, China.
4. Femininity was assessed by the extent to which you agree that it is more important for the wife to assist on her husband's career than to pursue on her own career and the degree to which you agree that the authority of the father should be respected at home, in any event.
   Individualism was evaluated by the extent to which you agree that it is not suitable to oppose majority's idea, even if one has different opinions and the degree to which you agree that one should not show his/her complain on others to get along well with them.
   Power distance was assessed by the extent to which you agree that the subordinate should obey the instructions from the boss despite her/his disagreement and the degree to which you agree that if the boss is capable, he or she should make all the decisions.
   Uncertainty avoidance was evaluated by the extent to which you agree that it is more desirable to have a life of risk and opportunity than to have an ordinary and steady life and the degree to which you agree that if spare money is available, I will invest into something with high returns but high risks.
   Admittedly, these measurements do not encompass the entire range of the dimensions, but they do cover certain aspects of the concept. For instance, individualism merely covers the dimensions related to expressive behaviors. However, Table 9.2 suggests that the existing measurements

are of predicative validity. For instance, individualism forms positive correlation with economy development at aggregate level.

5. Although the standard deviation scores of the four cultural dimensions suggest that cultural differences between different regions in China are not as large as that between countries, the results of ANOVA suggest that there exist statistically significant differences among them. Except power distance, η^2 for the other three cultural dimensions ranges from 0.10 to 0.16, meaning that the difference is modest (Tolmie, Muijs, & McAteer, 2011).

REFERENCES

Almond, G. A., & Verba, S. (1963). *The civic culture: Political attitudes and democracy in five nations.* Princeton, NJ: Princeton University Press.

Bandura, A. (2008). Social cognitive theory of mass communication. In J. Bryant & M. B. Olive (Eds.), *Media effects: Advances in theory and research.* New York, NY: Routledge.

Bian, Y., & Li, L. (2012). The Chinese general social survey (2003–8). *Chinese Sociological Review, 45*(1), 70–97. doi:10.2753/CSA2162-0555450104

Brehm, J., & Rahn, W. (1997). Individual-level evidence for the causes and consequences of social capital. *American Journal of Political Science, 41*(3), 999–1023.

Carpini, M. X. D., Cook, F. L., & Jacobs, L. R. (2004). Public deliberation, discursive participation, and citizen engagement: A review of the empirical literature. *Annual Review of Political Science, 7*(1), 315–344. doi:10.1146/annurev.polisci.7.121003.091630

Chan, J. M., & Zhou, B. (2011). Expressive behaviors across discursive spaces and issue types. *Asian Journal of Communication, 21*(2), 150–166. doi:10.1080/01292986.2010.543558

Cho, J., & McLeod, D. M. (2007). Structural antecedents to knowledge and participation: Extending the knowledge gap concept to participation. *Journal of Communication, 57*(2), 205–228. doi:10.1111/j.1460-2466.2007.00340.x

Dahl, R. (1989). *Polyarchy: Participation and opposition.* New Haven, CT: Yale University Press.

Delhey, J., & Newton, K. (2005). Predicting cross-national levels of social trust: Global pattern or Nordic exceptionalism? *European Sociological Review, 21*(4), 311–327. doi:10.1093/esr/jci022

Dowley, K. M., & Silver, B. D. (2002). Social capital, ethnicity and support for democracy in the post-communist states. *Europe-Asia Studies, 54*(4), 505–527. doi:10.1080/09668130220139145

Eveland, W. P., Morey, A. C., & Hutchens, M. J. (2011). Beyond deliberation: New directions for the study of informal political conversation from a communication perspective. *Journal of Communication, 61*(6), 1082–1103. doi:10.1111/j.1460-2466.2011.01598.x

Hofstede, G. H. (2001). *Culture's consequences: Comparing values, behaviors, institutions and organizations across nations.* London: SAGE.

Hox, J. (2002). *Multilevel analysis: Techniques and applications.* Mahwah, NJ: LEA.

Huang, H. (2005). A cross-cultural test of the spiral of silence. *International Journal of Public Opinion Research, 17*(3), 324–345. doi:10.1093/ijpor/edh065

Inglehart, R. F. (1990). *Cultural shift in industrial society.* Princeton, NJ: Princeton University Press.

Janda, K., Berry, J., & Goldman, J. (2008). *The challenge of democracy: American government in a global world.* Boston, MA: Wadsworth.

Kang, N., & Kwak, N. (2003). A multilevel approach to civic participation: Individual length of residence, neighborhood residential stability, and their interactive effects with media use. *Communication Research, 30*(1), 80–106. doi:10.1177/0093650202239028

Kim, Y.-C., & Ball-Rokeach, S. J. (2006). Community storytelling network, neighborhood context, and civic engagement: A multilevel approach. *Human Communication Research, 32*(4), 411–439. doi:10.1111/j.1468-2958.2006.00282.x

Kreft, I. (1996). *Are multilevel techniques necessary?: An overview, including simulation studies*. Unpublished Manuscript.

Kwak, N., Williams, A. E., Wang, X., & Lee, H. (2005). Talking politics and engaging politics: An examination of the interactive relationships between structural features of political talk and discussion engagement. *Communication Research, 32*(1), 87–111. doi:10.1177/0093650204271400

Letki, N., & Evans, G. (2005). Endogenizing social trust: Democratization in east-central Europe. *British Journal of Political Science, 35*(3), 515–529. doi:10.1017/S000712340500027X

Lipset, S. M. (1959). Some social requisites of democracy: Economic development and political legitimacy. *American Political Science Review, 53*(1), 69–105. doi:10.2307/1951731

Liu, Y.-I. (2012). The influence of communication context on political cognition in presidential campaigns: A geospatial analysis. *Mass Communication and Society, 15*(1), 46–73. doi:10.1080/15205436.2011.583179

Matsumoto, D. (2007). Culture, context, and behavior. *Journal of Personality, 75*(6), 1285–1320. doi:10.1111/j.1467-6494.2007.00476.x

McLeod, J. M., Bybee, C. R., & Durall, J. A. (1979). Equivalence of informed political participation: The 1976 presidential debates as a source of influence. *Communication Research, 6*(4), 463–487. doi:10.1177/009365027900600404

McLeod, J. M., Kosicki, G. M., & McLeod, D. M. (2010). Levels of analysis and communication science. In C. R. Berger, M. E. Roloff, & D. R. Roskos-Ewoldsen (Eds.), *The handbook of communication science* (pp. 183–202). Thousand Oaks, CA: Sage.

McLeod, J. M., Scheufele, D. A., & Moy, P. (1999). Community, communication, and participation: The role of mass media and interpersonal discussion in local political participation. *Political Communication, 16*(3), 315–336. doi:10.1080/105846099198659

Mondak, J. J. (1995). Media exposure and political discussion in U.S. elections. *The Journal of Politics, 57*(01), 62–85. doi:10.2307/2960271

Muller, E. N., & Seligson, M. A. (1994). Civic culture and democracy: The question of causal relationships. *American Political Science Review, 88*(3), 635–652.

Mutz, D. C. (2002). Cross-cutting social networks: Testing democratic theory in practice. *American Political Science Review, 96*(1), 111–126. doi:10.1017/S0003055402004264

Mutz, D. C. (2006). *Hearing the other side: Deliberative versus participatory democracy*. New York, NY: Cambridge University Press.

Mutz, D. C., & Martin, P. S. (2001). Facilitating communication across lines of political difference: The role of mass media. *American Political Science Review, 95*(1), 97–114. doi:null

Nie, N. H., Powell, G. B., & Prewitt, K. (1969). Social structure and political participation: Developmental relationships. *American Political Science Review, 63*(3), 808–832.

Pan, Z., Jing, G., Yan, W., & Zheng, J. (2010). *Understanding expressive engagement in urban China: Differentiating domains, settings, and media effects*. Paper presented at the Annual Conference of International Communication Association, Singapore.

Pan, Z., & McLeod, J. M. (1991). Multilevel analysis in mass communication research. *Communication Research, 18*(2), 140–173. doi:10.1177/009365091018002002

Pan, Z., Shen, L., Paek, H.-J., & Sun, Y. (2006). Mobilizing political talk in a presidential campaign: An examination of campaign effects in a deliberative framework. *Communication Research, 33*(5), 315–345. doi:10.1177/0093650206291478

Putnam, R. D. (1993). *Making democracy work: Civic traditions in modern Italy*. Princeton, NJ: Princeton University Press.

Putnam, R. D. (1995). Tuning in, tuning out: The strange disappearance of social capital in America. *PS: Political Science & Politics, 28*(4), 664–683. doi:10.2307/420517

Putnam, R. D. (2000). *Bowling alone: The collapse and revival of american community*. New York, NY: Simon & Schuster.

Scheufle, D. A., & Moy, P. (2000). Twenty-five years of the spiral of silence: A conceptual review and empirical outlook. *International Journal of Public Opinion Research, 12*(1), 3–28. doi:10.1093/ijpor/12.1.3

Scheufele, D. A., & Shah, D. V. (2000). Personality strength and social capital: The role of dispositional and informational variables in the production of civic participation. *Communication Research, 27*(2), 107–131. doi:10.1177/009365000027002001

Shah, D. V., Cho, J., Eveland, W. P., & Kwak, N. (2005). Information and expression in a digital age: Modeling internet effects on civic participation. *Communication Research, 32*(5), 531–565. doi:10.1177/0093650205279209

Shah, D. V., Cho, J., Nah, S., Gotlieb, M. R., Hwang, H., Lee, N.-J., … McLeod, D. M. (2007). Campaign ads, online messaging, and participation: Extending the communication mediation model. *Journal of Communication, 57*(4), 676–703. doi:10.1111/j.1460–2466.2007.00363.x

Shah, D. V., Mcleod, J. M., & Yoon, S.-H. (2001). Communication, context, and community: An exploration of print, broadcast, and internet influences. *Communication Research, 28*(4), 464–506. doi:10.1177/009365001028004005

Shah, D. V., Rojas, H., & Cho, J. (2008). Media and civic participation: On understanding and misunderstanding communication effects. In J. Bryant & M. B. Oliver (Eds.), *Media effects: Advances in theory and research* (pp. 207–227). New York, NY: Routledge.

Shen, F. (2009). *An economic theory of political communication effects: How the economy conditions political learning* (Doctoral Dissertation). Ohio State University, Columbus, OH.

Shen, F., & Liang, H. (2014). Cultural difference, social values, or political systems? Predicting willingness to engage in online political discussion in 75 societies. *International Journal of Public Opinion Research*. doi:10.1093/ijpor/edu012

Shoemaker, P. J., & Reese, S. D. (2014). *Mediating the message in the 21st century: A media sociology perspective* (3rd ed.). New York, NY: Routledge.

Snijders, T. A. B. (2012). Multilevel analysis. Retrieved from http://www.stats.ox.ac.uk/~snijders/MLB_new_S.pdf

Talhelm, T., Zhang, X., Oishi, S., Shimin, C., Duan, D., Lan, X., & Kitayama, S. (2014). Large-scale psychological differences within China explained by rice versus wheat agriculture. *Science, 344*(6184), 603–608. doi:10.1126/science.1246850

Tolmie, A., Muijs, D., & McAteer, E. (2011). *Quantitative methods in educational and social research using SPSS*. Maidenhead: Open University Press.

Vandello, J. A., & Cohen, D. (1999). Patterns of individualism and collectivism across the United States. *Journal of Personality and Social Psychology, 72*(2), 279–292. doi:10.1037/0022–3514.77.2.279

Weiner, M. (1971). Political participation: Crisis of the political process. In L. Binder, J. S. Colman, J. LaPalombara, L. W. Pye, S. Verba, & M. Weiner (Eds.), *Crises and sequences in political development* (pp. 159–204). Princeton, NJ: Princeton University Press.

CHAPTER ELEVEN

Israelis AND Foreign News

A 25-year Follow-up on Interest and Perceived Functions

AKIBA A. COHEN*

INTRODUCTION

Twenty-five years ago, during the first week of January 1991, just prior to the launch of Operation Desert Storm in Iraq, I conducted a survey among Jewish Israeli adults in an attempt to determine their interest in and attitudes towards foreign news. The study focused primarily on television, the medium that enjoyed high viewership levels for news.

In an article based on that study (Cohen, 1993), labeled as a "benchmark" by the Journal of Broadcasting and Electronic Media, I expressed the hope that scholars in other countries would pick up on these research questions thereby providing interesting and important comparative data. Unfortunately, this did not happen. Was it because my study was about Israelis and hence rather esoteric or because there has been relatively little interest altogether among scholars in studying the interest that people have in foreign news?

In any event, in describing the 1991 data concerning the interest of Israelis in foreign news my sense was that while they were naturally more interested in domestic news, they were also quite interested in foreign news. However, I had no yardstick to compare these data with that of other countries. This was unfortunate

* Akiba A. Cohen is Professor Emeritus of Communication at Tel Aviv University. Email akiba@tauex.tau.ac.il.

especially since dealing with foreign news by definition relates to other countries and hence reciprocity of interest might be a relevant issue worthy of study.

The present chapter presents the findings of a 25-year follow-up on my earlier study. While it does not compare Israel with other countries, which I have done in other studies, including one with Pamela Shoemaker (Shoemaker & Cohen, 2006), I felt that it would be worthwhile to do a "replication" of the initial study in order to examine whether or not changes that have taken place in Israel over the years in two main domains—the country's media ecology and its geopolitical situation—might have affected its citizens' interest in foreign news.

INTEREST IN FOREIGN NEWS

Overall, considerable research has been conducted on the contents of foreign news and significantly less on peoples' interest in it. In a landmark content analytic study, Galtung and Ruge (1965) proposed twelve criteria for the selection of foreign news. That study, based on four Norwegian newspapers, has been adopted and cited by numerous scholars regarding television news as well, often without even considering the inherent differences between the two media. A reassessment of these criteria was offered by Harcup (2001) who studied British newspapers. In-between the publication of those two studies, Chang and Lee (1992) surveyed newspaper editors to determine the criteria they claim to use in selecting foreign news. And of course, the work of Pamela Shoemaker on gatekeeping has also been central in this area (Shoemaker, 1991; Shoemaker & Vos, 2009).

When it comes to the public's interest in foreign news—the focus of this chapter—much less research has been done. In fact, only a handful of studies had been conducted prior to my 1991 Israeli study. In conjunction with the work of Galtung and Ruge, a survey was conducted in 1964 by Sande (1971) in three countries—Norway, France and Poland—in which respondents were asked about their perceptions of the previous days' foreign news. In America, in one of the earliest studies, Sparkes and Winter (1980) conducted a field experiment to test the factors that lead to increased interest in foreign news. A later survey conducted in the United States by Hargrove and Stempel (2002) showed that readers expressed greater interest in good vs. bad and in soft vs. hard news depicting international events. Recently, Sambrook, Terrington, and Levy (2013) showed that BBC viewers in Britain displayed significant interest in certain foreign news events that took place in 2010–2011. And yet, at about the same time, American data for 2011 and 2012 gathered by the Pew Research Center (2002) suggested that interest in foreign news was in decline.

In distinguishing between "domestic" and "foreign" news, it goes without saying that most people would be interested in domestic news, that is, in events that take place in their neighborhood, their town or city and their country, especially since this news category is clearly most dominant in news reporting. Also, one could assume (or at least hope) that there would be some interest expressed in exclusively foreign news, that is, in events and issues concerning neighboring or even faraway countries totally unrelated to one's own country. These patterns of interest in non-domestic news are important, particularly in our era of increased globalization and mutual interdependence among nations. Finally, it can be assumed that people would be concerned with "hybrid" news—foreign news with domestic involvement or domestic news with foreign involvement—that is, news about events and issues that link or have the potential of linking their own country with other countries: for example, conflicts between nations, worldwide terrorism, trade relations, natural disasters and visits by foreign dignitaries (Stępińska, Porath, Mujica, Xu, & Cohen, 2013).

Foreign and hybrid news, by definition, go beyond national boundaries. It therefore stands to reason that studying these genres—both in terms of their content and how publics relate to them—would be especially amenable to comparative research. Indeed, in the past quarter century or so there has been a growing trend of comparative research on news that included an interest component. As illustration, I briefly refer to three such collaborative studies in which I played a part.

In a study of the European Broadcasting Union's News Exchange Service (Cohen, Levy, Roeh, & Gurevitch, 1996) we examined the process, and contents in eleven countries. In five of the countries (Britain, France, Germany, Israel and the United States) we conducted focus groups in order to study perceived newsworthiness. We asked the participants to role play being the editor of three evening newscasts and to create their line-up based on an array of news items. They were also asked specific questions about their interest in domestic and foreign news of several categories (law and order, politics, sports, etc.). Finally, they were shown their country's actual version of the same three news reports—foreign to all—and asked to discuss them. Space does not permit a summary of the findings; suffice it to say that clear differences were found among the five countries.

A decade later, Pamela Shoemaker and I published the findings of a study of the contents and perceptions of news in central and peripheral cities of ten nations (Shoemaker & Cohen, 2006). In one part of the study 80 focus groups were conducted, four in each of the 20 cities. Each group consisted of either editors, public relations practitioners, low socioeconomic or high socioeconomic residents who were asked to assess how they perceived the newsworthiness of various news items that appeared in the cities' respective newspapers. Using rank correlations, we found that across the ten countries there was relatively high agreement about newsworthiness among the participants in the various focus groups but there was less agreement with the actual prominence of the items as they appeared in the cities' respective newspapers.

More recently, in a multination study of foreign news on television (Cohen, 2013), identical surveys were conducted in 13 countries (Brazil, Canada, Chile, China, Germany, Hong Kong, Israel, Poland, Portugal, Singapore, Switzerland, Taiwan and the United States). The respondents were asked about their interest in domestic and foreign events dealing with seven topics: accidents and natural disasters; social issues; relations between foreign countries; economics, business and commerce; crime and violence; and domestic politics of foreign countries. They were also asked about the perceived functions of viewing foreign news. Not surprisingly, there was significant variability among the countries in terms of interest regarding the various topics in both domestic and foreign news. Difference scores calculated for each country between domestic and foreign news revealed that in all the countries there was greater interest in domestic news regarding the seven topics compared with interest in foreign news about the same topics.

Particularly striking to me was that the difference scores were consistently the highest in Israel (Hanitzsch, Goodrum, Quandt, & von Pape, 2013). Regression analyses were done to predict interest in foreign news using several independent variables: perceived functions and evaluations of news (as reported by the respondents) as well as demographics and media exposure measures. The Israeli data stood out once again. Across the 13 countries, only 11.5% of the variance was explained in Israel in contrast with higher percentages in the other countries, up to 33.7% in the United States and 32.6% in Switzerland.

WHY STUDY ISRAEL?

So what if anything is special about Israel? Israel is a small country, ranked 99 in population and 154 in geographic size according to the *CIA Factbook* list of countries and territories.[1] But events in Israel and concerning it over the years have produced much more news relative to its size than any other country. For example, using data mining software, Segev and Blondheim (2013) measured the frequency in which both Israel and Palestine were mentioned in leading web sites of twelve countries (the United States, Europe, the Middle East and Asia). Based on a sample of more than 500,000 news items over nearly two years (2009–2010), they found that Israel was among the most prominent countries in online news; and when focusing on "top news", Israel was the second most prominent following the United States.

On the media front, several major changes took place in Israel between 1991 and the present time. First, television broadcasting began rather late in Israel, in 1968, with a single public service channel. There were no cable or satellite broadcasts. In the 1990s two commercial Hebrew channels were added along with cable television, while direct broadcast satellite channels entered the scene in 2000. Cable and satellite carry the domestic channels as well as dozens of foreign channels from many countries in numerous languages. Second, radio broadcasting expanded from two public service stations (one operated by the Israel Broadcasting Authority and one by the Israel Defense Forces) to a network of regional radio stations. Third, most of the political party newspapers that flourished in earlier years had folded, leaving Israelis with only a handful of secular newspapers as well as several published by religious factions. Finally, the Internet that did not exist in 1991 has become a major source of news both via domestic web sites and of course the availability of sites from across the globe. All this has made Israel a media-rich society comparable to that of other western nations and quite different from what it was a quarter century ago.

Israel's geopolitical situation has also changed over the years. For most of its existence, Israel had complex relations with many countries. Relationships with its neighboring Arab countries, ever since its establishment in 1948, have been troublesome. In fact, during its 68 years several major wars and numerous military campaigns have taken place and even after signing a peace treaty with Egypt in 1991 and with Jordan in 1994, tranquility has not come to the region. On the Palestinian-Israeli front, since the 1967 war, despite some periods of relative calm, there have been numerous waves of terror with varying levels of intensity. The first *Intifada* (uprising), which began in 1987, was followed by the Oslo Accords signed in Washington in 1993. The second *Intifada* started in 2000 which was considerably more violent and claimed many casualties on both sides and ended with an agreement in 2005, which was the precursor for Israel's unilateral disengagement from the Gaza Strip. During the eleven years since Israel's departure from Gaza, three major military operations took place (*Cast Lead* in 2008; *Pillar of Cloud* in 2012; and the longest and most fierce, *Protective Edge* in 2014). Finally, during 2016, another wave of attacks on Israeli civilians, mostly by individual Palestinians, has been raging.

Israel has had and continues to have complicated relations with the world powers—the United States, the United Kingdom, France, Germany and the former Soviet Union (now the Russian Federation)—as well as with other countries. Three examples relating to foreign countries illustrate these relationships: first, Israel's concern about Iran's nuclear program; second, the growing BDS (Boycott, Divestment and Sanctions) Movement, that since 2005 has attempted to increase economic and political pressure on Israel to end its occupation of Palestinian territories has been and continues to be a heated topic that was recently exacerbated with the decision of the European Union to require special labelling of products manufactured by Jewish settlements in the West Bank; and third, perennial resolutions passed by various international organizations, notably the United Nations, condemning Israel on various issues (or having failed to pass thanks to American vetoes).[2]

These factors and more—the fact that many Israeli citizens live outside the country (by some estimates as much as 10% of Israeli citizens) in addition to several million Jews in the "diaspora", and the fact that Israelis are well-known to be heavy travelers abroad as tourists—all these would also be expected to promote interest in foreign (or hybrid) news among Israelis. It was thus hypothesized that the combination of an expanded Israeli media ecology, including greater availability of world media, in addition to the increased interrelatedness of the country with other countries, its expatriates and with world Jewry, that there would be an increase in Israelis' interest in such news.

METHOD

As noted, the original survey was conducted in January 1991, shortly before the Gulf War.[3] In November 2015, just about a quarter century later, I commissioned a study to "replicate" the first one. Obviously, some essential adjustments in the survey questionnaire were mandated due to the changing nature of Israeli media (mainly the availability of news on the Internet that was not in existence in Israel or anywhere else back in 1991).

The original survey sample consisted of 758 Jewish Israeli adults, aged 18 and above, living in the urban parts of the country, which represented about 80% of the population (sampling was difficult in rural peripheral areas). The survey was conducted via landline telephones (mobile telephones were not even available then). The current sample—for lack of sufficient funds—consisted of only 501 respondents, and was also limited to the Jewish population 18 years of age and above, but was representative of all regions of the country. Moreover, in order to take account of the heavy use of mobile phones, 80% of the sample was based on landline phones and 20% on mobile phones.[4]

The same 16 questions appeared in both surveys.[5] The first two questions dealt with interest in domestic and foreign events[6] using 4-point scales ranging from "very interested" to "not interested at all". The next two questions requested respondents to indicate separately their main source of news about domestic and foreign news. Possible responses in the 1991 survey were: Israeli Radio; Israeli Television; newspapers; foreign television; foreign news magazines; and "other". These two questions were modified in the second survey due to the availability of the Internet. The new possible responses were: radio news; (Israeli) TV news; newspapers; foreign TV news; foreign news magazines, Israeli news web sites; foreign news web sites; social networks; and "other".

Two question asked respondents to indicate the frequency in which they watch television news (every evening; almost every evening; several times each week; hardly ever; never). This was followed by a question determining the extent to which the respondents watched a special weekly television program dedicated to foreign news (on a regular basis; sometimes; rarely; never).[7]

The next question was "What percentage of the nightly news *is* devoted to foreign news?" that was followed by "What percentage of the nightly news *should be* devoted to foreign news?" The response categories for both questions were: the entire newscast; about 75%; about 50%; about 25%; less than 25%; none.

The second half of the questionnaire dealt with the perceived functions of foreign news. Four questions presented statements to which the respondents were asked to indicate on 4-point scales the extent to which they agree or disagree. Each statement began with "Television broadcasts foreign news in order to..." and the functions were: inform the Israeli public of events happening abroad; create public opinion on Israel's foreign policy; show us that others also have problems; enable us to identify with the fate of other nations.

The last four questions also dealt with functions in a different manner, by relating them to a form of ethnocentrism. Respondents were asked to indicate their agreement on the same 4-point scales regarding statements that began with "Television *should* broadcast foreign news items ..." with the following four elements: if they are interesting even if they don't deal with Israel; if they deal with Jews living outside of Israel; if they deal with Israelis living outside of Israel; only if they deal with Israel and/or Israelis.

FINDINGS

Given the comparability of the two surveys, the findings are presented side-by-side in two tables. Table 11.1 presents the distributions of the responses to the questions dealing with consumption of and interest in both domestic and foreign news.

Table 11.1: Consumption of and Interest in Domestic and Foreign News

Question	Responses	Wave 1 (1991)	Wave 2 (2015)
In general, how interested are you in events taking place in Israel?	Very interested	59.5	56.8
	Somewhat interested	27.6	27.0
	Little interested	11.4	12.1
	Not at all interested	1.5	4.1
In general, how interested are you in events taking place in abroad?	Very interested	13.7	22.3
	Somewhat interested	35.9	30.3
	Little interested	45.1	31.8
	Not at all interested	5.3	15.6

Question	Responses	Wave 1 (1991)	Wave 2 (2015)
What is your main source of information on events taking place in Israel?	Israeli Radio / Radio news	22.5	10.8
	Israeli TV / TV News	26.9	40.2
	Newspapers	48.3	10.7
	Foreign television	0.9	*
	Foreign news magazines	0.6	*
	Other	0.8	*
	Israeli news portals	*	34.5
	Foreign news portals	*	1.4
	Social networks	*	2.5
What is your main source of information on events taking place abroad?	Israeli Radio	18.5	7.2
	Israeli Television	32.3	35.8
	Newspapers	44.8	10.8
	Foreign television	0.5	2.7
	Foreign news magazines	1.6	*
	Other	2.3	*
	Israeli news portals	*	32.4
	Foreign news portals	*	7.0
	Social networks	*	4.1
How often do you watch TV news?	Every evening	51.1	32.5
	Almost every evening	31.0	20.9
	Several times each week	9.6	17.0
	Hardly ever	4.6	12.8
	Never	3.7	16.8
How often do you watch the special weekly foreign news program?	On a regular basis	37.1	9.6
	Sometimes	35.9	29.8
	Rarely	9.3	15.7
	Never	17.7	44.9
What percentage of the nightly news *is* devoted to foreign news?	The entire newscast	0.4	2.9
	About 75%	5.8	4.8
	About 50%	25.4	19.4
	About 25%	49.2	39.2
	Less than 25%	18.6	31.3
	None	0.6	2.3
What percentage of the nightly news *should be* devoted to foreign news?	The entire newscast	0.0	3.5
	About 75%	4.7	3.9
	About 50%	29.6	28.5
	About 25%	51.0	36.1
	Less than 25%	13.8	21.6
	None	0.9	6.5

The interest expressed by the respondents in events taking place in Israel was remarkably similar in both waves, with nearly 60% expressing much interest (M_1=3.45 and M_2=3.37). As for interest in events taking place outside of Israel, that is, in foreign news, the mean scores for the two waves were also virtually identical

(M_1=2.58 and M_2=2.60) but there were some fluctuations in the high and low ends of the scales—a higher percentage of "very interested" as well as "not at all interested" in Wave 2 and lower percentages in the middle categories.

As for the main sources of information regarding domestic and foreign events, there were significant changes over time. While newspapers were claimed to be the main source for both domestic and foreign news in Wave 1 (48.3% and 44.8%, respectively), there was a sharp decline in Wave 2 down to nearly 11% for both types of news. Television, on the other hand, increased from 26.9% in Wave 1 to 40.2% in Wave 2 for domestic news and only slightly for foreign news (from 32.3% to 35.8%). While web sites were not an option in Wave 1 back in 1991, in Wave 2 Israeli web sites were mentioned by about one third of the sample: 34.5% regarding domestic news and 32.4% for foreign news. In addition, only 1.4% mentioned foreign web sites as their primary source of information on domestic events compared with 7.0% who mentioned foreign web sites regarding foreign news. Thus, taken together, nearly 40% mentioned web sites as their main source for foreign news.

At the same time, total viewing of television news declined dramatically between the two waves (M_1=4.21 to M_2=2.25). A Chi Square test between the two waves[8] was highly significant: χ^2=131.35; df = 4; $p < .001$. A similar picture was obtained regarding the special TV programs on foreign news (M_1=3.01 vs. M_2= 2.20 with χ^2=178.99; df = 3; $p < .001$).

The two questions dealing with the perceived actual and desired amount of foreign news in the newscasts also reveal some changes from Wave 1 to Wave 2. In both waves and for both the actual and desired portion of the newscasts devoted to foreign news, the modal response was "about 25%" of the newscasts. Moreover, in the first wave 14.7% said that the newscasts *should* devote less than 25% or none to foreign news, whereas in Wave 2 the comparable figure nearly doubled to 28.1% (χ^2=78.44; df = 5; $p < .001$).

Table 11.2: Perceived Functions of Foreign News

Question	Responses	Wave 1 (1991)	Wave 2 (2015)
Television broadcasts foreign news in order to inform the Israeli public of events happening abroad	Agree strongly	64	50
	Agree somewhat	29	37
	Disagree somewhat	5	9
	Totally disagree	2	4
Television broadcasts foreign news in order to create public opinion on Israel's foreign policy	Agree strongly	31	21
	Agree somewhat	35	30
	Disagree somewhat	18	30
	Totally disagree	16	19

Question	Responses	Wave 1 (1991)	Wave 2 (2015)
Television broadcasts foreign news in order to show us that others also have problems	Agree strongly	30	21
	Agree somewhat	24	26
	Disagree somewhat	20	26
	Totally disagree	26	27
Television broadcasts foreign news in order to enable us to identify with the fate of other nations	Agree strongly	16	15
	Agree somewhat	24	26
	Disagree somewhat	27	32
	Totally disagree	33	27
Television should broadcast foreign news items if they are interesting, even if they don't deal with Israel	Agree strongly	62	59
	Agree somewhat	26	25
	Disagree somewhat	8	9
	Totally disagree	4	7
Television should broadcast foreign news items if they deal with Jews living outside of Israel	Agree strongly	40	57
	Agree somewhat	27	24
	Disagree somewhat	18	10
	Totally disagree	15	9
Television should broadcast foreign news items if they deal with Israelis living outside of Israel	Agree strongly	34	48
	Agree somewhat	30	28
	Disagree somewhat	24	14
	Totally disagree	12	10
Television should broadcast foreign news items only if they deal with Israel and/or Israelis	Agree strongly	11	14
	Agree somewhat	13	12
	Disagree somewhat	25	18
	Totally disagree	51	56

The responses to the first four questions in Table 11.2 refer to perceived general functions of foreign news. The overall pattern found in the 1991 survey regarding the ranking of the four functions was repeated in the current survey. However, there was a significant decline in agreement from Wave 1 to Wave 2 for all functions except for the identification with the fate of others. The function most agreed with was that television news broadcasts foreign news "in order to inform the public about events happening abroad" (M_1=3.55 and M_2=3.33; χ^2=27.41; *df* = 3; $p < .001$) followed by "in order to create public opinion about Israel's foreign policy" (M_1=2.81 and M_2=2.53; χ^2=34.28; *df* = 3; $p < .001$), "in order to show us that others also have problems" (M_1=2.58 and M_2=2.41; χ^2=14.49; *df* = 3; $p < .01$), and finally, "in order to enable us to identify with the fate of other nations" (M_1=2.23 and M_2=2.29; χ^2=6.73; *df* = 3; *n.s.*).

The final responses in Table 11.2 refer to possible perceived ethnocentric factors as a function for TV reporting on foreign news. As with the previous four questions, the overall ranking pattern found in 1991 was repeated in 2015. However, the picture obtained regarding the differences between the two waves was quite different. The responses regarding whether or not the news should report on foreign events if they are interesting even though not related to Israel was highest in both waves (M_1=3.54 and M_2=3.36) while the difference between the two waves was not significant. Also not significant were the responses between the two waves concerning the obligation to broadcast foreign news items only if they deal with Israel or Israelis (both mean scores were 1.84). The patterns of responses to the other two questions were in the opposite direction, that is, greater agreement in Wave 2 compared with Wave 1. There was a higher expectation that TV news would report on foreign news that deals with Jews living outside Israel in Wave 2 (M_1=2.92; M_2=3.29; χ^2=41.71; df = 3; $p < .001$). Similarly, respondents in Wave 2 were more in agreement that the news should report foreign items dealing with Israelis living outside Israel (M_1=2.86; M_2=3.13; χ^2=31.38; df = 3; $p < .001$).

DISCUSSION

Israelis have traditionally been heavy news consumers, a fact that comes as no surprise given the tumults in the country that produce not only domestic news but also significant news that is reported around the world. As the expression goes, there is never a dull moment in Israel.

The quarter-century follow-up reveals several interesting points. The fact that Israelis are keenly interested in domestic events and issues—with 87% in Wave 1 and 84% in Wave 2 expressing much or quite a bit of interest—needs no explanation. It is also not surprising that interest in foreign news is significantly less, with only roughly 50% expressing much or quite a bit of interest. The increased polarity found in this respect in Wave 2 may be due to a more realistic worldview by some Israelis of their country's place in the global context and hence the need to follow world events, versus frustration and even desperation with the situation by others. What seems to be more striking, however, is the very significant decline in television news viewing in general—from a "whopping" 82.1% who watched the news nightly or almost every night back in 1991 to only 53.4% currently, which is still a high figure in a global perspective—but also a sharp decline in viewing the special programs devoted to foreign news (from 37.1% who used to watch it on a regular basis to only 9.6% today). In sum, the conclusive overall trend seems to be a declining interest in foreign news by Israelis, a finding that is corroborated with the Hanitzsch et al. (2013) study in which Israelis were ranked lowest among the 13 countries recently surveyed.

As for the perceived functions for broadcasting foreign news, here, too, there were significant declines in agreement from Wave 1 to Wave 2. The notion of informing about events abroad, which might be considered as a manifest function of foreign news, declined only slightly among those agreeing (from 93% to 87%).

In addition, two of the other three functions which may be considered as latent, also declined—creating public opinion about Israel's foreign policy and showing that others also have problems—and only one—identifying with the fate of other nations—remained the same at the lowest level of agreement.

As noted, the final four questions dealt with the extent to which interest in foreign news was related to elements of ethnocentrism, that is, interest in foreign news that relates to Israel, Israelis and Jews living abroad. A universal non-ethnocentric outlook was reflected in both the current wave as well as in the 1991 study as evidenced by the strong agreement with the notion that foreign news should be aired even if it has nothing to do with Israel. However, there were also indications that in Wave 2 there was an increment in the degree of interest in what would often be categorized as hybrid news, specifically relating to events concerning Israelis and Jews living abroad.[9]

While it is impossible to draw causal conclusions, these findings could possibly be explained by the fact that during the past quarter century the number of Israeli expatriates has grown significantly, thus their relatives who reside in Israel are interested in what happens with those living abroad. This factor may be compounded with regard to Jews living outside of Israel. In recent years, as noted earlier, Israel's geopolitical situation has deteriorated which may have prompted the recent rising of anti-Semitic incidents, mostly in some European countries but also from time to time in the United States. This may bring to mind the notion expressed by Jews over the centuries that all Jews are responsible for one another.

Given the changes that have taken place in Israel in terms of the availability of foreign news, thanks to its expanded cosmopolitan media ecology, and given the changes in the country's geopolitical circumstances, it was expected that interest in foreign news would have increased compared with the situation a quarter century ago. As the current data indicate, however, this did not seem to happen. And yet, along with the general decline, there was an increment in the perception that television news should broadcast foreign news items if they deal with Israelis and Jews living outside of the country. In other words, stories about the big wide world seem to be less relevant to Israelis but stories about their compatriots, wherever they may be, are definitely of interest to them.

This seeming ethnocentric worldview is reminiscent of a line in the biblical tale in which Balak, the King of Moab, orders Balaam, the diviner, to curse the Israelites, but at the will of God end up blessing them: "For from the top of the rocks I see him, and from the hills I behold him: lo, the people shall dwell alone, and shall not be reckoned among the nations" (Numbers, 23:9).

NOTES

1. See https://www.cia.gov/library/publications/the-world-factbook/
2. Just days ago, at the end of December 2016, as these lines are written, the United Nations Security Council, for the first time, passed a controversial resolution, with the US abstaining, demanding Israel to cease its settlement activities in the occupied territories.
3. At the time, there was tension in Israel because it was considered a potential victim and the goal of the major western coalition partners was to see to it that Israel remain on the sidelines and not become involved. Indeed, despite the fact that nearly forty Scud missiles were fired at Israeli targets by Iraq, Israel did not retaliate.
4. The circumstances during the current survey were also strained with a series of attacks by Palestinians against Israeli soldiers and civilians. The survey was initially scheduled for early October but was twice delayed due to the attacks for fear that the heavy news coverage of these domestic events would impact on peoples' interest in foreign news. However, due to the deadline for submitting this chapter, the survey was finally conducted despite the wave of attacks.
5. The first survey also measured perceived criteria of newsworthiness derived from Galtung and Ruge (1965) and formulated as survey questions. These questions did not appear in the second survey.
6. The wording of these questions referred to the events rather than to news about the events in order to avoid potential confusion.
7. The wording of this question in the two surveys contained the names of the specific programs: *Ro'im Olam* [Seeing the World] in Channel 1 (that has been on the air since the late 1980s until the present time) and *Seder Olami* (World Order) that is aired on Channel 2.
8. Chi Square test are presented for some of the analyses in addition to mean scores because they better reflect the nominal distributions of the two waves.
9. While the present study did not deal with the contents of television news in Israel, it should be noted that in the comparative study referred to above (Stępińska, Porath, Mujica, Xu & Cohen, 2013), Israel was ranked fifth among 17 countries in terms of the amount of hybrid news presented in its newscasts.

REFERENCES

Chang, T. K., & Lee, J. W. (1992). Factors affecting gatekeepers' selection of foreign news: A national survey of newspaper editors. *Journalism Quarterly*, *69*(3), 554–561.

Cohen, A. A. (1993). Israelis and foreign news: Perceptions of interest, functions and newsworthiness. *Journal of Broadcasting and Electronic Media*, *37*(3), 337–347.

Cohen, A. A. (Ed.). (2013). *Foreign news on television: Where in the world is the global village?* New York, NY: Peter Lang.

Cohen, A. A., Levy, M. R., Roeh, I., & Gurevitch, M. (1996). *Global newsroom, local audiences: A study of the Eurovision News Exchange*. London: John Libbey.

Galtung, J., & Ruge, M. H. (1965). The structure of foreign news: The presentation of the Congo, Cuba and Cyprus crises in four Norwegian newspapers. *Journal of Peace Research*, *2*(1), 64–90.

Hanitzsch, T., Goodrum, A., Quandt, T., & von Pape, T. (2013). Interest in foreign news. In A. A. Cohen (Ed.), *Foreign news on television: Where in the world is the global village?* (pp. 171–190). New York, NY: Peter Lang.

Harcup, T. (2001). What is News? Galtung and Ruge revisited. *Journalism Studies*, *2*(2), 261–280.
Hargrove, T., & Stempel, G. H. (2002). Exploring reader interest in international news. *Newspaper Research Journal*, *23*(4), 46–51.
Pew Research Center. (2002). Interest in foreign news declines. Retrieved December 30, 2015 from https://www.google.co.il/webhp?sourceid=chrome-nstant&ion=1&espv=2&ie=UTF-8#q=interest%20in%20foreign%20news%20declines
Sambrook, R., Terrington, S., & Levy, D. A. L. (2013). The public appetite for foreign newson TV and online. *Reuters Institute for the Study of Journalism.* Retrieved December 31, 2016 from https://www.google.co.il/webhp?sourceid=chrome-instant&ion=1&espv=2&ie=UTF-8#q=the+public+appetite+for+foreign+news+on+TV+and
Sande, O. (1971). The perception of foreign news. *Journal of Peace Research*, *8*(3/4), 221–237.
Segev, E., & Blondheim, M. (2013). Online news about Israel and Palestine: A cross-national comparison of prominence and trends. *Digital Journalism*, *1*(3), 386–398.
Shoemaker, P. J. (1991). *Gatekeeping*. Newbury Park, CA: Sage.
Shoemaker, P. J., & Cohen, A. A. (2006). *News around the world: Content, practitioners and the public.* New York, NY: Routledge.
Shoemaker, P. J., & Vos, T. P. (2009). *Gatekeeping theory*. New York, NY: Routledge.
Sparkes, V. M., & Winter, J. P. (1980). Public interest in foreign news. *Gazette*, *26*(3), 149–170.
Stępińska, A., Porath, W., Mujica, C., Xu, X., & Cohen, A. A. (2013). The prevalence of news: Domestic, foreign and hybrid. In A. A. Cohen (Ed.), *Foreign news on television: Where in the world is the global village?* (pp. 23–38). New York, NY: Peter Lang.

CHAPTER TWELVE

Network Analyses of Attention to Deviance and Social Significance Based on Gene and Culture Co-Evolution Theory

JONG HYUK LEE* AND YUN JUNG CHOI†

INTRODUCTION

Throughout the day, people are exposed to numerous news events through multiple media channels, and some of these events attract more attention than others. Although people encounter a vast amount of news, they only read a fraction of it. In such an environment, the question arises as to what determines people's attention to news events.

Studies on news values comprise the research area that is most relevant to this question. Harcup and O'Neill (2001) revised the research of Galtung and Ruge (1965), and suggested 10 news value indicators including surprise, relevance, bad news, celebrity, etc. Recently, Lee, Gil, Kang, and Choi (2014) found factors that news audiences use to evaluate news story values: social significance, visual novelty, audience relevance, and human interest. This implies that humans tend to pay spe-

* Jong Hyuk Lee is Associate Professor in the Communication & Media Department at Kyung Hee University, Seoul Korea. Email: jonghhhh@khu.ac.kr.

† Yun Jung Choi is Associate Professor in the Communication and Media Division at Ewha Womans University, Seoul Korea. Email: yunchoi@ewha.ac.kr.

cial attention to news events with those factors, but most news value studies have not clarified the question of why human beings come to pay attention to them.

Shoemaker's (1996) explication from the perspective of evolution is the most comprehensive theoretical discussion addressing this area. Shoemaker (1996) states that human beings are structured to pay special attention to deviance and social significance, and attention to deviance is explained under evolutionary psychology whereas attention to social significance is explained under cultural evolution theory. Shoemaker (1996) mentions the possibility of an interaction between attention to deviance and attention to social significance as follows: "An interest in news is probably the result of an interaction between these two pure models, with humans both innately interested in deviant events and socialized to attend to events that have some significance to their particular culture and society" (Shoemaker, 1996, p. 44).

Despite comprising a well-formulated conceptualization, Shoemaker's theory has not been expanded further nor empirically tested, and further applications are needed for evolution research on deviance and social significance. Shoemaker's conclusive hypothesis on the interaction between the two factors has not been tested through an empirical analysis. In 2006, Shoemaker and Cohen empirically showed that deviance and social significance for an event affect its prominence through a content analysis of 10 countries' media reports. However, the interaction between the two factors was not tested. Shoemaker and Cohen (2006) also suggested a new measure of complexity. Seven variables of deviance and social significance were dummy-coded (0=weak / 1=strong), with complexity referring to the number of variables out of seven that turned out to be strong. This complexity can explain the prominence of news events as well as the intensity of each variable. With this result, Shoemaker and Cohen (2006) indicate the need to approach integrative relationships between deviance and social significance rather than the individual effects of each factor.

This study aims to develop Shoemaker's (1996) idea in two ways. The first is by theoretically enriching the theories on deviance and social significance by introducing evolution theory further, including gene-culture co-evolution. Accordingly, the focus of this study is on the fundamental mechanisms that make human beings pay more attention to deviant and socially significant news events, rather than on their roles as news value indicators. Second, this study empirically examines the interaction between deviance and social significance by conducting network analyses. Network analyses are effective in visualizing and comparing the complex relationships among deviance and social significance indicators among different levels of attention to events.

ATTENTION TO DEVIANCE FROM BIOLOGICAL EVOLUTION PERSPECTIVES

Deviance is a major news value, as proposed by Shoemaker and colleagues (Shoemaker, 1996; Shoemaker, Chang, & Brendlinger, 1987; Shoemaker & Cohen, 2006; Shoemaker, Danielian, & Brendlinger, 1991). In particular, Shoemaker (1996) provides a theoretical account for why human beings pay special attention to deviant events. She uses evolutionary psychology to argue that special attention to deviance has evolved as a superior gene from our primitive ancestors to modern humans. In the Stone Age, human beings faced deviant events that threatened their lives, such as wild animals, fire, and the intrusion of other tribes. There was variation in the degree of attention to deviant events, and some human minds were equipped with a strong inclination to attend to deviant events while others had not developed it. As a result, deviant and threatening events killed those with little attention to deviance but spared those with greater attention to it. Through this process of natural selection, human beings with an inclination to attend to deviant events produced offspring from generation to generation. The psychological gene of attention to deviance continued to be passed down generationally, and human beings at present have inherited the instinct to pay attention to deviant events, which means that paying special attention to them occurs almost naturally with the help of genes rather than deliberate mental processes. Thus, this psychological process explains why people pay more attention to negative news than good news.

This explanation of deviance is mostly based on Charles Darwin's (1860/1936, 1871/1936) traditional theory of evolution, which states that within a species, multiple variations in the characteristics of individuals show up. Then, the variations compete for survival and reproduction through the natural selection process. A certain variation that fits the environment survives and is reproduced, and this variation in the form of genes is successfully transmitted to following generations. The variation here implies a trait of appearance or behavior of individuals.

Attention to deviance is a psychological mechanism, not a physical trait, consistent with the main focus of evolutionary psychology. Laland and Brown (2011) suggest that evolutionary psychology has three important concepts: Evolved Psychological Mechanism (EPM), Environment of Evolutionary Adaptedness (EEA), and Domain-Specific Mental Modules. First, EPM is an information-processing circuit in our brains. It includes context-specific emotions, preferences, and proclivities (Buss, 2009). Cosmides and Tooby (1987) argue that "natural selection cannot select for behavior per se; it can also select for mechanisms that produce behaviors" (p. 281). All humans have certain EPMs, but express them through various behaviors. For instance, fear of snakes is an EPM. Early mammals, including our ancestors, lived in an environment dominated by reptiles, which could have killed other living things. Human beings fearing reptiles had greater chance of survival than those who did not. Thus, this EPM has been successfully passed down to descendants. Now, fear of snakes, formerly an EPM of our ancestors, has become a universal instinct for all humans. However, the behaviors provoked by the fear vary from person to person.

Second, EEA is the environment in which our ancestors developed a certain EPM. According to Bowlby (1969), the tendency for young children to show a strong attachment to their mothers and feel distressed when they are separated from them is an EPM that evolved in a certain EEA in the past. Our ancestors were more likely to survive under the good care of their mothers than without it. This kind of EEA living condition is not necessarily true today. However, the psychological inclination to be attached to the mother is still present.

Third, each EPM has evolved as a domain-specific mental module. We have many EPMs, each of which operates in a specific area such as language, mate choice, parenting, friendship, disease avoidance, and social exchange. Humans, when they are faced with a certain-domain problem, call up the domain-relevant EPM and make appropriate judgments (Cosmides & Tooby, 1987). The human mind is often analogous to a "Swiss army knife", and each EPM is analogous to a single blade (Laland & Brown, 2011).

According to Shoemaker and Cohen (2006), deviance may be observed in news events that do not occur frequently, bring social changes, or violate norms. Since the Stone Age, humans were required to compete with one another to survive in a tough environment and learned to pay special attention to deviant events, and this special attention to deviance can be observed in human behavior today.

We come across a vast amount of news stories through news media, SNS, and the Internet. Among these news stories, we are especially attracted to deviant stories depicting violence, sex, war, protest, and disaster. Journalists are also interested in such stories, thus indicating that the EPM of special attention to deviance is still present for human beings today.

Now we can use evolutionary psychology to explain why journalists and audiences pay special attention to deviant news. Attention to deviance is a natural psychological mechanism that has been inherited from our ancestors from the Stone Age. It is a universal instinct for all humans.

ATTENTION TO SOCIAL SIGNIFICANCE FROM CULTURAL EVOLUTION

Social significance is another news value indicator proposed by Shoemaker and colleagues (Shoemaker, 1996; Shoemaker & Cohen, 2006). Shoemaker (1996) argues that attention to deviance has evolved biologically and that attention to social significance has evolved culturally. This raises the question as to whether culture can evolve and whether it has a replicator, such as a gene.

According to Laland and Brown (2011), cultural evolution was first developed as a theory of memes. This term, coined by Dawkins (1976), is defined as the unit of a replicator of culture (cultural gene). Each cultural aspect, such as fashion, diets, language, art, and technology, has been replicated by the transmission of a meme through competition. For instance, a new fashion design emerges in the market of retail clothes and competes for consumers' purchase. If this fashion, as a meme, appeals to a large number of people, this fashion-meme successfully evolves.

Scholars of cultural evolution argue that culture can be explained in terms of variation, competition, and inheritance, as with biological evolution (Boyd & Richerson, 1985; Cavalli-Sforza & Feldman 1981; Mesoudi, Whiten, & Laland, 2004). First, culture is extremely diverse. For example, Native American Indians exhibit 3,000 to 6,000 different culture elements, including pottery, bows, and shamanism, and U.S. patents for knowledge, technologies, and artifacts amount to 7.7 million since 1790 (Laland & Brown, 2011). Second, cultural competition is commonly observed. About 6,800 languages are spoken (Grimes, 2001), and more than 10,000 religious beliefs in the world have followers (Barrett, Kurian, & Johnson, 2001). Competition in cultural evolution is not a life-or-death struggle. Rather, it is a competition for limited slots as solutions to specific problems.

Third, cultural inheritance takes various forms. It can occur vertically (from parents to offspring), obliquely (from older to younger), or horizontally (within-generation transmission). Finally, cultural selection, similarly to natural selection in biological evolution, is defined as a process by which the frequency of a certain culture in society increases or decreases as a result of society members' adoption rates (Cavalli-Sforza & Feldman, 1981).

Then, how can the selection of social significance be explained in terms of cultural evolution? According to Shoemaker and Cohen (2006), social significance is perceived as something that is important politically, economically, culturally, and publicly. For instance, a presidential election, a change in interest rates, an international film festival, or a development of a new vaccine can have social significance if most members within a society agree that those events are important. The socialization process enables society members to distinguish between events with a high social significance and events with a low social significance. Human beings situated within a society learn what knowledge, norms, beliefs, and values are necessary and important for their society, and this learning is carried out through socialization, including conversations, experiences, social modeling, and systematic education. Based on this social process, each individual figures out the kinds of cultural events or artifacts that are important and selectively learns them. For instance, an election is a cultural event with several variations, including presidential elections, governor elections, county supervisor elections, town meeting member elections, elementary school secretary elections. These various elections compete for the society members' limited cognitive resources, and certain elections are finally chosen to have more attention, better memory, and higher evaluation. Based on this socialization, society members have come to agree that the presidential election is the most important election, and it receives more attention than any other election. This process can be regarded as cultural selection.

As previously discussed, attention to social significance arises from cultural evolution, and many variations in cultural events or artifacts compete to be selected to receive the public's attention. Once socially significant events or artifacts are chosen, they are spread out to all other members and younger generations through social systems and education.

ATTENTION TO DEVIANCE AND SOCIAL SIGNIFICANCE FROM GENE-CULTURE CO-EVOLUTION

Evolutionary psychologists have argued that genes and the environment strongly influence personality and behavior. In contrast, cultural evolutionists insist that the culture of a society better explains human psychology and behavior. However, it is likely that both genes and culture influence human behavior and psychology, and some studies have analyzed the interaction of genetic evolution and cultural evolution, with gene-culture co-evolution (Feldman & Cavalli-Sforza, 1989) or dual-heritance theory (Boyd & Richerson, 1985) as some examples (Laland &Brown). Lumsden and Wilson (1981) defined gene-culture co-evolution as "a complicated, fascinating interaction in which culture is generated and shaped by biological imperatives while biological traits are simultaneously altered by genetic evolution in response to cultural innovation" (p. 1). According to the authors, culture is created by biological necessity, and genetic change is made in response to cultural changes.

Gene and culture interfere with each other in the following way: First, the evolved gene helps humans adapt to a particular culture or information through selective action. Then, this selected culture or information is more likely to be adopted by most individuals in the society through social learning and adaptation. Next, those individuals who share culture and information are likely to undergo genetic changes adjusting to cultural changes. In short, genetic evolution affects cultural evolution, and cultural evolution leads to genetic evolution.

The co-evolution of the lactase gene and the dairy industry might serve as a good example (Feldman & Cavalli-Sforza, 1989). Most children do not have a problem drinking milk, but many adults cannot digest it because the lactase-decomposing enzyme is less activated in adults. This slight difference in the genetic code of the lactase gene is supposed to determine the digestibility, and more than 90% of people who live in a country with a developed diary industry digest lactose, whereas this proportion is no more than 20% in the group who live in areas where the dairy industry is not developed. Feldman and Cavalli-Sforza (1989) have verified that the frequency of milk digestion-related genes in adults depends on the probability that children drink milk. If this probability is high, the frequency of milk digestion-related genes increases significantly within 300 generations, which suggests that cultural evolution induces genetic evolution.

Studies on pro-social behavior also show the effects of mutual influence of genes and culture, and this topic raises the question of why animals or humans, who naturally have the tendency to deliver their genes to future generations, participate in public works for the common good of their society. According to Wynne-Edwards (1962), some individuals in groups of animals faced with a crisis of extinction from food shortages do not copulate or commit suicide to maintain the survival of their group. This happens because those animals judge that survival of their group at the expense of their individual gene extinction is better than the annihilation of the entire group. However, Boyd and Richerson (1982, 1985) argue that pro-social behavior should be explained in terms of cultural evolution rather than genetic evolution. A target of selection is a cultural behavior or artifact that passes through learning, not the gene. Suppose that a group chooses certain cultural behaviors of establishing barricades in preparation for war. Participating in this work is a pro-social behavior that requires each individual to forget selfish calculations, and in war, this group will receive less damage than the other groups. As a result, the group would succeed in preserving their population, and the act of building barricades would spread to other groups. Eventually, this pro-social behavior evolves through cultural selection, not by natural selection.

In light of discussing cultural and genetic evolution, let us try to explain why humans are interested in particular events or information. Human beings are supposed to pay special attention to deviant events and socially significant events, and the mechanisms for these two behaviors can be respectively explained in terms of genetic evolution and cultural evolution.

We now focus on the interaction between the attention to deviance and social significance from a perspective of gene-culture co-evolution. For example, gun violence receives a considerable amount of attention in American society. As discussed earlier, humans have evolved a psychological gene since the Stone Age directing special attention to deviance in order to avoid events that might threaten their breeding and genetic inheritance. This genetic apparatus explains people's immediate interest in gun violence. At the same time, American society has engaged in long historical discussions on gun control, and as such, gun violence has become a significant issue for society. Policy makers ignited the discussion of gun violence, and the importance of this issue has spread through institutional learning and various communication channels, making it a process of cultural selection and evolution. Thus, the special attention that the American public place on gun violence could be explained by a psychological gene and cultural selection. In this sense, this study uses gene-culture co-evolution theory to analyze the interaction of attention to deviance and attention to social significance.

Shoemaker and Cohen (2006) analyzed the interaction of deviance and social significance of an event through content analyses of news stories. The authors argued that journalists also pay particular attention to deviance and social significance when they determine the newsworthiness of events. This study goes one step further and applies the theory of gene-culture co-evolution to explore how the interaction between deviance and social significance of an event influences the degree of attention to it. We methodologically employ a network analysis and show the degree of co-appearance of deviance and social significance of an event. Then, we compare how networks of deviance and social significance differ for news events with different levels of attention. Therefore, we present the following research questions.

RQ 1: How does the relationship between deviance and social significance of an event show up in the network analysis?

RQ 2: How does the network of deviance and social significance of an event influence the extent to which a news event gets attention?

METHOD

To answer the proposed research questions, this study conducted a survey with 500 Korean participants. They were asked to read a news story on a fictitious event, to answer how much attention they paid to it, and how deviant and socially significant they thought it was.

First, we created 15 fictitious news stories, and each story described different news events. The events were designed to have a large variation in the extent to which they draw attention. Then, six journalists were asked to rank the 15 stories according to their judgment of the audience's attention levels to the news. The journalists who participated in this study included three newspaper staff-writers, two broadcast news reporters, and one weekly news magazine writer. Considering their evaluations, this study selected 10 stories with variations in attentive levels. Table 12.1 shows the headlines of the selected stories and attention rankings made by the journalists (A–F).

Next, this study recruited 500 survey participants using a quota sampling technique from panels of a Korean research firm. The participant's gender age ratios were similar to those of South Korea's population. Demographically, the number of male participants was 259 (51.8%) and that of female participants were 241 (48.2%). In terms of age, the proportion of respondents in their 20s was 29.6%, 30's was 34.2%, 40's-and-over was 36.2%. Education statistics showed that the majority of participants were college graduates (59.2%), and the others were high school graduates or lower (20.0%), college attendees (11.6%), and those with masters' or doctoral degrees (9.2%).

This study divided the 500 participants randomly to 10 groups of 50 and asked each group to read one of the 10 news stories. Then, the participants answered how much attention they paid to a given story on a scale of 1 to 10. The participants also assessed the degree of deviance and social significance of the story on a Likert-type scale of 1 to 5. Specifically, this assessment included seven statements that measured three types of deviance and four types of social significance (see Shoemaker & Cohen, 2006). The statements read as follows:

"The event in this story occurs rarely" (statistical deviance);
"... results in a change in society" (social change deviance);
"... violates social norms and ethics" (normative deviance);
"... is politically important" (political significance);
"... is economically important" (economic significance);
"... is culturally important" (cultural significance); and,
"... is important for the public" (public significance).

Table 12.2 shows the distribution of 500 participants according to their attention levels to the story. Most participants chose scores of 3 to 8. Nobody gave 10, and only 3.4% gave 1. Thus, this study used 8 groups of news stories with different attention levels ranging from level 2 to level 9. Table 12.3 shows the mean and standard deviation of the 7 types of deviance and social significance that participants rated for their story events. These scores were transformed into 0/1 dummy scores for network analyses. The scores of 1 to 3 were transformed into 0 while the scores of 4 and 5 were recoded into 1. In network analyses, a non-valued network with 0/1 links is easier to interpret than a valued network with links of continuous figures. In this study, it is important to examine the cases of both high deviance and high social significance rather than cases with numerical levels of deviance and social significance.

Table 12.1: News Story Headlines and Journalists' Evaluation

Story ID	Story headline	A	B	C	D	E	F	Mean
1	"FTA opposition" violent farmers protests / Throw stones at the police	15	9	15	15	15	13	13.67
2	Congress laid electoral amendments / Quarrel... brawl..."chaos"	14	12	14	12	14	8	12.33
3	Cancer-causing peppers distributed nationwide	11	8	12	14	6	15	11.00
4	Mr. Hongju Koh as new Yale law dean in US	6	14	5	8	10	6	8.17
5	Series of murders in China / 100 people sacrificed in a week	8	13	4	4	7	11	7.83
6	St. Petersburg hosts the world's summit meeting	5	7	3	6	12	9	7.00

Story ID	Story headline	A	B	C	D	E	F	Mean
7	CCTV parking control in January next year	10	6	10	3	2	7	6.33
8	Nude performance as a new fashion in theaters	2	5	8	10	8	4	6.17
9	Enjoy movie without advertisement	4	3	2	1	5	3	3.00
10	World record in living with centipede	3	1	1	5	4	1	2.50

Table 12.2: Distribution of Groups with Different Attention to News Story

Attention score	Number of respondents	Distribution (%)
1	17	3.4
2	28	5.6
3	59	11.8
4	46	9.2
5	107	21.4
6	53	1.6
7	100	2.0
8	57	11.4
9	33	6.6
10	0	.0
total	500	10.0

Table 12.3: Means and Standard Deviations of Deviance and Social Significance

	Mean	SD
Statistical deviance	3.25	.82
Social change deviance	3.95	.75
Normative deviance	3.92	.74
Political significance	3.78	.90
Economic significance	3.93	.87
Cultural significance	3.64	.84
Public significance	3.88	.88

Based on these data, this study carried out network analyses as follows. First, we analyzed data including 500 participants' ratings on 7 variables of deviance and social significance using a two-mode 500 × 7 matrix. Then, we transformed it to a one-mode 7 × 7 matrix by summing the cross-products to show the relationships between each of the seven deviance and social significance variables. The value in each cell indicates the degree of co-appearance between two corresponding variables. For example, if the cell between statistical deviance and political significance shows 200, this indicates that 200 participants out of 500 gave high ratings for both variables. Next, we divided all values in all cells by 500 to control the effect of the sample size. The values in the cells indicated the average co-appearance of two variables.

This study thus produced a network of seven variables of deviance and social significance with measures of network density and centrality. Then, this study showed 8 networks for 8 groups of different attention levels and compared the network measures among groups.

RESULTS

To answer the first research question, this study employed network analyses to evaluate the relationships among the seven kinds of deviance and social significance variables. We derived a network of seven variables from 500 participants (see Table 12.4 and Figure 12.1). Here, the nodes indicate seven variables, and the thickness of the link between them illustrates the extent to which two variables are strongly related. In other words, strong relationships (thick links) imply that the two variables frequently co-appear.

Table 12.4: Network Matrix and Centrality Measures of Seven Deviance and Social Significance Nodes for All Participants

	stat_dev	**change_dev**	**norm_dev**	**poli_sig**	**econ_sig**	**cult_sig**	**pub_sig**
stat_dev	.42	.34	.35	.30	.32	.29	.32
change_dev	.34	.77	.64	.56	.61	.51	.61
norm_dev	.35	.64	.76	.54	.58	.50	.59
poli_sig	.30	.56	.54	.66	.60	.49	.57
econ_sig	.32	.61	.58	.60	.72	.53	.62
cult_sig	.29	.51	.50	.49	.53	.60	.52
pub_sig	.32	.61	.59	.57	.62	.52	.71
normalized degree centrality	.32	.55	.54	.51	.54	.48	.54

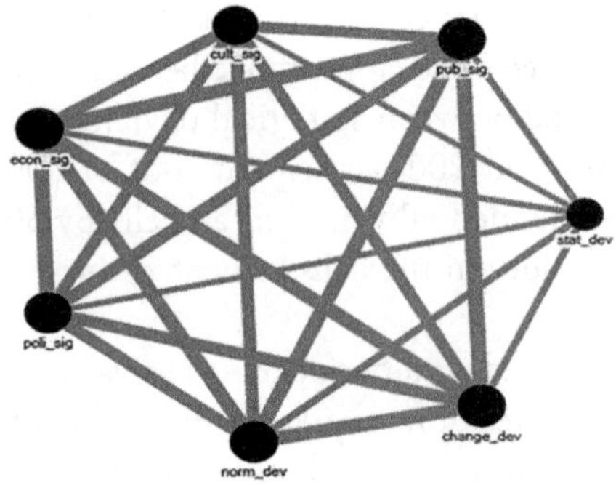

Figure 12.1: Networks of Seven Variables of Deviance and Social Significance

In the networks matrix (see Figure 12.1) the numbers in the cell between two different nodes range from .29 to .64. These numbers indicate the percentage of participants who reported high deviance and high social significance. For example, the connection between normative deviance and cultural significance was .50. That is, 250 out of 500 participants highly rated both variables. The size of the nodes in Figure 12.1 refers to the normalized degree centrality of each variable. The degree of centrality of a node is calculated as the extent to which the node is connected to all other nodes. For example, the degree centrality of statistical deviance is the sum of its connections to the other six nodes, which comes to 1.92 (.34 + .35 + .30 + .32 + .29 + .32), and the mean of the degree centrality is determined as the normalized degree centrality. In this way, the degree centrality of the statistical deviance comes to .32 (1.92 / 6). In other words, the normalized degree centrality indicates the average degree of a node associated with all other nodes. The bottom line of Table 12.4 shows the normalized degree centrality of the seven nodes.

Taken together, we can see the relationships between the seven variables. In terms of the strength of the connection (link thickness), social change deviance and normative deviance show the highest level of connection (.64) whereas statistical deviance and cultural significance show the lowest level of connection (.29). We observed a high level of connections (.61) between deviance and social significance, such as social change deviance and public significance, and social change deviance and economic significance. Looking at node centrality (node size), six variables showed a decent level of .48–.55 whereas statistical deviance showed a relatively low score of .32. In short, seven deviance and social significance variables were significantly inter-related, and statistical deviance showed a somewhat weak relationship. This implies that a significant percentage of participants assessed the event in a news story they read as having both high deviance and high social significance.

Research Question 2 asked how different relationships of deviance and social significance are shown among the eight groups with different attention levels. This study conducted network analyses in the same way for the eight groups, with attention levels ranging from level 1 to level 9. Figure 12.2 shows the respective group-specific networks.

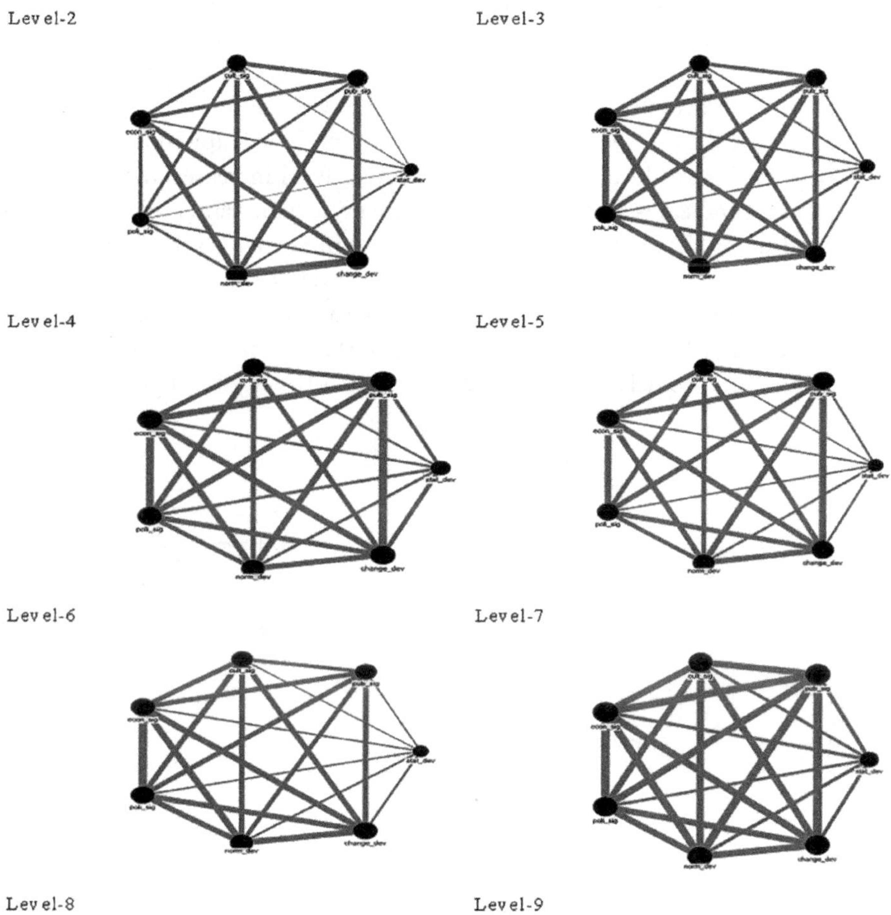

Figure 12.2: Networks of Eight Groups of Different Attention Levels

Let's first look at the degree of connection between nodes for each group. The links between nodes get thicker as the group's attention level increases. The average degree of connection shows .34 for level-2 and .40 and above for level-3 to level-6. It keeps increasing to .55, .64, and .78 for level-7, level-8, and level-9, respectively. This indicates that the co-appearance of two variables of deviance and social significance becomes stronger as the attention level increases. Another observation is that the node size also increases as the attention level increases. That is, the normalized degree centrality of the nodes tends to become larger as the attention level increases from level-2 to level-9. This indicates that a node is more strongly connected to other nodes for the group with a high attention level than for the groups with a low attention level. Taken altogether, these results imply that news events with both high deviance and high social significance levels tend to attract a higher degree of attention.

Finally, we analyzed the density and centralization of each group. The density refers to the overall degree of connection between all nodes in a group, and centralization indicates the extent to which some nodes occupy most connections in a group. As Figure 12.3 shows, as the attention level increases, the density also increases. This indicates that the co-appearance of deviance and social significance is observed more frequently as the attention level increases. On the contrary, centralization turns out to decrease as the attention level goes up. The groups with a high level of attention show a less hierarchical structure in which all variables are evenly connected. Taken together, we can argue that the news events with a high deviance and high social significance tend to attract the most attention.

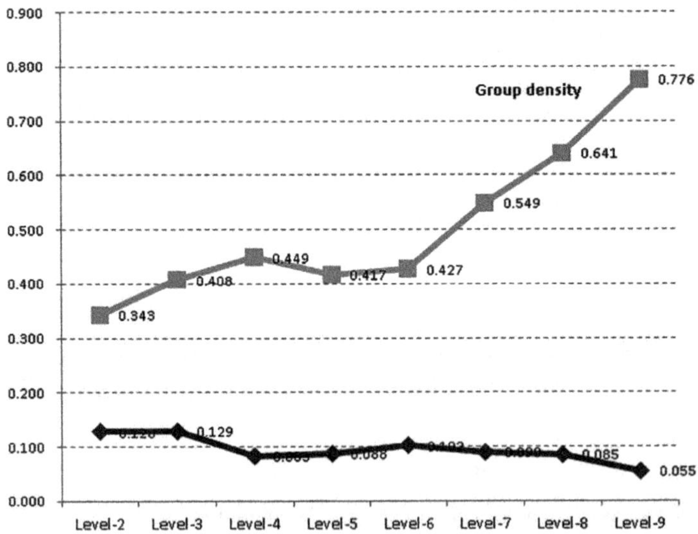

Figure 12.3: Network Density and Centralization of Groups with Different Attention Levels

DISCUSSION

This study suggested that humans pay special attention to news events that are deviant and socially significant. Attention to deviance is a psychological mechanism of genetic evolution, and attention to social significance is a cultural behavior that spreads among members of society through social learning and conformation.

However, a better explanation comes by considering the interaction of deviance and social significance according to the theory of gene-culture co-evolution. This requires us to focus on the relationship between deviance and social significance rather than the respective effects of each factor. In this sense, this study conducted network analyses and empirically provided some strong network relationships between deviance and social significance.

First of all, the network analysis for 500 participants' answers showed that seven variables for deviance and social significance were closely linked to each other. In particular, normative deviance and social change deviance showed a very strong connection with public significance and economic significance. In addition, the normalized degree centrality of each variable turned out to be .32 to .55, which is not a weak figure.

In the network, the connection degree between two variables refers to the extent to which news events are rated as both deviant and socially significant. A figure of .50 indicates that half of all participants rated events as being both deviant and socially significant. This reminds us that the events we learn about in news every day have deviance and social significance as attributes. There is almost no event that is only deviant or only socially significant. Thus, we should consider the two factors together or the relationship between the two to explain the attention to news events.

This study examined how deviance and social significance simultaneously affect attention to news events. The connection degree among the three variables for deviance and four variables for social significance increased as the level of attention increased. The network density also increased as the attention level increased. On the other hand, network centralization decreased, which implies that the event receiving the highest level of attention tends to have an equal amount of high deviance and high social significance. In short, this study showed that deviance and social significance of an event have an interaction effect on people's attention to the event.

This study discussed the attention to deviance and social significance from a perspective of human evolution following Shoemaker's (1996) footsteps. Attention to deviance has been explicated as an EPM (Evolved Psychological Mechanism) based on evolutionary psychology. That is, it is a psychological gene inherited from the Stone Age. Our ancestors faced dangerous EEA (Environment of Evolutionary Adaptedness), in which deviant events, such as a wild fire or predator's attack, occurred without any warning. Special attention to deviant events was needed to survive such environments, and human beings with this psychological mechanism were able to prolong their lives and leave descendants. Through this process, a superior gene that pays special attention to deviance was passed down from generation to generation. As a result, people today have an immediate reaction to deviant events or information, which is close to instinctive attention controlled by the gene.

Attention to social significance is considered as a cultural behavior chosen by a number of members of society, rather than by nature. In a society, when certain information is considered to be significant, more members come to attend and learn it, by which this information spreads out and becomes recognized as socially significant information by most members. As such, most cultural evolution is processed horizontally between members of society while genes are only transmitted vertically through generations. Taken together, we have two kinds of attention: attention to deviance from genetic evolution and attention to social significance from cultural evolution.

Furthermore, this study focuses on the interaction between the two kinds of attention based on gene-culture co-evolution. This theory argues that the relationship between genes and culture has a significant influence on human behavior and attitudes. As discussed earlier, human pro-social behavior can be explained by both genes and the society's culture. A better explanation for this can be found in the analysis of the interaction between genes and culture. Special attention to a certain event can also be explained in terms of coevolution. The deviance of an event activates genes in our DNA, and these genes cause us to respond. At the same time, the social significance of the event awakens members of society to attend and learn of it. Now, the most realistic explanation might be that these two processes work together.

This study is based on Shoemaker's (1996) evolutionary idea on deviance and social significance, and discusses the relationships between attention to deviance and attention to social significance. This study then expands the theory to gene-culture co-evolution and uses network analyses to show the interaction effect of deviance and social significance on news attention.

Nevertheless, this study has some limitations. First, evolution researchers have developed various mathematical models and have demonstrated the empirical effects of genes and culture on human behavior. However, this study did not provide a model explaining the relationship between evolution and attention to events. Second, although network analysis is suitable to determine complex relationships or interactions among variables, this method did not show the individual effects of each variable of deviance and social significance. Further research is needed in this respect.

REFERENCES

Barrett, D. B., Kurian, G. T. K., & Johnson, T. M. (2001). *World Christian encyclopedia: Religionists, churches, ministries: A comparative survey of churches and religions in the modern world.* Oxford: Oxford University Press.

Bowlby, J. (1969). *Attachment and loss.* New York, NY: Basic Books.

Boyd, R., & Richerson, P. J. (1982). Cultural transmission and the evolution of cooperative behavior. *Human Ecology, 10*(3), 325–351.

Boyd, R., & Richerson, P. J. (1985). *Culture and the evolutionary process.* Chicago, IL:

University of Chicago Press.

Buss, D. M. (2009). How can evolutionary psychology successfully explain personality and individual differences? *Perspectives on Psychological Science*, *4*(4), 359–366.

Cavalli-Sforza, L. L., & Feldman, M. W. (1981). *Cultural transmission and evolution: A quantitative approach* (No. 16). Princeton, NJ: Princeton University Press.

Cosmides, L., & Tooby, J. (1987). From evolution to behavior: Evolutionary psychology as the missing link. In J. Dupré (Ed.), *The latest and the best: Essays on evolution and optimality* (pp. 277–306). Cambridge, MA: MIT Press.

Darwin, C. (1936a). *The descent of man.* New York, NY: Random House (Original work published 1871).

Darwin, C. (1936b). *The origin of species.* New York, NY: Random House (Original work published 1860).

Dawkins, R. (1976). *The selfish gene.* Oxford: Oxford University Press.

Feldman, M. W., & Cavalli-Sforza, L. L. (1989). On the theory of evolution under genetic and cultural transmission with application to the lactose absorption problem. In M. W. Feldman (Ed.), *Mathematical evolutionary theory* (pp. 145–173). Princeton, NJ: Princeton University Press.

Galtung, J., & Ruge, M. H. (1965). The structure of foreign news: The presentation of the Congo, Cuba and Cyprus crises in four Norwegian newspapers. *Journal of Peace Research*, *2*(1), 64–90.

Grimes, B. F. (2001). Global language viability. *Endangered Languages of the Pacific Rim, Lectures on Endangered Languages*, *2*, 45–61.

Harcup, T., & O'Neill, D. (2001). What is news? Galtung and Ruge revisited. *Journalism Studies*, *2*(2), 261–280.

Laland, K. N., & Brown, G. R. (2011). *Sense and nonsense: Evolutionary perspectives on human behavior.* Oxford: Oxford University Press.

Lee, J. H., Gil, W. Y., Kang, S. M., & Choi, Y. J. (2014). A comprehensive and structural approach to news value in multimedia environment: Extraction of a structural model of news value. *Korean Journal of Broadcasting Research*, *27*(1), 167–212.

Lumsden, C. J., & Wilson, E. O. (1981). *The coevolutionary process.* Cambridge, MA: Harvard University Press.

Mesoudi, A., Whiten, A., & Laland, K. N. (2004). Perspective: Is human cultural evolution Darwinian? Evidence reviewed from the perspective of the origin of species. *Evolution*, *58*(1), 1–11.

Shoemaker, P. J. (1996). Hardwired for news: Using biological and cultural evolution to explain the surveillance function. *Journal of Communication*, *46*(3), 32–47.

Shoemaker, P. J., & Cohen, A. A. (2006). *News around the world: Content, practitioners, and the public.* New York, NY: Routledge.

Shoemaker, P. J., Chang, T. K., & Brendlinger, N. (1987). Deviance as a predictor of newsworthiness: Coverage of international events in the US media. In M. L. McLaughlin (Ed.), *Communication Yearbook10* (pp. 348–365). New York, NY: Routledge.

Shoemaker, P. J., Danielian, L. H., & Brendlinger, N. (1991). Deviant acts, risky business and U.S. interests: The newsworthiness of world events. *Journalism Quarterly*, *68*(4), 781–795.

Wynne-Edwards, V. C. (1962). *Animal dispersion in relation to social behavior.* New York, NY: Hafner.

CHAPTER THIRTEEN

From Gatekeeping to Bridge-Keeping

Gatekeeping Theory through the Lens of Micro-Documentary

NICK MICHAEL* AND TIM P. VOS†

GATEKEEPING AT THE BOUNDARIES OF DIGITAL JOURNALISM: GATEKEEPING FORCES AND MICRO-DOCUMENTARY

The world of short-form documentary is beleaguered by the popular sentiment that, given the proliferation of portable technology with built-in video capabilities, now "everyone is a journalist" and "everyone is a filmmaker". Indeed, the production and publication tools needed for short-form documentary, also called "micro-documentary" (Jetnikoff, 2008), continues to become more affordable and accessible to ever-widening socio-economic demographics, and the Internet now serves as a publication platform and distribution service for short-form documentaries that would otherwise be venue-less. Journalism organizations, corporations, non-profits, governments and other organizations are commissioning non-fiction, short-form videos (Jetnikoff, 2008). Employing the strategies and practices of documentary film, narrative film, broadcast news, advertising, video art, and advocacy, this short-form film industry creates work that bypasses traditional gatekeepers, although those traditional gatekeepers are quickly taking note and following suit (Micro-Documentaries, 2011).

* Nick Michael is a video producer for National Public Radio. Email: nicktmichael@gmail.com.

† Tim P. Vos is Chair and Associate Professor of Journalism Studies in the School of Journalism at the University of Missouri. Email: vost@missouri.edu.

These new micro-documentary filmmakers generally come from two institutional backgrounds, journalism or documentary filmmaking (Jetnikoff, 2008; Micro-Documentaries, 2011). Although both traditional journalism and documentary film seek to inform the public through storytelling, each does so with differing levels of immediacy and depth. In its ideal form, journalism contributes balance, criticism and accountability by investigating the "who, what, when, where and why" of events (Craft & Davis, 2016). In its ideal form, documentary film uncovers enduring tales of the human condition by delving deeply into characters, events, culture and phenomena (Aufderheide, 2007). Despite differences in their contexts of production (e.g., deadlines, organizational structure, cost, and funding models) and the final form of their messages, the audience and the interests of both journalism and documentary film have converged online. Both print and film have gone digital. They have done so in places such as the New York Times, whose Op-Docs have become an important and visible platform for micro-documentary (About Op-Docs, 2015).

In an era when journalism is increasingly being practiced outside of traditional newsrooms (Van Der Haak, Parks, & Castells, 2012), micro-documentaries represent a new entrant to the journalistic field. Many micro-documentarians worked as journalists and now embrace a format and approach that, they say, afford them more freedom. While they clearly contribute to the news ecology, they also practice a craft that not all of them want to call journalism (Micro-Documentaries, 2011). Nevertheless, having entered, even partially, the journalistic field, do micro-documentaries become subject to the same pressures from other social fields (Bourdieu, 1998) and from the same gatekeeping pressures (Shoemaker & Vos, 2009) as journalism? This chapter relies on in-depth interviews with micro-documentary producers to examine how they perceive the gatekeeping forces that shape the documentaries they produce.

A study of gatekeeping forces affecting micro-documentary production holds promise for untapped practical and theoretical value. Historically, the texts of films have been studied more often and more thoroughly than their production (Sperling, 2011). Beyond the application of a cornerstone media theory to an emerging field, research on the gatekeeping forces influencing micro-documentaries can aid in sensitizing gatekeeping theory to the complexities of the digital age.

DOCUMENTARY AND GATEKEEPING

While documentary popularity has boomed (Dowell, 2011; Schwab, 2010), newspaper circulation has declined. In addition to the consequent economic angst, many news organizations have faced an erosion of public confidence due to real or imagined corporate and political allegiances (Gans, 2003; Peters & Broersma, 2013).

Despite its skepticism, the public is increasingly finding its news online (Anderson, 2013). Given the multimedia potential of the web, many news organizations have increased video output to lure audiences to their news websites (Layton, 2007). Many news organizations have also put pressure on print reporters to collect audio-visual material in addition to their print stories (Kolodzy, 2006). In 2009, both CNN and MSNBC.com reorganized their websites to emphasize video (Project for Excellence in Journalism, 2011).

As newspapers have cut costs, documentary film has moved in to counterpoint (Diaz, 2005) or elaborate on (Kasson, 2010) stories that, under deadline and financial constraints (Shoemaker, Eichholz, Kim, & Wrigley, 2001), journalists find difficult to cover with equal depth or nuance. Of course, micro-documentary filmmakers also labor under financial constraints, lacking the capital of big news organizations. However, independent documentarians' passion for certain stories often serves as a different kind of capital. Because there is often little money in documentary film, documentary producers are more likely to tell stories that, driven by conviction rather than market sensibilities, they feel the public "needs" rather than "wants" to know (Ludtke, 2009).

While journalism and documentary have come with different institution histories and with different routines and different epistemological orientations, they nevertheless overlap in their commitment to basic truthfulness and to public affairs topics (Aufderheide, 2007). The similarities and differences come with requisite tensions. Because documentary film lacks an institutionalized ethical code to guide its practice, critics sometimes transfer their expectations of journalistic objectivity onto documentary films, criticizing them as "propaganda" (Barnouw, 1993, p. 345).

Gatekeeping. Defined broadly, gatekeeping is "the process by which the vast array of potential news messages are winnowed, shaped, and prodded into those few that are actually transmitted by the news media" (Shoemaker et al., 2001, p. 233). Gatekeepers are those people who "regulate the flow of information, language and knowledge" (Storm, 2007). Shoemaker and Vos (2009) posit that media gates exist at five levels of analysis: individual, routine, organizational, social institutional, and social systems (2009). Positive and negative forces—factors that promote and impede information's progress through a gate—influence each of these five levels (Shoemaker & Vos, 2009). Some forces may at first seem to act more to change the shape of a message, although this is likely a response to anticipated gates in the future. Historically, elites have exerted control over the flow of news and information; thus gatekeeping has largely explained a uni-directional and hierarchical flow of information (Barzilai-Nahon, 2008).

The Internet and digital technology have undermined that hierarchy and redistributed production power to the audience. Whether through citizen journalism, user-generated video, or amateur filmmaking, audiences have become producers and publishers (Wall, 2015). Storm (2007, p. 2) argues that this rise in the audience's production power constitutes a "reversal of the gatekeeping process through a convergence of content producers". Other scholars point to shifts in newsgathering (e.g., crowd-sourcing, citizen journalism) and distribution (e.g., social media) as more evidence of this reversal (Bowman & Willis, 2005; Cha, 2005). Shoemaker and Vos (2009) view all news consumers as gatekeepers.

This is not to say that the gatekeeping model has been undone (Vos, 2015a). Rather, Barzilai-Nahon (2008, p. 1495) proposes a "hybrid interpretation" called network gatekeeping that accounts for the overlap of the old and new models and the commerce of information between them. Barzilai-Nahon argues that traffic through the gates, no matter the source, is governed by information's salience, which is comprised in whole or part by four attributes: "(a) political power in relation to the gatekeeper, (b) information production ability, (c) relationship with the gatekeeper, and (d) alternatives in the context of gatekeeping" (2008, p. 1493). The higher the number and strength of these four attributes, the more likely information is to pass through a gate uncontested and unchanged. Other scholars maintain that salience is composed of social significance and deviance from three factors: deviance from the average, deviance from the social status quo, and deviance from social norms (Shoemaker & Cohen, 2006). Still, Barzilai-Nahon (2008) does not argue that traditional gatekeepers' power is undiminished. Rather she suggests a circularity to the gatekeeping process in which the former audience "produces information [while] taking into consideration reactions and feedback from gatekeepers and other stakeholders" and in which "gatekeepers are affected by the information produced and, in effect, change their stances" (Barzilai-Nahon, 2008, p. 1501). Crucially, gatekeeping theory's explanation of how the confluence of decisions, influences, and forces affect news sharing (Shoemaker et al., 2001) keeps the theory elastic enough to accommodate its application to online, digital media.

This reconceptualization of the gatekeeping process also applies to micro-documentary journalism. For decades, capital-rich corporate studios or networks served as the primary financiers and distributors of primarily long-form documentaries (Irwin, 2004). Although grant- and government-funded documentary productions existed or even thrived in some countries (e.g., Britain, Canada), in the United States prohibitive costs kept documentary production out of public hands as recently as the late 1980s, when film processing alone proved too costly (Delaney, 2009; Irwin, 2004). Additionally, the costs of insurance, broadcast or projection, and distribution were staggering, and elite gatekeepers controlled each of those stages (Lohmann, 2007). Today, micro-documentaries are produced by established media, the former audience, commercial directors, and quasi-journalistic third parties. The web guarantees that distribution is cheap and global (Christensen, 2007; Schwab, 2010; Wellman, 2004), and inexpensive digital photo, video and editing technology (Knight, 2007; Schwab, 2010) offer democratized access to production tools.

The gatekeeping forces affecting micro-documentaries exist in tension. Positive forces of increased audience appetite, democratized tech quality, rising visual culture, and diminished publishing gatekeepers compete with negative forces of high resource investment, high signal to noise ratio, wide range and high facility skill sets, and distracted web audiences. Additionally, web publication does not guarantee visibility online (Barzilai-Nahon, 2008; Knight, 2007), and although previous distribution models involved prohibitive cost, those models could at least monetize distribution, which has proven problematic for journalism or documentary online. Barriers to publication may be low, but those barriers are set by corporations (e.g., YouTube, Vimeo, Facebook) that control social, legal, and economic dynamics of user uploads and social sharing (Barzilai-Nahon, 2008).

Despite the techno-romantic myth of the equivalence of accessible technology and social progress (Curran, Fenton, & Freedman, 2012), documentary filmmakers' production choices are bound by more than equipment access. White's original gatekeeping study (1950) examined the agency of a specific gatekeeper, and in the same way this study means to examine the influence of gatekeeping forces on a filmmaker's agency, which can be channeled and bound by a variety of forces (Shoemaker & Vos, 2009). As the originator of the a micro-documentary "message", micro-documentary filmmakers base many production choices on their perception of the gatekeeping forces ahead, as evidenced by Aufderheide's and Jaszi's (2004) study on the chilling effect distributors' skepticism has on the employment of fair use. Nevertheless, attention to gatekeeping influences on documentary are rare (Vos, 2015b). Thus, we turn to a consideration of how gatekeeping forces come to bear on micro-documentarians at the individual, routine, organizational, and institutional levels of analysis.

Study Design

Gatekeeping forces are investigated through semi-structured interviews with 16 micro-documentary practitioners. Interviewees were chosen to maximize differentiation within a typology based on the following institutional production contexts: legacy journalism, commercial (agency), commercial (direct-to-client), broadcast, long-form, and self-publishing. Importantly, few micro-documentarians fit cleanly in a single institutional context, whether because they have held multiple jobs, their current institutional context overlaps multiple categories, or they work for clients in a variety of organizational contexts. Interviewees currently have or have had significant experience (whether a full-time job or a significant client) in the following organizational contexts: eight in legacy journalism, six in direct-to-client commercial work, four in long-form filmmaking, four in self-publishing, three in agency-driven commercial work, three in broadcast, and three in curatorial capacities. (Again, the numbers add to higher than 16 because the interviewees fit into more than one category.) The in-depth interviews lasted between 30 and 90 minutes, depending on the interviewee's availability. Nearly all lasted more than 60 minutes.

After the conclusion of all interviews, each interview was transcribed, and the transcripts coded for discrete phenomena according to a constant comparison method, as described by Corbin and Strauss (1990). These concepts were grouped into categories based on the five levels of gatekeeping analysis. However, only the first four levels will be considered here, mostly for space reasons and partly because this level proved little different from gatekeeping in traditional gated settings. Theories or primary findings were then produced based on interpretation of these concepts and categories. The analysis that follows includes concepts deemed noteworthy because of repeated presence in the coding. The conclusion includes concepts that micro-documentary theorists supplied but were "significantly absent" in interviews with practitioners (Corbin & Strauss, 1990, p. 7). The analysis includes all significant concepts and categories reported by one or more interviewees. Although this study cannot provide an exhaustive taxonomy of all relevant gatekeeping forces, it can provide an extensive interpretation of the gatekeeping forces perceived by micro-documentary practitioners.

Findings: Micro-Documentaries and Gatekeeping

"There is no gatekeeper" is an anthem common in the digital age. In fact, it was popular among this project's interviewees. Nine interviewees stated, more or less explicitly, that they believe there are no gatekeepers. Other interviewees believed that gatekeepers still exist but that they are changing, and others reported that everyone is now a gatekeeper. This breakdown illustrates the power of an interview-based research method to capture qualified answers. Although nine interviewees believe that no gatekeepers exist, all 16 provided a long list of "influences", "pressures", "requirements", "restrictions", "frustrations", "difficulties", "boundaries", and "possibilities" that affected their productions. Few of these are attached to gatekeepers, but all bind and channel the agency of micro-documentarians, thus constituting gatekeeping forces.

Interviewees typically equated embodied gatekeepers with "old media", meaning pre-Internet institutions where vested individuals shaped and approved messages for publication. Many of these old-media institutions have, with enthusiasm or reluctance, developed properties that publish online content. However, many of these online versions operate with similar editorial workflow to old media models, where a hierarchy of content producers and editors craft and queue messages for publication. Thus it is more appropriate to call these "gated" publications (Barzilai-Nahon, 2008).

Because these gated publications *publish* on the Internet, they exist alongside "gate-less" self-published content on platforms like YouTube, Vimeo, Facebook,

Wordpress, Tumblr, Twitter, Instagram, etc. Consequently, old media have "lost their total domination of the field", as one micro-documentarian put it, and must compete shoulder-to-shoulder with content the former audience is producing by and for itself. In effect, the Internet is a space where two gatekeeping models operate simultaneously: the new self-publishing model in which only gatekeeping forces (no embodied gatekeepers) positively and negatively affect a message's online visibility and an old "gated" model in which those same forces apply with the addition of one or more embodied gatekeepers. It would be convenient, but ultimately inaccurate, to call the self-publishing models "gate-less" for reasons explored below.

These two gatekeeping models are true for multiple media genres, including micro-documentary production. Indeed, under the new model, creating and sharing a micro-documentary has never been easier. A veteran long-form producer said: "The fact of the matter is it's no longer difficult to become a documentarian. Now anybody can pick up a camera". Among interviewees there existed a fundamental understanding that the production tools (e.g., smartphones, tablets, and digital single lens reflex [DSLR] cameras) and the publication platforms (e.g., YouTube, Vimeo and others) have made micro-documentary production more affordable and accessible for a wide socio-economic bracket. As one Emmy-winner put it, "I just don't see any barriers".

The removal of barriers has created a soup of undifferentiated content divorced from any single institutional production context. According to the interviewees, self-published films lack a built-in audience that content published by established "old-media" organizations might enjoy Authors of self-published content often must depend on publicity from elsewhere. In other words: "If you do it for yourself on Vimeo, you publish it. You're done, but you don't have an audience". It's always easy to publish, but it's often hard to be seen. The competition to be seen is fierce. Interviewees acknowledged that "everyone is a filmmaker", but understandably, many interviewees believed filmmaking required more than access to tools. Chief among those concerns is, in the words of a magazine video journalist, that simply "it's hard to create compelling stuff". What follows is an exploration of the gatekeeping forces that make it difficult for the micro-documentarians to create work that is as compelling as they would like. All forces listed were supplied in one form or another by interviewees, and all are organized based on the levels of gatekeeping analysis.

Admittedly, many gatekeeping forces bleed across level of analysis and are difficult to categorize given their interdependence on other forces. Additionally, the context of micro-documentary production creates variation across some of these levels of analysis, especially the individual, organizational, and institutional levels.

Individual Forces. Forces that micro-documentarians reported at the individual level included the difficulty of professional categorization, the density of the required skillset, and desired lifestyle. Most micro-documentarians reported they had difficulty categorizing themselves professionally as part of any singe organizational context, such as journalist, filmmaker, artist, activist, or a hybrid of those options. When asked how she described her job, one interviewee said, "I think I defy categorization only in the sense that I have to respond to that [question] in paragraph form, whereas more people tend to have a one-word answer". Interviewees were largely hesitant to define themselves by any single institutional context, often distinguishing between their background and their current job or between their professional title and their product. One interviewee said her initial interest was in film, but "once you start making documentaries, you tend to wade into journalism ethics". A journalist-turned-filmmaker said that he considers himself a "non-fiction storyteller" because he had shed his "journalistic balance" in the name of better storytelling. One filmmaker said she varies what she calls herself situationally, but she tends towards "filmmaking" because there are fewer assumptions associated with filmmaker than journalist. She felt comfortable describing her work as journalism only when it was published in a journalistic venue.

These categorization difficulties serve as a gatekeeping force by complicating how micro-documentarians identify with institutionalized practice, ethics and traditions; how they brand themselves both in interpersonal conversation and to potential clients and employers; and how and where they publish their work online. Micro-documentarians producing in hybrid genres or organizational contexts spend valuable time articulating their profession to themselves.

Micro-documentary production requires an increasingly wide range of skills for production and publication, especially for those micro-documentarians working alone. Interviewees list an impressive array of needed skills: creative and technical tasks including organizing pre-production, writing and negotiating contracts, capturing clean audio, capturing well-composed and thoughtful video, conducting an interview, managing a crew, protecting subject's interests, transcoding footage, navigating the technicalities of editing software, constructing a narrative arc, balancing conflicting stakeholder interests, uploading content, writing metadata and captions, connecting the piece with a network of gated publications, managing business financials, establishing a personal brand, and cultivating an audience. "There's all sorts of legal and also just business-financials… I don't even know what the right terminology would be". The more skills required of a micro-documentarian, the thinner that filmmaker must spread himself or herself across the production. Such a wide required skillset functions as a negative gatekeeping force by discouraging or eliminating new directors from the field.

Some interviewees mentioned lifestyle as a gatekeeping force. Calling the lifestyle "more precarious" than a desk job, one journalist-documentarian noted that most micro-documentarians are "not 9-to-5 kind of folks". Lifestyle preferences affect micro-documentary content by limiting the time and energy a director will spend on making work. Commitments to family or a desire to stay rooted in a particular community sometimes prevent micro-documentarians from taking jobs that require significant travel. Many micro-documentarians work as both artists and entrepreneurs, a combination that often requires them to work outside of conventional business hours. Conversely, that combination also allows them control over their work schedule.

Routine Forces. Routine forces involve technology, form, and conceptions of audience. As routine forces, these elements emerged as industry standards or common practice across a range of micro-documentarians. Admittedly, the micro-documentary is an emerging sub-genre, and as such, it and its gatekeeping forces at the routine level will evolve.

The interviewees say their routines revolve around using technology. Cheaper, more accessible and easier-to-use production equipment is the most commonly reported gatekeeping force among interviewees. However, the speed of technological advancement serves as a negative gatekeeping force. Micro-documentarians are forced to keep up with changes in equipment. As one interviewee said, "I'm always trying to predict the next thing, which is very hard and very time-consuming". As a vehicle for media, technology is often a driver of changes in storytelling. Lower costs, more ready access, and more user-friendly interfaces certainly expand the realm of possible storytellers. Although it is too often equated with aptitude, accessible technology is certainly one of the most significant gates lowered and consequently one of the largest contributing factors to the emergence of the micro-documentary.

Every journalistic form exhibits qualities and tendencies that seem to emerge from the medium itself. As one interviewee emphasized, good communicators have always matched a message's style, tone, length and more to its medium. The form includes a "multiplicity of [sub]genres". Interviewees describe particular micro-documentaries forms: "straight news", "short films", "derivative of direct cinema", "propaganda", "real people's stories", and "stand-alone reportorial products". Each comes with a range of expectations and limitations. The interviewees believed a micro-documentary should cover a story that "goes beyond your kitchen table", and this requires that filmmakers "make people ask questions that they're going to want to have an answer to". These beliefs forced films into routine treatments. One of the most debated micro-documentary form restrictions is length. Multiple interviewees expressed relief that the Internet has freed them from "the rigor of the clock" required by broadcast slots. However, many interviewees alluded to a clichéd three-minute rule, which limited the treatment of most topics. Coverage of topics favored by audiences and others can act as a positive gatekeeping force that creates opportunities to tell similar stories. Coverage of taboo topics has served as a negative gatekeeping force by endangering personal and professional possibilities.

One of the most critical gatekeeping forces affecting micro-documentary filmmakers is conceptions of audience, which affects story selection, story construction, and distribution. Although most interviewees said they rarely think about audience during production, many expressed definite opinions about what audiences are looking for in micro-documentaries. As one interviewee put it, when you're editing "you have this little bird on your shoulder telling you, 'They're not going to click on Facebook if you don't make this more interesting.'" Despite the audience's unpredictability, many interviewees spoke of share-ability: "Our main strategy I guess is to make [them] as shareable as possible". A filmmaker's over-emphasis on share-ability places significant boundaries on the tone, length and topic of micro-documentaries. Catering a message to a mass, attention-deficit, and distracted audience would likely produce a micro-documentary that differs substantially from the personal standards filmmakers reported. As a gatekeeping force, "share-ability" operates in tension with filmmaker's visions of their best work. In striking any balance between the two, they acknowledged key gatekeeping forces.

Organizational Forces. Organizational gatekeeping forces revealed themselves through differences in production and distribution mechanisms between organizational contexts. Critically, these differences are attributable to the organizational locus of production rather than idiosyncrasies of individual producers. The documentarians worked mostly in three organizational contexts: broadcast, web journalism, and self-publishing. The organizational context bears significantly on the gatekeeping forces affecting production.

Although there are "very few outlets" that broadcast micro-documentaries, the context of broadcast production provides a counterpoint to the Internet's "clocklessness", its loose rights considerations, and low editorial thresholds. One of the most restrictive gatekeeping forces for broadcast is the time slot. Documentarians are given very precise restrictions on the running time of their films. Rights acquisition also functions very differently in the broadcast space. Many broadcast organizations require filmmakers to sign liability contracts stating that they have licenses for all audio-visual material and releases for all identifiable subjects in the film. Broadcast outlets also often assert editorial rights. They do this for a variety of reasons, but mostly to avoid controversy and to target niche audiences. Broadcast distribution is a highly regulated platform that requires specific lengths, rights management, and commitments to either advertisers or editorial standards. Documentarians, if they seek a broadcast outlet, must be prepared to play by broadcasters' rules.

Given their ties to legacy media, web journalism organizations come with staff hierarchies, story-gathering methodologies, financial models, organizational resources, and divisions of labor. Consequently, traditional gatekeeping theories can explain much of the micro-documentary production context in web journalism organizations, although gatekeeping forces affecting micro-documentary distribution have changed dramatically. Interviewees sometimes expressed surprise at the respect and resources allotted to video inside their organizations. Compelling video gets attention. This deference to video described by video-journalists operates as a gatekeeping force by raising their political capital within their respective organizations. Despite that deference, the journalists reported having little influence over which stories they produce. Beyond story choice itself, an interviewee said she believed that she "had agency to suggest" possible stories as well as control over the visual direction for all stories she produced. Interviewees also reported greater access to elite sources when working for a traditional journalism outlet compared to their work for independent distribution.

Self-published projects are free of many of the traditional gatekeeping forces associated with media publishing. Indeed, that is their appeal. Interviewees spoke of publishing "personal projects" or "passion projects" in this way, and one interviewee had made a living, in part, by self-publishing micro-documentaries. A majority of interviewees believed that in this space either there are no gatekeepers or the only gatekeepers are filmmakers themselves. Most of the gatekeeping forces reported around self-publishing pertain more to distribution than publication. Thus the gatekeeping forces associated with production in the self-publishing space are marked by absence, often in relief to other organizational contexts. In self-publishing, often there are no organizational resources, no staff hierarchies, no mentorship, no deadlines, no responsibility to audience, no responsibility to advertisers, and low to no financial compensation. Still, filmmakers in the self-publishing space often trade a lack of organizational gatekeeping forces for a lack of organizational resources. Many of those resources are desirable, however; such as protections for external pressures and access to elite sources.

Social Institutional Forces. Interviewees reported a variety of institutional forces affecting their work, from legacy media to legal regimes to audiences. Only two institutional forces will be highlighted here: market considerations and the Internet. Interviewees say micro-documentaries need a "mix of funding sources", which requires filmmakers to "be more of an entrepreneur" and "hustle a little bit more". Although market demand for micro-documentaries is growing, there does not yet exist a standard funding model. In addition, there is often little financial "return on investment". All this creates negative gatekeeping pressure on micro-documentaries in general. This force is mitigated by the fact that the interviewees generally don't expect to make a profit. Some interviewees mentioned geographic market as a force affecting their work. A filmmaker/consultant reported meeting and making clients purely by virtue of the city he lives in. However, being located there also results in competition from fellow documentarians in the same city.

As a social institution, the Internet can be considered a significant, if not primary, contributor to the rise of micro-documentaries. It has enabled relatively easy publishing, immediate global availability, and relatively permanent display. The Internet has become the "obvious" and "easiest" publication venue for documentary films. As a viewing environment, the Internet forces micro-documentarians to consider the length, style, structure and topicality of their videos. Thus like every other medium before it, the Internet makes unique demands on the messages it spreads. As a gatekeeping force, the Internet represents both a welcoming platform and difficult viewing environment for micro-documentaries. The Internet also allows an unprecedented precision in measuring an audience's engagement with video. As a journalist-turned-filmmaker noted, individuals and organizations producing video are now able to "measure things we've never been able to measure before".

Because the Internet is a seemingly gatekeeper-less space with ever more abundant content, micro-documentarians depend in part on social media to connect their content to interested audiences. This is a unique capacity of the web that allows individuals to share content with a network of friends, colleagues and followers. In fact, when pressed to name a gatekeeper, many interviewees responded with social media circles. A gatekeeper can be "some kid in middle-America who's super-passionate about a film", and in fact that single kid might have the power (or luck) to "share that idea and that thing sort of explodes and multiplies and other people…go on to share it".

CONCLUSIONS

Through semi-structure interviews with micro-documentary producers, this study uncovered a catalogue of gatekeeping forces affecting micro-documentary production at four levels of analysis: individual, routine, organizational, and social institutional. Aside from the forces already identified above, the consideration of micro-documentaries as an emergent variation of digital journalism raises an important concern relevant to theorizing about gatekeeping: the de-corporeality of gatekeeping.

When asked whom they considered their gatekeepers, many interviewees found it difficult to provide an answer. When pressed, most interviewees stated, more or less explicitly, that they believe there are no gatekeepers anymore, or that gatekeepers still exist but that they are changing, or that everyone is now a gatekeeper. Of course, these answers make sense only in the context of the Internet. Within organizations, gatekeepers certainly exist in the form of supervisors and colleagues, as interviewees suggested. However, when one micro-documentarian was asked if she saw gatekeepers for her stories outside of her organization, she responded with "Isn't that outside of the gate?"

Indeed, in previous gatekeeping models, established publication points enjoyed pockets of dedicated readers or viewers, and publishing meant reaching that audience. Under the traditional gatekeeping model, if you "get past the gatekeeper, you have their audience", as one interviewee put it. Thus under the new model, the potential audience is much larger, but the guaranteed audience is in most cases much smaller. Today and especially online, the primary gate has shifted from one between the communicator and the platform to one between the platform and the audience. Traversing that second gate has more to do with visibility than publishing. In keeping with this shift, interviewees discussing gatekeeping spoke less about people and more about "influences", "pressures", "requirements", "restrictions", "frustrations", "difficulties", "boundaries", and "possibilities" that affected their productions. When interviewees did actually supply a gatekeeper, they listed Vimeo, Vimeo's Staff Picks, Facebook, Reddit, Google, or YouTube. They also referenced popular blogs, social media, and other online sources that were "trusted" or had "taste". No interviewee mentioned an established news organization—broadcast or print—as a current gatekeeper. Referencing his own media consumption habits, a journalist-turned-filmmaker said "I don't care where it is as long as it's what I want and when I want it,...I don't see any gatekeeper. I'm not loyal to anybody".

The central metaphor of gatekeeping theory—that of an individual standing between a message and its audience—applies only in limited contexts today. The original gatekeeping study involved a single editor selecting wire stories for inclusion in a small town newspaper (White, 1950). Subsequent articulations of the theory have adapted to the complexities of the media ecosystem, and now the theory addresses multiple levels of analysis (Shoemaker & Vos, 2009) and the overlap of old and new media models (Barzilai-Nahon, 2008). Based on this study's analysis, gatekeeping theory should address gatekeeping's de-corporeality, meaning the transfer of gatekeeping power from elite individuals to emergent forces. This would be consistent with Lewin's (1951) observation that gatekeepers do not always have to be human being—sometimes they can be disembodied rules. It would also be consistent with Gans' (1979) argument that the construction of news emerges from a process of routines and organizational contexts, rather than from individual journalists or publishers.

Online, there is no one tending the gate between publisher and platform; that gatekeeper is no one and everyone. As one interviewee noted, gatekeeping traditionally assumes an "active agent" or "purposeful blockage", whereas today content producers are presented with an array of "passive phenomena" that comprise an "ecosystem of challenges". Indeed, many of the reported gatekeepers—designers of Facebook's interface, Internet service providers, developers of search algorithms—are in fact content-neutral. Rather than keeping a gate whose fundamental nature is blockage, they keep a bridge whose fundamental nature is passage. Rather than selectively permitting passage based on a collection of standards particular to a message's content, new gatekeepers—or bridge-keepers—regulate the flow of information from producer to consumer. The old chief value was selecting a program of relevant content in scarce publication space; the new chief value is maximizing a library of relevant content in abundant publication space. Thus the new gatekeepers care less about what a message says and more about whether it has been said at all.

Considering these findings, gatekeeping theory must evolve. At least in the micro-documentary genre, bridge-keeping entities and gatekeeping forces both bind and channel the agency of micro-documentary filmmakers. Online, gatekeepers are disembodied and their power transferred to a distributed network of forces, hidden and conspicuous, strong and weak, citizen and corporate. The major players are the same—source, author, and audience—but a message's path from player to player has changed significantly. Gatekeepers, in this setting, are no longer required.

Like the medium that supports them, online micro-documentaries are evolving rapidly. A changing media landscape and its attendant gatekeeping forces have implications for both the quality and nature of the messages the public receives. As a part of that evolving media landscape, micro-documentaries have implications for the reality that the public perceives to be true. This is the same reality that informs the public's actions, choices, beliefs, habits, prejudices, and future. Told with honesty and skill, micro-documentaries can inspire change when the public realizes the world they have just watched is their own. By illuminating such gatekeeping forces, this chapter has grounded gatekeeping theory in micro-documentarians' working experience, and further articulated gatekeeping theory in the digital age.

REFERENCES

About Op-Docs. (2015, January 22). *New York Times.* Retrieved from http://www.nytimes.com/ref/opinion/about-op-docs.html

Anderson, C. W. (2013). *Rebuilding the news: Metropolitan journalism in the digital age.* Philadelphia, PA: Temple University Press.

Aufderheide, P. (2007) *Documentary film: A very short introduction.* Oxford: Oxford Press.

Aufderheide, P., & Jaszi, P. (2004). Untold stories: Creative consequences of the rights clearance culture for documentary filmmakers. *Center for Social Media.* Retrieved from http://www.acsil.org/resources/rights-clearances-1/nps240.tmp.pdf

Barnouw, E. (1993). *Documentary: A history of the non-fiction film.* New York, NY: Oxford.

Barzilai-Nahon, K. (2008). Toward a theory of network gatekeeping: A framework for exploring information control. *Journal of the American Society for Information Science & Technology, 59*(9), 1493–1512.

Bourdieu, P. (1998). *On television.* New York, NY: New Press.

Bowman, S., & Willis, C. (2005) The future is here, but do news media companies see it? *Nieman Reports.* Retrieved from http://www.nieman.harvard.edu/reports/article/100558/The-Future-Is-Here-But-Do-News-Media-Companies-See-It.aspx

Cha, A. E. (2005, July 2005). Do-it-yourself journalism spreads: Web sites let people take news into their own hands. Other articles don't. *The Washington Post.* Retrieved from http://www.washingtonpost.com/wp-dyn/content/article/2005/07/16/AR2005071601359.html.

Christensen, C. (2007, May). *Political documentaries, grassroots distribution and online organization: The case of brave new films.* Paper presented at the International Communication Association, San Francisco, CA.

Corbin, J. M., & Strauss, A. (1990). Grounded theory research: Procedures, canons, and evaluative criteria. *Qualitative Sociology, 13*(1), 3–21.

Craft, S., & Davis, C. N. (2016). *Principles of American journalism: An introduction* (2nd ed.). New York, NY: Routledge.

Curran, J., Fenton, N., & Freedman, D. (Eds.). (2012). *Misunderstanding the Internet.* London; New York, NY: Routledge.

Delaney, E. J. (2009, August 14). The rise of documentaries and the fall of newspaper series. [Web log comment]. Retrieved from http://documentarytech.com/?p=50

Diaz, P. (2005). The political documentary in America today. *Cineaste, 30*(3), 33–34.

Dowell, B. (2011, June 5). Steve James hails a "golden age of documentary film-making". *The Guardian.* Retrieved from http://www.guardian.co.uk/film/2011/jun/06/steve-james-golden-age-documentary

Gans, H. J. (1979). *Deciding what's news: A study of CBS evening news, NBC nightly news, Newsweek, and Time.* New York, NY: Pantheon Books.

Gans, H. J. (2003). *Democracy and the news.* New York, NY: Oxford University Press..

Irwin, J. R. (2004). On digital media as a potential alternative cinema apparatus: A marketplace analysis. *Atlantic Journal of Communication, 12*(1), 4–18.

Jetnikoff, A. (2008). Making a micro-documentary on a shoestring budget. *Screen Education, 51,* 98–104.

Kasson, E. G. (2010). The message is the medium: The difference between documentarians and journalists. [Web log comment] Retrieved from http://www.documentary.org/magazine/message-medium-difference-between-documentarians-and-journalists

Knight, J. (2007). DVD, video and reaching audiences. *Convergence: The Journal of Research into New Media Technologies, 13*(1), 19–41.

Kolodzy, J. (2006). *Convergence journalism: Writing and reporting across the news media.* Lanham, MD: Rowman & Littlefield.

Layton, C. (2007). The video explosion. *American Journalism Review, 29*(6), 24–32.

Lewin, K. (1951). *Field theory in social science: Selected theoretical papers.* New York, NY: Harper.

Lohmann, F. (2007). Fair use, film, and the advantages of Internet distribution. *Cinema Journal, 46*(2), 128–133.

Ludtke, M. (2009). Long-form multimedia journalism: Quality is the key ingredient. *Nieman Reports, 63*(1), 20–24.

Micro-Documentaries. (2011). *Micro-Documentaries.com.* Retrieved from http://www.micro-documentaries.com/

Peters, C., & Broersma, M. J. (Eds.). (2013). *Rethinking journalism: Trust and participation in a transformed news landscape.* New York, NY: Routledge.

Project for Excellence in Journalism. (2011). The state of the news media 2011: An annual report on American journalism. Retrieved from http://stateofthemedia.org/

Schwab, T. (2010). Does it still feel real? Documentary film as media, market and message: 1980–2010. *Global Media Journal: Australian Edition, 4*(2), 1–7.

Shoemaker, P. J., & Cohen, A. A. (2006). *News around the world: Content, practitioners, and the public.* New York, NY: Routledge.

Shoemaker, P. J., Eichholz, M., Kim, E., & Wrigley, B. (2001). Individual and routine forces in gatekeeping. *Journalism & Mass Communication Quarterly, 78*(2), 233–246.

Shoemaker, P. J., & Vos, T. P. (2009). *Gatekeeping theory.* New York, NY: Routledge.

Sperling, J. (2011). Reframing the study of American visual culture: From national studies to transnational digital networks. *Journal of American Culture, 34*(1), 26–35.

Storm, E. (2007, May). *The endurance of gatekeeping in an evolving newsroom: A multimethod study of web-generated user content.* Paper presented at the International Communication Association, San Francisco, CA.

Van Der Haak, B., Parks, M., & Castells, M. (2012). The future of journalism: Networked journalism. *International Journal of Communication, 6*, 2923–2938.

Vos, T. P. (2015a). Revisiting gatekeeping theory during a time of transition. In T. P. Vos & F. O. Heinderyckx (Eds.), *Gatekeeping in transition* (pp. 3–24). New York, NY: Routledge.

Vos, T. P. (2015b). Documentary film and gatekeeping forces. *Visual Communication Quarterly, 22*(1), 20–24.

Wall, M. (2015). Citizen journalism: A retrospective on what we know, an agenda for what we don't. *Digital Journalism, 3*(6), 797–813.

Wellman, B. (2004). Connecting communities: On and offline. *Contexts, 3*(4), 22–28.

White, D. M. (1950). The "gate-keeper": A case study in the selection of news. *Journalism Quarterly, 27*, 383–390.

CHAPTER FOURTEEN

Stuck IN THE Second Tier

News Coverage of the Non-Frontrunners in the 2012 Presidential Campaign

ELIZABETH A. SKEWES*

In the "year of Trump", some pundits speculated that at least some credit for the success of Donald Trump's non-traditional campaign was due to the media's fascination with him, especially during the pre-primary phase of the campaign from June 2015 through early January 2016. During this period, Trump benefitted from a dominating 34 percent of news coverage of the Republican race (Patterson, 2016), and most of that coverage was positive, according to a study by the Tom Patterson at the Shorenstein Center on Media, Politics and Public Policy at Harvard University (Patterson, 2016). In contrast, the next closest Republican contender—at least in terms of news coverage—was Jeb Bush at 18 percent, who garnered about half of the coverage received by Trump. Marco Rubio and Ben Carson each got 14 percent of the news coverage, Ted Cruz got 13 percent, John Kasich got 7 percent, and the remaining 11 candidates—people like Chris Christie, Carly Fiorina, Lindsey Graham, Bobby Jindal and Rick Santorum—didn't get enough coverage to even merit mentioning in Patterson's study. None of these candidates really managed to break out of the second tier in coverage, which damaged their ability to be seen as viable in the eyes of the voting public.

* Elizabeth A. Skewes is Associate Professor of Journalism and Media Studies at the University of Colorado Boulder. Email: elizabeth.skewes@colorado.edu.

While there are many things that are unique about Trump's run for the White House and the divisiveness in the Republican Party in 2016, one thing that was not unusual was the presence of a large number of qualified candidates who were relegated to the second tier by media outlets covering the campaign. So although 2016 saw a field of 17 candidates vying for the Republican nomination—and the attention of the media in the critical pre-primary season—it was similar in scope to previous election cycles that have seen a long list of candidates explore a presidential run and test the waters in events like the Iowa straw poll and in the media in the year before the first nominating contest. But like Kasich, Fiorina, Jindal and the rest of the 2016 candidates, the vast majority of those contenders barely got a mention in media coverage, or if they did get mentioned, it was only for a brief moment in the long campaign season.

The road to the White House is a long one, and it's made even longer by media coverage that starts looking ahead to the next campaign even before the Election Day signs have been taken down and the last of the confetti has been swept up. While some scholars bemoan the front-loading of the primary season, which has the nominating process largely concluded by early March (Busch & Mayer, 2004; Schneider, 1999), the fact is that the race for the presidency starts much sooner and that news coverage of the candidates that gears up long before the primary season starts is shaping public perception of the candidates before voters have a chance to weigh in. So although the election season grows longer, the very fact that news coverage winnows the field to frontrunners so quickly also means that candidates have a small window of time in which to make a big impression.

This study examines the problem of being stuck in the second tier through a content analysis of media coverage of candidates in the 2012 Republican primary. It finds that only a handful of candidates got a significant and sustained amount of coverage during the pre-primary season and going through May 2012, when Mitt Romney accrued enough delegates to effectively lock up the nomination. It also finds that there are changes in how some candidates are covered over time, particularly those who are put forward in the media as strong challengers to the frontrunner.

BACKGROUND AND THEORY

In the 2012 election, there were 131 people who filed for the Republican presidential nomination with the Federal Election Commission. Many were people who filed in only one or perhaps a handful of states, and others were minor characters in national politics. But there were many who had national profiles, and many of those who also had significant political experience, who still were considered by the media to be second tier candidates from the start and who never broke out of that pack in terms of the coverage they got—among those were George Pataki, Bobby Jindal and John Kasich. And there were others, like Michele Bachmann, Rick Perry and Herman Cain, who rose on the media radar for a brief time, only to fade quickly and then be permanently relegated to the second tier for the rest of the campaign season. There were reasons for all of this, of course. Some of the second tier candidates simply never polled well, which for journalists means that they have no shot of winning the nomination and therefore aren't worth much time, attention or space, all of which are limited resources in the current media environment (Meyrowitz, 1995). Other second tier candidates would show promise, like Bachmann, who came out of the August 2011 straw poll in Iowa as a frontrunner, but then would fade due to falling poll numbers or some self-inflicted wound, like Perry's "oops" moment in the Republican candidates debate on November 9, 2011, when he couldn't remember the three agencies he said he would shut down or Cain's problem when a number of women came forward to accuse him of sexual harassment. But the impact of being deemed unworthy of media attention is devastating for a candidate and campaign stuck in the second tier. And for the voting public, the impact of coverage that focuses only on frontrunners challenges the democratic ideal of having a robust debate about the merits of all of the qualified candidates who run for the White House.

Election studies by the Pew Research Center's Project for Excellence in Journalism document the disparity in coverage among the candidates. In a report on the pre-primary season coverage of the Republican Race, Pew found that Herman Cain, Ron Paul and Rick Santorum were generating the least coverage, showing up in only 2 percent of the stories that were studied from May through October of 2011, and Jon Huntsman showing up in only 3 percent of stories about the election (Pew Research Center, 2011) (It's worth noting that a candidate needed to be mentioned in at least half of the story in order to be considered a newsmaker in a particular story). In that same time period, the candidates who were dominating the coverage were Rick Perry, with 17 percent, Mitt Romney with 13 percent and Michele Bachmann with 10 percent. Perry benefitted from a late entry into the race in August 2011, which made him something new and therefore noteworthy. Bachmann was most noted for her win in the Iowa straw poll in August, but quickly moved "back where she started, an unlikely contender discounted in the narrative" (Pew Research Center, 2011, p. 3).

By the official start of the primary season in January 2012, the media narrative had narrowed to a handful of candidates, focusing on Romney as the likely nominee—especially after his primary win in his home state of Michigan on Feb. 28—and on those who could pose a serious challenge to him. Those two candidates, Santorum and Newt Gingrich, saw their coverage spike with some notable victories. Following his January 21 primary victory in South Carolina, Gingrich got a positive bump both in the amount of his coverage, going from a significant presence in less than 20 percent of election stories in early January to about 65 percent of the election stories in late January, and in the tone, which was more positive than negative for about two weeks (Rosenstiel et al., 2012). Despite polling numbers that ranged from the mid-teens to low 20s leading up to the South Carolina primary, Gingrich's win there positioned him—at least in the minds of the media—as the candidate most likely to offer a strong challenge to Romney, which translated briefly into more and more positive news coverage. But as Gingrich's fortunes fell, Santorum's rose. Early in January, after a win in the Iowa caucuses, Santorum got a short burst of coverage, but he quickly faded and was being featured in about 6 percent of election stories by the end of the month. A third-place finish in South Carolina contributed to both a drop in the amount of his coverage and an increase in a negative tone (Rosenstiel et al., 2012). Victories in Colorado, Minnesota and Missouri on February 7 pushed Santorum back into the headlines and he hovered there for several weeks, but as journalists saw the delegate count going to Romney, the amount of coverage given to Santorum and its tone began to wane (Rosenstiel et al., 2012).

What all of this points to is a need for journalists to ensure that news coverage is replete with conflict and drama. In order to keep the news interesting, there has to be a viable contest, but that contest quickly winnows down to the frontrunner and his or her most likely challenger. It happened in 2000 when Bill Bradley was raised out of the small group of Democrats running against then-Vice President Al Gore. It happened in 2008, when the race on the Democratic side was narrowed in the fall of 2007 to a contest between Hillary Clinton and Barack Obama, and the race on the Republican side was a contest between John McCain and a range of candidates who flirted with success early on, including Rudy Giuliani and Mike Huckabee, before Romney became McCain's primary challenger. But in a world of limited resources, news organizations will focus on only two or three candidates in either race since they cannot cover every candidate (Meyrowitz, 1995). As Zaller and Hunt (1994) note in their work on the 1992 run of independent candidate Ross Perot, reporters ignore third-party candidates because they think that voters don't care about candidates who will not have a direct impact on their lives, and journalists think that covering candidates who won't or can't win the election may reduce their own status as media professionals. But that leads to what Kirch calls "a chicken-and-egg dilemma" for lower tier candidates: "they do not receive news coverage because reporters view them as losers, but they may be losing elections because they do not receive news coverage" (Kirch, 2015). Whether it's driven by a perception among journalists that voters aren't interested in second tier candidates or by a scarcity of newsroom resources or both, the lack of coverage of candidates who aren't at the top of the polls results in a kind of "spiral of silence" about them that renders them invisible to the electorate (Noelle-Neumann, 1974).

For candidates in the second tier, the problem is that even in an era when social media is a significant part of the communication picture, voters still rely on traditional media for information about the election. A candidate's fortunes—political and financial—therefore, depend on getting the attention of the press very early in the process. The reliance on the media for political information isn't new, but the role of the media in the electoral process has grown over time, and especially with the declining influence of political parties in the nominating process and in voters' lives during the 1970s and 1980s (Blendon et al., 1998; Davis, 1992; Patterson, 1993).

> [T]he media's role today in helping to establish the election agenda is different from what it was in the past. Once upon a time, the press occasionally played an important part in the nomination of presidential candidates. Now its function is always a key one. The news media do not entirely determine who will win the nomination, but no candidate can succeed without the press. The road to the nomination now runs through the newsrooms. (Patterson, 1993, p. 33)

Journalists, by their training and by their nature, are skeptical about those in power and often see it as their duty to provide an important check on those in political office, or at least to take what candidates are saying and doing and provide the political backdrop for those actions (Clymer, 2001; Weaver et al., 2007). Add to that the fact that life on the campaign trail, with its very limited access to the candidates and battle for control of the message that gets into the media, leads to an increasingly adversarial relationship between the media and the campaigns (Skewes, 2007), and voters are left with campaign coverage that is much more focused on the horse race and much more negative in tone. Patterson's (1993) study of campaign coverage found that during the 1960 election, 75 percent of the references to either John Kennedy or Richard Nixon were positive, but three decades later during the 1992 campaign, only 40 percent of the references to either Bill Clinton or George H. W. Bush were positive. Patterson (1993; see also Dautrich & Hartley, 1999) concluded that some of the increase in negative news coverage was a result of stories that focus on public opinion polls, candidate character coverage and campaign strategies—something that journalists call "inside baseball" stories.

The content and tone of political matters because, as many scholars argue, it is contributing to an increasingly alienated electorate as evidenced by turnout that hovers at just more than half of the eligible voters. In the 2000 election between George W. Bush and Al Gore, arguably one of the closest contests in U.S. history, voter turnout among all eligible voters was 55.6 percent (Althaus, 2005). Four years later, in the wake of a presidential contest that was decided by the U.S. Supreme Court, turnout bumped up to 56.7 percent of eligible voters, but more than half of that increase was due to gay marriage referenda that were on the ballots in 11 states in 2004 (Althaus, 2005). Even the historic election of 2008, which resulted in the first African American being elected to the presidency and was marked by a high degree of optimism, saw turnout at 58.2 percent, which was still significantly below the 62.8 percent mark reached in 1960, when television started to play a major role in campaigns by bringing the debate between Kennedy and Nixon into American homes.

The reality is that most people have little interest in politics and end up paying attention—on the rare occasions when they do pay attention—out of a sense of civic duty. For these people, the topics and tone of political coverage can be critical in whether and how they process political information. This occurs through several processes—agenda setting, priming and framing. Agenda setting typically is applied to issues and holds that those topics that get covered more in the media become more important to the public (McCombs, 2004; McCombs & Shaw, 1972), but in the current study it also is important in its ability to communicate to readers and viewers, simply by the volume of news coverage, which candidates are worth their attention and which are deemed "unelectable" and, therefore, not worth considering.

The media also influence the public by raising the salience of some candidate attributes in the public view, leading to candidate evaluations that rely more on those attributes (Sheafer, 2007). By focusing on specific attributes, the media prime voters to use those characteristics in their electoral decisions by making them more accessible for the individual (Iyengar & Kinder, 1987). But beyond accessibility, "the media influence affective priming through the affective compelling arguments effect, in which they attach an evaluative tone (i.e., positive, negative, or neutral) to objects or issues. In other words, the media help people in assigning affective attributes to these issues" (Sheafer, 2007, p. 26). The evaluative tone is attached to a candidate through the process of framing, or how the issue or candidate is presented in the news. These frames play into existing models of understanding politics that voters already have, and they are "invaluable tools for presenting relatively complex issues, such as stem cell research, efficiently and in a way that makes them accessible to lay audiences because they play into existing cognitive schemas" (Scheufele & Tewksbury, 2007, p. 12).

The streamlining of politics by the media end up casting elections as contests between frontrunners and the one or two candidates who are closest to them in the polls, even though other candidates may still be in the race. And it does this early on in an election season, long before the vast majority of voters are paying attention, which leaves the media in a powerful position to set the electoral agenda and frame candidates as viable or not through the amount of coverage and the tone of coverage that candidates receive. This study examines those issues in the context of the 2012 Republican primary. It examines the following hypotheses:

> H1: Second tier candidates will receive less coverage and less positive coverage than first tier candidates.
>
> H2: Second tier candidates will be afforded fewer opportunities to speak in news coverage.

H3: The amount of coverage of non-frontrunners will vary over time as new candidates are elevated to "strong challenger" status to the frontrunner.
H4: The tone of coverage of non-frontrunners will vary over time as new candidates are elevated to "strong challenger" status to the frontrunner.

METHODOLOGY

While there were 131 Republican candidates who filed for the presidency with the Federal Election Commission, this study is narrower in its scope. It focuses on media coverage in six newspapers of the 31 candidates who were mentioned as either a potential or declared candidate between January 2011 and May 2012, when Romney secured enough delegates to lock up the nomination. In order to generate a sample of stories for the study, four random dates were selected from each of the 17 months in the study and all stories in the six newspapers on those four dates were included for analysis. The sampling resulted in a total of 754 stories—317 from *The New York Times*, 184 from *The Washington Post*, 132 from the *Houston Chronicle*, 24 from the *Chicago Sun-Times*, 24 from the *San Francisco Chronicle*, and 71 from *USA Today*.

Stories were coded for the total number of sentences that mentioned of each of the 31 candidates, as well as the tone of each of those mentions. Additionally, coding included the number of sentences from a candidate that were direct quotes, reflecting the ability of candidates to speak for themselves in an era of a shrinking sound bite (Patterson, 1993). Stories also were coded for the prominence of each candidate within the story. For this variable, it was noted where the candidate was first mentioned—in the lead, in the first third (but not the lead), in the second third or in the bottom third. Intercoder reliability was calculated using Scott's pi, with values that ranged from .76 on tone to .98 on placement.

RESULTS

Not surprisingly, Romney was mentioned in the most stories—35 percent—in the 2012 primary season (see Table 14.1, numbers bold in black are used for the top five candidates in each category of coverage). He came into the 2012 campaign as a second place contender in the 2008 Republican primary, with victories in 11 states in 2008, and 22.2 percent of the votes cast during the primary season, surpassing Mike Huckabee who won eight states and wound up with 20.1 percent of the primary votes cast (though Huckabee did end up with 278 delegates to Romney's 271). Their relatively strong finishes in 2008 meant both Romney and Huckabee were seen as contenders early on in the 2012 election cycle, and while Huckabee initially considered another presidential run in 2012, he announced in May 2011 that he wasn't going to seek the nomination.

That decision by Huckabee left Romney as the other likely candidate coming out of the 2008 field and put him at the top of the polls coming into the pre-primary year of 2011. Romney held the lead in the polls, by as much as 13 percentage points, through early 2011 and held his lead—except for one week in April when he was in a tie at 11 percent with Gingrich—until August when Perry entered the race and dominated the polls for about a month. Still, Romney never fell out of double digits in polling, sending a signal to journalists that he was still a contender. So Romney continued to get covered in the fall of 2011, even as people like Bachmann and then Perry picked up support, and overall Romney got mentioned in more stories and was mentioned more often in those stories, setting him up as a strong contender in the minds of prospective voters. Other candidates at the top of the polls did get mentioned in many of the stories, but other than Romney, none of the other four candidates who showed up in the most number of stories scored highly on any of the other measures related to news coverage in 2012, while Romney was among the top five candidates for all five measures—the total number of stories in which he was mentioned, the average number of sentences in which he was mentioned per story, the average number of both negative and positive sentences in each story and, perhaps most importantly, the average number of quotes per story.

As a more colorful and outspoken candidate, Chris Christie got mentioned more often in the stories that did mention him, with a mean of 14 sentences, and more positively, with a mean 2.83 positive sentences, but he was mentioned in only 2 percent of the stories in the sample. The only candidate to receive more mentions per story and more positive mentions was Buddy Roemer, a former Louisiana governor, who got a mean of 16 sentences per story and six positive and four negative sentences per story. However, all of those mentions came in the one feature story that he was cited in, and it was a feature on "outside" candidates that ran in the style section of *The Washington Post* just before the start of the primary season. Other candidates who were high in mentions per story or positive or negative sentences were, like Roemer and Christie, candidates who got mentioned in relatively few stories overall. The only candidate who got mentioned in a relatively high number of stories (8.6 percent of the sample) who also scored high in any other measure was Santorum. He was sixth among the 31 candidates in terms of total number of stories in which he was mentioned, and when he was in a story, he got a higher mean quote average than Romney (2.75 quotes per story for Santorum to Romney's 2.58). And as a precursor to the 2016 election season, it's worth noting that Donald Trump, who wasn't a candidate, got mentioned as a potential candidate in 16 stories, or 2 percent of the sample. More to the point, when he was in a story, he got to talk a lot. His mean quote count was 3.29, which is higher than Romney's or Santorum's. The only candidate with a higher quote count is Mike Pence, but

Pence was mentioned in only two stories, so he never got out of the second tier in terms of news coverage in 2012.

In all, the data in Table 14.1 show support for the first hypothesis. Candidates who were frontrunners, even briefly, did get mentioned in more stories, and typically got mentioned more frequently, than candidates considered to be in the second tier. And while the top five candidates measured by the amount of mentions they obtained did receive more positive coverage than many in the pack of 31 candidates, only Romney was in the top five for overall positive mentions. Other than Romney and Christie, however, the other three candidates who received generally positive coverage—Roemer, Pence and Marco Rubio—also received mentions in only a handful of stories.

Table 14.1: Candidate Mentions in News Stories, Coverage Valence and Candidate Quotes

Candidate	**No. of Stories (N=754)**	**Mean sentences per story**	**Mean negative sentences**	**Mean positive sentences**	**Mean quotes**
Romney	**238**	**10.81**	**2.14***	**1.82**	**2.58**
Perry	**176**	9.27	1.79*	1.27	1.92
Bachmann	**112**	5.79	1.08	1.11	1.40
Gingrich	**93**	7.38	1.65*	1.06	1.88
Paul, Ron	**68**	4.85	0.98*	0.86	1.16
Santorum	65	6.91	1.64*	1.30	**2.75**
Pawlenty	63	4.30	1.14*	0.39	1.13
Huntsman	62	5.79	0.90	1.03	1.79
Palin	54	5.91	1.19*	0.68	1.17
Cain	52	6.17	1.33*	1.26	2.41
Huckabee	22	1.45	0.17	0.42	0.12
Christie	16	**14.00**	1.83	**2.83**	3.00
Trump	16	8.56	**1.91***	0.83	**3.29**
Ryan	13	2.15	0.67*	0.40	0.73
Daniels	10	5.50	0.30	1.09	0.50
Giuliani	10	2.00	**2.00***	0.20	1.00
Barbour	8	1.63	0.50*	0.00	1.70
Paul, Rand	7	6.57	1.57*	1.00	**3.00**
DeMint	5	2.80	0.20	0.20	1.67
Rubio	5	**11.20**	**2.71***	**1.80**	0.80
McCotter	4	1.00	0.25*	0.00	0.00

Candidate	No. of Stories (N=754)	Mean sentences per story	Mean negative sentences	Mean positive sentences	Mean quotes
Johnson	3	8.00	0.50*	0.00	2.00
Bush	2	4.50	0.00	1.50	1.00
Pence	2	**12.00**	1.00	**2.00**	**4.00**
Bolton	1	1.00	0.00	0.00	0.00
Nader	1	3.00	0.00	0.00	2.00
Pataki	1	4.00	0.00	0.00	1.00
Roemer	1	**16.00**	**4.00**	**6.00**	0.00
Thune	1	1.00	0.00	0.00	1.00

The data in Table 14.1 also show support for the second hypothesis, with Romney again among the top candidates for overall speaking time, but his quote average per story of 2.58 is the lowest of the top five candidates on that measure. On this scale, as with the number of mentions, two of the top candidates—Pence and Rand Paul—were both mentioned in fewer than 10 stories out of the 754 in the sample, so despite getting to speak more, they were largely invisible in news coverage overall. Trump, as noted above, got quoted in an average of 3.29 sentence per story, and Santorum who remained the last challenger standing, got quoted in 2.75 sentences per story. This may be an artifact of his being the final candidate to pose a threat to Romney since, by late spring of 2011, there were only a few candidates still in the race and all but Romney and Santorum had been written off by the press.

The other measure in Table 14.1 deals with negative sentences. Here Romney, again, is among the top five candidates with an average of 2.14 negative sentences per story. And two other candidates who were found to have a higher number of negative sentences on average—Giuliani at 2 sentences per story and Trump at 1.91 sentences per story—were among the candidates who got mentioned in at least 10 stories overall. In fact, among the 16 candidates who received the 10 or more mentions in stories, 11 of them had a higher number of negative sentences on average than positive sentences (noted by asterisks). The two candidates who got the highest negative scores—Roemer and Rubio—were mentioned in only one and five stories, respectively, and while they were featured prominently in those stories, they did not break into first tier coverage during the 2012 election. But the relative level of negative coverage among the most-covered candidates supports the findings of others that media coverage of campaigns generally is more negative than positive (McGowen & Palazzolo, 2014; Patterson, 1993).

The third hypotheses concern changes in the amount of coverage over time. And here there are only six candidates who saw significant increases in the amount of coverage they received over the course of the campaign (see Table 14.2). For this hypothesis, time was converted to a ratio variable of number of days out from the start of the data collection period in January 2011. Also, due to the large number of candidates studied, many of whom did garner much coverage or who did not see shifts in coverage, Table 14.2 focuses only on the candidates who saw significant shifts in coverage over the span of the campaign season. The table shows that Santorum saw the biggest increases in coverage ($r = .71$), which is consistent with the findings of the Pew Research Center study showing that Santorum "was largely ignored by the press" through 2011 and until he won the Iowa caucuses on January 3, 2012 (Rosenstiel et al., 2012). And the media still waffled in covering Santorum until his February 7, 2012, victories in Colorado, Minnesota and Missouri. At that point, his coverage spiked for roughly four weeks, with Santorum being mentioned in anywhere from 42 to 60 percent of news stories about the election (Rosenstiel et al., 2012).

Other candidates who saw increases in their amount of coverage over time included Romney, who had a slow and steady increase in media coverage as he continued—through the pre-primary and primary seasons—to poll well and raise money, both of which are cues the media use to assess a candidate's viability (Skewes, 2007). Two other candidates who saw increases in coverage over time were Gingrich and Herman Cain, both of whom saw spikes in coverage when they outperformed expectations. For Gingrich, there were two spikes in his coverage—one in mid-December 2011 that corresponded with a brief polling bump that put him in frontrunner status, and another in late January 2012 when he won the South Carolina primary and appeared in roughly 65 percent of stories that week. He also saw a more modest bump in coverage, in early to mid-March 2012, showing up in about 35 percent of stories. Some of those were about his March 6 win in Georgia, but many were about his overall poor performance and involved speculation about whether he would drop out of the race. As it turns out, he stayed in officially until May 2, 2012, when he suspended his campaign.

Herman Cain, on the other hand, had faded from coverage long before the first primary occurred. Cain, a businessman and Tea Party supporter, campaigned heavily in the early primary states in 2010 and came into 2011 with some support, but still a longshot. His fortunes started to shift upward—as did the amount of his news coverage—as Perry fumbled and got relegated to second tier status in September. Cain's coverage jumped in late September from mentions in about 23 percent of stories earlier in the month to 35 percent of stories heading into October. The spike in coverage corresponded with increasing poll numbers, and late in October, following a strong showing in a straw poll in Florida in late September, Cain was being considered a top tier candidate. In November, several women accused Cain of sexual harassment and Cain's fortunes fell, as did his coverage. Less than a month later, on December 3, 2011, Cain suspended his campaign. Ron Paul and Jon Huntsman also saw upticks in their coverage over the course of the campaign, but despite being mentioned nearly as much as some of the candidates who did ascend to temporary frontrunner status, neither was covered as a candidate who had a serious chance at winning and more often than not, both Huntsman and Ron Paul were mentioned in summary paragraphs about what other candidates were doing that came lower in news stories and relegated them to also-ran status.

Candidate	r	Sig.
Cain	.39	.004
Gingrich	.44	.001
Huntsman	.45	.001
Paul, Ron	.50	.001
Romney	.36	.001
Santorum	.71	.001

Table 14.2: Pearson Correlations of Amount of Coverage of Candidates to Time

When considering how the tone of candidate coverage changed over time, there is a lot of variance among the candidates, providing some support for the fourth hypothesis (see Table 14.3). Again, time is treated as a ratio variable here. It was coded by recording the year, then the month then the date that each story appeared, so May 12, 2011, became 110512, for example, and January 8, 2012, became 120108. The data show that Romney, who was always in the mix as a frontrunner or potential frontrunner, saw his negative coverage increase more over time than his positive or neutral coverage. The same pattern emerged for Ron Paul, despite the fact that he never broke out of the second tier in terms of his treatment by the media. For Cain, his negative coverage increased over time, mostly as a result of the sexual assault allegations against him, as well as a particularly poor performance in a videotaped interview with the editorial board of the Milwaukee *Journal Sentinel.* Perry also saw his negative coverage increase over time, and also as a result of underperforming, based on media expectations, in some early straw polls and his widely lampooned "Oops" moment at the November 9, 2011, Republican debate when he forgot the name of the third government agency he would shut down. The little coverage that Huntsman got was increasingly positive over time. As a non-contender in the eyes of the media, he benefitted from some sympathetic treatment as a candidate who was bucking the odds as he headed into the primary season. Huntsman, who put most of his political resources into the New Hampshire primary, finished third there on January 7, 2012, and stayed in the race through the January 21 primary in South Carolina. But after finishing in seventh place in South Carolina, he withdrew from the race and endorsed Romney. The only other candidate to see significant increases in the positive tone of coverage over the course of the pre-primary and primary season was Santorum, largely as a result of a good showing in Iowa and later in the Midwest. But Santorum, who tacked to the Christian conservative side of the Republican Party, also saw an increase in his negative coverage over time. So as he started to score a few primary victories in 2012 and was put under the media microscope, the tone of his coverage grew both more positive and more negative.

Candidate	Positive coverage	Neutral coverage	Negative coverage	F	Sig.
Cain	111450.35	111133.99	112379.89	3.53	.030
Huntsman	115515.13	111731.40	113647.00	7.21	.001
Perry	111302.23	111731.35	113295.76	8.15	.001
Paul, Ron	112114.36	113301.96	116273.04	7.03	.001
Romney	113569.69	114371.05	115649.63	3.73	.025
Santorum	118764.46	115798.56	118056.97	5.28	.006

Table 14.3: One-Way Analysis of Variance of Tone of Candidate Coverage Over Time

While amount of coverage and tone of coverage certainly reveal a lot about the state of the 2012 race—at least from the journalists' perspectives—the question of where candidates showed up in stories, which is a measure of their prominence, also provides evidence of the fall of grace for some presidential candidates. Although the evidence is not as strong as it is for other measures, there were some significant differences in the placement of a handful of candidates in news stories about the election (see Table 14.4). For Jim DeMint, who was discussed as a possible candidate but who ultimately didn't run, his mentions quickly moved to the bottom third of a story before disappearing altogether. Giuliani also started out strong, making it into the lead in many stories, but when the buzz about him didn't materialize into a campaign, he became a pundit for the Republican Party and the mentions about him dropped in prominence into the middle or bottom third of news stories when he was mentioned. Similarly, Huckabee and Huntsman both saw slight shifts to lower placement in news coverage over the course of the campaign as they moved from potential candidates to declared candidates to second tier candidates.

Candidate	Lead	Top third	Middle third	Bottom third	F	Sig.
DeMint		110178.00	118194.80	120113.00	10.18	.006
Giuliani	120160.00	110796.80	113911.83	113114.00	3.04	.051
Huckabee	116854.33	110832.82	112701.64	111649.55	2.99	.044
Huntsman	114044.36	111348.29	112269.85	112286.82	2.47	.052

Table 14.4: One-Way Analysis of Variance of Placement of Candidates in News Stories Over Time

DISCUSSION

The data and finding presented here reinforce the idea that news organizations, especially in an era of shrinking resources, will opt—during the pre-primary and primary seasons—to cover only the candidates that they think have a chance of becoming the nominees of the two major political parties (Meyrowitz, 1995; Skewes, 2007). This calculation is based partly on journalists' assessment of the interests of news consumers (Zaller & Hunt, 1994) and partly on the unwieldy number of candidates who consider a run or who actually file for the presidency (Busch & Mayer, 2004). But the effect of not getting coverage early on, or of being relegated to second tier status, can be an artificially limiting one. Some Republican candidates in the 2012 presidential race were largely absent from the media radar early on. Although Cain had been campaigning in early primary states in 2010, he was largely ignored by media outlets until after both Bachmann and Perry stumbled in the late summer and early fall of 2011. Likewise, Santorum, struggled to get media coverage throughout 2011, though he ended up being a central figure in the campaign once the primary season started in January 2012. Had these candidates been covered earlier in the race, voters would likely have known about Cain's problems with women long before the fall of 2011 and Santorum might have been assessed based on his positions on issues, rather than as a possible roadblock to a smooth run to the nomination for Romney.

The frames that journalists use to define candidates, including the "frame" of little or no coverage because the candidate isn't a contender, can prime for the public a sense of how they should feel about the candidates.

> By making certain issues, candidates and characteristics of candidates more salient, the media can contribute significantly to the construction of a perceived reality that voters rely upon in making decisions about whether to vote and for whom to vote. (Weaver, 2004, p. 349)

News organizations need to simplify the narrative (Skewes & Plaisance, 2005), so the field quickly gets winnowed down to a handful of candidates who are deemed "electable" by the media. Once that happens, those who haven't been polling as well or raising as much money—typically the markers that the media use to assess electability—find that the journalistic "pack" covering them can be loaded into a Chevy Suburban rather than a convoy of press buses. And the decisions about how to allocate scarce media resources to cover an election are made as early as three years before a campaign officially starts. The problem is that those decisions end up marginalizing lesser-known candidates, which hampers their ability to then grow a war chest or rise in the polls. It's back to the chicken-and-egg problem that Zaller and Hunt (1994) described, and it contributes to a spiral of silence regarding some candidates that keeps them stuck in the second tier for the duration of the election season.

Indeed, the concern about the media's failure to provide somewhat equivalent coverage to primary candidates is at the heart of the debate over Trump's nomination in 2016. Examinations of coverage once Trump entered the race show him dominating the coverage throughout 2015, getting the equivalent of roughly $55 million in free media—and most of it positive—compared to $36 million in free media for Jeb Bush, his closest competitor in the media coverage race, and $16 million for John Kasich, who landed squarely in the second tier throughout the 2016 nominating season (Patterson, 2016). So even early analysis of the 2016 election is revealing some similar patterns that have persisted over contemporary presidential nominating contests. The goal of any candidate has to be a strong start in the run up to announcing a presidential bid in order to avoid being cast as a secondary character for the duration of the election season.

Of course, this study is examining only one election cycle. A more thorough explanation of the role of the media and the candidates—as well as the political calendar—as influences on media content would come from looking at other elections, including the 2016 campaign season. Also, additional variables, such as candidate fundraising and public opinion poll ratings, would add to the understanding of media coverage in the pre-primary year. It also would help to introduce more data regarding newsroom resources and the increasing role of social media in determining how to cover candidates and which candidates to cover.

Still, the patterns that emerge here—early favorite status for those who get in the race several years before the election, and an increasing tendency to inject affective tone into campaign coverage—are significant as we try to understand why campaign coverage looks the way it does and as we seek ways to make it better serve the electorate.

REFERENCES

Althaus, S. L. (2005). How exceptional was turnout in 2004? *Political Communication Report, 15* (1), 1–5. Retrieved March 20, 2016 from http://www.ou.edu/policom/1501_2005_winter/commentary.htm

Blendon, R. J., Young, J. T., Brodie, M., Morin, R., Altman, D. E., & Brossard, M. (1998). Did the media leave the voters uninformed in the 1996 election? *Harvard International Journal of Press/Politics, 3*(2), 121–130.

Busch, A. E., & Mayer, W. G. (2004). The front-loading problem. In W. G. Mayer (Ed.), *The making of the presidential candidates 2004* (pp. 1–43). Lanham, MD: Rowman & Littlefield.

Clymer, A. (2001). Better campaign reporting: A view from the major leagues. *PS: Political Science and Politics, 34*, 779–784.

Dautrich, K., & Hartley, T. H. (1999). *How the news media fail American voters: Causes, consequences, and remedies.* New York, NY: Columbia University Press.

Davis, R. (1992). *The press and American politics: The new mediator.* White Plains, NY: Longman.

Iyengar, S., & Kinder, D. R. (1987). *News that matters: Television and American opinion.* Chicago: University of Chicago Press.

Kirch, J. (2015). Why news reporters ignore third-party candidates. *Newspaper Research Journal, 36*(4), 399–414.

McCombs, M. (2004). *Setting the agenda: The mass media and public opinion.* Cambridge: Polity.

McCombs, M. E., & Shaw, D. L. (1972). The agenda-setting function of mass media. *Public Opinion Quarterly, 36*(2), 176–187.

McGowen, E. B., & Palazzolo, D. J. (2014). Momentum and media in the 2012 Republican presidential nomination. *Presidential Studies Quarterly, 44*(3), 431–446.

Meyrowitz, J. (1995). The problem of getting on the media agenda. In K. E. Kendall (Ed.), *Presidential Campaign Discourse: Strategic Communication Problems* (pp. 46–47). Albany, NY: State University of New York Press.

Noelle-Neumann, E. (1974). The spiral of silence: A theory of public opinion. *Journal of Communication, 24* (2), 43–51.

Patterson, T. E. (1993). *Out of order.* New York, NY: Alfred A. Knopf.

Patterson, T. E. (2016, June). Pre-primary news coverage of the 2016 presidential race: Trump's rise, Sanders' emergence, Clinton's struggle. Retrieved from http://shorensteincenter.org/pre-primary-news-coverage-2016-trump-clinton-sanders/

Pew Research Center. (2011). The media primary: How news media and blogs have eyed the presidential contenders during the first phase of the 2012 race. Retrieved from http://www.journalism.org/2011/10/17/cr/

Rosenstiel, T., Jurkowitz, M., & Sartor, T. (2012, April 23). How the media covered the 2012 primary campaign. *Pew Research Center.* Retrieved from http://www.journalism.org/2012/04/23/romney-report/

Scheufele, D. A., & Tewksbury, D. (2007). Framing, agenda setting, and priming: The evolution of three media effects models. *Journal of Communication, 57*, 9–20.

Schneider, W. (1999, July 18). Whatever happened to voting? *Los Angeles Times*, p. M1. Retrieved March 17, 2016 from http://web.lexis-nexis.com

Sheafer, T. (2007). How to evaluate it: The role of story-evaluative tone in agenda setting and priming. *Journal of Communication, 57*, 21–39.

Skewes, E. A. (2007). *Message control: How news is made on the presidential campaign trail.* Lanham, MD: Rowman & Littlefield.

Skewes, E. A., & Plaisance, P. L. (2005). Who's news? A new model for media coverage of campaigns. *Journal of Mass Media Ethics, 20*(2&3), 139–158.

Weaver, D. H. (2004). Media agenda setting and elections: Voter involvement or alienation? *Political Communication, 11*(4), 347–356.

Weaver, D. H., Beam, R. A., Brownlee, B. J., Voakes, P. S., & Wilhoit, G. C. (2007). *The American journalist in the 21st century: U.S. news people at the dawn of a new millennium.* Mahwah, NJ: Lawrence Erlbaum Associates.

Zaller, J., & Hunt, M. (1994). The rise and fall of candidate Ross Perot: Unmediated versus mediated politics—Part 1. *Political Communication, 11*(4), 357–390.

CHAPTER FIFTEEN

The Psychometry of Sexting

Non-Normative Psychic Desire as a Predictor of Sexual Text Message Engagement

JOHN WOLF*

Sexting (or the sending and receiving of sexual text messages) represents a novelty in computer-mediated communication of a sexual nature, an area of mass communications that researchers have only recently begun to explore empirically. This behavior can be attributed, in part, at least, to the now widespread adoption rate of digital information and communication technologies (ICTs) like cell phones, smartphones, tablets, and laptops (Anderson, 2015). The high adoption rates of these kinds of technologies have resulted in the digital routinization of numerous areas of activity that once required, to some varying degree, person-to-person interaction (e.g., banking [Smith, 2015], shopping [Greengard, 2015], education [Soukup, 2015], etc.). Sexual activity is a prime example of one such area, the routines of which are being renegotiated by digital technologies.

While there exists no shortage of studies showcasing the impact that contemporary digital technologies are having on everyday tasks (e.g., Barkhuus & Polichar, 2011; Gardner & Davis, 2014; Wallace, 2016), less well understood is the adoption of these technologies for the purposes of sexual activity. This lack of understanding isn't due to want of effort nor can it attributed to the sensitivity of the topic. On the contrary, sexting has been the focus of a number of recent academic studies (several are reviewed in the present study), the findings of many of which seem to generate more questions than they provide empirical data to answer, due, in

* John Wolf is Assistant Dean of the College of Science and Liberal Arts at the New Jersey Institute of Technology in Newark. Email: john.m.wolf@njit.edu.

no small part, to their exploratory nature (which is attributable to the recency of the phenomenon itself). Thus, although research into sexting hasn't been scant, it remains incomplete, with a particular dearth in the literature concerning psychosocial forces like motivation, need fulfillment, and personality (Cooper, Quayle, Jonsson, & Svedin, 2016).

Likewise, although the topic is taboo—or perhaps *because* it is taboo (e.g., Shoemaker & Reese, 2014, pp. 75–77)—sexting has appeared frequently in the popular press (Ricketts, Maloney, Marcum, & Higgins, 2015), which often employs alarmist and sensationalist rhetoric to characterize the behavior (Judge, 2012). News media coverage of sexting tends to emphasize themes such as teenage rebellion and extreme risk-taking (Hasinoff & Shepherd, 2014; Mitchell, Finkelhor, Jones, & Wolak, 2012), criminality (Karaian, 2014), and negative mental health repercussions (Klettke, Hallford, & Mellor, 2014), which, collectively, convey the message that sexting is an act of social deviance.

That the news media have emphasized deviance in their framing of sexting invites further empirical exploration. Because sexting is constructed as an act that violates norms related to the appropriateness of sexual expression, individuals' associations with other sexual behaviors that have been historically coded as deviant (e.g., non-monogamy [Conley, Moors, Matsick, & Ziegler, 2013]; anal intercourse [Halperin, 1999]; non-procreative sexual encounters [Hubbard, 2000]) may offer key insight into the psychosocial forces that coalesce to engender this behavior. Using a purposive sample of more than 2,000 respondents, the present study seeks to fill a gap in the extant literature by exploring the relationship between sexting engagement and the appeal of non-normative (i.e., deviant) sexual acts and relationship types.

SEXTING: A CONCEPT EXPLICATION

The first step in working towards a better understanding of sexting is to deal with the operationalization of the concept itself. In other words: What—empirically—constitutes sexting? Drouin, Vogel, Surbey, and Stills (2013) note that "the greatest inconsistency in the limited sexting literature concerns the definition of the *content* of sex messages" (p. 26, emphasis in the original). At issue is what to include under the umbrella of sexting (i.e., sexually explicit text, photos, and/or videos), and studies seeking to quantify the prevalence and correlates of the behavior have repeatedly observed the lack of a mutually agreed upon operational definition (e.g., Klettke et al., 2014; Lounsbury, Mitchell, & Finkelhor, 2011; Strohmaier, Murphy, & DeMatteo, 2014).

Although the word now appears in English language dictionaries (e.g., *Oxford English Dictionary*, *Merriam Webster*), many prior studies neglect to include an analysis of the different kinds of sext-related behaviors that empirically exhibit covariation. Using in-depth interviews with a research population of 15- to 20-year-olds, Walker, Sanci, and Temple-Smith (2013) found that "[a]lthough sexting is a term used by legislators, law enforcement, educators, and mass media… young people do not use this term. Moreover, there was no one word that described the phenomenon for all young people" (p. 699). Burkett (2015) confirms this finding, observing that young adults seldom used the term sexting when discussing the phenomenon, preferring instead to employ a vocabulary referencing specific acts (e.g., "'pictures', 'naked photo', 'topless photo', 'naked selfies', and 'sex video,'" p. 844) rather than a more general, all-encompassing term.

Prevalence

Perhaps due to the lack of a mutually agreed upon operational definition, the reported prevalence of sexting varies considerably from one study to the next. Conducting a meta-analysis of literature dealing with the phenomenon, Klettke et al. (2014) ascertain that the prevalence of sexting among adolescents and adults differs depending on the sampling design as well as the operational definition used by the researchers. Studies employing a random sampling design found that, among adolescents aged 10–19 years, the prevalence of sending or receiving sexually suggestive text messages or photos was 10.2% for sending and 15.64% for receiving (p. 46). Using a non-representative sample, one study found that the prevalence of sending and receiving sexts was 17% among the same age cohort. For adults aged 18 to 30 years, studies using non-representative convenience samples found that the prevalence of sending or receiving sexually suggestive text messages or photos was 53.31% for sending (p. 48) and 56.59% for receiving (p. 49).

It's important to note that, of all the studies investigating the prevalence of sexting among adults, only one used random sampling, finding that the prevalence of receiving sexually suggestive text messages or photos was 33%, while the prevalence of sending (10%) was given only for sexually suggestive or explicit photos alone (Associated Press & MTV, 2009, p. 14). The difference in prevalence among studies using representative samples versus non-representative samples is noteworthy, with the latter demonstrating an inflated prevalence among all age cohorts. The inflation of sexting prevalence among non-representative samples is most likely attributable to self-selection among respondents. The second observation that merits consideration is that no study—not even those using a random sample—has failed to observe the phenomenon, meaning that studies seeking to characterize the behavior should focus more on frequency of engagement rather than a preoccupation with prevalence.

Correlates of Sexting Engagement

Since statistics regarding the prevalence of sexting are inexact and varying, it is equally productive to consider the correlates that, in past research, have been found to predict engagement. I will begin by looking at the demographic predictors of sexting before considering behavioral and attitudinal correlates.

Demographic predictors. Klettke at al. (2014) offer a good starting point for considering which demographic variables have demonstrated empirical relationships with sexting engagement in past research. Before considering these findings, however, it is important to note that all of the following studies involve adult populations 18 years or older and that all make claims based on results derived from self-selecting (i.e., non-random) samples.[1]

Although much prior research has focused on age, the researchers found that among seven studies examining age as a factor, six concluded that it was *not* a predictor of engagement. The sole remaining study found that age was a predictor of engagement when measuring the prevalence of the sending of nude or sexually suggestive or explicit photos.

Studies measuring gender differences in engagement were less conclusive overall. Among the 12 studies that measured gender differences in adult sexting, six indicated no differences between males and females, while, of the remaining six, three found that males were more likely to receive sexts, two found that females were likely to send sexts, and one found that males were more likely to engage in sexting overall.

The impact of race, sexual orientation, and relationship status has also been considered, although less extensively than gender and age. Among studies measuring engagement differences by race, one study found that identifying as white was a positive predictor of engagement, one found that identifying as Asian or Pacific Islander was a negative predictor of engagement, while one found no difference in engagement by racial identification.

Few studies have investigated the relationship between sexting and sexual orientation, and the ones that have leave many questions unanswered. One study (Wysocki & Childers, 2011) found that LGBTQ women demonstrated a higher likelihood of sending and receiving sexts, but—it's worth noting—that the same study observed a gender difference for engagement, with females indicating higher prevalence overall regardless of sexual orientation. It remains unclear if the researchers controlled for gender when investigating sexual orientation as a predictor. Another study (Grov, Breslow, Newcomb, Rosenberger, & Bauermeister, 2014), focused on self-identified gay and bisexual men's use of the Internet more generally rather than sexting per se, observed that, increasingly, mobile technology is "an environment gay and bisexual men are using for sexual purposes" (p. 390). If, within the gay community, mobile technology is, indeed, becoming a prominent space to meet and engage with potential sex partners, it may be logical to assume that gay or bisexual self-identification among men is a predictor of sexting engagement. Bauermeister, Yeagley, Meanley, and Pingel (2014) confirm this finding, concluding that sexting was more frequent among sexually active men who have sex with men; in the same study, sexting was also found to be predictive of insertive (but *not* receptive) anal intercourse.

Finally, among studies that investigated relationship status as a predictor of sexting, all five concluded that individuals in relationships were more likely to engage in sexting behaviors. For individuals in relationships, thus, sexting engagement may serve as a kind of relationship maintenance or a contemporary means to exchange intimacies. Whether engagement varies by relationship type (e.g., gay versus straight, serious versus casual, etc.) remains unknown.

Behavioral predictors. Sexting is, by definition, a form of sexual engagement, as any operational definition of the concept involves the sending and receiving of sexually suggestive or explicit content (it is, recall, in the specification of content in which operational definitions can vary considerably). Thus, sexual histories are likely to be an important consideration in reviewing the behavioral correlates of sexting engagement. A 2015 study of Canadian young adults observed that individuals who have engaged in sexting are likely to be older by about one year and have had, on average, more lifetime and monthly sex partners than individuals who have never engaged in the behavior (Champion & Pedersen, 2015, p. 207). Other studies have demonstrated similar findings (e.g., Benotsch, Snipes, Martin, & Bull, 2013; Crimmins & Seigfriend-Spella, 2014).

In one study, individuals who viewed Internet pornography were four times more likely to sext, indicating that sexting may be merely another form of sexual expression, which, along with other behaviors, comprises a broad range of digitally routinized sexual habits (Crimmins & Seigfriend-Spella, 2014). Other studies have linked sexting with high-risk sexual behaviors, including penetrative sex (both vaginal and anal) without a condom (Benotsch et al., 2013), regretted sexual encounters (Burkett, 2015), and sexual experiences under the influence of drugs and alcohol (Champion & Pedersen, 2015). Additionally, recreational drug use—chiefly in the form of alcohol and marijuana—was higher among individuals who reported sexting engagement over the same time period, thus further establishing a link between sexting and high-risk behaviors (Benotsch et al., 2013).

Attitudinal predictors. Attitudes serve a dual purpose: they can help to elucidate why individuals engage in certain kinds of behavior, and, furthermore, they can reveal participatory intention regarding future behaviors. Along with subjective norms and motivation, attitudes are an essential component of any psychometric model, the purpose of which is to offer a prototype for behavioral engagement.

Multiple studies have demonstrated that favorable attitudes about sexting are among the strongest predictors of engagement (Byers & Shaughnessy, 2014;

Champion & Perdersen, 2015; Hudson & Fetro, 2015). Attitudes towards sexting are commonly measured by indexing participants' responses across three dimensions (Hudson & Fetro, 2015; National Campaign to Prevent Teen and Unplanned Pregnancy, 2008): opinions about sexting behaviors (e.g., How much do you agree or disagree that each of the following adjectives describes the behavior of sexting? Flirty, gross, hot, lame, fun, dangerous, etc.); opinions about the perceived consequences of sexting behaviors (e.g., potential for embarrassment; concern over disappointing family, friends, or teachers; anticipatory regret; etc.); and opinions about individuals who engage in sexting (e.g., How much do you agree or disagree that each of the following adjectives describes people who sext? Flirty, lame, confident, cool, desperate, insecure, slutty, etc.).

In addition to attitudes, findings from previous studies commonly demonstrate that subjective norms also positively predict sexting engagement. With respect to sexting, subjective norms reference the perceived prevalence of the act among participants' friends and peers, as well as perceived expectations regarding sexting partners (i.e., the partner with whom one engages in sexting). Motivation is also key in predicting sexting and can be especially germane when considering individuals' likelihood to engage in the behavior at some point in the future. The extant literature (e.g., Champion & Pedersen, 2015) on this subject, though limited, indicates that the most common reasons cited for sexting engagement include relationship maintenance and individuals' desire to showcase their sexual appeal to a current or potential sex partner. To a lesser degree, findings also demonstrate that sensation seeking is a common motivation among individuals who engage in sexting.

EXPLORING SEXTING THROUGH NON-NORMATIVE PSYCHIC DESIRE

Considering the identified correlates of sexting, it is apparent that there exists a link between the phenomenon and deviant behaviors and attitudes. Deviance doesn't reflect a value judgment; rather, it signifies an action or a thought that violates normative boundaries—something that threatens to disrupt the status quo (e.g., Shoemaker & Reese, 2014, p. 75). In other words, many of the behaviors and attitudes that have been demonstrated to correlate with sexting are non-normative insofar as they transgress the prescriptive expectations that have been established—whether implicitly or explicitly—by the dominant culture. It stands to reason, thus, that deviant attitudes and behaviors are likely to be predictive of sexting, especially as this relationship has already been established anecdotally by the news media (as already identified in the current study). Thus, this study will explore this relationship by investigating the ways in which non-normative (i.e., deviant) sexual desires influence sexting engagement.

Data were collected from 2,013 respondents from May through September 2011. Respondents were recruited using a variety of sampling plans. The largest share of respondents was recruited randomly from the email directory of a large, Northeastern university. A subset of LGBTQ respondents was recruited purposefully by emailing LGBTQ community groups across the United States and Canada and asking them to distribute digitally to their mailing lists an invitation to participate in the survey. Finally, respondents were recruited using convenience sampling by sharing the survey on the social media sites Facebook and Twitter.

Respondents participated in a web-based questionnaire administered by an online survey software platform. Given the potentially sensitive nature of the topic, respondents were made aware of the study's focus during recruitment as well as in the informed consent text, the content of which respondents had to agree to before beginning the survey. The questionnaire took, on average, 15 minutes to complete. After completing the survey, respondents were invited to enter a drawing for a $50.00 gift card by entering their email into an online drawing. If respondents chose to enter the drawing, they clicked on a link that took them away from the website hosting the survey so that their email addresses could not be linked with their responses.

Operational Definitions

Demographics. Demographic measures included age, gender, and relationship status. The average age was 24.73 (SD = 8.06). Gender was dichotomously coded into female (63.1%) and male (34.9%). Slightly more than one-quarter (27.9%) of the sample indicated that they were in a relationship, while nearly half (53.1%) identified as single (never married); otherwise, the remaining 19% of respondents indicated other relationship statuses (e.g., married, partnered, divorced, etc.). Sexual identity was assessed by instructing respondents to select the term that they would use to describe their own sexual identity. Responses included choices included "bisexual", "gay", "heterosexual", "homosexual", "lesbian", "queer", "straight", and "other". Duplicate terms (e.g., straight and heterosexual) were collapsed during data cleaning to arrive at the following categories: bisexual (11.3%), gay (8.2%), lesbian (5.4%), and straight (75.1%).

Liberal sex attitudes. Liberal attitudes about sex were by using items from the revised Sociosexual Orientation Inventory (Penke, 2011). Using a 9-point Likert scale (9 = "strongly agree"), respondents were asked to rate their agreement on items such as, "Sex without love it OK". Items were then indexed to provide a single score indicative of liberal attitudes about sex (Cronbach's α = .81).

Sexual preoccupation. Sexual preoccupation was adapted from the sexual preoccupation index from the Sexuality Scale (Snell & Papini, 1989). Using a 5-point Likert scale (5 = "strongly agree"), respondents were asked to rate their agreement on items such as, "I am more sexual than most people". Items were then indexed to provide a single score indicative of the degree to which respondents thought of themselves as more or less sexual (Cronbach's α = .76).

Social currency. Sexual experiences as social currency or the need to discuss sexual experiences with friends was measured by asking respondents to provide their opinions on items like, "It's important that I can share my sexual desires and thoughts with others". Respondents indicated the degree to which each item was important using a 5-point Likert scale (5 = "very important"). Items were then indexes to provide a single score indicative of the value respondents assigned to sexual experiences as social currency (Cronbach's α = .79).

Sexual histories. Respondents were also asked about their sexual histories, including: the number of lifetime sexual partners; the number of sexual partners with whom respondents had sexual experiences on only one occasion; the number of sexual partners with whom respondents had sexual experiences without having an interest in a long-term committed relationship. Responses for all three measures were numeric.

Sex frequency. Respondents were asked to report, on average, about how often they had sex during the past year. Frequency was measured using an 8-point Likert scale (1 = "not at all"; 8 = "4 times or more a week").

Pornography use. Respondents were asked to indicate how frequently they viewed pornographic materials during the past year. Pornographic materials were defined as referring to any material viewed specifically for the purposes of sexual excitement or arousal. Frequency was measured using an 8-point Likert scale (1 = "not at all"; 8 = "everyday").

Technology use. Technology use was measured by assessing the frequency with which respondents used different technological devices. Mobile phone use was measured by asking respondents to estimate the frequency with which they use a mobile, cellular telephone during a typical week. Use was measured with a 5-point Likert scale (5 = "very frequently").

Internet use was measured by asking respondents to estimate how many hours they spend using the internet for personal (i.e., non-work related activities) on an average day.

Text messaging ("texting") was measured by asking respondents to report two separate items: (1) the number of text messages sent on an average day and (2) the number of text messaged received on an average day. Responses to the two items were then combined to form the variable texting (Cronbach's α = .96).

Cruising. In addition to sexting, respondents were also asked to indicate how frequently they used technologies like smartphones, laptops, and tablets to search for potential sex partners, to chat with potential sex partners, and to meet sex partners (i.e., individuals they met using the aforementioned technologies with whom they then had sex). Collectively, these behaviors were referred to as "cruising" (i.e., the search for and subsequent rendezvous with sex partners). The items were then indexed to form a single score indicative of cruising frequency (Cronbach's $\alpha = .81$).

Non-normative psychic desire. Non-normative psychic desire was measured by assessing respondents' opinions about non-normative sexual behaviors as well as different types of romantic relationships. All the following behaviors and scenarios were labeled "non-normative" because they disrupt the norm that "sex must involve a meaningful material and emotional exchange based on procreative sexual intercourse", branding "deviant" those who participate in such activities (Hubbard, 2000, p. 197).

The appeal of non-normative sexual desire was measured by asking respondents to gauge the appeal of numerous sex acts and scenarios, including anonymous sex and group sex. The appeal of anal intercourse was measured by indexing respondents' evaluation of performing and receiving six acts (i.e., digital stimulation, oral stimulation, and penetrative sex) related to anal intercourse (Cronbach's $\alpha = .91$). For all non-normative sexual desire, appeal was measured using a 4-point, forced choice Likert scale (4 = "very appealing").

The appeal of non-normative relationship prototypes was measured by asking respondents to rate the appeal of consensual non-monogamy ("where you and your partner agree to have sex with one another as well as other people") and non-consensual non-monogamy ("where you and/or your partner engage in sex outside the relationship without receiving permission or informing one another of the event"). Definitions were provided as a part of the questionnaire. Appeal of both relationship prototypes was measured using a 4-point, forced choice Likert scale (4 = "very appealing").

Sexting. Sexting engagement was assessed using six, 5-point Likert scale items (5 = "very frequently") gauging the frequency with which respondents used a mobile phone (smartphone or otherwise) to send and receive sexually explicit text messages, nude or sexually explicit photos, nude or sexually explicit videos. The architecture of sexting engagement, as measured by these items, is discussed in detail below.

THE ARCHITECTURE OF SEXTING

In order to construct a valid measure of sexting, the six sexting behaviors measured in the study were collectively assessed using correlation analysis, exploratory factor analysis, as well as reliability analysis.

As displayed in Table 15.1, correlation analysis revealed that all six behaviors were predictive of one another, although the strength of the relationship varied significantly from one pair of behaviors to the next. Notably, each "send" behavior (i.e., a behavior in which the respondent was the sender of whatever content was being measured) demonstrated the strongest relationship with its "receive" behavior counterpart (i.e., the behavior in which the respondent was the receiver of the same content). So, for example, sending sexually suggestive or explicit text messages was most strongly correlated with how frequently an individual receives them ($r = .93$, $p < .001$). This finding was also true in the case of sending and receiving sexually suggestive or explicit photos ($r = .75, p < .001$) as well as videos ($r = .72, p < .001$). In terms of overall predictive strength, the sending of sexually suggestive or explicit videos was the weakest among the six. Even so, it's important to note that sending sexually suggestive or explicit videos was still a statistically significant predictor of the five other sexting behaviors. Moreover, the magnitude of statistical significance was uniform among all possible bivariate relationship combinations ($p < .001$).

Since the behaviors demonstrated a wide range of predictive power, it was necessary to use additional statistical tests in order to explore the empirical architecture of sexting as a construct. Specifically, it was clear from the correlation analysis that although the sending and receiving of sexually suggestive or explicit texts were strongly predictive of the sending and receiving of sexually suggestive or explicit photos, the relationship between text, photos, and the sending and receiving of sexually suggestive or explicit videos necessitates further validation. Exploratory factor analysis was used to investigate dimensional specificity among the six behaviors. An oblique rotation revealed two factors based on the criteria used for extraction (i.e., Eigenvalues ≥ 1.00). Factor 1, accounting for 61.20% of the variance, shows a factor in which all six behaviors are reflective of the same construct. Factor loadings fluctuate between .68 and .83. Factor 2, accounting for 19.45% of the variance, is mainly reflective of a construct that is empirically bound to the sending and receiving of sexually suggestive or explicit videos. Notably, however, the factor loading scores for sending as well as receiving sexually suggestive or explicit videos were higher for Factor 1 than for Factor 2. Thus, it seems apparent from the results of the factor analysis that the best way to conceptualize the phenomenon is to consider all six behaviors as indicative of the same overarching construct. Subsequent reliability analyses confirm this supposition. Thus, the six behaviors were indexed to form a single score indicative of sexting frequency (Cronbach's α = .86). See Table 15.1 for a detailed display of these results.

Table 15.1: Statistical Architecture of Sexting

	Text (S)	*Text (R)*	*Photos (S)*	*Photos (R)*	*Videos (S)*	*Videos (R)*	*Factor 1*	*Factor2*
Text (S)	1.00						.83	-.49
Text (R)	.93***	1.00					.82	-.49
Photos (S)	.59***	.56***	1.00				.83	-.02
Photos (R)	.56***	.61***	.75***	1.00			.84	.00

	Text (S)	*Text (R)*	*Photos (S)*	*Photos (R)*	*Videos (S)*	*Videos (R)*	***Factor 1***	***Factor2***
Videos (S)	.31***	.31***	.51***	.45***	1.00		**.68**	**.61**
Videos (R)	.34***	.35***	.43***	.55***	.72***	1.00	**.70**	**.57**
Eigenvalue							3.67	1.17
% of Variance							61.20%	19.45%
***Cronbach's* α**							.86	.83

Note: *(S) = send; (R) = receive;* *** *indicates* $p < .001$; $N = 2{,}013$.

THE EFFECT OF NON-NORMATIVE PSYCHIC DESIRES ON SEXTING ENGAGEMENT

Hierarchical regression analysis was used in order to test the effects of non-normative sexual desires on sexting engagement. In order to assess the nuances of direct and indirect effects, variables were entered in four blocks to produce four models, beginning with the focal variables. For all models, linear independence was evaluated using the variance inflation factor (VIF) for multicollinearity. Skewness, kurtosis, and scatter plots revealed no heteroscedasticity or violations of normality otherwise.

Model 1 analyzes the relationship between sexting engagement and each of non-normative sexual desires as well as the two attitudinal measures about the non-monogamous relationships. This model reveals that all five variables are predictive of sexting. Overall, the model accounts for 8% of the sample variance. Standardized coefficients were used to evaluate relative effect size. The appeal of anal intercourse was the strongest predictor of sexting engagement ($\beta = .12, p < .001$) followed by the appeal of group sex ($\beta = .10, p < .001$). The remaining variables all indicated predictive capabilities, but their magnitude began to wane: appeal of non-consensual non-monogamy ($\beta = .07, p < .01$); appeal of anonymous sex ($\beta = .06, p < .05$); and appeal of consensual non-monogamy ($\beta = .05, p < .05$). Thus, Model 1 indicates that there exists an empirical relationship between non-normative sexual desires and sexting engagement.

Model 2 demonstrates that the addition of attitudinal variables results in a predictive model that accounts for 15% of the sample variance, a 7% increase from Model 1. Three out of the five non-normative variables from Model 1 fail to predict sexting according to Model 2, with only the appeal of anal intercourse ($\beta = .08, p < .001$) and the appeal of non-consensual non-monogamy ($\beta = .06, p < .05$) retaining any predictive power for the outcome variable, suggesting that the effects witnessed in Model 1 may actually be the result of mediation. Elsewhere, the strongest predictors of sexting engagement were sexual preoccupation ($\beta = .19, p < .001$) and the importance individuals attach to sexual experiences as social currency ($\beta = .14, p < .001$). Attitudes about sex was also a significant predictor of engagement ($\beta = .08, p < .01$), with liberal attitudes predicting higher engagement.

The addition of behavioral variables in Model 3 results in a 10% change in the amount of sample variance accounted for by the model for a total of 25%. By Model 3, the appeal of non-consensual non-monogamy is the only one of the original non-normative sexual desire variables to retain its predictive capabilities ($\beta = .05, p < .05$), and it is among the weakest predictive variables with respect to comparative effect size. Among the strongest predictors were the frequency with which respondents use technology to seek out and meet sex partners ("cruising"; ($\beta = .25, p < .001$) and how frequently respondents indicated having sex during the past year ($\beta = .24, p < .001$). Other strong predictors included and the importance individuals attach to sexual experiences as social currency ($\beta = .14, p < .001$) and sexual preoccupation ($\beta = .09, p < .001$). Among the weaker predictors, in addition to the appeal of non-consensual non-monogamy, were how frequently respondents indicated looking at pornography ($\beta = .06, p < .01$) and the number of one-time sex partners respondents indicated having had ($\beta = -.08, p < .05$), with the latter demonstrating an inverse relationship with the outcome variable. In other words: as respondents' number of one-time sex partners decreased, sexting engagement increased, potentially indicating some support for the idea that sexting is a form of relationship maintenance.

Finally, demographic, sexual identity, and technology use variables are added to Model 4, which, in total, accounts for 33% of the sample variance, an 8% increase from Model 3. Notably, in the final model, two of the non-normative sexual desire variables from Model 1 demonstrate predictive capabilities for sexting engagement: the appeal of anal intercourse ($\beta = .06, p < .01$) and the appeal of non-consensual non-monogamy ($\beta = .05, p < .01$). The frequency with which respondents use technology to seek out and meet sex partners ("cruising") remained the strongest predictor of engagement ($\beta = .25, p < .001$) followed once again the frequency with which respondents indicated having had sex during the past year ($\beta = .17, p < .001$). Other behavioral predictors included how frequently respondents viewed pornography ($\beta = .11, p < .001$), the number of lifetime sex partners ($\beta = .14, p < .01$), and the number of one-time sex partners ($\beta = -.08, p < .05$). Among the demographic variables, age ($\beta = -.14, p < .001$), gender ($\beta = -.12, p < .001$), and relationship status ($\beta = .11, p < .001$) were all significant predictors of engagement, with the model indicating that sexting engagement was higher among younger respondents, female respondents, and respondents in a romantic relationship. Among the technology use variables, sending and received text messages was a strong predictor of engagement ($\beta = .16, p < .001$) followed by mobile phone use ($\beta = .05, p < .01$) and then internet use ($\beta = .05, p < .05$). Finally, sexual preoccupation ($\beta = .09, p < .001$) and the importance individuals attach to sexual experiences as social currency ($\beta = .07$, $p < .01$) were also significant predictors of engagement.

Table 15.2: Hierarchical OLS Regression Models Predicting Sexting Engagement

	Model 1			*Model 2*			*Model 3*			*Model 4*		
	b	*S.E.*	β	*b*	*S.E.*	β	*b*	*S.E.*	B	*b*	*S.E.*	β
Anonymous Sex	0.04	0.02	0.06*	-0.01	0.02	-0.02	-0.02	0.02	-0.04	-0.01	0.02	-0.01
Group Sex	0.05	0.02	0.10***	0.03	0.02	0.05	0.02	0.02	0.04	0.03	0.01	0.04
Anal Intercourse	0.09	0.02	0.12***	0.06	0.02	0.08***	0.00	0.02	0.00	0.05	0.02	0.06**
Non--Monogamy (C)	0.03	0.02	0.05*	0.00	0.02	0.00	0.00	0.02	0.01	0.01	0.01	0.01
Non--Monogamy (NC)	0.08	0.03	0.07**	0.06	0.02	0.06*	0.05	0.02	0.05*	0.06	0.02	0.05**
Liberal Sex Attitudes				0.02	0.01	0.08**	0.01	0.01	0.02	0.00	0.01	0.01
Sexual Preoccupation				0.15	0.02	0.19***	0.07	0.02	0.09***	0.07	0.02	0.09***
Social Currency				0.09	0.02	0.14***	0.09	0.01	0.14***	0.05	0.01	0.07**
# Lifetime SP							0.00	0.00	0.02	0.01	0.00	0.14**
# One-Time SP							0.00	0.00	-0.08*	-0.01	0.00	-0.08*
# No--Relationship SP							0.00	0.00	0.06	0.00	0.00	0.03
Sex Frequency							0.06	0.01	0.24***	0.05	0.01	0.17***
Cruising							0.28	0.03	0.25***	0.28	0.02	0.25***
Porn Frequency							0.02	0.01	0.06**	0.03	0.01	0.11***
Age										-0.01	0.00	-0.14***
Gender[1]										-0.16	0.03	-0.12***
Sexual ID[2]										-0.07	0.01	-0.03
Relationship Status[3]										0.15	0.03	0.11***
Texting										0.00	0.00	0.16***
Mobile Phone Use										0.02	0.01	0.05**
Internet Use										0.01	0.00	0.05*

	Model 1			*Model 2*			*Model 3*			*Model 4*		
	b	*S.E.*	*β*	*b*	*S.E.*	*β*	*b*	*S.E.*	B	*b*	*S.E.*	*β*
Intercept	0.98***	0.04		0.56***	0.05		0.29***	0.05		0.44***	0.07	
F value	35.08***			46.66***			50.11***			50.04***		
Total R^2	.08			.15			.25			.34		
Adj. R^2	.08			.15			.25			.33		
R^2 change				.07***			.10***			.08***		

Note: *N = 2,013;* indicates p < .05; ** indicates p < .01; *** indicates p < .001*
1: For "Gender" males = 1, ELSE = 0
2: For "Sexual ID" gay and bisexual males = 1, ELSE = 0
3: For "Relationship Status" respondents in a relationship = 1, ELSE = 0

NON-NORMATIVE PSYCHIC DESIRE AND SEXTING: AN INDIRECT EFFECTS MODEL

Model 1 demonstrates that non-normative psychic desires, when considered in the absence of any control variables, affect sexting engagement positively, meaning that as the appeal of non-normative desire increases, so, too, does sexting frequency. However, much of this impact (with the exception of the appeal of anal intercourse and non-consensual non-monogamy) is explained away by the control variables introduced in subsequent models.

The introduction of attitudinal measures in Model 2 results in a more predictive overall model, but also witnesses the decreased predictive capabilities of the non-normative psychic desire variables, suggesting mediation. Indeed, subsequent analysis reveals strong correlations for the relationships between liberal sex attitudes and the appeal of anonymous sex ($r = .60, p < .001$), liberal sex attitudes and the appeal of group sex ($r = .52, p < .001$), and liberal sex attitudes and the appeal of consensual non-monogamy ($r = .53, p < .001$). The relationship between liberal sex attitudes and the appeal of anal intercourse ($r = .30, p < .001$) as well as the relationship between liberal sex attitudes and the appeal of non-consensual non-monogamy ($r = .31, p < .001$), while statistically significant, are comparatively weaker, which may explain why these were the only two of the original five non-normative psychic desire variables to retain their predictive relationship with sexting. Furthermore, while relationships among the other attitudinal predictors and the non-normative psychic desire variables were also statistically significant, they were also much weaker (i.e., $r \geq .30$).

The addition of the behavioral variables in Model 3 precipitated the disappearance of the direct effects of all the non-normative psychic desire variables with the exception of the appeal of non-consensual non-monogamy, the effect of which was diminished considerably. It is noteworthy that liberal sex attitudes, which was the primary mediator for the appeal variables in Model 2, no longer has a direct effect on sexting engagement, which suggests that one or more of the behavior variables introduced in Model 3 is acting as mediator for both attitudes and appeal. Subsequent analysis reveals that the frequency of pornography exposure seems to be the primary mediator for both liberal sex attitudes ($r = .35, p < .001$) and the non-normative sexual appeal variables: anonymous sex ($r = .42, p < .001$), group sex ($r = .51, p < .001$), anal intercourse ($r = .44, p < .001$), and consensual non-monogamy ($r = .31, p < .001$). The appeal of anal intercourse also demonstrates moderate-strength relationships with cruising ($r = .36, p < .001$), the number of lifetime sex partners ($r = .33, p < .001$), and the number of one-time sex partners ($r = .28, p < .001$), indicating that these three behavior variables also act as mediators for the effect of anal intercourse appeal, although to a lesser degree than frequency of pornography exposure.

Interestingly, among the non-normative psychic desire variables, the appeal of anal intercourse becomes once again a significant predictor of sexting engagement upon the addition of demographic and technology use variables in Model 4. This is likely due to a suppression effect from the addition of the dichotomously coded sexual identity variable in which gay and bisexual males are used as the control group. In other words, the addition of gay and bisexual males suppresses some of the error variance of the anal intercourse appeal variable, which results in the latter's increased predictive capabilities. Subsequent correlation analyses confirm this reasoning.[2] Thus, even though sexual identity is not itself a predictor of sexting, it nonetheless acts as a moderator for the appeal of anal intercourse. Similarly, the standardized effect for frequency of pornography exposure almost doubles when the demographic and technology use variables are added to the model. Gender, acting as a moderator, is the most likely explanation for this observation. A subsequent correlation analysis reveals a strong relationship between gender and pornography exposure (whereby males are much more likely to view pornography more frequently), which confirms this supposition.[3]

Relationship status was also a significant predictor of sexting engagement, whereby individuals in a relationship indicated more frequent sexting when compared to their single counterparts, offering evidence to support the idea that sexting serves as an important means of contemporary relationship maintenance. Motivation is also key in explaining the relationship between sexual preoccupation and sexting engagement, whereby individuals who are more focused on sex as a part of their identity are more likely to use the medium in order to showcase and display their sexual appeal to potential or current sex partners.

Finally, across all four models, the strongest predictor of sexting was cruising via internet enabled information and communication technologies. Furthermore, a post-hoc analysis revealed that cruising likely acts as a mediator for sexual identity.

We can derive from this the conclusion, then, that sexual identity alone has little to do with directly predicting sexting engagement; rather, sexual identity acts as a predictor of behavior (i.e., cruising) and non-normative psychic desire, which, in turn, are positively correlated with sexting engagement.

This analysis demonstrates that although non-normative psychic desires do not have a direct effect on sexting, there is strong evidence to suggest that they indirectly affect engagement. Namely, as appeal of non-normative desires increases, attitudes about sex become more liberal, and, in turn, frequency of engagement in sexual acts or behaviors also increases. This finding is consistent with an understanding of attitudes as a precursor to behavior, but one that also demonstrates that behavior is not reducible to attitudes alone. Indeed, it is apparent from these findings that sexting cannot be understood apart from the psychosocial system of behaviors, attitudes, and motivations—many of which have been and continue to be coded as deviant—of which it is but one manifestation.

NOTES

1 Unless otherwise specified, summary statistics for sexting engagement by age, gender, race, sexual orientation, and relationship status are all taken from Klekkte et al.'s (2014) meta-analysis of the extant literature on the topic (Section 3.1.2. *Adults*, p. 49).

2 For example, using bivariate correlation we can garner that the relationship between sexting engagement and the appeal of anal intercourse ($r = 0.20$) is stronger than the relationship between sexting engagement and gay and bisexual identified males ($r = 0.10$). The relationship between gay and bisexual identified males and the appeal of anal sex is, comparatively, much stronger ($r = 0.49$).

3 The relationship between gender and pornography exposure is, indeed, strong as evidenced by Pearson's r ($r = 0.61$).

REFERENCES

Anderson, M. (2015, October 29). Technology device ownership: 2015. Retrieved from http://www.pewinternet.org/2015/10/29/technology-device-ownership-2015/

Associated Press & MTV. (2009). MTV Digital Abuse Survey, Executive Summary. Retrieved from http://surveys.ap.org/data/KnowledgeNetworks/AP_Digital_Abuse_Topline_092209.pdf

Barkhuus, L., & Polichar, V. E. (2011). Empowerment through seamfulness: Smart phones in everyday life. *Personal and Ubiquitous Computing, 15*(6), 629–639.

Bauermeister, J. A., Yeagley, E., Meanley, S., & Pingel, E. S. (2014). Sexting among young men who have sex with men: Results from a national survey. *Journal of Adolescent Health, 54*(5), 606–611.

Benotsch, E. G., Snipes, D. J., Martin, A. M., & Bull, S. S. (2013). Sexting, substance use, and sexual risk behavior in young adults. *Journal of Adolescent Health, 52*(3), 307–313.

Burkett, M. (2015). Sex(t) talk: A qualitative analysis of young adults' negotiations of the pleasures and perils of sexting. *Sexuality & Culture, 19*(4), 835–863.

Byers, E. S., & Shaughnessy, K. (2014). Attitudes toward online sexual activities. *Cyberpsychology: Journal of Psychosocial Research on Cyberspace*, *8*(1), article 10.

Champion, A. R., & Pedersen, C. L. (2015). Investigating differences between sexters and non-sexters on attitudes, subjective norms, and risky sexual behaviours. *The Canadian Journal of Human Sexuality*, *24*(3), 205–214.

Conley, T. D., Moors, A. C., Matsick, J. L., & Ziegler, A. (2013). The fewer the merrier?: Assessing stigma surrounding consensually non-monogamous romantic relationships. *Analyses of Social Issues and Public Policy*, *13*(1), 1–30.

Cooper, K., Quayle, E., Jonsson, L. S., & Svedin, C. G. (2016). Adolescents and self-taken sexual images: A review of the literature. *Computers in Human Behavior*, *55*, 706–716.

Crimmins, D. M., & Seigfriend-Spella, K. C. (2014). Peer attachment, sexual experiences, and risky online behaviors as predictors of sexting behaviors among undergraduate students. *Computers in Human Behavior*, *32*, 268–275.

Drouin, M., Vogel, K. N., Surbey, A., & Stills, J. R. (2013). Let's talk about sexting, baby: Computer-meditated sexual behaviors among young adults. *Computers in Human Behavior*, *29*(5), A25–A30.

Gardner, H., & Davis, K. (2014). *The app generation: How today's youth navigate identity, intimacy, and imagination in a digital world.* New Haven, CT: Yale University Press.

Greengard, S. (2015). *The internet of things.* Cambridge, MA: The MIT Press.

Grov, C., Breslow, A., Newcomb, M., Rosenberger, J., & Bauermeister, J. (2014). Gay and bisexual men's use of the Internet: Research from the 1990s through 2013. *Journal of Sex Research*, *51*(4), 390–409.

Halperin, D. T. (1999). Heterosexual anal intercourse: Prevalence, cultural factors, and HIV infection and other health risks, Part I. *AIDS Patient Care and STDs*, *13*(12), 717–730.

Hasinoff, A. D, & Shepherd, T. (2014). Sexting in context: Privacy norms and expectations. *International Journal of Communication*, *8*, 2932–2415.

Hubbard, P. (2000). Desire/disgust: Mapping the moral contours of heterosexuality. *Progress in Human Geography*, *24*(2), 191–217.

Hudson, H. K., & Fetro, J. V. (2015). Sexual activity Predictors of sexting behaviors and intentions to sext among selected undergraduate students. *Computers in Human Behavior*, *49*, 615–622.

Judge, A. A. (2012). "Sexting" among U.S. adolescents: Psychological and legal perspectives. *Harvard Review of Psychiatry*, *20*(2), 86–96.

Karaian, L. (2014). Policing 'sexting': Responsibilization, respectability and sexual subjectivity in child protection/crime prevention responses to teenagers' digital sexual expression. *Theoretical Criminology*, *18*(3), 282–299.

Klettke, B., Hallford, D. J., & Mellor, D.J. (2014). Sexting prevalence and correlates: A systematic literature review. *Clinical Psychology Review*, *34*(1), 44–53.

Lounsbury, K., Mitchell, K. J., & Finkelhor, D. (2011, April). *The True Prevalence of "Sexting"*. Durham, NC: Crimes against Children Research Center.

Mitchell, K. J., Finkelhor, D., Jones, L. M., & Wolak, J. (2012). Prevalence and characteristics of youth sexting: A national study. *Pediatrics*, *129*(1), 13–20.

National Campaign to Prevent Teen and Unplanned Pregnancy. (2008). Sex and tech: Results from a survey of teens and young adults. Retrieved from https://thenationalcampaign.org/sites/default/files/resource-primary-download/sex_and_tech_summary.pdf

Penke, L. (2011). The revised sociosexual orientation inventory. In T. D. Fisher, C. M. Davis, W. L. Yarber, & S. L. Davis (Eds.), *Handbook of sexuality related measures* (3rd ed.; pp. 622–625). New York, NY: Routledge.

Ricketts, M. L., Maloney, C., Marcum, C. D., & Higgins, G. E. (2015). The effect of internet related problems on the sexting behaviors of juveniles. *American Journal of Criminal Justice, 40*(2), 270–284.

Shoemaker, P. J., & Reese, S. D. (2014). *Mediating the message in the 21st century: A media sociology perspective* (3rd ed.). New York, NY: Routledge.

Smith, A. (2015, April 1). Chapter three: A "Week in the Life" analysis of smartphone users. Retrieved from http://www.pewinternet.org/2015/04/01/chapter-three-a-week-in-the-life-analysis-of-smartphone-users/

Snell, Jr., W. E., & Papini, D. R. (1989). The Sexuality Scale: An instrument to measure sexual-esteem, sexual-depression, and sexual-preoccupation. *The Journal of Sex Research, 26*(2), 256–263.

Soukup, P. A. (2015). Smartphones. *Communication Research Trends, 34*(4), 3–37.

Strohmaier, H., Murphy, M., & DeMatteo, D. (2014). Youth sexting: Prevalence rates, driving motivations, and the deterrent effect of legal consequences. *Sexuality Research and Social Policy, 11*(3), 245–255.

Walker, S., Sanci, L., & Temple-Smith, M. (2013) Sexting: Young women's and men's views on its nature and origins. *Journal of Adolescent Health, 52*(6), 697–701.

Wallace, P. (2016). *The psychology of the internet* (2nd ed.). New York, NY: Cambridge University Press.

Wysocki, D. K., & Childers, C. D. (2011). "Let my fingers do the talking": Sexting and infidelity in cyberspace. *Sexuality & Culture, 15*(3), 217–239.

The "Mediated" Method

CHAPTER SIXTEEN

Documenting THE "Mediated Message"

The Art and Science of Content Analysis Research

ERICA SCHARRER*

As media consumers, we are often struck by the content features of what we encounter on television, film, radio, the newspaper, the Internet, in print, and in video games. Content can make us laugh, cry, fearful, angry, or joyful. It can make us feel connected to others or it can make us feel isolated or distant. It can inform us and it can persuade us. It is always teaching us something about the world around us, and the events and people—as well as the values, experiences, and points of view—that make up that world. What, exactly, we encounter through news and entertainment outlets, as well as what we ourselves create and distribute, has much to tell about our culture and the world in which we live.

Content analysis is a social scientific tool that allows for the documentation of the content features of the media and other cultural artifacts in order to better understand them, to determine whether the content we encounter represents broad patterns or is more idiosyncratic in nature, and to begin to consider how and why content features function as they do as cultural products with particular uses, users, and audiences. The method examines the artifacts of culture as an important locus of inquiry in their own right and also has the potential to reveal a great deal about both why and how those cultural artifacts take the shape they do and how individuals might create, use, and/or be influenced by them.

* Erica Scharrer is Professor in the Department of Communication at the University of Massachusetts Amherst. Email: scharrer@comm.umass.edu.

Content analysis has a special place in the field of Communication and Media Studies, since an understanding of messages sent and received through technological means and the meaning making engaged in by both content creators and content consumers is a foundational aspect of the discipline. The method illuminates and potentially interrogates those messages, thereby lending insights into the very heart of the communicative process. To borrow from the phrasing in the title of the Shoemaker and Reese (1991, 1996, 2014) seminal book, content can be considered, therefore, to be a message or series of messages that is/are "mediated" in both meanings of the term, distributed through media channels and inevitably altered as a result of this intermediary step.

The shift of the individual from audience member to content producer in the face of mobile and Internet technologies only makes the need for content analysis more acute and the possibilities more interesting. With a greater array of content creators that goes well beyond the traditional large media conglomerates that have historically had the means to distribute messages to audiences to now include individuals themselves, how does content change? Systematic study is needed to provide an answer.

THE ART AND SCIENCE OF CONTENT ANALYSIS

Many textbooks exist that outline the logic and the pragmatic considerations of quantitative content analysis research design. Klaus Krippendorff's *Content Analysis: An Introduction to Its Methodology* (2013); Daniel Riffe, Stephen Lacy, and Frederick G. Fico's *Analyzing Media Messages: Using Quantitative Content Analysis in Research* (2014); and Kimberley Neuendorf's *Content Analysis Guidebook* (2002) have long been essential reading on the "how to" of the methodology as well as on the underlying assumptions behind its use. Krippendorff's (2013) definition of content analysis—"a research technique for making replicable and valid inferences from texts (or other meaningful matter) to the contexts of their use" (p. 24)—reveals the central position for the logic of the scientific method with its emphasis on observation, validity, and reliability. Indeed, content analysts know that they must be systematic in every stage of the process, beginning with making unitizing decisions (determining the unit of analysis in the research design and figuring out how to know whether any available content meets the definition necessary to be observed and documented) and sampling decisions (deciding, among the universe of units, on which limited set will be observed). The ways in which they operationalize their concepts must also be clear, comprehensive, and systematic, and judgments of coders about how to apply those operationalizations to the content they encounter must be consistently made and mathematically tested to ensure a high rate of agreement among multiple coders. Of course, the statistical analysis that proceeds from this point in the process of content analysis design is governed by hypothesis testing, research question exploration, description, explanation and inference, all clear markers of the scientific method that defines the methodology.

Thus, pioneers and practitioners of content analysis point out ways in which the method is, indeed, a science with precise rules, standardized steps, and systematic approaches. The principles and practices of content analysis methodology that include sound sampling toward the goal of generalizability, conceptualization and operationalization of variables to work toward reliability and validity, and intercoder agreement to make some claim on objectivity and replicability all speak directly to the science of the method. Yet, despite the standardization of the steps involved in carrying out content analysis and its close relationship to quantitative methods, there is room in the method, as well, I argue, for a bit of art in the process, a modest degree of subjectivity, creativity, and interpretation.

In some of my prior studies, for instance, I have combined the quantitative approach to the study of media content with a discussion of qualitative exemplars to illustrate not just the quantity of particular portrayals but the vividness, tone, and tenor—the qualities—of a subset as well. In Scharrer (2002), for instance, I examined the treatment of Hillary Rodham Clinton in newspaper coverage during the time of her transition from First Lady of the United States to candidate for the U.S. Senate. The study uses a systematic sampling technique to randomly select from the full population of U.S. newspaper articles archived in the LexisNexis database produced using the search term "Hillary (Rodham) Clinton" that circulated between the unofficial and official announcement of her Senate run, resulting in 342 articles. An additional 96 articles about Senate candidate opponent Rudy Giuliani that ran concurrently with a subsection of the Clinton stories was also systematically sampled to allow for comparisons. The quantitative results of the study found that the majority of criticism printed in the news coverage of both Senate candidates pertained to the issues at hand, thereby showing the press performing its watchdog role, questioning the candidates' stances on the economy, foreign affairs, and other issues. The campaigns themselves were also subject to scrutiny in the press, especially for Clinton, comprising 32% of all negative statements about Clinton and 16% of all negative statements about Giuliani in the sample. Yet beyond those general parallels, disparities surfaced in the themes that elicited negative coverage by candidate, with 16.6% of all negative statements about Clinton calling into question her likelihood of winning, 15% bringing up her "carpetbagger" status (both, therefore, challenging the legitimacy of her candidacy), as well as 11.9% critiquing Clinton for violating traditional gender roles (for instance, by being too careerist) or, conversely, for not being sufficiently feminist (for instance, for putting up with President Clinton's affairs).

Qualitative exemplars examined alongside these numerical estimations shed further light on these and other sources of "bad press" that Hillary Clinton was attracting at the time. Although it occupied only a small percentage of the coverage analyzed in the sample (4.3% of all negative statements about Clinton among the 342 articles), for instance, the qualitative quotes that implied it was audacious for Clinton to run for elected office at all provided some of the most vivid illustrations of critique in the press during the period. For instance, *Washington Post* columnist Judy Mann wrote that "Mrs. Clinton is turning her back … on the very great honor that the American people bestowed upon her when they made her husband president" and E. J. Dionne, appearing in the *Denver Post*, called Clinton's move from First Lady to Senator "the most improbable political leap in our history". I interpreted these remarks as clear indicators of negative fallout for Clinton's crossing of traditional boundaries. Similarly, the qualitative data on the more explicitly gender-related comments Clinton received in news coverage, although comprising just 11.9% of all the negative statements garnered in the sample, are evocative, as well, as seen in reporter David Daley's claim in the *Milwaukee Journal Sentinel* on December 19, 1999 that some members of the public find Clinton to be "a frustrating feminist who mocked Tammy Wynette for standing by her man, then did just that during the humiliating impeachment drama" or in this quote from author Danielle Crittenden, in a *Boston Globe* article on December 26, 1999: "Whether you're a Democrat or a Republican, you have to be sick of this Lady Macbeth character we now have in the White House, and look forward to having a First Lady who will be happy in the traditional role and secure in a good marriage". By integrating quantitative data with qualitative exemplars, the meaning behind the numbers that surfaces from a solely quantitative approach to content analysis can be enhanced, thereby bolstering, as well, the validity of the study.

In other content analysis studies, the art form of the methodology is made apparent in relatively subjective interpretations of content that—through careful coder training and the application of the coding scheme to sample content to work continually toward shared understandings of the application of major concepts—can eventually result in a convergence of coding decisions necessary to meet intercoder reliability standards. In doing so, content analytic researchers need not rely fully on manifest aspects of content that nearly everyone would agree on given their surface-level presence, but also can extend into observations of more latent aspects of media depictions, those that require some interpretation and judgment regarding their coding, so long as the latter are sufficiently precise in definition as to render agreement among multiple coders. (Note here that this view diverges from the advice of Riffe and colleagues (2014), who suggest quantitative content analysis limit itself to manifest forms.)

In my study of gender and violence in video game ads (Scharrer, 2004, outlined in more detail in a subsequent section, below), I was interested in exploring whether print ads that marketed video games would differ in their depictions of male and female video game characters. Some variables were relatively straightforward to code, including how much of their bodies the attire of the characters revealed. But, I also asked coders to note the attractiveness of the primary characters appearing in the ads from 1 (not attractive at all, intentionally disgusting or repulsive looking) to 5 (extremely attractive, very beautiful or exceptionally handsome characters), a request open to a fair degree of subjectivity. Coders also noted the sexiness of each primary character—from 1 (not sexy at all, not intended to be a sexual being, no emphasis on sexuality) to 5 (highly sexualized, emphasis on sexual body parts or provocatively posed)—again, a coding decision spurring potentially differential interpretation on the part of the coders. I do recall extensive discussion of these judgments in the training of the six graduate student coders, but with time and practice using sample content and the coding instrument, we were able to arrive at just-this-side of acceptable 66% agreement for the sexiness variable and 70% for the attractiveness variable across each of the pairs of the coders. These were the lowest intercoder agreement coefficients among the 27 variables coded in the study, thereby showing the ongoing challenge of reliably coding latent variables that require extrapolation and interpretation beyond the surface-level dimensions of content. And yet, they are validated by additional variables that also tapped into the sexualization and appearance of the characters and that produced higher rates of intercoder agreement.

In a different study, my graduate students and I examined the interplay between aggression and humor in television commercials, prompted by the observation that movie trailers, promos for television programs, and depictions of accidents and injury in commercials for products and services are a less studied but still important source of potential audience exposure to aggression that is difficult to anticipate or avoid (Scharrer, Bergstrom, Paradise, & Ren, 2006). (More personally, my own experience as a mother concerned about my child's exposure to the content of ads that popped up unexpectedly during even "family friendly" programming fueled this particular study.) Sampling 536 primetime commercial messages that featured injury to characters and/or aggression, unitized from the well over 4,000 ads that appeared in the week of primetime programming from which this sample was selected, the coding scheme required "determining if the commercials featuring aggression or injury were intended to be humorous to the viewing audience…indicated by circling yes, no, or uncertain" (p. 624). Another variable required making note of whether the humorous element of the commercial derived from one of three "grand theories" of humor: incongruity (laughing at the unexpected), superiority (derision or parody), or psychoanalysis (an explanation for why we tend to laugh at other people's pain or discomfort). In this study, despite the inherent subjectivity involved in determining whether something is funny and why it's funny, Scott's pi intercoder reliability coefficients, averaged across all coder-by-coder pairs among the three graduate student coders, was a respectable .88 for humorous intent of the commercial, likely enhanced by the yes or no nature of the question. The type of grand humor theory variable was also sufficiently reliable at a Scott's pi of .78. From these examples, therefore, we see that with careful definitions of concepts and operationalizations and sufficient training, even relatively subjective coding decisions can be made somewhat uniformly among trained coders and can lend depth to the aspects of content that are the subject of content analysis research.

THE POLITICS OF CONTENT ANALYSIS

Content analysis can be used to expose the limits of mainstream commercial media and its means of representing individuals, social groups, issues, and events. In doing so, I argue that we can consider the use of the method to be a political act of challenging and potentially disrupting the status quo, a possibility more often associated with critical social science and qualitative methods than with positivism and quantitative social science (Gunter, 2000). Indeed, in a scenario in which cold, hard numbers and the scientific method often carry with them the force of authority, a content analysis can be used as evidence to reveal biases, distortions, and problematic portrayals in media content to set the stage to advocate for more fair, accurate, and nuanced depictions. It can also be used to identify sources of positive and forward-thinking depictions that should be applauded for their sensitivity, complexity, nuance, and accuracy.

Pamela J. Shoemaker and colleagues were pioneers in examining the determinants of newsworthiness that explain the prominence of particular items that will become "the news" amid the massive number of events and other possible entries into the news media agenda. The body of scholarship that extends from these analyses points to many sources of influence at play in the creation and distribution of the news media agenda, including the event's perceived deviance and social significance as key factors (Shoemaker & Cohen, 2006) within the wider gatekeeping process (Shoemaker & Vos, 2009). A wealth of meticulously conceived and rigorous empirical observations across a number of decades, from early studies by Shoemaker, Danielian, and Brendlinger (1991) to more recent analyses by Zhang, Shoemaker, and Wang (2013), provide the empirical basis on which this ongoing theory building rests, regarding the ways in which what becomes "the message" sent to news audiences is mediated, modified, and molded by forces and factors that range from those individuals to those more ideological in nature (Shoemaker & Reese, 2014). The resulting consideration of news formation as a construction whose final form takes shape in large part from the structural formations imposed by an advertising-based commercial system in a context of economic competition and rapid conglomeration of ownership at the same time that it considers micro-level judgments of individuals involved in the news gathering process as well as meso-level factors, such as organizational norms and cultures in the newsroom, is a prime example, I would argue, of the ways in which content analysis can be used to illuminate the limits and opportunities of existing social structures and systems of power.

In my own work, I have a series of studies of representations of gender in media content whose findings, taken together, point toward the narrowness of the ways in which gender roles are represented in entertainment media content that ranges in from video games ads (Scharrer, 2004), to police and detective television programs (Scharrer, 2001a, 2012), to wide-circulating pornography (Bridges, Wosnitzer, Scharrer, Sun, & Liberman, 2010; Sun, Bridges, Wosnitzer, Scharrer, & Liberman, 2008), to commercials featuring housework and domestic chores (Scharrer, Kim, Lin, & Liu, 2006). Yet, at the same time, some aspects of these studies show evidence of progress away from restrictive roles and toward greater fluidity among gender depictions compared to past analyses. In either case, whether depictions can generally be considered restrictive or more open or—more likely—some combination thereof, content analysis methodology is useful in revealing systems of social order, norms, and values at a particular moment of cultural context.

In Scharrer (2012), for instance, various markers of masculinity were examined among the major male characters in the ever-popular police and detective television genre over time. Sampling "every police or detective drama from the first dramatic programs broadcast on television to those offered at the turn of the millennium on broadcast or cable rated among the top 15 for at least one year in the total run of the program", (p. 94), with the exception of some missing data not accessible through the television archive, the process resulted in a sample size of 210 major male characters that were the unit of analysis for the study. Results found stable and high levels of physical aggression and somewhat lower but also consistent rates of verbal aggression carried out by those male characters over time, thereby demonstrating the persistent link between masculinity and aggression in the genre. There was a trend from the 1950s through the 1980s toward greater emotional sensitivity among male characters, however, as well as movement away from the isolated, loner depiction accompanied by emotional stoicism toward more social integration and emotional expression. Yet, the programs from the 1990s—the most recent decade examined in the study—showed a return to a greater degree of isolation and stoicism among the major male characters. The study unveiled, therefore, some stable components of this enduringly popular genre and its treatment of masculinity as well as some ways in which masculine gender roles have generally shifted over time away from a more traditional notion of masculinity toward a newer, more sensitive form, and then took a regressive step back in the final decade examined.

Scharrer, Kim, Lin, and Liu (2006) studied 477 commercials appearing within a week of primetime network television programming, coding every commercial airing during that heavily viewed time slot that featured a depiction of housework performed in and around the home. Findings revealed that the male characters carried out many fewer chores, performed them less satisfactorily, and elicited a negative response from other characters for their housework efforts more often than female characters. In fact, the performance of chores by men was frequently depicted as humorous, with male characters more likely than females to be poked fun at due to their chore performance, reinforcing the ostensible limits to domesticity associated with masculinity. Here we see a relatively restrictive role for men, depicted as ineffectual and rather uninvolved in domestic life.

Scharrer (2004) obtained a sample of print ads for video games by subscribing to major video game fan magazines for a period of six months. Every ad for a video game, console, or gaming equipment within those magazine issues was coded, resulting in a sample size of just over 1,000 ads, 96% of which were for games themselves. Results showed male characters outnumbered female characters by more than a 3:1 ratio, just over half of the ads (55%) contained a depiction of at least one act of violence, and there was an average of 2.49 weapons, 1.52 violent acts, 2.17 violent words, and 0.85 violent threats per ad. Female characters were more scantily clad and were rated by coders as both more attractive and sexier than male characters (recall from the paragraphs above the borderline reliability of these attractiveness and sexiness measures). Male characters were determined to be more muscular, and although the number of male humans depicted in the ads was not related to the violence variables, those ads with masculine non-humans (robots, monsters, and other anthropomorphized beings) were more likely to have violent words and images. In this study, we see a reliance on the sexualization and ornamentation of women in this media form as well as a severe underrepresentation of female characters appearing in the ads. We also see the consistent presence for violence and aggression in the manner in which video games are marketed, and some indication of the relatively greater tendency to associate masculine non-human characters with the use of violent words and actions.

Finally, in two interrelated studies (Bridges et al., 2010; Sun et al., 2008), I was the methodologist working with an interdisciplinary team of psychologists and media studies scholars to examine the ways in which men and women were presented within a sample of 50 randomly selected top-selling and most frequently rented "adult" films according to a compilation maintained by Adult Video News. We found a total of 3,375 acts that met our definition of aggression in the study, and found that males perpetrated 70% and females were on the receiving end of an overwhelming 94% of the total number of aggressive acts. In only 2.7% of the total number of aggressive acts did the recipient of the aggression express pain or displeasure, thereby sending a facilitative message about aggression within the context of sexual activity to the audience, and female recipients of aggression were less likely than male recipients to express displeasure in response to aggression.

The implications of this work in light of the socialization potential of media are socially significant and suggest that gender stereotypes persist among many forms of our cultural artifacts well into the most recent decades. Yet, there are aspects of each of these studies that also can be construed as progress toward more flexibility and freedom in gender role enactment within the characters that appear in popular media forms. The content analysis methodology employed in these studies and others allows for important observations of the messages about gender—as well as about a host of other themes and topics in the wider literature, of course—that audiences receive through media. With media use at very high levels among the public and given the role of the media in both reflecting and shaping social norms and behaviors, these are important inquiries with critical political implications.

CONSIDERING MEDIA CONTENT AS A DEPENDENT VARIABLE

Shoemaker and Reese's path-breaking book, *Mediating the Message: Theories of Influence on Mass Media Content* (1991; 1996; retitled to *Mediating the Message in the Twenty-first Century: A Media Sociology Perspective* for its third edition in 2014), was a landmark contribution to the scholarly practice of considering the forces and factors that are at play in the creation of media messages, resulting in messages being imbued with the particular features and attributes we later encounter as audiences. Not satisfied with taking media content as a given or merely as a starting place preceding effects, as is so often the case in communication research, Shoemaker and Reese delivered a groundbreaking explanation of the spheres of influence ranging from micro-level processes to macro-level cultural conditions and used their own scholarship to put that explanation into practice in analyses of the news environment.

Of course, the hierarchy of influences on news media content is just one application of a larger theme championed in Shoemaker's larger body of work. Decades ago, Shoemaker and Reese (1990, p. 650) wrote, "The media are not just channels. Media impose their own organizational, institutional and ideological logic on information, shaping it into a product that offers a specific view of social reality. We cannot fully understand the effects of that version of reality if we do not understand the forces that shape it". Today those words still ring true, and perhaps the greatest legacy of Shoemaker's work is its theorization and empirical exploration of precisely this, the interplay of influences that result in media content taking the shape that is packaged and delivered to audiences, a critically important inquiry that can be applied to any form of media content, including both news and entertainment forms.

In my research, using the premise established by Shoemaker and colleagues that the principles and practices that shape news and entertainment content should be the subject of rigorous social science inquiry, I have theorized about the ways in which entertainment television content both reflects and helps shape social norms, as seen in a number of studies in which television content is compared against real-world social patterns. In Scharrer, Kim, et al. (2006), for example, my co-authors and I compare and contrast the performance of domestic duties among heterosexual couples in the United States with the depictions of the same among characters appearing in commercials airing during primetime television. While real-world statistics show increased domestic responsibilities of males in U.S. households with heterosexual couples, they also continue to demonstrate that the females in that context still spend more time engaged in such activity. Amid the depictions on commercials examined through content analysis, we found nearly twice as many female characters engaged in chores in and around the house than male characters, and—perhaps most interestingly—we found that half of the domestic chores taken on by male characters ended up being depicted as humorously inept. Thus, the television world is out of step with many aspects of the modern realities of U.S. households, and gives short shrift to the real-world fathers and other adult men who do more and more (but still not most) of the child care, cleaning, cooking, and other duties to maintain the family and the home.

In an earlier content analysis study, I examined the depiction of father figures in televised sitcoms from the 1950s through the 1990s, theorizing that the rise in economic status of women in the U.S. workforce as seen through national social statistics was concurrent with the evolution of sitcom dads from the sage and measured parental figures of the *Father Knows Best* era to the bumbling buffoon dads of *The Simpsons*, *Married with Children*, *Home Improvement* and other more recent shows (Scharrer, 2001b). This study positions humor and joke telling as a manifestation of power between mother figures and father figures, as well as between the father figure and other characters, in domestic situation comedies centered on family life. Within the 136 episodes of 29 domestic sitcoms rated among the top 25 programs at the time of their viewing, the study finds a linear increase in the depiction of "foolishness"—defined by a series of semantic differential adjective pairs judged holistically across the episode—over time from the 1950s to the 1990s, and an increase in the overall proportion of jokes in the episodes made at the expense of the father as well as in the specific proportion of jokes told by the mother at the expense of the father. The argument put forth in the study is that this television depiction can be considered a dependent variable shaped by the changing economic realities of U.S. families in which mothers increasingly joined fathers as breadwinners, thereby undermining fathers' previously privileged status. In other words, I argue, when fathers were the sole breadwinners, their economic role in the household was so critically important that perhaps they were above scrutiny and criticism, a situation disrupted by the emerging economic power of wives and mothers.

Connecting Content and Effects

James A. Anderson (2012) suggests, "Content analysis can play an important (and often neglected) part in audience effects studies…Most effects studies are rather cavalier in the selection of content with the researcher selecting the content with an 'of course it's true' approach that this content is violent, sexy, gender based or whatever the issue. It would be much better if we adopted a more sophisticated analysis of the content and could point to the properties by which the genre claim is made" (p. 279). Anderson's words are reminiscent of similar observations made by Shoemaker and Reese (1990) over two decades prior, in which they outlined four particular ways of integrating the study of media content with the study of media effects: greater specificity in effects studies measuring media exposure that shows what content features such exposure encompasses, more sound social science in content analysis itself (better standardization, greater claims to both reliability and validity), deeper understanding of what factors among those that influence media content are most important from the audience reception point of view, and additional exploration of how much audience members know about the factors that influence media content.

Influenced a great deal by this line of thinking, my own dissertation work involved conducting two interrelated studies on the topic of hypermasculinity and violence in media. Under the guidance of a dissertation committee comprised of George Comstock, Pamela J. Shoemaker, and Carol Liebler, I performed a content analysis of the relative presence or absence of the indicators of hypermasulinity (Mosher & Sirkin, 1984)—sensation seeking, emotional control/toughness, romantic/sexual callousness, and a reliance on violence or aggression—among major male characters in police and detective television programs over time (Scharrer, 2001a). From that analysis of 75 episodes of 29 programs and 321 characters, I chose the single most aggressive and hypermasculine example, an episode of the television program *Miami Vice*, to serve as the treatment group stimulus in the experiment I conducted to determine whether exposure to content that combines violence with the tough and callous hypermasculine male character might trigger an aggressive response among college-aged males (Scharrer, 2001c). In doing so, the goal of integration of content and effects was, I hope, achieved.

CONCLUSIONS AND NEW TRENDS IN CONTENT ANALYSIS: INTERACTIVE MEDIA AND BIG DATA

New media forms represent both new opportunities and new challenges for content analysis. One challenge is the dynamic nature of interactive media. How can one claim to say something essential about media content if that content changes based on the ways in which users interface with it? Indeed, one of the defining features of newer technologies is the customizable ways in which the decisions of users negotiating various features and affordances change what is presented to the user on the screen.

Video games are a prime example of interactive media that can be difficult to tie down long enough to sustain reliable systematic content analysis (Schmierbach, 2009). If you and I play the same opening screens of *Call of Duty Black Ops III*, for instance, we will see different content depending on how we navigate our avatar in the virtual world. Researchers have taken various strategies in an attempt to address or circumvent this problem. In my own case, I opted for circumventing the dynamic and interactive nature of video games entirely and decided, instead, to study the static features of the ways in which games are advertised in video game fan magazines (Scharrer, 2004), as described above. Others have recorded periods of game play to assess the presence and absence of content features (Downs & Smith, 2010; Williams, Martins, Consalvo & Ivory, 2009), and yet, even these analyses are, of course, shaped by the decisions of the players themselves. Indeed, Matthews and Weaver (2013) found considerable differences in the instances of violence derived by relatively skilled compared to unskilled video game players after recording their play of a *Call of Duty* and a *Grand Theft Auto* game. Specifically, Matthews and Weaver found those with more video game playing skill and experience played these games in a manner that produced more violence in the resulting content than those with less playing skill and experience, thereby demonstrating important variability in what can be considered to be "content" in video games.

The massive amounts of data produced by social media and other information sources in the digital age also pose particular opportunities and obstacles for scholars interested in the systematic documentation of cultural artifacts. The age of "big data" generated by Facebook, Twitter, and other sources and the corresponding development of computer algorithms to capture and describe those data are a relatively new but already important component of social scientific explorations of messages circulating in contemporary discourse. Computers can be used to not only identify the presence of particular words and phrases within huge stores of data, but they can also provide information about tone through sentiment analysis and they can shed light on context through cluster analysis and on relationships between and among multiple sources of content through social network analysis (Grimmer & Stewart, 2013; Lacy, Watson, Riffe, & Lovejoy, 2015; Zamith & Lewis, 2015). Although the lure of automaticity and the command of huge samples can produce highly (perhaps technically even purely) reliable results on a host of topics, scholars and practitioners of these approaches caution against replacing human coders too soon, given human coders' unique ability to understand more complex textual structures, connotations, meanings, and inferences (Lacy et al., 2015; Zamith & Lewis, 2015).

Analyses of the content produced through social media and other Internet sources also reflect the move away from media companies and corporate conglomerates as the sole or perhaps primary producers of what becomes known as media content toward the ability of everyday citizens to create and distribute content themselves in the digital age. YouTube is, of course, a prime contemporary outlet for blogs, web video, and other citizen-produced content, and a cursory glance through recent published articles shows a number of content analyses of the web channel, representing a wide range of topics investigated among videos posted to the site and the comments they elicit, from those pertaining to health topics such as obesity (Yoo & Kim, 2012) or organ transplants (Tian, 2010), to those pertaining to identity and diversity (Kopacz & Lawton, 2013) and teenage sexuality (Cunningham, 2014).

Whether one considers newer forms of media or those that have been around for decades and whether one incorporates more recent techniques in the systematic study of content or those more traditional and longstanding in nature, all signs point to continued growth and critical importance for the documentation of "the message" sent through technological means. Rigorous social science in the exploration of not just what becomes media content but also how that content develops and for whom and how it matters continues to be timely and socially significant. I have argued in this chapter that the blending of scientific objectivity with an acknowledgement of power, politics, context and subjectivity in content analysis methodology can result in scholarship that both reflects the social and cultural context in which it is produced and also has the potential to spur social change.

Despite the near-revolutionary advancements in the media landscape that have taken place since its writing, I end with a quote from a *Journalism Quarterly* piece by Shoemaker and Reese published in 1990, that is just as relevant today as it was at the time of its publication. It's a call for social scientists to continue to pursue the systematic study of media content.

> If we are to understand the role of the mass media in shaping social processes and peoples' lives, we must do more to bring media content into our studies. It isn't enough to study only exposure to, use of, attention to, attitudes about, or effects of the mass media. We must study what people are exposing themselves to, using, attending to, thinking about, or being affected by. Although many content analyses have been carried out on newspapers, television, and magazines, these have been largely descriptive and are not often linked in any systematic way to either the forces that created the content or to its effects. We must integrate the study of mass media content with the study of mass media effects, a step that will facilitate the growth of mass communication theories. (Shoemaker & Reese, 1990, p. 649)

REFERENCES

Anderson, J. A. (2012). *Media research methods: Understanding metric and interpretive approaches.* Thousand Oaks, CA: Sage.

Bridges, A., Wosnitzer, R., Scharrer, E., Sun, C., & Liberman, R. (2010). Aggression and sexual behavior in best-selling pornography videos: A content analysis update. *Violence against Women, 16*(10), 1065–1085.

Cunningham, C. M. (2014). Sixteen and not pregnant: Teen-created YouTube parody videos and sexual risk taking in the United States. *Journal of Children and Media, 8*(1), 53–68.

Downs, E., & Smith, S. L. (2010). Keeping abreast of hypersexuality: A video game character content analysis. *Sex Roles, 62*, 721–733.

Grimmer, J., & Stewart, B. M. (2013). Text as data: The promise and pitfalls of automatic content analysis methods for political texts. *Political Analysis, 21*, 267–297.

Gunter, B. (2000). *Media research methods: Measuring audiences, reactions and impact.* London: Sage.

Kopacz, M. A., & Lawton, B. L. (2013). Talking about the YouTube Indians: Images of Native Americans and viewer comments on a viral video site. *Howard Journal of Communications, 24*(1), 17–37.

Krippendorff, K. (2013). *Content analysis: An introduction to its methodology* (3rd ed.). Los Angeles, CA: Sage.

Lacy, S., Watson, B. R., Riffe, D., & Lovejoy, J. (2015). Issues and best practices in content analysis. *Journalism & Mass Communication Quarterly, 92*(4), 791–811.

Matthews, N. L., & Weaver, A. J. (2013). Skill gap: Quantifying violent content in video game play between variably skilled users. *Mass Communication & Society, 16*(6), 829–846.

Mosher, D. L., & Sirkin, M. (1984). Measuring a macho personality constellation. *Journal of Research in Personality, 18*(2), 150–163.

Neuendorf, K. (2002). *The content analysis guidebook.* Thousand Oaks, CA: Sage.

Riffe, D., Lacy, S., & Fico, F. (2014). *Analyzing media messages: Using quantitative content analysis in research* (3rd ed.). New York, NY: Routledge.

Scharrer, E. (2001a). Tough guys: The portrayal of aggression and hypermasculinity in televised police dramas. *Journal of Broadcasting & Electronic Media, 45*(4), 615–634.

Scharrer, E. (2001b). From wise to foolish: The portrayal of the sitcom father, 1950s-1990s. *Journal of Broadcasting & Electronic Media, 45*(1), 23–40.

Scharrer, E. (2001c). Men, muscles, and machismo: The relationship between television violence and aggression in the presence of hypermasculinity. *Media Psychology, 3*(2), 159–188.

Scharrer, E. (2002). An "improbable leap": A content analysis of newspaper coverage of Hillary Clinton's transition from first lady to Senate candidate. *Journalism Studies, 3*(3), 393–406.

Scharrer, E. (2004). Virtual violence: Gender and aggression in video game advertisements. *Mass Communication & Society, 7*(4), 393–412.

Scharrer, E. (2012). More than "just the facts"? Portrayals of masculinity in police and detective programs over time. *Howard Journal of Communications, 23*(1), 88–109.

Scharrer, E., Bergstrom, A., Paradise, A., & Ren, Q. (2006). Laughing to keep from crying: Humor and aggression in television commercial content. *Journal of Broadcasting & Electronic Media, 50*(4), 615–634.

Scharrer, E., Kim, D. D., Lin, K., & Liu, Z. (2006). Working hard or hardly working?: Gender, humor, and the performance of domestic chores in television commercials. *Mass Communication & Society, 9*(2), 215–238.

Schmierbach, M. (2009). Content analysis of video games: Challenges and potential solutions. *Communication Methods and Measures, 3*(3), 147–172.

Shoemaker, P. J., & Cohen, A. A. (2006). *News around the world: Practitioners, content and the public.* New York, NY: Routledge.

Shoemaker, P. J., Danielian, L., & Brendlinger, N. (1991). Deviant acts, risky business and U.S. interests: The newsworthiness of world events. *Journalism & Mass Communication Quarterly, 68*(4), 781–795.

Shoemaker, P. J., & Reese, S. D. (1990). Exposure to what? Integrating media content and effects studies. *Journalism & Mass Communication Quarterly, 67*(4), 649–652.

Shoemaker, P. J., & Reese, S. D. (1991). *Mediating the message: Theories of influences on mass media content.* White Plains, NY: Longman.

Shoemaker, P. J., & Reese, S. D. (1996). *Mediating the message: Theories of influences on mass media content* (2nd ed.). White Plains, NY: Longman.

Shoemaker, P. J., & Reese, S. D. (2014). *Mediating the message in the twenty-first century: A media sociology perspective* (3rd ed.). New York, NY: Routledge.

Shoemaker, P. J., & Vos, T. P. (2009). *Gatekeeping theory.* New York, NY: Routledge.

Sun, C., Bridges, A., Wosnitzer, R., Scharrer, E., & Liberman, R. (2008). A comparison of male and female directors in popular pornography: What happens when women are at the helm? *Psychology of Women Quarterly, 32*(3), 312–325.

Tian, Y. (2010). Organ donation on web 2.0: Content and audience analysis of organ donation videos on YouTube. *Health Communication, 25*, 238–246.

Williams, D., Martins, N., Consalvo, M., & Ivory, J. D. (2009). The virtual census: Representations of gender, race, and age in video games. *New Media & Society, 11*(5), 815–834.

Yoo, J. H., & Kim, J. (2012). Obesity in the new media: A content analysis of obesity videos on YouTube. *Health Communication, 27*(1), 86–97.

Zamith, R., & Lewis, S. C. (2015). Content analysis and the algorithmic coder: What computational social science means for traditional modes of media analysis. *The Annals of the American Academy of Political and Social Science, 659*(1), 307–318.

Zhang, D., Shoemaker, P. J., & Wang, X. (2013). Reality and newsworthiness: Press coverage of international terrorism by China and the United States. *Asian Journal of Communication, 23*(5), 449–471.

CHAPTER SEVENTEEN

Just THE Facts, Ma'am

Merging Media Content Analysis with Survey Research

MICHAEL J. BREEN*

INTRODUCTION: THE SHOCK OF THE SAVI REPORT

In 2002, a group of Irish academics undertook a telephone survey to examine the lifetime experience of sexual abuse and violence in Ireland. It was to be a ground-breaking piece of work. The team interviewed, by telephone, some 3,130 respondents, achieving a response rate of 71.44 percent. The full report, Sexual Abuse and Violence in Ireland (SAVI) is available online and provides immense detail on the sampling and survey methodologies employed.[1]

As the authors put it, in the Executive Summary of the SAVI Report

> The prevalence of sexual violence in Ireland is unknown. Incomplete evidence from crime statistics, previous research reports and service uptake figures is insufficient to understand the nature and extent of the problem and to plan and evaluate services and preventive interventions. The main aim of the SAVI study was to estimate the prevalence of various forms of sexual violence among Irish women and men across the lifespan from childhood through adulthood. (McGee, Garavan, de Barra, Byrne, & Conroy, 2002, p. 31)

It was a courageous undertaking, broad in its scope, ambitious in its intent, and detailed in its design. The questionnaire used was wide-ranging and probing, seeking gently to explore each respondent's lifetime experience of sexual abuse. The data generated provide an extraordinary insight into an element of Irish life, hidden

* Michael J. Breen is Dean of Arts at Mary Immaculate College at the University of Limerick in Ireland. Email: Michael.Breen@mic.ul.ie.

and denied for decades. The detailed analysis makes for very distressing reading but one single reported outcome has stood out for many readers as encapsulating the core of SAVI.

> Child Sexual Abuse (defined as sexual abuse of children and adolescents under age 17 years)
> • Girls: One in five women (20.4 percent) reported experiencing contact sexual abuse in childhood with a further one in ten (10.0 percent) reporting non-contact sexual abuse. In over a quarter of cases of contact abuse (i.e. 5.6 percent of all girls), the abuse involved penetrative sex—either vaginal, anal or oral sex.
> • Boys: One in six men (16.2 percent) reported experiencing contact sexual abuse in childhood with a further one in fourteen (7.4 percent) reporting non-contact sexual abuse. In one of every six cases of contact abuse (i.e., 2.7 percent of all boys), the abuse involved penetrative sex—either anal or oral sex. (*op. cit. p. 32)*

The findings are devastating, a veritable tsunami of sexual abuse in a nation that has prided itself on the sobriquet of the "Island of Saints and Scholars". More than a decade later, it is possible to look back at the media coverage of this topic, not just of sexual crime but also of SAVI itself. What is beyond question is that there is no shortage of stories of sexual abuse, but very little about SAVI and what it had to say to the Irish public. Over the last 13 years, fewer than 200 references to SAVI have appeared in the mainstream Irish press compared to more than 20,000 stories relating sexual crime. The issue is very much a live one: within 24 hours of tweeting about Donald Trump's taped lascivious comments, Kelly Oxford received some 9.7 million responses referencing personal experience of sexual assault.

MEDIA COVERAGE OF SEXUAL ABUSE

Mass media play a role in the formation of public opinion, are selective in the messages transmitted, and are directive in trying to shape and mold opinion (Shoemaker & Reese, 2014). While there are clearly external forces at work in terms of what enters the news, it is abundantly evident that there is much left to the choices of the individual editor or journalist, as well as many influences that act from within media organizations (Altheide, 1976; Bass, 1969; Breed, 1955; Dimmick & Coit, 1982; Gross & Merritt, 1981; Luttberg, 1983; Pan & McLeod, 1991; Peterson, 1981; Salwen & Garrison, 1989; Schudson, 1989; Shoemaker & Reese, 2014; Stempel, 1985; Todd, 1983; Weaver, 1984; White, 1950). Gatekeeping theory suggests that it is important to understand what "gates" apply in relation to the coverage of various issues, in terms of examining what is covered, to what extent, and what is omitted from coverage (Shoemaker & Vos, 2009).

Media coverage of sexual abuse, as in the case of all serious news coverage, serves several social functions: apart from making people aware of the issue, it serves as a constant reminder of the levels of sexual abuse in society. Hawkins,

McDonald, Davison, and Coy (1994) have written about how the prevention of sexual abuse requires a measure of public education. The need to focus on research and intervention strategies is seen as particularly important (Brawley, 1995). On the other hand, coverage can also represent a disservice, with both Franklin and Horwath (1996) and Goddard and Saunders (2000) arguing that media coverage can sometimes be abusive in itself, a major disservice to victims, and an enormous threat to society where vigilantism has led to attacks on innocent citizens.

In December 2001, the News of the World, (a UK tabloid newspaper since closed down because of other scandals) retreated from its "name and shame" campaign targeted against British pedophiles, with the stated aim of publishing details of all 100,000 of them. The Independent had referred to the campaign as the more extreme folly that continued to engage in scare mongering, sensationalism and incitement to vigilante action. In the wake of the News of the World campaign, some parents in Portsmouth had their children carrying banners saying, "Kill Them" and vigilantes gathered outside the homes of suspected pedophiles, shouted abuse and threw stones. An innocent man with a name similar to one of those listed by the newspaper had his windows broken and abuse hurled at him. Two vigilantes were jailed for life at the Old Bailey for murdering a retired sea captain whom they wrongly suspected of being a pedophile, by firebombing his flat in Grimsby. In another incident, a suspected pedophile was battered to death with a toaster, frying pan and iron bar by vigilantes in Glasgow. In Gwent, a group of protestors, who could not tell the difference between a pediatrician and a pedophile, hounded Dr. Yvette Cloete, a respected pediatrician, from her home.

The widespread condemnation of "name and shame" campaigns in the U.K. as well as the mixed public reaction to the "outing" of pedophiles after release from prison has given rise to concern about the nature of some elements of media coverage, as well as mixed reactions by members of the public. Kitzinger (1996, 2001) and McDevitt (1998, 1999) have written on the nature of sexual abuse as constructed in media reports in Ireland and elsewhere. Many scholars have all raised questions about moral panics in respect of sexual abuse reportage (Hunter, 2008; Jenkins, 1998; Jewkes & Wykes, 2012; Kaplan & Manicavasagar, 2001; Wilczynski & Sinclair, 1999). As Adler and Polk (2001) contend: "the gradual evolution of an internationalised media, capable of the instantaneous transfer of 'infotainment' around the globe… (has created) a special appetite for the bizarre and unusual". Neil (2006) has evidenced the need to understand perpetrator gratifications. The use of sexual abuse reportage in this context has generally not been conducive to public education (Franklin, 2014; Franklin & Horwath, 1996; Tomison, 1997).

The media, however, play a critical role in covering sexual abuse in general and child sexual abuse in particular. Weatherred (2015) demonstrates how media framing of child abuse stories has changed over time and how such changes have an impact on policy, practice and public perception of the issue. McCartan, Kemshall, and Tabachnick (2015) report on how media coverage of high profile sexual assault cases, such as those involving Jimmy Saville in the UK or Jerry Sandusky in the US, confront the public with difficult social questions and help to generate a debate that moves beyond simple blame to a consideration of cause, extent, and response. Mejia, Cheyne, and Dorfman (2012) focus on the shortcoming of media reportage on sexual assault on children, wherein high profile cases are reported without sufficient attention to prevention or understanding. The ongoing media representations of pedophiles as overtly monstrous is criticized by Mayer and Furlong (2010) who, while recognizing the role of the media in contributing to social policy discourses, sees some news reportage as misrepresentative, sensationalist, and insufficient.

SEXUAL CRIME REPORTAGE IN IRISH NEWSPAPERS

The nature of newspaper reportage of sexual crimes is well documented in the academic literature. There are a number of scholarly perspectives on media coverage of sexual abuse and sexual crime. Hawkins et al. (1994) indicate that the prevention of sexual abuse requires an educated public. Brawley (1995) emphasizes research on intervention strategies as a central element in how mass media can combat abuse. Scholars also detail how media coverage can sometimes be abusive in itself: when such coverage is sensational or voyeuristic, it can render a disservice to victims rather than either provide support or education (Franklin & Horwath, 1996; Goddard & Saunders, 2000; Lonne & Parton, 2014; Niner, Ahmad, & Cuthbert, 2013; Saint-Jacques, Villeneuve, Turcotte, & Drapeau, & Ivers, 2012).

The reportage of sex crimes can be as much about social control as about public information. Kitzinger (2000) references the use of media templates as a form of media routine as defined by Shoemaker and Reese (2014). According to Kitzinger (2000), such templates are routinely used to stress one clear objective, and serve as rhetorical shorthand/shortcuts and help audiences and producers to contextualize stories. These templates shape narratives around specific issues, guide public opinion and discussion, and set the frame of reference for future media coverage, which in turn reinforces the templates themselves.

Breen's (1997, 2000, 2004, 2007, 2008) studies of sexual crime reporting in the USA, UK and Ireland showed that between 1993 and 2002, in the ten years pre-SAVI, there were twice as many stories about child sexual abuse as adult abuse, that they tended to be significantly longer than those about adult sexual abuse, and that female victims predominated in both categories. In addition, stories of abuse by authority figures predominated, with a clear predominance of stories of abuse by clergy. Familial incest was underplayed and often unnamed. There was a major gap between national prevalence statistics and newspaper reporting: for example, 75 percent of all stories of child sexual abuse in The Irish Times sample referred to clergy whereas the SAVI report indicates that clergy and religious teachers are responsible for about 3.2 percent of all child sexual abuse.

A serendipitous confluence of events allowed for a natural experiment related to Irish coverage of sexual crime. The Irish Catholic bishops commissioned an independent research agency—the Health Services Research Centre (HSRC) at the Department of Psychology, Royal College of Surgeons in Ireland (RCSI)—to undertake a program of research on its behalf. This included a national telephone survey (N=1,081) (Goode, McGee, & O'Boyle, 2003). The survey itself took four months to complete. About half-way through the data collection period in 2002, the main UK public service television channel (BBC2) screened a documentary entitled "Suing the Pope", dealing with the crisis of sexual abuse in the Irish church. Some 600 participants had responded to the survey before the screening and 481 afterwards. The subsequent analysis of attitudes pre- and post-screening supported the view that the screening of a documentary on a particular topic, particularly one as repulsive as child sexual abuse by clergy, along with the concomitant public discussions that followed, has significant impact on a wide range of variables, both those related directly to the topic of the documentary and those tangential to it. Media content has a direct bearing on public attitudes.

MEDIA OMISSIONS

It is evident that high profile cases are over-reported with a disproportionate level of coverage. This is typified by the Jon Benét Ramsey case in the U.S., Jamie Bulger in the U.K., and Sophie McColgan in Ireland. All of these cases are heinous examples of child abuse and were deeply shocking to the public in each country. While clearly newsworthy and important they are also singular events. To a large extent, the ongoing substrate of abuse is ignored. While it is not possible to give equal coverage to every episode of child sexual abuse, it is important to ensure that the topic itself is reported in a balanced way that will help educate and advise the public beyond a simple fear response (Breen, 2008).

Just as with adult sexual abuse, child sexual abuse reporting can retraumatize victims. A typical example of this in a different medium was seen in Ireland on a popular daytime radio program. The host asked a man, who had been molested as a child, about the precise nature of the abuse he had experience. When his guest declined to provide details, the host answered for him, telling the nation in detail what had happened. The risk of behavior such as this, as well as lengthy detail in media reports of abuse, is that it can readily be abusive of the victims and their families, and sometimes as traumatic as the original abuse. This requires redirection by media professionals.

The extent of child sexual abuse in particular and child neglect in general is mostly ignored. While there is a focus on child abuse by specific groups of people (e.g., teachers, clergy, strangers), there is an overall lack of coverage as to the extent of abuse in society. Prevalence studies are rarely reported, and, even where reported, rarely referenced in subsequent reports. The lack of emphasis on child neglect, as opposed to child sexual abuse is particularly troublesome. Prevalence studies indicate that many more children are neglected than are sexually abused, but their plight rarely receives prime time coverage except when a particularly heinous case comes to light as a result of social system failure, as in the case of Victoria Climbé in the UK.

The inadequacy of coverage has significant outcomes as it prevents the development of appropriately directed public outrage and it allows abuse, especially family-based abuse, to continue. It also works against the production of effective public policies. A solution requires courage from policy makers, victims, support groups, child welfare professionals, media professionals and others. Problematizing the few, and driving the problem underground, does not solve the problem, ease the pain, protect children or advance social development and justice.

THE REALITY OF SEXUAL CRIME: MEDIA, POLICE STATISTICS, AND SURVEY DATA

A wide ranging search[2] of news stories in The Irish Times using Nexis-Lexis yielded 1,127 stories between 1993 and 2002 (pre-SAVI) using a random sample of five weeks in every year. When filtered to remove non-relevant stories (e.g., overseas reporting, rape as a crop), some 495 stories were entered in a database for analysis, representing an approximate 10 percent sample. Reports of sexual crime against children were twice as common as stories about crimes against adults. Apart from a general category of sexual assault (60 percent of all stories), rape was the most common crime covered (30 percent). In those stories where the gender of the victim or the perpetrator was identified, 71 percent of victims were female, whereas 76 percent of perpetrators were male. Of those child victims whose gender is identified, 29 percent are male and 35.8 percent female, compared to 11.8 percent for adult males and 77 percent for adult females. In terms of reporting then, it would appear that boys and girls have about equal levels of sex crime against then whereas sex crimes against adults are six times more likely to be against a woman than a man. In those stories where the profession of the perpetrator was identified (163 stories), clergy or religious constituted 58 percent of cases, with teachers at 6.2 percent.

The official police statistics present a rather different picture. The Garda Siochána (the Irish police force) publishes crime statistics annually. Between 1993 and 2002, the most common crime against children is sexual assault (67.29 percent). The same is true of the content analysis data (66.4 percent). The figures for rape in relation to children are also broadly similar, 18.8 percent in the official statistics and 16.9 percent in the media reports. Incest accounts for 2.2 percent of the official statistics but 5.1 percent of the media reports. In relation to adults, the official figures indicate that sexual assault is the most common offense (64.3 percent) whereas the media reports have rape as the most frequent (67.3 percent). In the comparisons between adults and children, a different picture emerges. In the official figures rape is committed almost three times as often against adults as against children (73.1 percent v. 26.9 percent) whereas in the media reports it appears twice as often (62.6 percent v. 37.4 percent). According to the Gardaí, the majority of victims of sexual assault are adults (63.9 percent) whereas media reports imply that children are overwhelmingly more commonly such victims (85.8 percent).

The Gardaí statistics show 3,072 offenses against children between 1993–1997 and 2000–2002 (data were recorded differently for children in 1998/1999), and in the period 1993–2002 some 10,510 against adults. This contrasts strongly with the Irish Times reports, extrapolating from the 10 percent sample, of 4,940 offences overall, with 3,211 being against children and 1,611 against adults (120 unspecified). Of the more than 13,000 cases reported in the official statistics, less than one third were covered in the Irish Times. Bearing in mind that many of the Irish Times reports were reports on court cases at different stages, with multiple stories linked to one sexual crime, the gap between media coverage and actual crime is vast.

If we turn to the SAVI report, published in 2002, it become clear that the discrepancy between media reports and the official crime statistics is minor compared to the discrepancy with the lifetime experience of sexual assault of the survey respondents. SAVI would seem to indicate that the official sexual crime statistics are the tip of an iceberg. SAVI indicates that 20.4 percent of women and 16.2 percent of men reported contact sexual abuse as children. The Irish census data report that in 2002, there were 1,007,260 males and 907,768 between the ages of 25 and 65. Applying the SAVI percentages to these numbers gives an approximation of 353, 539 individuals who might have experienced contact sexual abuse as children. Averaging that out on a basis of an average age of 45 would indicate an annual rate of 7,834 sexual crimes against children, on a very conservative approximation. The official police statistic suggests 384 such crimes annually. The survey data suggest a rate more than 20 times as much.

SAVI also reports the data for adult sexual assault.

> Adult Sexual Assault (defined as sexual violence against women or men aged 17 years and above)
>
> - Women: One in five women (20.4 percent) reported experiencing contact sexual assault as adults with a further one in twenty (5.1 percent) reporting unwanted non-contact sexual experiences. Over a quarter of cases of contact abuse in adulthood (i.e. 6.1 percent of all women) involved penetrative sex.

- Men: One in ten men (9.7 percent) reported experiencing contact sexual assault as adults with a further 2.7 percent reporting unwanted non-contact sexual experiences. One in ten cases of contact abuse in adulthood (i.e. 0.9 percent of all men) involved penetrative sex.

Using the same mechanism as above, this extrapolates to 293,534 individuals being sexually assaulted as adults, conservatively approximating to 6,522 crimes annually. The official police average is 1,051 such crimes annually, indicating an under-reportage by a factor of 6.

Finally, there is a major discrepancy between SAVI and the media in respect of the perpetrators of sexual crime. Within the media reports of sexual crimes against children, 15.6 percent of such crime is attributed to parents or family members, 3 percent to strangers and 45 percent to authority figures, including clergy and teachers. This contrasts very strongly with the SAVI figures which suggest that strangers are responsible for about 20 percent of child abuse, 16.8 percent by family members (fathers, uncles, cousins, siblings) and 4.6 percent by authority figures.

THE SAVI REPORT AS TOUCHSTONE

As indicated above, the SAVI report makes for very uncomfortable reading. Based on a rigorous methodology, its findings are unimpeachable. It holds up a mirror to Irish society in general and the reflection is deeply unattractive. It also implicitly challenges the media construction of sexual crime.

> Although more recent estimates by the public of the prevalence of sexual abuse are not available, the heightened media attention given to the issue internationally has led to what has been called a "moral panic" about the (violent) nature of the world we now live in (Goddard & Saunders, 2000). Kemp (1998) have described contemporary society as being preoccupied with child sexual abuse. In considering the role of the media, Kitzinger (1996) has examined the construction of UK media reports. Intrafamilial stories of child sexual abuse are under-emphasised while those of a more sensationalist nature, e.g. those involving paedophile rings, are highlighted. A similar Australian analysis showed that stories focused on unusual and extra-familial cases (Wilczynski & Sinclair, 1999). This fosters the notion of "stranger danger" rather than considering the lack of safety afforded by the home environment for many (children and adults) who are at risk of sexual violence. (McGee et al., 2002, p. 13)

But SAVI itself provided a critical opportunity for the mainstream media, given its forensic detail. Unfortunately, little use has been made of it in the Irish media, with 197 newspaper articles referencing the data between 2002 and 2015. The Irish Times, Ireland's newspaper of record, has 85 references in this time frame, 20 of which related to the launch of the report or its immediate aftermath. Between 2003 and 2015, Ireland's premier newspaper has referenced the SAVI data less than 6 times per year on average.

CONCLUSION

The figures alluded to in the earlier part of this work indicate that the sexual crime in Ireland is not well represented in the mainstream media, that some types of sex crimes are prioritized in reporting above others, and that the representation of sex crime perpetrators is deeply unrepresentative of the reality. With respect to the official police statistics, it is clear that the level of sex crime actually reported to the civil authorities is a fraction of what actually happens in Irish society. The SAVI report brings home the reality and extent of the lifetime experience of sexual abuse in the population, against both adults and children. The SAVI data are unpalatable. Apart from dealing with a type of crime that most right thinking people regarded as "particularly heinous", the SAVI report is an indictment of Irish society. Just as Irish society contains victims, it also contains the perpetrators. While the figures in Ireland are on par with those in the USA—29 percent of women in the USA had experienced sexual abuse as children and 30 percent of Irish women said they had been sexually abused as children, according to David Finkelhor of Crimes against Children Research Centre (Holland, 2002)—there is scant comfort in knowing that the problem is as bad elsewhere. The issue is compounded by the fact that victims are very reluctant to report these crimes to the authorities: just 1 percent of men and 7.8 percent of women had disclosed the abuse to the police.

Given the media interest in sexual crimes, it seems somewhat surprising that more use has not been made of the SAVI report by the media. At this point, we lack hard data on why this is so. There is a world of difference between diagnosis and prescription: much of the media reportage tells us about deviant behavior, but does very little to either challenge or to help readers understand it. The work of Shoemaker and Cohen (2006) may well provide a way forward. At the heart of this disconnect between news coverage and social reality lie two distinct things—the news (including all the dimensions that go into news constructions) and the consumer. Personal salience and social significance/deviance also come into play. But that research is for another day.

NOTES

1. Accessible at http://www.drcc.ie/wp-content/uploads/2011/03/savi.pdf
2. (sex* w/2 (abuse or assault or attack or offence or harassment or molestation)) or rape or bestiality or buggery or incest or (gross w/1 indecency) or paedophil* or (child* w/3 molest*).

REFERENCES

Adler, C., & Polk, K. (2001). *Child victims of homicide.* Cambridge: Melbourne.

Altheide, D. L. (1976). *Creating reality: How TV news distorts events.* Beverly Hills, CA: Sage Publications.

Bass, A. Z. (1969). Refining the "gatekeeper" concept: A UN radio case study. *Journalism Quarterly, 46*(1), 69–72.

Brawley, E. (1995). *Human services and the media.* New Brunswick, NJ: Harwood Academic Publishers

Breed, W. (1955). Social control in the newsroom: A functional analysis. *Social Forces, 33*(4), 326–335.

Breen, M. J. (1997). Deviance as a trigger for intermedia agenda setting: A case study of clergy and sex abuse. *Journalism and Mass Communication Quarterly, 74*(2), 348–356.

Breen, M. J. (2000). The good, the bad and the ugly: The media and the scandals. *Studies: An Irish Quarterly Review, 89*(356), 332–338.

Breen, M. J. (2004). Depraved paedos and other beasts: The media portrayal of child sexual abusers in Ireland and the UK. In P. L. Yoder & P. M. Kreuter (Eds.), *Monsters and the monstrous: Myths and metaphors of enduring evil.* Oxford: Interdisciplinary Press.

Breen, M.J. (2007). Through the Looking Glass: How the mass media represent, reflect and refract sexual crime in Ireland. *Irish Communications Review*, Vol. 10.

Breen, M. J. (2008). Deconstructing media reports of sexual abuse: An analysis of framing in Irish print media coverage of sexual abuse 1993–2002. In W. Huber, M. Böss, C. Maignant, & H. Schwall (Eds.), *Ireland: Representation and responsibility* (Irish Studies in Europe, Vol. 1). Trier: Wissenschaftlicher Verlag.

Dimmick, J., & Coit, P. (1982). Levels of analysis in mass media decision making: A taxonomy, research strategy, and illustrative data analysis. *Communication Research, 9*(1), 3–32.

Franklin, B. (2014). Citizen journalists or cyber bigots? Child abuse, the media and the possibilities for public conversation: The case of baby P. In S. Wagg & J. Pilcher (Eds.), *Thatcher's grandchildren? Politics and childhood in the twenty first century.* Basingstoke: Palgrave.

Franklin, B., & Horwath, J. (1996). The media abuse of children: Jake's progress from demonic icon to restored childhood. *Child Abuse Review, 5*(5), 310–318.

Goddard, C., & Saunders, B. J. (2000). The gender neglect and textual abuse of children in the print media. *Child Abuse Review, 9*(1), 37–48.

Goode, H., McGee, H. M., & O'Boyle, C. A. (2003). *Time to listen: Confronting child sexual abuse by Catholic clergy in Ireland.* Dublin, Ireland: Liffey Press.

Gross, H. E., & Merritt, S. (1981). Effect of social organizational context on gatekeeping in lifestyle pages. *Journalism Quarterly, 58*(3), 420–427.

Hawkins, R., McDonald, A., Davison, S., & Coy, S. (1994). The prevention of child abuse: Strategies to change attitudes and behavior. *Children Australia, 19*(4), 33–39.

Holland, K. (2002, April 20). Study shows sex abuse figures here higher than Europe, US. *Irish Times.* Retrieved from http://www.irishtimes.com/news/study-shows-sex-abuse-figures-here-higher-than-europe-us-1.1085729

Hunter, J. (2008). The political use and abuse of the "pedophile". *Journal of Homosexuality, 55*(3), 350–387.

Jenkins, P. (1998). *Moral panic: Changing concepts of the child molester in modern America.* New Haven, CT: Yale University Press.

Jewkes, Y., & Wykes, M. (2012). Reconstructing the sexual abuse of children: 'cyber-paeds', panic and power. *Sexualities, 15*(8), 934–952.

Kaplan, R., & Manicavasagar, V. (2001). Is there a false memory syndrome? A review of three cases. *Comprehensive Psychiatry, 42*(4), 342–348.

Kemp, A. (1998). *Abuse in the Family: An Introduction.* Pacific Grove, CA: Brooks Cole Publishing Company.

Kitzinger, J. (1996). Media representations of sexual abuse risks. *Child Abuse Review, 5*(5), 318–333.

Kitzinger, J. (2000). Media templates: Patterns of association and the (re)construction of meaning over time. *Media, Culture & Society, 22*(1), 61–84.

Kitzinger, J. (2001). Transformations of public and private knowledge: Audience reception, feminism and the experience of childhood sexual abuse. *Feminist Media Studies, 1*(1), 91–104.

Lonne, B., & Parton, N. (2014). Portrayals of child abuse scandals in the media in Australia and England: Impacts on practice, policy, and systems. *Child Abuse & Neglect,* 38(5), 822–836.

Luttberg, N. R. (1983). News consensus: Do United-States newspapers mirror society's happenings. *Journalism Quarterly, 60*(3), 484–488.

Mayer, M. J., & Furlong, M. J. (2010). How safe are our schools? *Educational Researcher, 39*(1), 16–26.

McCartan, K. F., Kemshall, H., & Tabachnick, J. (2015). The construction of community understandings of sexual violence: Rethinking public, practitioner and policy discourses. *Journal of Sexual Aggression, 21*(1), 100–116.

McDevitt, S. (1998). Media trends in child abuse reporting: The United States and the Republic of Ireland. *Journal of Child Centred Practice, 5*(2), 11–28.

McDevitt, S. (1999). Children speak: Children trauma and social work. *Families in Society-the Journal of Contemporary Human Services, 80*(6), 664–665.

McGee, H., Garavan, R., de Barra, M., Byrne, J., & Conroy, R. (2002). *The SAVI Report: sexual abuse and violence in Ireland: A national study of Irish experiences, beliefs, and attitudes concerning sexual violence.* Dublin: Liffey Press.

Mejia, P., Cheyne, A., & Dorfman, L. (2012). News coverage of child sexual abuse and prevention, 2007–2009. *Journal of Child Sexual Abuse, 21*(4), 470–487.

Neil, V. (2006). Cruelty's rewards: The gratifications of perpetrators and spectators. *Behavioral and Brain Sciences, 29*(3), 211–224.

Niner, S., Ahmad, Y., & Cuthbert, D. (2013). The 'social sunami': Media coverage of child abuse in Malaysia's English-language newspapers in 2010. *Media, Culture & Society, 35*(4), 435–453.

Pan, Z. D., & Mcleod, J. M. (1991). Multilevel analysis in mass communication research. *Communication Research, 18*(2), 140–173.

Peterson, S. (1981). International news selection by the elite press: A case study. *Public Opinion Quarterly, 45*(2), 143–163.

Saint-Jacques, M. C., Villeneuve, P., Turcotte, D., Drapeau, S., & Ivers, H. (2012). The role of media in reporting child abuse. *Journal of Social Service Research, 38*(3), 292–304.

Salwen, M. B., & Garrison, B. (1989). Press freedom and development: United States and Latin American views. *Journalism Quarterly, 66*(1), 87–91.

Schudson, M. (1989). The sociology of news production. *Media, Culture & Society, 11*(3), 263–282.

Shoemaker, P. J., & Cohen, A. A. (2006). *News around the world: Content, practitioners, and the public.* New York, NY: Routledge.

Shoemaker, P. J., & Reese, S. D. (2014). *Mediating the message in the 21st century: A media sociology perspective* (3rd ed.). New York, NY: Routledge.

Shoemaker, P. J., & Vos, T. P. (2009). *Gatekeeping theory.* New York, NY: Routledge.

Stempel, G. H. (1985). Gatekeeping: The mix of topics and the selection of stories. *Journalism Quarterly, 62*(4), 791–808.

Todd, R. (1983). New York "Times" advisories and national/international news selection. *Journalism Quarterly, 60*(4), 705–708.

Tomison, A. M. (1997). Overcoming structural barriers to the prevention of child abuse and neglect: A discussion paper. *New South Wales Child Protection Council, Sydney.*

Weatherred, J. L. (2015). Child sexual abuse and the media: A literature review. *Journal of Child Sexual Abuse, 24*(1), 16–34.

Weaver, D. (1984). Media agenda-setting and public opinion: Is there a link? In R. N. Bostrom (Ed.), *Communication Yearbook 8* (pp. 680–691). Newbury Park, CA: Sage.

White, D. M. (1950). The "GateKeeper": A case study in the selection of news. *Journalism Quarterly, 27*, 383–390.

Wilczynski, A., & Sinclair, K. (1999). Moral tales: Representations of child abuse in the quality and tabloid media. *Australian and New Zealand Journal of Criminology, 32*(3), 262–284.

CHAPTER EIGHTEEN

Content Analysis AND Social Justice

Mediated Erasure and News Coverage of Missing Children

CAROL M. LIEBLER*

> It was the silences that told us something; it was what wasn't there. It was what was invisible, what couldn't be put into frame, what was apparently unsayable that we needed to attend to. If you want to ask "what can content analysis teach you?" well, one of the questions you have to ask is, "what about the people who appear to have no context at all—who are just pure form, just pure invisible form?" (Hall, 1992)

Silences. Stuart Hall (1992) writes of absence in relation to cultural representation, and although his theory and method are rooted firmly in cultural studies, his conceptualization is relevant to quantitative inquiry of contemporary mass media portrayals. Indeed, a related concept, symbolic annihilation, highlights how some members of society are trivialized or absent from media content entirely (Gerbner & Gross, 1976; Tuchman, Daniels, & Benét, 1978). What each of these approaches addresses is a lack of representation that is political and/or ideological in nature.

As scholars, it is critical to examine who or what isn't included in the news, as otherwise we are culpable in further perpetuating their cultural erasure. I suggest here that Hall's conceptualization should be explicitly embraced in quantitative content analyses, systematically highlighting absences, providing generalizable results and theorizing about their meanings. Such an emphasis has implications for addressing social justice as it manifests in media content. As Hall (1992, p. 14) as-

* Carol M. Liebler is Professor at the S.I. Newhouse School of Public Communications at Syracuse University. Email: cmlieble@syr.edu.

serts, "You can count lexical terms if they're there; but you need a different approach if you really want, as it were, to read a society and its culture symptomatically".

Thus, using the example of news coverage of missing children, this chapter suggests that content analysis should be used as one means of studying those who are absent in order to better understand news practices of exclusion. However, such an endeavor necessarily takes us to material outside of media content. It is through the analysis of such extra-media variables (Shoemaker & Reese, 2014), that we can better extend our inquiry to examining predictors of news invisibility. Characteristics of those who are absent may, for example, comprise the independent variables of our study; this is in contrast to individuals, groups or topics being excluded from content analyses because they don't appear frequently enough in news content. It is also in contrast to studies that note absences or low frequencies, but then focus on that which dominates the news. This chapter emphasizes that content analysis is not a mere mechanism for assessing manifest content, but a vehicle for turning a spotlight on mediated opportunity and privilege.

THE CASE OF MISSING CHILDREN

Children go missing every day. In fact, the U.S. National Crime Information Center reports that 460,699 children under age 18 were reported missing in 2015. Many of these children were runaways, some were subject to custody disputes and family abduction, and for others, their disappearances signaled something more nefarious still. Most of us, however, will never hear of any of these children because the vast majority of them will not be deemed newsworthy. Certainly, news media can't cover every child who goes missing, nor do the circumstances under which a child disappears necessarily call for media attention. It appears, however, that media gatekeepers select some children for coverage, while symbolically annihilating others.

Yet news coverage of missing children may be critical to helping find them. According to Davies and Davies (1990, p. 184), who participated in the 1981 search for 6-year-old Adam Walsh who went missing in a Florida shopping mall and was later found murdered, "there is no denying the effectiveness of media, especially television, when dealing with a missing child case …the importance of media in such cases cannot be overstated". Indeed, the importance of media attention is evidenced in the Amber Alert Program created in 1996, which is coordinated by the US Department of Justice, and partners with broadcasters and others to publicize serious child abduction cases and ensure rapid dissemination of information to the public. Amber Alerts are also sent via cell phones, pagers and the internet, all because children's lives may be saved by quick notification and public involvement. Steidel (2000, p. 183) calls local media "instrumental in raising awareness of a case and soliciting valuable information from the public". Conversely, it follows that a lack of media attention may hinder a child's chances of being found.

Of note, of the thousands of children who go missing every year, 86 percent of them are runaways; far fewer children are abducted—1 percent of missing children are non-family abductions and an additional 10 percent are family abduction (NCMEC, 2016). While the public may fear such abductions most (Fritz & Altheide, 1987), runaway children are also likely to be at significant risk. Indeed, the National Center for Missing and Exploited Children states that at least one in five endangered runaways are victims of sex trafficking. The New York Times highlighted the problematic existence of runaways in its October, 2009 series, "Running in the Shadows". The series revealed that many children use sex in exchange for food, drugs and a place to stay, leading to more formal prostitution. Many of these children were running from troubled homes.

In 1984, when President Ronald Reagan announced the creation of the National Center for Missing & Exploited Children (NCMEC) and Congress passed the Missing Children's Assistance Act, the NCMEC was designated as the National Resource Center and Clearinghouse on Missing and Exploited Children. Twenty-five years later in 2009 when the National Center for Missing & Exploited Children celebrated its 25th anniversary, it had helped to recover 135,00 children. As of 2016, that number had risen to 227,000. According to NCMEC, its mission "is to help find missing children, reduce child sexual exploitation, and prevent child victimization". (NCMEC, 2016).

NEWS COVERAGE OF MISSING CHILDREN

There is both anecdotal and scholarly evidence to suggest that particular children, those who are white and attractive, receive the most attention in the news. The coverage of missing children such as Elizabeth Smart in 2002, Natalie Halloway in 2005, and Chelsea King in 2010 blanketed the airwaves from the moment their disappearances were made public, continuing through the search efforts in Holloway's case, and legal proceedings in Smart's case. Indeed, when it comes to abducted children, news media create "moral panics", with disproportional coverage of sensational cases relative to their occurrence in daily life (Duvall & Moscowitz, 2016).

There are a variety of studies that point to disparities in news coverage of missing children when it comes to race and gender. There is evidence that missing African-American children are underrepresented in national news, with their representations falling short of their proportions in national data bases (Min & Feaster, 2010; Simmons & Woods, 2015). One case study of two missing female college students revealed print and broadcast news media privileged a missing blond, middle class girl whereas a working class African American girl was largely ignored until her dismembered body was discovered (Liebler, 2004). When it comes to gender, print news media have been found to report on abducted girls in greater depth than boys (Taylor, Boisvert, Sims, & Garver, 2013).

Studies of news coverage of missing adults tend to report similar findings. The practice of privileging white, attractive and typically middle class young women in news coverage has been highlighted as "the Missing White Woman Syndrome" (Liebler, 2010; Stillman, 2007); such bias functions within a patriarchal paradigm that emphasizes physical appearance and femininity and systematically excludes missing women of color (Moody, Bruce, & Harriet, 2009). In Canada, also, missing or murdered Aboriginal women are marginalized in news coverage (Gilchrist, 2010; Jiwani & Young, 2006).

PHYSICAL APPEARANCE

Studies referenced above emphasize gender and race, but it seems logical that appearance may also play a role in whether a missing child is visible in the news. Indeed, a significant body of literature has found that appearance matters across a variety of venues. Across 11 meta analyses of over 900 studies, Langlois, Kalakanis, and Rubenstein (2000) found: (1) agreement across attractiveness ratings; (2) assessments of attractiveness did not vary across cultures and (3) being considered attractive was a significant advantage for both children and adults in every context the authors examined. The authors conclude that attractiveness is comparably important for children and adults, and for males and females. Of particular relevance to the present study is the authors' suggestion that differential parental solicitude theory explains their results for children. In short, the theory predicts that adults will invest more in children they find attractive than in children they do not. In the present context, that investment may come in the way of increased police or media attention.

Media content reinforces the notion that beauty is necessary for success (Labre and Walsh-Childers, 2003) and that physical attractiveness is rewarded (e.g., Baker-Sperry & Grauerholz, 2003; Fouts and Burggraf, 1999; Greenberg, Eastin, Hofschire, Lachlan, & Brownell, 2003; Herbozo, Tantleff-Dunn, Gokee-Larose, & Thompson, 2004). Significantly, a white, thin beauty ideal for women and girls is dominant across media genres (e.g., Baker-Sperry & Grauerholz, 2003; Frith, Shaw, & Cheng, 2005; Jung & Lee, 2009), with girls often being sexualized (Durham, 2008; Hautton & Trautner, 2011; Lamb and Brown, 2006). For boys and men, the emphasis is on muscularity, physique and toning of the body (Frederick, Fessler, & Haselton, 2005; Leit, Pope, & Gray, 2001; Maisey, Vale, Cornelissen, & Tovee, 1999). Notably, it is within this cultural environment that editors make decisions about which missing children are newsworthy.

NEWS TYPIFICATIONS AND HYPOTHESES

A number of scholars (e.g., Berkowitz, 1992; Chiricos & Eschholz, 2002; Tuchman, 1978) have advanced the notion that news is created via typifications. The notion of typification dates back to Alfred Schutz (1967), who stated that we understand the world in terms of ideal types. Typification as a news production value encourages journalists and reporters to use story templates that "reflect existing social structure, appear logical in terms of commonsense understandings of the ways the world operates…and mesh easily with long-standing stereotypical images, including those grounded in belief systems that reflect and nourish race and gender stratification" (Lundman, Douglass, & Hanson, 2004, p. 251).

Tuchman (1978, p. 46) integrated this concept into her study of the social construction of news, suggesting that typifications help journalists distinguish among "a glut of occurrences". That is, journalists put items "into a predictable scheme of actors, settings, and story plots" (Berkowitz, 1992). Typification in turn allows journalists to predict and gauge expected audience reaction, thereby guiding future story coverage that results in journalists across publications and platforms constructing a shared definition of what is considered news (Sumpter, 2000).

I propose here that the thousands of missing children each year represent this "glut of occurrences" and that news workers use typifications in order to make sense of them. As a result, some children fit into the story plot, while others fall outside it. These absent children are silenced, culturally erased from the public domain. Drawing upon the above literature and theory the following research question is posed: What are the characteristics of the children who are absent in the news coverage? This question is addressed via content analysis of the missing children's posters.

Additionally, the following hypotheses are tested by using characteristics of the missing children (obtained from the posters) as the independent variables and news visibility as the dependent variables (operationalized as the number of news stories in the first week of a child's absence).

H1: There will be significant differences in news visibility among types of missing children, with endangered missing children being the most visible.
H2: There will be significant differences in news visibility between missing white children and those of other races, with white children being the most visible.
H3: There will be significant differences in news visibility between missing younger children and older children, with younger children being the most visible.
H4: There will be significant differences in news visibility between missing female children and male children, with female children being the most visible.
H5: There will be significant differences in news visibility between missing attractive children and unattractive children, with attractive children being the most visible.

METHOD

Missing children posters were downloaded from the National Center for Missing and Exploited Children's website twice daily, January 2009 to April 2009. The NCMEC does not archive the posters, and posters are removed as soon as a case is resolved; i.e., a child is found alive or dead. It was therefore necessary to monitor the site carefully, with the hope that all cases would be obtained as the NCMEC was not able to provide posters. The posters provide photos as well as demographic information about each child. The NCMEC data base is more comprehensive than the National Missing and Unidentified Missing Person System (NAMUS), which although it provides access to posters, relies upon law enforcement, case workers or others to enter cases.

Independent variables were obtained by content analyzing missing children posters. These included each child's age, sex, race, and nature of disappearance. Satisfactory coder reliability on these nominal-level manifest variables was achieved with Krippendorf's alpha. A photo was also obtained from each poster. No objective measure of attractiveness (e.g. symmetry of facial structure, waist-to-height ratio) was deemed appropriate to these data. As news gatekeepers make decisions based on perception every day, a perceptual measure of attractiveness was used here. A child's attractiveness was based on a rating of his/her photo on a scale of 10=very attractive and 1=not at all attractive. Between 9 and 16 advanced reporting students rated each child's photo. Children's photos were randomly presented and the order varied to control for any order effect. Raters were not aware which children had received coverage, nor why they were rating the photographs. The mean rating was then assigned to each case.

In order to assess news visibility, the dependent variable, each child's name was entered into Google, and the Lexis-Nexis and Ethnic NewsWatch databases. Coverage was monitored for several months after each child's disappearance. It is important to note, however, that the most critical coverage in a missing child case is often in the immediate aftermath of the disappearance and it is this coverage that is analyzed here. Therefore, visibility was operationalized as the number of stories during the first week after disappearance in the following media outlets: local newspaper, local TV, national newspaper, national TV, wire services, radio, and online. Online news included news exclusive to online outlets, such as the The Huffington Post. Restricting the coverage to the first week facilitated control for cases that were resolved quickly.

RESULTS

Table 18.1 provides demographic information by nature of disappearance. Children were more likely to be runaways than any other type of disappearance (89.8 percent). Endangered missing children account for a mere 5.5 percent of cases. Missing children were more likely to be female (69.1 percent), rather than male. Forty-five percent (44.9 percent) of the sample was white, and 34.5 percent was African American; 76.7 percent of the missing children fell in the 15- to 17-year-old range.

Table 18.1: Demographics of Missing Children by Nature of Disappearance

	Endangered Runaway (n=821)	Endangered Missing (n=50)	Family Abduction (n=12)	Missing* (n=11)	Non-Specific/ Other** (n=20)	Percent of Total Cases
Female	70.0%	68.0%	50.0%	72.7%	45.0%	69.1%
Male	30.0%	32.0%	50.0%	27.3%	55.0%	30.9%
						100.0%
White	44.1%	56.0%	41.7%	36.4%	55.0%	44.49%
African American	36.7%	12.0%	0%	27.3%	25.0%	34.5%
Hispanic	11.4%	24.0%	0%	27.3%	10.0%	12.1%
Biracial	6.1%	4.0%	41.7%	9.1%	10.0%	12.1%
American Indian	0.1%	4.0%	0%	0%	0%	1.1%
Asian	.6%	0%	16.7%	0%	0%	0.8%
						100.0%
0–4 years old	0.2%	20.0%	33.3%	27.3%	0%	2.1%
5–9 years old	0%	30.0%	50.0%	9.1%	0%	2.4%
10–14 years old	19%	18.0%	0%	27.3%	20.0%	18.8%
15–17 years old	80.8%	32.0%	16.7%	36.4%	80.0%	76.6%
						100%

* Some children were labeled as "Missing", but being endangered was not specified.
** The circumstances for some children were not specified.

Of the sample, 877 (95.5 percent) received no media coverage during the first week of their disappearance, meaning the vast majority of the children were completely absent from local, national or online news. Children least likely to appear in the news were African American runaways who were 15 years of age or older, and especially if they were perceived to be unattractive.

Because so few children received coverage, when analyzing the entire sample, hypotheses 1–4 were tested with nonparametric tests as it was determined that the data as a whole deviated too far from normality for parametric statistics. Analyses on those children who did receive coverage (n=41) were tested with correlation analysis and analysis of variance or t-tests.

Hypothesis 1 predicted significant differences in visibility among case types. This hypothesis was supported. A greater proportion of endangered missing children received coverage than those in other groups, as shown in Table 18.2 (c^2 =144.69, *df* = 4, $p < .001$). This hypothesis was further tested with the Kruskal Wallis test for the overall sample (n = 914) and results indicated that endangered missing children were significantly more visible in terms of total news hits than were other children (H=149.11. $p < .001$).

Of the children who received coverage (n = 41), in contrast to the other groups, endangered missing children were significantly more visible in online news ($F = 3.49$, *df* = 3, $p < .05$) and in terms of total news hits ($F = 4.01$, *df* = 3, $p < .05$). Local print and local TV news also both approached significance. Means are provided in Table 4.

The second hypothesis predicted that white children would be more visible than children of other races. This hypothesis received partial support. As shown in Table 18.2, white children were overrepresented among children receiving coverage, while African American children were underrepresented. Children of other races were covered more proportionately relative to their representation in the sample. These differences were significant (c^2 = 22.88, *df* = 6, $p = .001$). A Kruskal Wallis test was also significant for race and total news hits (H=22.22, $p < .001$), with white and Asian children ranked the highest.

However, among the children who received coverage, there were no significant differences for race in terms of the mean number of news hits.

Hypothesis 3 was supported. Younger children were more visible in the news, and significantly so. As shown in Table 18.2, older children were proportionately underrepresented; the converse is true of younger children (c^2 =34.49, *df* = 3, $p < .001$). Younger children were also ranked higher on total news hits (H = 35.71, $p < .001$).

Table 18.2: Percentage of Total Cases Receiving Coverage

	Percentage of total cases by group (n=914)	**Percentage of total who received coverage by group ***	**Percent difference**
Endangered Runaway	89.8%	34.1%	-55.7
Endangered Missing	5.5%	48.8%	+43.3
Family Abduction	1.3%	12.2%	+10.9
Missing	1.2%	0%	-1.2
Non-Specific/Other	2.2%	4.9%	+2.7
Female	69.1%	68.3%	-0.8

	Percentage of total cases by group (n=914)	Percentage of total who received coverage by group *	Percent difference
Male	30.9%	31.7%	+0.8
White	44.9%	73.2%	+28.3
African American	34.5%	7.3%	-27.2
Hispanic	12.1%	14.6%	+2.5
Biracial	6.6%	0%	-6.6
American Indian	1.1%	0%	-1.1
Pacific Islander	0.1%	0%	-0.1
Asian	0.8%	4.9%	+4.4
0–4 years old	2.1%	17.1%	+15.0
5–9 years old	2.4%	19.5%	+17.1
10–14 years old	18.8%	19.6%	+.7
15–18 years old	76.7%	43.9%	-32.8

* Nominal variable indicating at least one story ran within first week after disappearance

Moreover, among the children who received coverage, there were significant negative correlations for age and local print news ($r = -.39, p < .05$); national print news ($r =-.37, p < .05$); national TV news ($r = -.49, p = .001$), and total news hits ($r = -.41, p < .05$). In other words, the older the child, the less visible s/he was.

Contrary to expectations, Hypothesis 4 was not supported. Girls were not more visible in the news, with one exception. Among endangered missing children (n = 50), girls (41.1 percent) were more likely to be covered than boys (31.3 percent), but even this difference was not statistically significant (see Table 18.3).

Table 18.3: Percentage of Children Who Received Coverage* by Demographics and Case Type

	Overall (n=914)	Endangered Runaway (n=821)	Endangered Missing (n=50)	Family Abduction (n=12)	Missing (n=11)	Non-specific/ Other (n=20)
Sex						
Female	4.43%	1.73%	44.1%	16.7%	0%	22.2%
Male	4.61%	1.45%	31.3%	66.7%	0%	0%
Race						
White	7.30%	3.31%	50.0%	60.0%	0%	9.0%

	Overall (n=914)	Endangered Runaway (n=821)	Endangered Missing (n=50)	Family Abduction (n=12)	Missing (n=11)	Non-specific/ Other (n=20)
African American	0.95%	0.33%	33.3%	0%	0%	0%
Hispanic	5.41%	1.1%	8.33%	0%	0%	50.0%
Biracial	0%	0%	0%	0%	0%	0%
American Indian	0%	0%	0%	0%	0%	0%
Asian	0%	0%	0%	0%	0%	0%
Age						
0–4 years old	28.6%	0%	0%	100%	0%	0%
5–9 years old	36.8%	0%	60.0%	25.0%	0%	0%
10–14 years old	36.4%	0%	26.6%	66.7%	0%	0%
15–18 years old	4.65%	2.56%	22.2%	0%	0%	66.7%
Overall	2.57%	1.50%	50.0%	0%	0%	0%

*Nominal variable indicating at least one story ran within first week of disappearance

The fifth hypothesis predicted that attractive children would be more visible than unattractive children. This hypothesis was supported for endangered missing children, the group who proportionately garnered the most media attention. There are significant positive correlations ($p < .05$) between attractiveness and total news hits (.38), local TV (.39), local print (.39), and online news (.37). In other words, the more attractive the child was rated, the more news coverage he or she obtained.

A t-test further reveals that endangered missing children who received any coverage at all during the first week of their disappearance were rated significantly more attractive than those who did not ($t = -3.319$, $df = 3$, $p < .005$).

This hypothesis was further tested for runaway children. A random sample of children who did not receive coverage was compared to those who did ($n = 34$). There were no significant relationships between attractiveness and number of news hits, but this is most likely because there is so little variance on these variables. The mean for total news hits across five media types is 2.11, and runaways were not covered at all by national media.

However, as with the endangered missing children, a t-test showed that endangered runaways who received any coverage at all during the first week of their disappearance were rated significantly more attractive than those who did not ($t = -2.15$, $df = 32$, $p < .05$).

Analyses were not run on the other groups due to the small number of children who had received coverage.

Table 18.4: Mean Number of Stories* for Children Who Received Coverage, by Demographics

	Local TV	Local Print	National TV	National Print	Online	Radio	Wire	Total #
Sex								
Female	2.75	1.79	1.50	0.25	1.25	0.04	1.39	8.96
Male	3.85	2.54	0.54	0.23	0.85	0.62	1.00	9.61
Race								
White	2.80	2.07	0.37	0.33	1.20	0.30	1.03	8.10
African American	1.00	1.67	0	0	2.00	0	1.00	5.67
Hispanic	5.33	0.67	5.67	0	0.33	0	2.67	14.7
Biracial	0	2.0	0	0	0	0	0	2.0
American Indian	0	0	0	0	0	0	0	0
Pacific Islander	0	0	0	0	0	0	0	0
Asian	4.00	6.00	2.00	0	1.00	0	1.00	14.0
Age								
0–4 years old	4.29	1.43	1.14	0.43	0.71	0.71	1.14	9.86
5–9 years old	5.50	4.13	4.75	0.75	3.13	0.50	5.00	23.8
10–14 years old	2.00	0.88	0.13	0	0.75	0	0.13	3.88
15–18 years old	2.06	1.83	0.11	0.06	0.56	0	0.17	4.78
Overall	3.10	2.02	1.20	0.24	1.12	0.22	1.27	9.17

* Based on coverage for the first week after disappearance.

DISCUSSION

This chapter explored the mediated (in)visibility of missing children, suggesting that it is important to step outside of news content to truly assess who or what is being silenced, to better understand cultural patterns of exclusion. Thus, the chapter examined the extent to which sex, age, race and physical appearance affect likelihood of coverage by starting with the children themselves.

The findings here are clear: If a child is young, attractive, and endangered missing, s/he is more likely to attract media attention. Conversely, a child is most likely to be absent in news coverage if s/he is a teenaged runaway who is considered unattractive. The data further suggest that the likelihood of white children garnering coverage exceeds that of African American children. These findings reinforce those of earlier research (Liebler, 2004; Min & Feaster, 2010; Simmons & Woods, 2015)

Although the original sample had 914 children, only 41 of these children were visible in the news media during the first week of their disappearance. Most children are not covered by the news media, even when circumstances might warrant such attention. Here, 877 children were completely erased from the public eye, a finding illuminated via content analysis of the children's posters. It is not the mere fact that so many children did not receive coverage; the patterns found here reveal how dominant ideology manifests in the news, with some children considered more valuable than others. As Hall (1992) put it, absences are "media-mediated".

I suggest that a runaway does not fit neatly into newsmakers' typification for a missing child. Indeed, only 1.5 percent of runaways received any coverage at all, and of these 14 children, only four of them had more than two total news hits during the first week of their disappearance; the highest was twelve hits. In these latter cases, the children may have been considered newsworthy due to circumstances surrounding their disappearance: one was thought to be with a man she had met on the internet, another was in need of medical attention, and a third was thought to be in the company of an unknown male adult. Perhaps runaways are thought to be culpable in their own disappearance, and only circumstances that suggest otherwise result in media attention. Notably, of the 14 runaways with news visibility, 12 were white. Yet white children comprise 57 percent of runaway/thrownaway children (Hammer, Finkelhor, & Sedlak, 2002) so their disappearance is certainly not more unusual than that of children of other races. Here and elsewhere, the data are suggestive of a practice whereby it is easier for white children to obtain news visibility than it is for children of color.

Endangered missing children fared much better in terms of news visibility. Although these children are but a small percentage of those who go missing, their total news visibility ranged from one to 64 hits. The data suggest, therefore, that it is these children upon whom news typifications may be based. So although runaways are considered at risk, other endangered missing children are the ones who capture journalists' attention and the public's imagination. They are, in the words of Duvall and Moscowitz (2016), the ones most likely to cause a moral panic.

Results indicate that newsmakers do not attend to all endangered missing children, however. Those who are young are more visible, perhaps because they are perceived as the most vulnerable. Also provocative is the finding that physical attractiveness is related to news coverage. While congruent with research linking physical appearance and success, and parental solicitude theory (Langlois et al., 2000), the notion that some missing children may be ignored because of how they look is concerning.

Counter to the hypothesis, sex did not make a difference in news visibility. Boys and girls were comparably visible, indicating that a gender bias may not exist for missing children in the same way it has been suggested for adults.

The measure of attractiveness began with each child's photograph, which was then viewed by reporting students. Each missing child was rated multiple times and assigned the mean value of the rating; students' perceptions of what was attractive are likely congruent with those of reporters and editors as they are based in cultural norms. The logical conclusion, therefore, is that the photograph of a child matters. The NCMEC recommends that parents have an up-to-date good quality photo of their child in case s/he goes missing (NCMEC, 2016). In fact, parents may want to ensure that the photograph shows their child to his or her best advantage, as this may help to catch the eye of an editor or news director.

Exploration of the missing children who did not appear in the news is at the heart of a consideration of mediated absences. Had this study not begun with content analyzing the children's posters, analyses would have necessarily centered purely on the 41 children who appeared in the news. The study would have revealed nothing about the large number of "invisible" children, nor been able to provide data that highlighted patterns of exclusion. Certainly media coverage is not necessary or appropriate to every missing child case. The findings suggest, however, that newsmakers rely on news typifications that privilege some children over others, and that in order to truly understand such news practices we must consider those who are absent via analysis of non-news content.

REFERENCES

Baker-Sperry, L., & Grauerholz, L. (2003). The pervasiveness and persistence of the feminine beauty ideal in children's fairy tales. *Gender Society, 17*(5), 711–726.

Berkowitz, D. (1992). Routine newswork and the what-a-story: A case study of organizational adaptation. *Journal of Broadcasting & Electronic Media, 36*(1), 45–60.

Chiricos, T., & Eschholz, S. (2002). The racial and ethnic typification of crime and the criminal typification of race and ethnicity in local television news. *The Journal of Research in Crime and Delinquency, 39*(4), 400–420.

Gerbner, G., & Gross, L. (1976). Living with television: The violence profile. *Journal of Communication, 26*(2), 172–194.

Davies, L. C., & Davies, L. C. (1990). Working together: Law enforcement and the missing children's organization. In M. L. Forst (Ed.), *Missing children: The law enforcement response* (pp. 181–189). Springfield, IL: Charles C. Thomas Publisher.

Durham, G. M. (2008). *The Lolita effect: The media sexualization of young girls and what we can do about it.* Woodstock, NY: Overlook Press.

Duvall, S. S., & Moscowitz, L. (2016). *Snatched: Child abductions in U.S. news media.* New York: Peter Lang.

Forst, M. L. (Ed.) (1990) *Missing children: the law enforcement response.* Springfield, IL: Charles C. Thomas.

Fouts, G., & Burggraf, K. (1999). Television situation comedies: Female body images and verbal reinforcement. *Sex Roles, 40*(5/6), 473.

Frederick, D. A., Fessler, D. M. T., & Haselton, M. G. (2005). Do representations of male muscularity differ in men's and women's magazines? *Body Image, 2,* 81–86.

Frith, K., Shaw, P., & Cheng, H. (2005). The construction of beauty: A cross-cultural analysis. *Journal of Communication, 55*(1), 56–70.

Fritz, N. J., & Altheide, D. L. (1987). The mass media and the social construction of the missing children problem. *The Sociological Quarterly Berkeley, 28,* 473–492.

Gilchrist, K. (2010). "Newsworthy" victims? Exploring differences in Canadian local press coverage of missing/murdered Aboriginal and White women. *Feminist media studies, 10(*4), 373–390.

Greenberg, B. S., Eastin, M., Hofschire, L., Lachlan, K., & Brownell, K. D. (2003). Portrayals of overweight and obese individuals on commercial television. *American Journal of Public Health, 93*(8), 1342–1348. doi:10.2105/ajph.93.8.1342

Hall, S. (1992). Race, culture, and communications: Looking backward and forward at cultural studies. *Rethinking Marxism, 5*(1), 10–18.

Hammer, H., Finkelhor, D., & Sedlak, A. J. (2002) *Runaway/Thrownaway children: national estimates and characteristics.* Washington, DC: The Office of Juvenile Justice and Delinquency Prevention.

Hautton, E., & Trautner, M. N. (2011). Equal opportunity objectification: The sexualization of men and women on the cover of *Rolling Stone. Sexuality and Culture, 15,* 256–278.

Heider, D. (2004). *Class and news.* New York, NY: Rowman & Littlefield.

Herbozo, S., Tantleff-Dunn, S., Gokee-Larose, J., & Thompson, J. K. (2004). Beauty and thinness messages in children's media: A content analysis. *Eating Disorders, 12*(1), 21–34.

Jiwani, Y., & Young, M. L. (2006). Missing and murdered women: reproducing marginality in news discourse. *Canadian Journal of Communication, 31*(4), 895–917.

Jung, J., & Lee, Y-J. (2009). Cross-cultural examination of women's fashion and beauty magazine advertisements in the United States and South Korea. *Clothing & Textiles Research Journal, 27*(4), 274–286.

New York State Division of Criminal Justice Services. (2009). *Governor Paterson proclaims Monday, May 25 as Missing Children's Day in New York State* [Press release]. Retrieved from http://criminaljustice.state.ny.us/pio/press_releases/2009-05-22_pressrelease.html

Labre, M. P., & Walsh-Childers, K. (2003). Friendly advice? Beauty messages in web sites of teen magazines. *Mass Communication Society, 6*(4), 379–396.

Lamb, S., & Brown, L. M. (2006). *Packaging girlhood: Rescuing our daughters from marketers' schemes.* New York, NY: St. Martin's Press.

Langlois, J., Kalakanis, L., & Rubenstein, A. (2000). Maxims or myths of beauty? A meta-analytic and theoretical review. *Psychological Bulletin, 126*(3), 390–423.

Leit, R. A., Pope, H. G., & Gray, J. J. (2001). Cultural expectations of muscularity in men: The evolution of playgirl centerfolds. *International Journal of Eating Disorders, 29*(1), 90–93. doi:10.1002/1098-108x(200101)29:13.3.co;2–6

Liebler, C. M. (2004). Tales told in two cities: When missing girls are(n't) news. In D. Heider (Ed.), *Class and news* (pp. 199–212). New York, NY: Rowman & Littlefield.

Liebler, C. M. (2010). Me(di)a culpa?: The "Missing White Woman Syndrome" and media self-critique. *Communication, Culture & Critique, 3*(4), 549–565.

Lundman, R. J., Douglass, O. M., & Hanson, J. M. (2004). News about murder in an African American newspaper: Effects of relative frequency and race and gender typifications. *Sociological Quarterly Berkeley, 45*(2), 249–272.

Maisey, D. S., Vale, E. L. E., Cornelissen, P. L., & Tovee, M. J. (1999). Characteristics of male attractiveness for women. *The Lancet, 353*(9163), 1500.

Min, S., & Feaster, J. C. (2010). Missing children in national news coverage: Racial and gender representations of missing children cases. *Communication Research Reports, 27*(3), 207–216. doi:10.1080/08824091003776289

Moody, M., Bruce D., & Harriet, B. (2009). How national media framed coverage of missing black and white women. *Media Report to Women, 37*(4), 12–18.

NCMEC. (2016). *FAQ: National center for missing & exploited children general information.* Retrieved from http://www.missingkids.com/missingkids/servlet/PageServlet?LanguageCountry=en_US&PageId=2817

Schutz, A. (1967). *Phenomenology of the social world* (1st ed.). Chicago, IL: Northwestern University Press.

Shoemaker, P. J., & Reese, S. D. (2014). *Mediating the message in the 21st century: A media sociology perspective* (3rd ed.). New York, NY: Routledge.

Simmons, C., & Woods, J. (2015). The overrepresentation of White missing children in national television news. *Communication Research Reports, 32*(3), 239–245.

Steidel, S. E. (Ed.). (2000). *Missing and abducted children: A law-enforcement guide to case investigation and program management.* Arlington, TX: National Center for Missing and Exploited Children.

Stillman, S. (2007). The Missing White Girl Syndrome: Disappeared women and media activism. *Gender and Development, 15*(3), 491–502.

Sumpter, R. S. (2000). A case study: how to get on (or stay off) the front page. *Newspaper Research Journal, 21*(3), 39–50.

Taylor, J., Boisvert, D., Sims, B., & Garver, C. (2013). An examination of gender and age in print media accounts of child abductions. *Criminal Justice Studies, 26*(2), 151–167.

Tuchman, G. (1978). *Making news: A study in the construction of reality.* New York, NY: Free Press.

Tuchman, G., Daniels, A. K., & Benét, J. W. (1978). *Hearth and home: Images of women in the mass media.* New York, NY: Oxford University Press.

Reflections on the Transitional Age

CHAPTER NINETEEN

Sixty Years of Challenging Dubious Conclusions

GUIDO H. STEMPEL III*

As a graduate student at Indiana and Wisconsin, I read a lot of press criticism and political theory, two things I had not been much concerned about as an undergraduate. I came to realize that a lot of conclusions in both areas were not based on solid research. Some of those conclusions did not seem reasonable, and were contrary to what I had observed as a journalist and a user of media. I also became aware that it was unusual for academic researchers and media professionals to collaborate on research.

Those two findings set the agenda for me for 60 years. I wanted to challenge dubious conclusions, and I wanted to work with media people and help bring academia and media professions closer together. I was to have some success on both counts.

A (NON)PARTISAN PRESS

The first issue that drew my attention was the "one-party press". President Harry Truman coined the phrase in the 1948 campaign. Trailing Republican Thomas E. Dewey badly in the polls, Truman embarked on a whistle-stop campaign in October with emphasis on two issues—one-party press and the do-nothing 80th congress. With those two issues, Truman came from behind to win a clear victory.

* Guido H. Stempel was Professor Emeritus in the School of Journalism at Ohio University, where he had formerly served as director.

What did Truman mean by one-party press? Sixty-eight percent of the daily newspapers in the U.S. had endorsed Dewey editorially, and 15 percent had endorsed Truman. Truman contended that the news columns were just as stacked against him. He offered no evidence of that, and researchers did not test it. What there was evidence of was that claiming bias by the press was effective politics. What those who made the claim did not recognize was that the reporters who wrote the news stories did not write the editorials and that on most newspapers these were separate functions.

Because one-party press had worked in 1948, it came back in 1952. The endorsement ratio was almost the same as it had been in 1948—67 percent to 14 percent in favor of the Republican candidate Dwight Eisenhower. The Democratic candidate Adlai Stevenson picked up where Harry Truman left off. The one-party press question became large enough that after the election the Society of Professional Journalists had a committee look into making a study of press coverage. It decided, however, that it was impractical to begin the study after the campaign was over.

A few state studies were made on the 1952 election, but the issue remained alive, and a group of researchers made a proposal to the Ford Foundation in 1955 for a study of coverage of the 1956 campaign. The foundation sent the proposal to major newspapers and asked for reaction. The response was mostly negative, and the foundation decided not to fund it. That left it up to individual researchers to deal with the issue.

I was at Penn State then, and James Markham and I were among those who did state studies. We analyzed coverage by 24 randomly selected Pennsylvania dailies for the last five weeks of the campaign. The average for space was 45 percent for the Democrats and 55 percent for the Republicans with neutral space excluded. However, the Democrats led 51–49 in frequency of mention of issues.

The several state studies of 1956 did not resolve the issue, but as the 1960 election approached it was evident that there was less interest in it. I decided to do a national study, but wondered what newspapers to study. A survey of editors by the magazine *Practical English* provided a sensible answer. The magazine asked editors which newspapers were "most superior for news coverage, integrity and public service".

The papers selected were *The Atlanta Constitution, The Baltimore Sun, The Chicago, Daily News, The Chicago Tribune, The Christian Science Monitor, The Des Moines Register, The Kansas City Star, The Los Angeles Times, The Louisville Courier-Journal, The Miami Herald, The Milwaukee Journal, The New York Times, The St. Louis Post-Dispatch, The Wall Street Journal* and *The Washington Post.* I tagged this group The Prestige Press.

I analyzed coverage of the same papers in 1964 and 1968. In 1980 John Windhauser and I analyzed this group except for *The Chicago Daily News,* which had ceased publication. In 1984 we added *The Dallas News, The Portland Oregonian* and *The San Francisco Chronicle* to get more regional balance. We kept them in 1988.

Back in 1960 the traditional start of the presidential campaign was Labor Day, so I analyzed those 15 papers from Labor Day to the day before the election. I measured space and size of headlines. Excluding neutral space, these newspapers gave 50.2 percent of their space to the Democrats and 49.8 percent to the Republicans. Twelve of the 15 papers had between 45 percent and 55 percent Democratic space. All five of the papers that supported Kennedy editorially gave the Democrats more space, but so did three of the nine papers that supported Nixon editorially.

In 1964, the space allocation was almost as even as it had been in 1960, with the Democrats getting 51.9 percent and the Republicans getting 48.1 percent. Eleven of the 15 papers gave the Democrats more space. The overall margin was as close as it was because *The Chicago Tribune* gave the Republicans 64 percent to 36 percent for the Democrats.

In 1968 we had something that we had not had in 1960 and 1964—a third-party candidate. George Wallace was the nominee of the American Independent Party, and his presence affected coverage. Although he was on the ballot in all 50 states, he did nearly all of his campaigning in the South. That showed in the vote—he took four southern states and nothing else—and in the coverage by these newspapers. Overall, the American Independent Party received 22 percent of the space while the Democrats received 41 percent *and* the Republicans received 37 percent. The American Independent Party had 30 percent of the space in *The Louisville Courier-Journal* and *The Christian Science Monitor* and 29 percent in *The Atlanta Constitution*, but less than 22 percent in nearly all the other newspapers. Twelve of the 15 Newspapers gave the Democrats more space than they gave the Republicans. Endorsements were split evenly, with six for Democrat Hubert Humphrey, and six for Republican Richard Nixon, with three newspapers not endorsing. Five of the six newspapers that endorsed Nixon gave the Democrats more space. One of them, *The Los Angeles Times,* had a 48 percent to 33 percent margin for the Democrats.

By 1980, one of the prestige press newspapers, *The Chicago Daily News,* had folded. There was a third-party candidate again, John Anderson, and he did get an endorsement from one of these newspapers, *The Miami Herald.* Anderson, however, got only 7 percent of the popular vote and did not win any state. He received only 14 percent of the space from *The Herald* and 12 percent from all the newspapers.

Overall the Republicans received 45 percent of the space, and the Democrats received 42 percent. It was the first time in the four studies we made that the Republicans had the edge in space. Eight newspapers gave the Republicans more space, and six gave the edge to Democrats. Four of the nine newspapers that endorsed Democrat Jimmy Carter gave the Republicans more space.

The studies and I did of the 1984 and 1988 campaigns became part of a book that provided a wider view of the campaigns (Stempel & Windhauser, 1991). We included network television news and news magazine coverage. We also had articles by David S. Myers analyzing editorials in the 17 newspapers. We also included a survey of respondents in Louisville and Chicago in 1984 by Hugh Culbertson and me. The purpose was to assess the influence of editorials of endorsement.

Thirteen of the 17 newspapers had more stories about the Democrats in 1984. Coverage was more even in 1988, with 9 of the 17 newspapers having more Democratic stories, and the median percentage of Democratic stories being 51 percent. There was little indication either year that coverage correlated with endorsement. In 1984, of the seven newspapers that gave the Democrats the most coverage, three endorsed Democrat Walter Mondale, two endorsed Republican Ronald Reagan and two did not endorse. In 1988, two of the newspapers most favorable to the Democrats endorsed Republican George H.W. Bush.

Government and politics and candidate strength were the two issues covered by most of the papers in both years. Coverage of economic activity was minimal, and coverage of health, science and education was virtually non-existent. In 1988, the Republicans were criticized for not discussing issues, but Bush pointed out the Republicans had released 200 issue statements. The media, however, had largely ignored them.

For television news, our unit of analysis was the news segment. Our analysis was of the early evening newscasts of ABC, CBS and NBC. The number of Democratic and Republican stories was nearly even for all three networks in both elections. NBC had 53 percent Democratic stories in 1974, and ABC and CBS had 49 percent Democratic stories. In 1988 all three networks gave the Democrats slightly more stories. It was CBS with 55 percent, ABC with 52 percent, and NBC with 50 percent. In 1984, there were five times as many favorable stories as unfavorable stories, but in 1988 the ratio of positive to negative was about 3.5 to 1. On issue coverage, politics and government and candidate strength led, as was the case with newspapers.

We analyzed news coverage by three news magazines—*Newsweek, Time* and *U.S. News and World Report*—for the 1984 and 1988 campaigns. Previous studies led us to hypothesize that all three would favor the Republicans. We also hypothesized that *U.S. News and World Report* would be the most favorable and *Newsweek* least favorable. *U.S. News and World Report* was most favorable to the Republicans in 1984, with *Newsweek* a close second. However, the most striking thing about the coverage was that for all three magazines combined 45 percent of the stories were neutral. In 1988, *U.S. News and World Report* was most favorable to the Republicans by a narrow margin over *Newsweek.* For both years combined, *Time* had 31 articles favoring the Republicans, 30 favoring the Democrats and 40 neutrals.

Our surveys of newspaper subscribers in Chicago and Louisville in late October and early November 1984 found that most did not know which candidate had been endorsed by the newspaper they read. Most surprising was that only 46 percent of the subscribers of *The Chicago Tribune* knew it had endorsed Reagan. The Tribune was a major player in getting Abraham Lincoln, the first Republican president, elected in 1860 and had endorsed every Republican nominee since. Only 27 percent of *The Chicago Sun-Times* readers knew it also endorsed Reagan. Results in Louisville where only 31 percent of *Courier-Journal* subscribers knew it had endorsed Mondale and only 19 percent of subscribers to *The Louisville Times* knew it endorsed Mondale. In both cities those who knew which candidate the paper they read had endorsed, a majority thought that paper's news coverage favored the endorsed candidate.

There was considerable variation in editorial topics both years. A little more than a third of the space overall was on domestic issues. The economy was next in space, but *The San Francisco Chronicle* had nothing on it. And while nearly one fourth of the editorial space in *The Des Moines Register* was on foreign affairs, 14 papers had less than 10 percent, including three that had no editorials at all on foreign affairs. In 1988 *The Dallas Morning News* had 74 percent of their editorial space on international trade and *The Los Angeles Times* had 58 percent of its space on the combination of international trade and international finance. Yet 10 newspapers had nothing on either topic. *The Christian Science* gave 57 percent of its editorial space to national defense, but 13 newspapers had nothing on that topic. With the variation there was, it was difficult to verify influence of editorials on the outcome of the election.

What had we learned from six studies of election coverage? First, coverage overall was reasonably balanced. It looked as if there was an effort toward achieving that. Second, there seems to be an indication that media are striving for even coverage. Third, there is little indication that the editorial position affects news coverage. We were studying campaigns that were slightly more than two months long. By 2016, the campaign was more than 18 months long. Complaints about coverage will continue, and there may be more studies, but the volume of material in campaigns nine times as long, and with more media, will make it difficult to draw conclusions about overall coverage.

(NON)STANDARD COVERAGE

At the same time one-party press emerged as an issue standardization of media was getting a lot of attention. Warren Breed (1955), in an article in *Journalism Quarterly*, said that among other things the decline in the number of wire services, wire service budget messages, and play messages obviously produced standardization. The budget message is a list of major stories sent at the beginning of the wire cycle. It obviously cannot include breaking news. Play messages are brief descriptions of the Page One play of a few major newspapers.

I tested Breed's complaint by analyzing use of the United Press International TTS wire for one week by six dailies in Michigan that used only that wire. I found 764 UPI stories in those newspapers. Only eight were used by all six newspapers. The number of stories used by each of these papers varied from 122 to 383. I did the comparisons of each possible pair of newspapers and found agreement between pairs averaged about a third. Those findings suggested that budget messages did not lead to much standardization. A study I made of use of the AP A-Wire five years later found an average of 23 percent of the stories the wire transmitted were used. That study also showed considerable variation from one newspaper to the next in the proportion of national and international wire news.

Along with standardization, there was concern about monopoly. The impression was created by some observers that the country was full of cities where there was only one daily newspaper, one radio station and one television, with all three owned by the same person or company. I decided to see how many such cities there were and went through the *Broadcasting Yearbook* and *Editor & Publisher Yearbook* to ascertain the ownership of every daily newspaper, radio station and television station in the United States. And how many of these monopoly cities did I find in the entire U.S.? One! In Zanesville, Ohio, 60 miles from my office.

I wrote an article for *Columbia Journalism Review* and then was contacted by the Twentieth Century Fund, which offered to fund a study. Zanesville was the obvious focus, and I matched it with two Ohio cities of comparable size and number of media—Portsmouth and Steubenville. We did surveys and content analyses in all three. We did find that news coverage was less in Zanesville, and the newspaper took editorial stands less often than the newspapers in the other two cities. However, we found reasonable acceptance of the Zanesville media by the public.

(RE)FORMATTING THE NEWS

In the 1960s, there was a revolution in newspaper layout. It was partly because of the move from letterpress to offset and partly because the people working with layout thought it was time for some new ideas, such as five-or-six-column pages, increasing white space and replacing vertical formats with horizontal formats. Amazingly, there was virtually no research on the public acceptance of these new designs. Bill Click and I had slides made of some traditional pages and some new format pages. We showed each slide for a minute to students in freshman speech classes at Ohio University. We then had students rate the pages on 20 semantic differential scales.

The result was that students liked the new format pages better, except that on the ethical scales the modern pages did not do so well.

After we published these results, we were contacted by Galen Rarick, head of the ANPA Research Bureau. He wondered if our results indicated that the modern pages were seen as sensational and said ANPA Research would fund a study using general population respondents rather than students. We agreed and showed our slides and asked for responses from intact groups in three states. Those groups included service clubs, social clubs and church groups. The results were completely positive including the items on the ethical factor.

This did lead to the most unusual survey I ever did. Mario Garcia had done a redesign for the newspaper in St. Cloud, Minnesota. On a Friday, I got a call from Max McCombs, head of the ANPA News Research Center. The new format was to be unveiled Monday. Garcia wanted the immediate reaction of the St. Cloud readers done Monday and Tuesday. I agreed to do a survey about response to a format that I had not even seen. Garcia described the changes over the phone, and I put together a questionnaire that apparently made sense to respondents in St. Cloud that we interviewed by phone. They liked the new format.

(RE)CALCULATING THE COURT

Another matter I addressed was voting patterns of the U.S. Supreme Court. Much was said about the complexity of the issues and the difficulty this posed for the justices. I decided to test this by using Guttmann scaling with the votes of justices. This procedure tests the consistency of T scores. If, for example, you had a math test that consisted of an arithmetic problem, a geometry problem and a calculus problem, you would expect that the person who got just one right got the arithmetic problem right, and the person who got two right got the arithmetic problem and the geometry problem right. You would not expect a person who got only one right to have gotten the calculus problem right. I analyzed the votes on First Amendment media cases from 1971 to 1981, a period in which there was no change in the composition of the court. That meant there were eight justices for that decade, and I analyzed the votes of those eight. I found a wide range in support of media First Amendment rights. William Rehnquist voted for the press 21 percent of the time, while Justice William Brennan voted for the press 87 percent of the time.

The votes met the Guttmann criteria. The coefficient of reproducibility was .94. In other words, 94 percent of the votes fit the model described with the math test. When you knew the vote, you knew with reasonable accuracy how each justice had voted. The votes of the justices formed a unidimensional scale. What was that dimension? I suggested it was political orientation.

The Roberts Court has gone out of its way to prove my point. When you heard that the vote on Obama Care was 6–3 in favor in June 2015, you knew that Antonin Scalia, Clarence Thomas and Samuel Alito had voted against it, and the other six justices had voted for it. If the vote had been 5–4, then you would have known how seven justices had voted, and would have had to guess how Justices Anthony Kennedy and John Roberts had voted. Nothing very complicated about that.

I updated the study five years later when Chief Justice Warren Burger resigned. The votes over that five-year period again met the Guttmann criterion with 95 percent reproducibility. Rehnquist voted for the press 20 percent of time these five years, while Brennan voted for the press 80 percent of the time, and Thurgood Marshall voted for the press 85 percent of the time.

(RE)CREATING APPLIED RESEARCH

Bringing the media and academic researchers together was not an easy task. I did reader interest surveys for a handful of newspapers, but each of those was for one newspaper and was proprietary and therefore not published. Another effort was the column on research I wrote for *Presstime* between 1984 and 1994. Each column provided 100 to 200-word summaries of research in mass communication journals. I wrote 54 columns and therefore informed readers of *Presstime* about more than 150 research studies with results pertinent for newspapers.

The opportunity to be part of a much more significant academic-industry effort came out of the blue in October 1992. The Scripps Howard News Service contacted the Ohio University School of Journalism and asked if we would be willing to do a survey with them the week of the presidential election. Why did they want to we do a survey then? Because it looked as if the 1992 election would be the first one in which less than half the adults in the United States would vote. Since 1968 there had been a steady decline in voter turnout. It was almost a straight line, and if you drew the line from 1988 to 1992 it dropped below 50 percent.

I agreed to do the survey. On the Friday before the election, Thomas Hargrove of the Scripps Howard News Service arrived in Athens. We had never met, knew little about each other, but a week later we would send to 400 Scripps Howard News Service a story explaining what had happened in the election. We put together a questionnaire, prepared a national sample and recruited interviewers in time to begin interviewing at 7 p.m. Election Day. We interviewed for three nights, and by 10 p.m. Thursday we had completed 600 interviews. Friday morning we went over the results.

Turnout had not been the predicted low, but instead had been 56 percent, the highest since 1968. Our questionnaire was not stacked to the low turnout side, and we could explain the high turnout. Our story, which went out at noon Friday, said that voters felt Perot had made the campaign more interesting and informative. That was why voter turnout was so high. When it dropped to 49 percent four years later that seemed to confirm our findings.

That survey turned out to be the first of 43 national surveys Hargrove and I did over the next 19 years. A month or so after our 1992 election survey, Hargrove phoned me and asked me if I would be interested in doing another survey. I agreed and we were on our way. We were a good combination. We both had survey experience, but we each knew some things the other did not know. Together we knew more and we were good at utilizing our combined knowledge.

We did the 1992 survey with paper questionnaires and paper sample lists. We keyboarded the responses into our SPSS system. Six years later we got computer-assisted interviewing terminals, which meant that we did away with paper questionnaires and sampling lists. The interviewer keyboarded responses directly into the SPSS system. Hargrove and I emailed questions back and forth as we developed the survey questionnaires and emailed the data sets when the survey was completed. He no longer had to come to Athens as he had done on earlier surveys. We had the help of two journalism faculty members, Joseph Bernt and Thomas Hodges, my son Carl, a sociologist at California State East Bay, and Robert Owens, manager of the Scripps Survey Research.

In 2003 we created a web site with the assistance of Robert Stewart. The Scripps Howard Foundation provided funding for this. The web site contains a brief write-up on each survey, a list of questions and answers, and the survey data made accessible for anyone who wanted to use it. Users included a professor from a university in France, who was interested in the survey in which we asked about the Bush administration's role in the war with Iraq. We emailed the data to her.

Several stories were written on each survey and made available to the 400 Scripps Howard News Service. We were able to document for any one survey that the stories reached 15 to 20 million readers. However, there was no way we could track use by all 400 newspapers, so the number reached was undoubtedly more than 20 million.

We sought to ask questions that had not been asked on topics that were being discussed. So we asked unmarried respondents if they thought they would get married. It turned out that more men than woman saw themselves as getting married. That was a finding that surprised a lot of editors, and the story got good play. The result was not a surprise to sociologists because it reflected the fact that women could now have economic security without being married.

In 1993 we asked respondents if they thought flying saucers were real. That was not a new question, but it had not been asked recently. We thought perhaps the flying saucer era was over, but half our respondents said it was somewhat likely or very likely the saucers were real. Four years later was the 50th anniversary of the first sighting of a saucer in Roswell, New Mexico. We discovered, not surprisingly, that Roswell was having a big celebration in June. We had a survey planned for June, so we put our saucer question in the survey. However, there was another player. The Defense Department had no only insisted there were no saucers, but expressed considerable annoyance at the discussion of saucers. For the 50th anniversary the Defense Department commissioned an anti-saucer book. They had a press conference to announce the release of it. That press conference fell right in the middle of our survey. Our survey showed only a slight decline in number of people believing saucers were real, but more significant it showed that more people believed saucers were real after the Pentagon press conference than had before it.

We were aware of the annual Gallup surveys for Phi Delta Kappa, the education professional fraternity that showed when you asked people about the performance of schools in their community and schools nationally, local schools came out ahead in double digits. Was that true only of schools, or might it be true of other things? We asked about police, courts, roads, doctors, and banks. Sure enough it was the same story—people thought the institutions and people in their own community were better than those in the country as a whole. That even was true for air quality. We suggested the familiar adage should be changed to "The grass is greener on this side of the expressway".

We then sensed that spouse abuse was a hidden issue, so we went after it in a survey. We didn't ask, "Do you still beat your wife?" We asked respondents if they were aware of spouse abuse among people they knew. Nearly half said they did. In some cases, the respondent may have been thinking of his or own experience, but we did not pursue that. We did, however, help get some attention for the issue, and at about the same time a congressional committee had hearings about it.

We did ask people who they intended to vote for in presidential elections, but we were doing so out of curiosity, not out of effort to predict. We were usually on target, with one exception. In 2004, we made a survey in mid-October. We showed John Kerry ahead by 7 percent. If you looked at other surveys at that time, they had similar results. Then as October ended, George W. Bush pulled ahead in virtually all the polls. What happened? Well one thing that happened was that Osama Bin Laden released one of his ugly, threatening tapes. It increased emphasis on national security as a campaign issue, and the Republicans took advantage of it.

We were back on track in 2008, showing Barack Obama ahead by 7 percent. He actually won by 4 percent. Our survey was actually made in the latter part of September. We had the good fortune to do our survey after the bad day in the stock market, which was followed the next day by John McCain brushing aside the market hit as unimportant. McCain went into that day leading in most polls and came out trailing. He never made up that loss.

Sometimes the impact of a poll result surprised us. In 2005 we asked respondents whether or not they had a tattoo. Most interesting was the result we got when we cross-tabulated by age. Three percent of the elderly had tattoos, 9 percent of the middle-aged people did, and 28 percent of those under 35 years of age did. It had in fact tripled from generation to generation. That suggests that more than 80 percent of those born in this century will have tattoos, but we did not predict that. We did, however, hear from researchers who studied tattoos and who were amazed at our figures. There was a bigger surprise, however. A little more than a year after our study, the Department of the Army announced an easing of restrictions on tattoos for recruits. The only explanation for the change was a reference to our survey.

The most surprising result, however, came from a poll we did in 2006 in which we asked respondents if they thought it was very likely, somewhat likely or not likely that "People in the federal government either assisted in the 9/11 attack or took no action to stop the attack because they wanted the United States to go to the war in the Middle East".

I have looked at this question many times since and wondered if we should have made it two questions, one asking "assisted" and the other asking "overlooked". Was this double barreled? Well, the situation was doubled barreled. To begin with we had heard rumors on the day of 9/11 that it was bombs planted in one or all of the buildings that caused them to blow up. There had been indications that some government officials were considering military action. By the time we did our survey there were dozens of conspiracy rumors. Some were about assisting and some about ignoring.

The 9/11 Commission, headed by former New Jersey governor Thomas Kean and Indiana Congressman Lee Hamilton, had completed their investigation. In their report they said they found it difficult to come to conclusions about 9/11 because government officials were not candid and not always truthful. The only definite finding was that the failure of the FBI and CIA to communicate with each other was a major problem.

This was the context in which we asked that question five years after 9/11. The result was that 16 percent of our respondents said it was very likely and 20 percent said it was somewhat likely. A little more than a third felt it was at least somewhat likely that people in the government had either aided the attackers or ignored warnings of the attack.

This result made it around the world. We know it appeared in newspapers in Canada, Great Britain, Russia, China, and Japan. It stayed alive for a long time. Finally, nearly two years after the survey, *The New York Times* asked the Department of State to react. The result was a front-page story denying any aiding or ignoring. Of course, the *Times* had to explain why they were asking, so the second paragraph of the story was about our survey, including mention of the Scripps Survey Center.

These surveys all produced news-feature stories, but in addition we wrote five journal articles and a chapter in an encyclopedia as well as including results in my book *Media and Politics in America* (Stempel, 2003). The Scripps Survey Research Center is no longer operating because of tight budgets at Ohio University and the

Scripps Howard News Service. Yet we did show that academic-professional collaboration can work. Two universities, Elon in North Carolina and Quinnipiac in Connecticut have gone into survey research and are getting considerable recognition because of their surveys. The need for research is still there. The difficulty media are having in making online news dissemination financial viable is a major example. Academic researchers can find answers that professionals have not thought of.

REFERENCES

Breed, W. (1955). Social control in the newsroom: A functional analysis. *Social Forces, 33*(4), 326–335.

Stempel, G. H. (2003). *Media and politics in America: A reference handbook.* Santa Barbara, CA: ABC-CLIO.

Stempel, G. H., & Windhauser, J. W. (1991). *The media in the 1984 and 1988 presidential campaigns.* New York, NY: Greenwood Press.

CHAPTER TWENTY

Queen Bees, Beekeepers, Hives and Ecosystems

The Social Forces Influencing Gender and Diversity in Public Relations and Communication Management

BRENDA J. WRIGLEY*

INTRODUCTION

In *How to Build Social Science Theories*, Shoemaker, Tankard, and Lasorsa (2004) challenge scholars to push their work beyond descriptive research and build new theory. This challenge is vital to the growth and value of mass communication scholarship (Shoemaker et al., 2004). The theory of cognitive dissonance reduction termed Negotiated Resignation is one such theory that the author developed in response to that challenge. Others have taken up the theory and tested it in their own research. The theory grew from dissertation research on the glass ceiling for women in public relations and communications management (Wrigley, 2002). While public relations theory development has been steadily growing, research in the area of gender and diversity in the field has not.

EVOLUTION OF THEORY IN GENDER AND DIVERSITY IN PUBLIC RELATIONS AND COMMUNICATION MANAGEMENT

Prior to the mid-1980s, little attention was paid to issues of gender—let alone diversity—in public relations. Why? No one was saying, "We have to have more men in the field" prior to the 1980s. But they're saying it now, when easily 80% of

* Brenda Wrigley is Associate Professor in and Chair of the Department of Marketing Communication at Emerson College. Email: brenda_wrigley@emerson.edu.

public relations practitioners are female. The handwringing over a "feminization of the field" (translation: majority female) stemmed from a concern that too many women meant the field wouldn't have the respect of top management (translation: men), that salaries would become depressed or stagnate (translation: women are paid less than men) and we wouldn't have the variety of opinions (translation: male opinions) in the field that we should.

Why was there a glass ceiling for women in public relations and communication management? Was it because individual women did not work hard enough, did not have the right skill set, were taking time off to have children, or a host of other individual factors? Was it just the routines that develop in organizations that set the stage for discrimination? Or were organizations themselves structured to predetermine the opportunities for women? Could the social institutions in place determine the prospects for women in the work force? What societal forces are at work perpetuating this discrimination and why would anyone—especially women—tolerate it?

Shoemaker and Reese's (2014) levels of influence on media content give us an opportunity to learn how other fields deconstruct influence and power. Early public relations research put the onus on the individual women and urged them to gain advanced credentials, work with men to reshape the roles of women in the workplace and even take up golf to be "one of the boys".

Such strategies ignored that the reasons for women's lack of advancement in the field might lie in their organizations, the ways of doing business (routines), the social institutions in place that perpetuated gender roles and expectations, and the social systems designed to keep men in power and women in lesser roles.

The theory of Negotiated Resignation describes a process by which women accept discrimination rather than challenge its limitations because, to do so, their jobs or their mental well-being could be in jeopardy. This self-convincing behavior helps them cope with the discrimination they face in their careers. However, it places this discrimination solely on their shoulders, making the individual the one to deal with the discrimination rather than the larger forces at work. Clearly, this self-blaming accomplishes little because improving oneself to get ahead, working harder, and faulting oneself for not advancing in a career shifts focus away from the broader levels of influence (Wrigley, 2002).

Shoemaker and Reese's (2014) work translates well to these questions in public relations and communications management. Blaming individual women for not negotiating their salaries, not trying hard, not forgoing child bearing, not seeking out mentors, being "bitchy" (Queen Bees) and a host of other excuses gives the routines, organizations, social institutions and social systems a "free pass".

Most public relations and communication management scholars subscribe to the liberal feminist framework—women need to work with men to change laws, work within the system, and build consensus. This approach has stalled real change.

Hillary Clinton would not have talked about salary inequities in the presidential race if the problem were fixed. Her husband's campaign office signs said when he ran for president, "It's the economy, stupid", and for women in public relations and communications management, "It's the structure..."

Researchers are asking the wrong questions. Instead of asking women to "lean in" and try harder to adapt, researchers should question why so few of those many women have ascended to the top management roles in public relations and communications management and why they tolerate second-class citizenship in a field that is billed as welcoming to women?

In her book chapter, "How feminist theory advanced the practice of public relations", Dr. Elizabeth Toth, credits feminist theory with calling attention to issues of gender discrimination in public relations (Toth, 2001). To the extent that feminist theory asked us to notice issues of gender in the field, that is true. But liberal feminist theory settles for a structure that exists—not a dismantling of a social system that is broken. Radical feminism is the surgeon excising a diseased organ; liberal feminism recommends a treatment that leaves the dysfunctional organ continuing to debilitate the patient. The patient may live, but with a vastly reduced quality of life.

Just as we should not settle for resting on the theories in communication that have brought us this far, we should not settle for the injustices that keep those working in the communication industries stuck in neutral, at best, or rolling backwards, at worst. For too long, pats on the head from white, male and comfortable management have kept those who are oppressed in our fields from gaining traction. Questions about the structure and the social systems that perpetuate that structure are the only ones that make sense. Patterns of deflection, such as pointing out that Queen Bees (women who advance to management and make it difficult for other women to advance) are at fault, ignore the beekeepers, those who are really in charge of the power and money in organizations—and in the larger social system. How simple it is to tell women (insert here: people of color, those of LGBTQ communities, those from limited social means) to be agentive and suck it up. Work hard and you will be rewarded. If hard work worked, these women, people of color, LGBTQ persons, and those from limited social means would be ruling the communications industry boardrooms. But they are not.

> As long as women don't get mad about sex discrimination, the hegemonic train rolls on. As long as mass media devote stories on this topic to a few shining stars, women who have "made it", the rest of us will ignore the fact that most of use haven't. We'll believe there's still hope for us, ignoring the reality that progress is moving at a snail's pace. We are placated. (Wrigley, 1999, p. 311)

Developing theory that explains discrimination should make people uncomfortable, if it's doing its job. The unease we cause in others when we step outside the lines tells us we may be on to something that could change our way of thinking about a problem or finding a solution. Safe, comfortable, and mainstream theories won't get us there. Developing new theories may. Early studies of women in public relations, beginning in the mid-1980s, largely focused on their increasing numbers in the field and the impact that has had on the profession (Toth, 2001, p. 237). Bravo to these early researchers who asked us to pay attention to women in the field and what they were experiencing. This use of standpoint epistemology was an important contribution to our understanding of the field and its evolution. It's easy today to dismiss using feminist theory as a rather minor leap forward, but at that time it was considered a bold step (Wrigley, 2010). Recognizing a glass ceiling is the first step in shattering it. Unfortunately, that hasn't happened yet.

Grunig, Toth, and Hon (2001) concluded their book on women in the field of public relations with this warning:

> Most feminist treatises end with the notion that the solution to sex discrimination hinges on political, institutional, and organizational policies. Women alone, even women aligning themselves with like-minded men, cannot overcome either the blatant or the subtle sexism we have described...We agree. We also acknowledge, as have most writers before us, that societal transformation is not so easy as it might seem on paper. Change takes longer than anyone expects. Without moving toward equity for women in public relations, however, the field risks losing the talents of well more than half of what we have established as its most effective practitioners. (Grunig et al., 2001, p. 360)

Just as the earlier feminist movement was criticized for revolving around the oppression of white, heterosexual women, so, too, did the scholarship in public relations and communications management begin with examining how women (specifically, white women) were experiencing the workplace. Scholars like Linda Aldoory (2001) and Jennifer Vardeman-Winter and Natalie Tindall (2010) have urged the field to explore issues of race, sexual orientation, class and more. By doing so, existing theory is tested using the experience of others to see what we can learn about societal forces that shape stereotypes and channel certain practitioners into roles that may or may not be satisfying for them.

This type of research should be complicated. Isolating just gender or just race misses the notion of intersectionality, a theory that examines the effect of multiple identities and "intersecting forms of domination [that] produce both oppression and opportunity" (Zinn & Dill, 1996, p. 327). This theory is fascinating, because it forces us to examine identity as having layers of meaning and representation. It has the potential to help us understand the experience of professionals in communications.

This more complex way of examining the field of communications forces us away from dichotomies and takes people as they are, at face value, with all of the things that make them unique. It also moves from reducing people to a single category and moving to a notion of social identity—something that, by its very nature, is constructed by larger social systems. Shoemaker's theory of media sociology may not be the direct contributor to some of this theoretical development in public relations and communications management, but the linkage to examining society's role in all this is clear.

REFERENCES

Aldoory, L. (2001). Making health messages meaningful for women: Factors that influence involvement. *Journal of Public Relations Research, 13,* 163–185.

Grunig, L. A., Toth, E. L., & Hon, L. C. (2001). *Women in public relations: How gender influences practice.* New York, NY: The Guilford Press.

Shoemaker, P. J., & Reese, S. D. (2014). *Mediating the message in the 21st century: A media sociology perspective* (3rd ed.). New York, NY: Routledge.

Shoemaker, P. J., Tankard, J. W., & Lasorsa, D. L. (2004). *How to build social science theories.* Thousand Oaks, CA: Sage.

Toth, E. L. (2001). How feminist theory advanced the practice of public relations. In R. L. Heath (Ed.), *Handbook of public relations* (pp. 237–246). Thousand Oaks, CA: Sage Publications.

Vardeman-Winter, J., & Tindall, N. T. J. (2010). Toward an intersectionality theory of public relations. In R. L. Heath (Ed.), *The Sage handbook of public relations* (pp. 223–236). Los Angeles, CA: Sage.

Wrigley, B. J. (1999). *The ceiling's made of structural steel, not glass: Barriers to advancement of women in public relations and communications management* (Doctoral dissertation, Syracuse University, 1999).

Wrigley, B. J. (2002). Glass ceiling? What glass ceiling? A qualitative study of how women view the glass ceiling in public relations and communications management. *Journal of Public Relations Research, 14*(1), 27–55.

Wrigley, B. J. (2010). Feminist scholarship and its contributions to public relations. In R. L. Heath (Ed.), *The Sage handbook of public relations* (pp. 247–260). Los Angeles, CA: Sage.

Zinn, M. B., & Dill, B. T. (1996). Theorizing difference from multiracial feminism. *Feminist Studies, 22,* 321–331.

REFERENCES

CHAPTER TWENTY-ONE

The Intellectual Craftsman in a Digital World

STEPHEN D. REESE*

The life of the mind is under attack from many directions. Concentrated in communities of higher education, this life makes an easy target for critics of academia who think it should conform more closely to business values and productivity metrics. And the irrational forces in the larger culture undermine reason itself, diminishing the importance of rational arguments and casting doubt on even issues of scientific consensus. More insidious pressures arise, however, from the inside, with the distractions of always-on information streams that make it harder to carve out space for serious reflection and quality work. There are enough external threats without being self-defeating.

As "information workers" are scholars contending with the same pressures they always have, or have we entered a new era with greater demands on information handling abilities than ever before—requiring new skills and different forms of personal discipline? I think the latter, and want to consider the habits of mind, workflows and tools in the academic routine. There is a vast amount written on the general subject of productivity, but in this essay I review the special challenges we face in the academic world in keeping up with professional demands, put them in the context of that larger productivity conversation, and share some of the routines and tools that I've found useful. My emphasis is on the daily needs we have in common in staying organizing and keeping up with the academic workflow,

* Stephen D. Reese is the Jesse H. Jones Professor of Journalism in the School of Journalism at the University of Texas at Austin. Email: steve.reese@austin.utexas.edu.

leaving aside the more specific pedagogical and methodological skills also required for the job.

Writing about productivity implies that I myself have some credibility in this area. I don't profess to have it all figured out, but having been promoted through the ranks at my own institution, I hope that I have learned a few things worth sharing. In the length of my career and as an early adopter I've seen the remarkable changes technology has brought to the academic workplace, and been obliged to adapt to them. I do regularly take stock of my own routines and update them, particularly at the beginning of a new year and as office moves have forced some organizing and down-sizing. Above all, I take seriously the life of the mind and have been privileged to be allowed to pursue it, so I want to do everything I can to get better at it and help others do the same. These strategies are not usually taught in graduate school, and how we organize ourselves is a very personal side of life, one that can be a source of potential embarrassment and sensitivity.[1] People cobble together some system they think works for them and are resistant to changing it, especially after it's been rooted in place for many years. These are not issues we often share with our colleagues, much like teaching once was, where new teachers were thrown into the classroom with little preparation. That has changed fortunately, and perhaps it's time to have more conversation with how to get better organized as well. As technology has raced ahead, I think they are becoming ever more crucial to success.[2]

THE INTELLECTUAL CRAFTSMAN

Academic productivity should not be separated from the deeper professional mission. C. Wright Mills, with his scathing critique of the social sciences in *The Sociological Imagination* (Mills, 1959), was concerned that the field was becoming too obsessed with data-gathering and losing the larger picture. The emerging form of bureaucratized research, he feared, was diminishing the role of the autonomous "intellectual craftsman". For many years I have assigned in my research seminars the appendix to that volume, "On intellectual craftsmanship", in which Mills takes a somewhat different perspective with his critique, providing a practical "how to" essay on how he himself went about thinking about his projects. His insights inspired me early on in my career, and it seems that it may be an opportune time to revisit its useful guidance on life-structuring as young scholars contend with the pressing demands of career expectations and the digital firehose of information. Mills works through a specific research question to examine his "actual ways of working", but here I'll deal with more general organizational habits.

What does Mills mean to be an "intellectual craftsman"? This seems like a term better suited to manual, blue-collar work than the rarified space of the academic professional. According to him, for those who feel themselves "part of the classic tradition, social science is the practice of a craft" (p. 1). The craftsman in this sense does not fetishize theory and methods but absorbs and puts them in the service of "problems of substance". The intellectual craftsman does not separate work from life but has been given the privilege and opportunity to design not just a career but a life. To fully take advantage of the potential for this life, one cannot shirk the responsibility to be constantly managing one's self, and must take seriously the need to construct one's character based on the "qualities of good workmanship". Thus, craftsmanship, the careful curation and awareness of one's intellectual capital, is at the center of all one's projects.

In this respect, scholarship is like any other kind of creative work. In a fascinating book, *Daily rituals* (Currey, 2013), the author documents the working routines of a wide variety of writers and artists. Although they differ in many ways, they have created a structure for their lives to guide their work. Inspiration can strike unexpectedly, but successful people don't leave it to chance. They treat creative effort as a job and report to work on a schedule. A well-organized life does not happen by chance either but takes some pro-active steps to construct the optimal conditions for success.

OCCUPATIONAL HAZARDS OF ACADEME

The broader social trends that affect the intellectual craftsman are familiar. The explosion of information, the pace of life, and the always-on nature of work make the challenge of organizing for productivity more urgent. Email is a familiar example of the pressures of the workplace that threaten creative space. As widely observed, technology merges the domains of workplace and home, making it necessary to find "life" strategies that cover activities both at home and at work, wherever and whatever we're doing, and reduce the friction in shifting from one domain to another. Even just the past few years have brought major changes in the technology of productivity, which even the most committed Luddites must engage at some level if they are to remain competitive.

Academic workers are not the only ones who perceive that time has accelerated. Our time gets plugged up with multiple overlapping projects that we have greater capacity to be aware of and alerted to. Judy Wajcman's recent book, *Pressed for Time* (Wajcman, 2014) provides important insights for academics who never feel they have enough time to get what they want done. We are particularly susceptible, even more than other knowledge workers, to a feeling of being "harried", in part by also being part of a social stratum where busyness is a sign of status. And as part of our work we are "always on" via "multimodal connectivity", feel a norm of "responsiveness" to what we receive from that connectivity, and are immersed in never-ending tasks, all of which Wajcman says contribute to that harried feeling. That requires not an avoidance of digital tools but leveraging them for better mindfulness.

The Changing Information Worker

In an early line of my own research, I was interested in the "information worker", and how different types of work affected the use of technology. According to one classification scheme I drew on, *knowledge producers* included scientists, engineers, doctors, and lawyers, who marketed their knowledge through *knowledge distributors*, which included educators, professional communicators, and librarians. *Market specialists* served as the planning and control apparatus for the economy, and so on to the clerically-oriented *information processors* (Reese, 1988). Scholars aspire to be knowledge producers, and to some degree distributors, but if not careful relegate themselves to being mindless drones, shuttling information around networks. We've already been obliged to take on clerical tasks we once outsourced to others (typing, receiving messages, etc.), and there is no going back. But we are at risk of losing the habits of mind that characterize the knowledge creators, even as we use the same technology and have similar workflows as information workers in general.

As academics, we are drawn into the world of the corporate and hi-tech information worker but rewarded most for intellectual creativity. Significant work happens in teams with colleagues, requiring participation in the same bureaucracies faced by other information workers. As administrative pressures take more time, the routines associated with other office workers threaten to pull on us, impose their own template, and limit the kind of quality creative work we need to succeed. Intellectual labor remains our focus as largely independent knowledge entrepreneurs, even as the demands on our attention from other tasks have exploded.

Finally, given all these challenges it may not be surprising that academics are in a high-risk profession for mental illness, and have not been immune from the precariousness affecting other workers. Graduate students who aspire to the profession are particularly prone to anxiety and isolation, with pressures to perform getting stronger, performance metrics more visible (and more obsessively noted), and the path to success not particularly clear. In spite of the common public perception that college professors don't work very hard, surveys show they put in far more than 40 hours a week, and administrative demands have increased. Thus, far from being a professional quirk or geeky obsession, a well-organized life is a matter of professional survival. The main challenge lies in setting long-term goals, preserving creative spaces, capturing valuable insights, and growing intellectual fruit. This places even greater importance on being self-directed, resisting the perceived norm of instantaneous response, bounding off priority projects, and ignoring others' boasts of busyness.

Responding to Those Pressures: Profhacks

Personal productivity advice has become big business, especially in the corporate world and high-tech community. Technology professionals have embraced the personal "hack", or "workaround" culture, turning their natural problem-solving orientation toward their own work practices. How can these strategies best be deployed by the intellectual craftsman?

Some academic readers may be tempted to dismiss the various systems for productivity as only for helping middle managers process paperwork more quickly. Perhaps the best known such systems is the "Getting Things Done" work by David Allen (Allen, 2015). His system, through books, and related seminars and software support, has become highly popular (even cult-like), especially at the middle-management level where the volume of workflow is great, coming from all sides—and from top and bottom. And indeed it does seem to appeal to a corporate-world audience, with university people underrepresented in general from my unscientific survey of the productivity-oriented podcasts, blogsites, and books. Artistic types, of which academic workers are a class, may resist getting organized as a regimentation harmful to the free exercise of their gifts, but just the opposite proves true. As Allen (2015) has argued, the crucial value of getting organized and managing distractions is to free up space for creative reflection, and he has attracted fans in the creative world from Howard Stern to noted *Atlantic* writer James Fallows.[3]

The basics of GTD are easily applied to academic work—easily explained but difficult to implement without real commitment. Basically, life can be divided into "projects", defined as any activity that requires more than one action. Thus, identifying those projects and the "next action" item in each helps define and move things along. Classes and papers are the natural "projects" in academia, but they extend to much more than that. A crucial insight of Allen (2015) (borrowed from cognitive psychology) is that by relentlessly capturing and organizing the tasks and commitments that are "on our mind" into a trusted system, we free our minds for more creative work. The email analog of this idea is "in-box zero", where email is processed, deleted, dealt with, delegated or deferred into the trusted system for later action. Regular reviews (weekly, monthly, etc.) of the projects ensure that they are lined up with one's areas of focus and long-range goals.[4]

Among the relatively few academic-oriented productivity writers, Georgetown computer science professor Cal Newport speaks directly to the challenge of intellectual craftsmanship. He argues that "deep work" is increasingly more valuable for success while the conditions of modern life make it ever more difficult to carry out (Newport, 2016). Distractions must be managed, but at the same time the practice of deep work must also be actively cultivated. As one concerned scientist observed, the pressures on the craft seem to actively oppose real creativity: "The pace of academic life and research has become so frenetic that activity and motion have come to replace thought" (Loehle, 1990, p. 127). I've written on this concern myself, arguing that the ever-increasing pressures toward productivity privilege the appearance of outward action, what may seem like research "hyperactivity", making disciplined reflection more difficult (Reese, 2014). The business of sustained depth thinking is hard and easily avoided, so we have to carve out those spaces where it can happen.[5]

Organizing for Intellectual Work

In this section, I will lay out some practical considerations for the academic life. I've always been interested in how to get myself better organized, with better time management and the latest technology. My first organizational tool in grad school was limited to a large desktop blotter-style calendar and, later, a chalkboard on my assistant professor office wall, on which I listed my research projects with a current action alongside them. Later I adopted the Daytimer notebook system, then a computer-based calendar, then PalmPilot, replaced now by a combination of software and platforms: the office-only desktop giving way to the laptop, IPad, and Iphone. With mixed success I've tried to save time where I can to make more room for the tasks I enjoy.

The first thing needed is a general, personal organization strategy. Successful academics are by nature self-starters, or else they don't thrive in the often ambiguous environment of scholarly creativity. But even those accustomed to goal setting and self-direction need to pay attention, lest the demands of the workplace undermine the very source of our success: ideas and discovery. Thus, one of the critical strategies is to have a general system for helping balance immediate and long-term activities, building in time for personal renewal and planning. Stephen Covey (1989) made a fortune with his book, *Seven Habits of Highly Effective People*, but it provided good advice for working on setting priorities, keeping things in balance, and finding time to "sharpen the saw". The intellectual craftsman has to start there.

The workplace is highly mobile, of course, as indicated by the shrinking size of typical faculty offices and more use of the "third places", like Starbucks, for doing work. As a practical matter that makes it essential to have a system with devices and tools that can sync across locations. The whenever-wherever online world has made in short order some basic tools necessary to work effectively, which I review next. Of course, for keeping work securely backed up "Dropbox" has become a standard tool, which also facilitates the sharing across multiple platforms. That multi-site syncing is a must to allow working wherever and whenever the need arises. The important thing is to exploit the ability to take advantage of those otherwise unproductive spaces in the day, or double up on blocks of time (e.g., exercising while listening to Podcasts), while preserving those other creative spaces from distractions by keeping a clear set of goals in mind.

Productivity requires finding a trusted system and committing to it so that habits will develop, and we're certain where to look for the things we need. As my work has moved more and more online, I still at times find myself wondering where an important piece of information is stored (physical files--rarer, or increasingly on my computer). And even online, information is still stored across multiple applications, so they need to be coordinated with a consistent system. "Evernote" has quickly become a valuable tool (and emerging standard) in helping organize all the details of life, syncing and making searchable across multiple platforms. Notes can take the form of written notes, pictures, PDFs, web clippings, or audio files. My internet browser is set up with an Evernote button to permit quick clipping of information I want to save, or I can email something to Evernote and sort it out later. Tips for using Evernote are easily found online, but because relatively few academics share their routines, there doesn't appear to be any one strategy. In any case, ways of using Evernote will be unique to each user, but I've been using it myself to keep track of information I think may be valuable for classes and various research projects, in addition to things like travel, setting up a separate notebook for each trip and saving to it copies of airline and hotel reservations, emails from colleagues with phone numbers and addresses, and conference agendas or programs.

Mills (1959) recommends the intellectual craftsman adopt a playful approach in reviewing physical paper files from time to time in a concrete way, allowing new connections to be found among various materials. Electronic files and systems for organizing them make this process easier, finding connections that would have been impossible with paper files. If the habits of self-reflection are cultivated, with a number of research problems never far from mind, then a vast range of insights can be pulled together with greater ease, especially if materials are properly stored from the beginning.

Once the raw materials, details of life, and general resources have been safely stored away, a way is needed to keep track of the project agenda. This avoids the pitfall of only working out of the email inbox and creates rather a "dashboard" for monitoring goals and projects. For me the system is "OmniFocus", an OSX product developed with GTD in mind (I've heard that "Things" does something similar). (Some use Evernote to keep track of to-do lists, but I've found it easier to keep the "To Do" world separate from the "Keeping track of" world (the things I'll do vs. the things I have). OmniFocus allows syncing across devices, with versions for the laptop, iPad, and iPhone. It's tempting to let the email inbox serve as the to-do list, but that makes us too reactive to the agenda of others (There are lots of guides elsewhere to taming the email beast). Email originating tasks can be processed into a program like OmniFocus, forcing decisions about "next actions" and context. Areas of responsibility (class, research, administrative, home) can be used to set up a number of folders, which contain a series of projects (specific classes, specific projects, buy a new computer, etc.), within which any number of "actions" can be listed, with deadlines and additional resources linked as necessary. This list is reviewed and updated at least weekly. There is a vast literature on GTD software and related personal systems, but the important thing is to be able to quickly identify what needs attention, and to be able to access it anywhere. As David Allen (2015) advocates as a core principle, getting things off your mind and into a trusted system lets your mind focus on the task at hand.

Creative intellectual work, in particular, needs this kind of clarity and concentration. For reasons discussed earlier, academic work may not lend itself as well to the discipline of something like OmniFocus, and I find myself being less disciplined as the seasons of the academic calendar change. Class schedules and conference deadlines impose their own underlying series of urgent To-do lists, but having a reliable system is important to resist the non-scholarly flood of demands on our time that threaten the creative space. GTD organization means both having a system and developing habits of mind. Even in the pre-productivity software days, I would ask myself what I had done—even if just a small step—each day to advance one of my projects, and I suppose that's a typical GTD "next action" perspective. Also, even if not fully disciplined in my OmniFocus system, I find I have absorbed the GTD mentality in the sense that I try to be ruthless in getting things off my mind if I can possibly do it at the moment they present themselves (the "2-minute rule" suggests if something can be done within that time, it should be, rather than deferred for later). I try to empty my email (at least into an action folder) each day, and quickly dispense with something if I can without letting it linger.

THE ACADEMIC WORKFLOW SIMPLIFIED CHRONOLOGY

With that general strategy in mind, we can consider productivity tools and routines in relation to the creative process. A linear assembly-line process oversimplifies how we work, especially in a networked context, but it helps to think about what is most useful at each stage. We gather information, form it into organized structures, and create formally published products, which are then fed back into our professional networks. Living in a network society means participating in multiple levels of connectivity as we receive information, make sense of it, and ourselves contribute to the conversation. That's always been the case, but the difference now lies in the intensity and volume of that communication. And previously our information strategies were more institutionally oriented; that is, we relied more directly on a core of institutional authorities to help organize our information for us. Now, practical necessities require developing our own networks tailored to individual needs, and less organized around a few key institutional outlets.

Hunting and Gathering

In the process of writing and preparing classes, we take in a huge volume of information, an intake that is both targeted and general. For both it's helpful to visualize a "personal learning network", sources of information that have been identified as likely to provide useful information, sources to whom we also contribute in our "personal teaching network". These networks combine to form communities of mutual learning and teaching, but which don't necessarily overlap. Therefore, it's important to use social networks strategically in order to tame the information tide. Large corporations form boards of directors to help monitor the environment, alerting them to potential threats and opportunities, and we are doing the same when we select others as members of our social networks, whether Facebook, Twitter, or on more focused services like academia.edu. (LinkedIn seems less useful for academics in general). So choose them with care. These sources then help push valuable information to us from the news and scholarly worlds, making things available that we would otherwise never have time to hunt down.

For my own media monitoring, a tablet device quickly has become an important tool. News and information feeds can be customized and browsed quickly, using a variety of aggregation apps. Once we've been alerted to information, it's helpful to delay and displace reading into other dayparts with tools like "Pocket" that allow saving articles quickly in a cloud-based list for reading on whatever platform is handy. There's a Pocket icon on my web browser, and Pocket available on other services for clipping material. And, of course, the ability to quickly share what we read with our networks should be set up to be as frictionless as possible, posting useful articles to Twitter or Facebook, etc. (or further organized for our personal use with other organizing tools—below). This routine supports curation and the participatory ethic of sharing, increasing our social capital within our personal learning-teaching networks. Newport (2016) is highly dubious about the value of social networking platforms as distractions with little added value for deep work, but certainly those of us in the communication field have a harder time dismissing them. They are a key focus of research but also, I would certainly argue, have their place in supporting productivity.

Archiving and Annotating

A more serious form of hunting and gathering involves the scholarly literature that we search in feeding our own research. Online library resources are familiar to most. Products like "Endnote" have become important time-saving tools for maintaining bibliographies and quickly citing works while writing. After much frustration at the time wasted in chasing down copies of articles in my files, I'm more systematic now about archiving them electronically in Mendeley (migrating my citations from

Endnote), a cloud-based application that (with the also popular Firefox-based "Zotero") allows storage, annotation, and—increasingly valuable—sharing with social media and class group features. (Other colleagues have spoken highly of "Papers", which allows similar functions). Although some have developed systems for storing Pdfs on Evernote, I've kept the formal academic archiving separate in Mendeley, saving Evernote for less formal resources (news and web clippings) gathered for projects and teaching and, of course, "everything else".

Scholarly Writing

Next we produce something based on our research. Microsoft Word has become the de facto standard, but an outline-based tool to help write and organize papers makes the process much more efficient. I became sold on using an outline processor early on in my career, beginning with an MD-DOS program called "MaxThink", and I've stuck with them ever since. The manual that came with that early program, even if relatively primitive, made a compelling case for its value of outlines in supporting critical thinking: synthesis, evaluation, and clear inductive and deductive reasoning. Writing from an outline up makes it easier to quickly see how a paper should best be put together, with logical flow, completeness, and hierarchical integrity (after satisfactorily organized and annotated, the entire outline is exported to Word for final clean-up).

A number of websites have reviews of various "outliner" products, but I've been using the well-regarded "OmniOutliner" for OSX, and prior to that "Inspiration" (for either Mac or PC). Some writers also have adopted more visual tools, prior to the outline stage, that support "mindmapping". It's a matter of personal preference, with Inspiration, for example, being able to toggle back and forth between a mindmap and hierarchical outline view. (I used "IThoughts HD" for the iPad to organize this essay, before exporting to "WriteRoom", a simple word processor I've been trying out because I like its full-screen green-on-black format that reminds me of the early days on my IBM AT. To finish it up I'll use Word.)

A relatively recent writing tool that I've tried is "Scrivener", which supports outlining and structure in more than one perspective and has been well reviewed in the *Chronicle of Higher Education*. Scrivener allows the writer to assemble the raw material for an article (interviews, research articles, etc.) along with one's own writing into a saved Scrivener "project", which allows side-by-side screens and generally helps keep the relevant materials readily accessible. Once the writing is finished it can easily be exported to Word for final polishing. The important thing about outline support is that thinking is encouraged, rather than distracting the writer prematurely with decisions about fonts, margins, and other superficial, cosmetic elements which properly belong at the end of the process, not the beginning.

Professional Promotion

Finally, back to the professional networks, there's making work public and promoting it. Academics have little choice but to embrace the networked world, especially in giving some thought to their "online professional presence", and there are a number of resources available for guidance. No one template will work for everyone, but the visibility that allows one to participate effectively in the professional world means keeping published work and professional activities easily findable online, an essential part of success nowadays. Productivity metrics are based on citations to our work, and others can't cite that work if they can't find it. At the least, a personal-professional website helps archive publications and other information and can be combined with blogsite and Twitter feed. I haven't found the best mix of these, but there are a number of tools that help consolidate one's various online feeds. At least I've tried to have a fairly comprehensive faculty site, with links to and among a more personal blogsite and class blogs. I use both Academia.edu and ResearchGate as an easy way to post current papers and projects, saving the primary site for finished publications, but these sites can be used for that too. I'm a relatively inactive Twitter user, but I recognize that a steady presence there can bring academics to prominence as a complement to and even beyond their published work. The online professional presence brings suggestions from others and other interaction that feeds back into all the other stages above.

CONCLUSION

A proper system won't guarantee productivity, and indeed it's easy to get absorbed, as I can attest, with finding the perfect system and coolest apps. But without a good workflow routine, a trusted system, and some technology-supported discipline, too much of the creative space is taken up by distractions, tedium, and wasted time. Intellectual work is precious capital and needs to be captured, organized, and easily retrieved. Doing so makes creative space more available and resistant to the encroaching demands on limited attention. One is never done with this process. There are enough external impediments in this life without disarming unilaterally. I take from the writing of C. Wright Mills (1959) that it is an ongoing challenge and serious responsibility to elevate the habits of one's own work to the status of craftsmanship. Only then can they be put in the service of problems of real significance.

NOTES

1. For example, I've tried to organize my wife, but she has been reluctant to adopt my systems for some reason, and I've had mixed results with offering advice elsewhere.

2. This essay connects to Pam Shoemaker's career in a few ways. She has obviously been a productive scholar, but I also observed her as an early adopter of personal computers and followed her lead, as new assistant professors at Texas. I also recall at that time her self-declared fondness for office supplies. As a graduate student I had limited myself to a large desk blotter that displayed month at a time, on which I would mark everything of importance, but when professor life quickly became more complex I followed Pam's adoption of the Daytimer line of appointment books. On a more intellectual level, the large survey project we were involved with in the early 1980s, from which we co-authored several studies, led me to pursue questions about the information worker, which relates to some of the issues discussed here.
3. I have used the techniques for several years, attended an Allen-led workshop in Dallas a few years ago (no other academics present) and even bought a copy of his most recent edition for students in my last graduate seminar.
4. The cognitive science foundation for the GTD methodology has been elaborated in a very helpful book by Daniel Levitin, *The organized mind* (2014).
5. It's hard for me to imagine, but I was among the first of my graduate student cohort to write my dissertation using a word processor. But the catch was that the terminal was connected to the mainframe computer and only available at one of the university's main computer centers. So, I had to walk there from my office, with plenty of time to think about what I was going to write—and plenty of time in the spartan and utilitarian computer center to do it, free of distraction and friends.

REFERENCES

Allen, D. (2015). *Getting things done: The art of stress-free productivity.* New York, NY: Penguin Press.

Covey, S. R. (1989). *The 7 habits of highly effective people.* New York, NY: Free Press.

Currey, M. (2013). *Daily rituals: How artists work.* New York, NY: Knopf.

Levitin, D. (2014). *The organized mind: Thinking straight in the age of information overload.* New York, NY: Plume.

Loehle, C. (1990). A guide to increased creativity in research: Inspiration or perspiration? *BioScience, 40*(2), 123–129.

Mills, C. W. (1959). *The sociological imagination.* New York, NY: Oxford.

Newport, C. (2016). *Deep work: Rules for focused success in a distracted world.* New York, NY: Grand Central.

Reese, S. D. (1988). New communication technologies and the information worker: The influence of occupation. *Journal of Communication, 38*(2), 59–70.

Reese, S. D. (2014, March 14). When productivity becomes hyperactivity. *Inside Higher Ed.* Retrieved from https://www.insidehighered.com/advice/2014/03/14/cautionary-words-about-academic-productivity-and-problem-hyperactivity-essay

Wajcman, J. (2014). *Pressed for time: The acceleration of life in digital capitalism.* Chicago, IL: University of Chicago.

Contributors

Michael J. Breen is Dean of Arts at Mary Immaculate College at the University of Limerick in Ireland. He is widely published, and his interests include public opinion formation, survey design, and quantitative data analysis. His most recent books are a statistical analysis of public opinion polls dealing with constitutional referenda issues in Ireland, an analysis of the Irish data of the European Social Survey, and an edited volume of European Social Survey-based research papers.

Yun Jung Choi is Associate Professor in the Communication and Media Division at Ewha Womans University, Seoul Korea. She received her B.A. from Ewha Womans University, her M.A. from the University of Missouri, and her Ph.D. from Syracuse University. Her research interests include television effects, social viewing, and online communication. She worked as a television producer at SBS productions, one of three television networks in Korea.

Akiba A. Cohen (Ph.D., Michigan State University) is Professor (Emeritus) of Communication at Tel Aviv University. He is a Fellow and former president of the International Communication Association. His main interest has been the comparative study of television news. He is coauthor with Pamela Shoemaker (Routledge, 2006) of *News around the World: Content, Practitioners and the Pubic.* His latest edited volume is *Foreign News on Television: Where in the World Is the Global Village?* (Peter Lang, 2013).

Marcos Paulo da Silva is Professor of Journalism Studies at Federal University of Mato Grosso do Sul (UFMS), Campo Grande, Brazil (since 2013). He received his Ph.D. in social communication from the Methodist University of São Paulo,

Brazil (2013), which included a doctorate internship at the Newhouse School of Public Communication at Syracuse University (fall 2011). He is a coauthor of *Critérios de noticiabilidade: problemas conceituais e aplicações* (Editora Insular, 2014) *and* conducts research on the theoretical aspects of journalism and newsworthiness.

Gang (Kevin) Han, Ph.D., is Associate Professor in the Greenlee School of Journalism and Communication at Iowa State University. Han received a doctorate from Syracuse University, and taught at the State University of New York and Fudan University previously. Han's research interests include framing, social networking, health risk, and strategic communication. Han's articles have appeared in *Journalism & Mass Communication Quarterly, Health Communication, Mass Communication & Society, Public Relations Review, Asian Journal of Communication*, among others.

Dominic L. Lasorsa is Associate Professor in the School of Journalism at the University of Texas at Austin. He received a doctorate in communication from Stanford University, a master of arts in journalism from the University of Texas at Austin, and a bachelor of arts in journalism from St. Bonaventure University.

Jong Hyuk Lee is Associate Professor in the Communication & Media Department at Kyung Hee University, Seoul Korea. He received his B.A. in communication from Seoul National University, his M.A. from the University of Missouri, and his Ph.D. at Syracuse University. His research interests include news values, political communication, and digital journalism. He worked as a reporter at *Chosun-Ilbo*, the most influential daily newspaper in Korea.

Suman Lee is Associate Professor in the Greenlee School of Journalism and Communication at Iowa State University. His research centers on international and global issues of public relations. He has published numerous articles and book chapters on international public relations, image/reputation building processes, public diplomacy, and international newsworthiness. He received his Ph.D. in mass communication from Syracuse University, his M.A. in Communication from San Diego State University, and his B.A. in English literature from Yonsei University.

Carol M. Liebler (Ph.D., University of Wisconsin) is Professor of Communication in the S.I. Newhouse School of Public Communications at Syracuse University. Her research centers on media and diversity issues, and particularly on gender as it intersects with race, ethnicity, and class. Her work has appeared in a variety of journals including *Journal of Communication, Communication Culture and Critique*, and the *Asian Journal of Communication.*

Gina Masullo Chen (Ph.D., Syracuse University) is Assistant Professor in the School of Journalism at the University of Texas at Austin. She spent 20 years as a newspaper reporter and editor before joining academia. Her research focuses on the online conversation around the news with a particular interest in uncivil debate. She is a co-editor of *Scandal in a Digital Age* (Palgrave Macmillan, 2016) and author of *Online Incivility & Public Debate: Nasty Talk* (Palgrave Macmillan, 2017).

Maxwell McCombs is the Jesse H. Jones Centennial Chair in Communication Emeritus in the School of Journalism at the University of Texas at Austin. He is the co-founder with Donald Shaw of agenda-setting theory. His B.A. is from Tulane University and his M.A. and Ph.D. are from Stanford University.

Nick Michael is a video producer for National Public Radio in Washington, D.C., and co-founder, partner and producer for 1504, a video studio specializing in narrative content. He completed his master's at the University of Missouri in 2014, and his chapter is based on his master's thesis.

Paromita Pain is a doctoral student in the School of Journalism at the University of Texas at Austin. Her research interests include examining the participatory media process, citizen journalism and women's empowerment via mobile technologies. She has a B.A. from the University of Calcutta, a M.A. from the University of Madras, and a M.A. from the University of Southern California, and is finishing a Ph.D. in communication at the University of Texas at Austin.

Shuya Pan (Ph.D., University of Southern California) is Assistant Professor in the School of Journalism and Communication at Renmin University of China. Her research interests include health communication and journalism.

Stephen D. Reese has been on the University of Texas at Austin faculty since 1982, where he is now the Jesse H. Jones Professor of Journalism. His research focuses on press performance, including the sociology of news, media framing of public issues, and the globalization of journalism. He received his Ph.D. from the University of Wisconsin–Madison, from which he received the Harold L. Nelson Award in 2015 for distinguished contribution to research and education in journalism and mass communication.

Erica Scharrer, Professor in the Department of Communication at the University of Massachusetts Amherst, studies media content, opinions of media, media effects, and media literacy, especially regarding the topics of violence and gender. The editor of the Media Effects/Media Psychology volume of the *International Encyclopedia of Media Studies* (Wiley-Blackwell, 2013), her work has appeared in *Communication Research*, *Human Communication Research*, *Journal of Children and Media*, and other journals.

Hyunjin Seo (Ph.D., Syracuse University) is Associate Professor and Docking Faculty Scholar in the William Allen White School of Journalism and Mass Communications at the University of Kansas. Seo's research interests lie at the intersection of digital media, international communication, and strategic communication. Seo has conducted research on how social collaborative networks, often facilitated by digital communication technologies, catalyze social movements and address social issues at local, national, and international levels.

Josh Shear is a senior producer for Advance Digital's National Desk, a co-creator of the Josh & Kelvin World Domination Podcast, and the creator of Josh: The Podcast. A writer and podcaster with nearly 20 years' experience in print and online media, he is also an early adopter of blogs and social media, often helping coach others to success.

Elizabeth A. Skewes is Associate Professor of Journalism and Media Studies at the University of Colorado Boulder. Her research focuses on media sociology and news practices, the media's role in electoral politics, and politics in popular culture. She has a B.A. in political science from University of California, Los Angeles, a M.A. in journalism from Ohio State University, and a Ph.D. in mass communications from Syracuse University.

Guido H. Stempel III (Ph.D. University of Wisconsin) was Professor Emeritus in the School of Journalism at Ohio University, where he had formerly served as director. A former editor of *Journalism & Mass Communication Quarterly* and a Paul H. Deutschmann award winner, Stempel was a prolific researcher and legendary journalism professor. Stempel died on May 31, 2016.

Elena Vartanova is Full Professor of Media Theory and Media Economics and Dean and Chair of the Faculty of Journalism, Lomonosov Moscow State University. She is the president of the Russian National Association of Mass Media Researchers (NAMMI). Her research focuses on Russian and foreign media systems, media economics and media management, information society, digital divide, journalism and media theory, science communications, media education, and Russian language in media.

Tim P. Vos (Ph.D., Syracuse University) is Chair, Associate Professor of Journalism Studies, and Coordinator of Global Research Initiatives at the University of Missouri School of Journalism. He is co-author of *Gatekeeping Theory* (2009), co-editor of *Gatekeeping in Transition* (2015), and author of more than 30 journal articles and book chapters.

Xiuli Wang (Ph.D., Syracuse University) is Associate Professor in the School of Journalism and Communication at Peking University. Her research interests include social media and public diplomacy.

John Wolf (Ph.D., Syracuse University) is Assistant Dean of the College of Science and Liberal Arts at the New Jersey Institute of Technology in Newark, where he also teaches in the Science, Technology, and Society Program. His research focuses on technology adoption, human-computer interaction, and social change.

Brenda Wrigley, Ph.D., is Associate Professor in and Chair of the Department of Marketing Communication at Emerson College, Boston. She has 20 years of university teaching and administrative experience, and more than 21 years of professional experience as a broadcast journalist, as well as experience in broadcast advertising sales, sales management, and corporate communications management. She teaches and conducts research in the areas of gender and diversity, public relations, corporate communications, crisis communications and management.

Di Zhang (Ph.D., Syracuse University) is Associate Professor in the School of Journalism and Communication at Renmin University of China. His research interests include public relations and health communication.

Pei Zheng is Assistant Professor in the Roy H. Park School of Communications at Ithaca College. Her research focuses on political communication, new media technologies and the media's social impacts. She has a B.A. from Tsinghua University and a M.Phil. from the Chinese University of Hong Kong, and is finishing a Ph.D. in communication at the University of Texas at Austin.

Index

A

B

C

D

E

F

G

H

I

J

K

L

M

Q

R

S

Mass Communication and Journalism

Lee B. Becker, *General Editor*

The Mass Communication and Journalism series focuses on broad issues in mass communication, giving particular attention to those in which journalism is prominent. Volumes in the series examine the product of the full range of media organizations as well as individuals engaged in various types of communication activities.

Each commissioned book deals in depth with a selected topic, raises new issues about that topic, and provides a fuller understanding of it through the new evidence provided. The series contains both single-authored and edited works. For more information and submissions, please contact:

Lee B. Becker, Series Editor | *lbbecker@uga.edu*
Kathryn Harrison, Acquisitions Editor | *Kathryn.Harrison@plang.com*